# Designing Experiments for the Social Sciences

Sara Miller McCune founded SAGE Publishing in 1965 to support the dissemination of usable knowledge and educate a global community. SAGE publishes more than 1000 journals and over 800 new books each year, spanning a wide range of subject areas. Our growing selection of library products includes archives, data, case studies and video. SAGE remains majority owned by our founder and after her lifetime will become owned by a charitable trust that secures the company's continued independence.

Los Angeles | London | New Delhi | Singapore | Washington DC | Melbourne

# Designing Experiments for the Social Sciences

## How to Plan, Create, and Execute Research Using Experiments

**Renita Coleman**

*University of Texas at Austin*

Los Angeles | London | New Delhi
Singapore | Washington DC | Melbourne

FOR INFORMATION:

SAGE Publications, Inc.
2455 Teller Road
Thousand Oaks, California 91320
E-mail: order@sagepub.com

SAGE Publications Ltd.
1 Oliver's Yard
55 City Road
London EC1Y 1SP
United Kingdom

SAGE Publications India Pvt. Ltd.
B 1/I 1 Mohan Cooperative Industrial Area
Mathura Road, New Delhi 110 044
India

SAGE Publications Asia-Pacific Pte. Ltd.
3 Church Street
#10-04 Samsung Hub
Singapore 049483

Printed in the United States of America

ISBN 978-1-5063-7732-2

Acquisitions Editor: Helen Salmon
Development Editor: Chelsea Neve
Editorial Assistant: Megan O'Heffernan
Production Editor: Olivia Weber-Stenis
Copy Editor: Diane Wainwright
Typesetter: C&M Digitals Ltd.
Proofreader: Jennifer Grubba
Indexer: Jean Casalegno
Cover Designer: Ginkhan Siam
Marketing Manager: Susannah Goldes

This book is printed on acid-free paper.

MIX
Paper from
responsible sources
FSC® C008955

18 19 20 21 22 10 9 8 7 6 5 4 3 2 1

# PRAISE FOR THIS BOOK

"This book offers many examples and hands-on instruction that can help students learn how to conduct experiments."

—Francis O. Adeola, University of New Orleans

"This book is a must for learning about the experimental design—from forming a research question to interpreting the results, this text covers it all."

—Sarah El Sayed, University of Texas at Arlington

"This text provides students with an excellent explanation of experimental methodology: not just descriptions of elements of the experiment method, but understanding of where those elements came from, how and why they work together, and how students can become scholars."

—Kyle J. Holody, Coastal Carolina University

"This is a comprehensive text on experiments, clearly and engagingly written, with many excellent examples. Renita Coleman has included everything the student will need to develop, design, and execute a methodologically sound experiment."

—Glenn Leshner, University of Oklahoma

"This textbook is detailed and well organized, with each topic progressing logically to build on foundational knowledge. Students will find it easy to master research concepts and practice using the exercises and examples provided. The 'Study Spotlight' scenarios and practical examples are effective tools to demonstrate research designs, and the 'Test Your Knowledge' quizzes reinforce student learning."

—Janet Reid-Hector, Rutgers University

"This book is well-written and readable. If you need to grasp concepts of experimental designs, this book guides you as to what the experimental designs are, and what you should keep in mind in conducting your studies."

—Ji Hoon Ryoo, University of Virginia

# BRIEF CONTENTS

# DETAILED CONTENTS

# PREFACE

"There are excellent books and courses of instruction dealing with the statistical manipulation of experimental data, but there is little help to be found on the methods of securing adequate and proper data to which to apply statistical procedure."[1]

Forty years after W. A. McCall wrote this statement, Don Campbell and Julian Stanley said, "This sentence remains true enough today."[2]

More than fifty years have passed, and I say this *still* remains true today, especially for the social sciences.

This book is about securing adequate and proper data.

It is different from most other experimental design books in two ways: First, it concentrates on the methodological and design issues of planning an experiment rather than on analyzing data with various statistics after the data are collected. Careful design of studies from the beginning is the key to good research. That is nowhere more the case than with experiments. This book is about how to effectively *design* experiments rather than how to *analyze* them. It focuses on the stage where researchers are making decisions about procedural aspects of the experiment, before interventions and treatments are given.

It will help readers learn how to plan and execute experiments from the beginning by walking step-by-step through deciding whether to use a single-factor or factorial design, how to assign subjects to groups, choosing and collecting a sample, creating the stimuli and instrument, doing a manipulation check, applying for approval from the Institutional Review Board (IRB), and doing a pilot study, as well as other choices along the way. It gives guidelines for deciding which elements are best used in the creation of a particular experiment and things to consider when making the inevitable trade-offs. It is practical and applied.

*Designing Experiments for the Social Sciences* only briefly covers the statistics aspect of experiments, for they are inextricably linked. However, the focus is mainly on enabling readers to learn how to design experiments from the beginning. The inner workings of the statistics, formulas, and how to calculate them by hand or using software is not part of this book. In-depth knowledge of statistics is not required to understand the material. This book is confined to helping readers understand which statistics are appropriate for what kinds of analysis and level of measurement, but it is very basic. I recommend taking a traditional experimental design class, statistics courses, or reading such a book that focuses on statistics in addition to this one.

The second way in which this book is different from others is that it is aimed at social scientists broadly. Readers will find examples beyond psychology ranging from political science, business, economics, information sciences, social work, education, sociology, health fields, advertising, and more. My discipline is journalism and the larger field of communication. My first experimental design class had students enrolled from journalism, advertising, public relations, radio, television, film, political, and interpersonal communication. Experiments are becoming more prevalent throughout the social sciences as researchers discover the importance of understanding cause and effect to their discipline. With the introduction of easy-to-use software (such as SPSS, G*Power, Qualtrics) and greater access to human subjects (such as Mechanical Turk), experimental designs are becoming more prevalent. This book speaks directly to these researchers with examples from their own worlds. It also explores some of the challenges facing specific disciplines—for example, objections to random assignment common in education, reporting of response rates with samples in political science, and the use of observations or performance-based measures rather than self-reports in economics.

Many researchers in the social sciences learn by working with another experimentalist one-on-one. This book is written to be a supplement to those learning this way, a guidebook for those working on their own, or a textbook for an organized class. It came about when I first taught an experimental methods class at the University of Texas and could not find a book that did exactly what I wanted. That course is the foundation for this book. I envisioned it as a core textbook for stand-alone experimental design methods courses. It will also be a good supplementary text for general research methods courses in the social sciences where experiments are prominent—for example, advertising, political science, health sciences, and others.

I wrote *Designing Experiments for the Social Sciences* with graduate students in mind, although my fifteen years as a professional journalist have taught me how to write for a general audience. This book is written in easy-to-understand language so that undergraduate students can understand it too. It is not appropriate for the totally uninitiated, however; it is more suited to an educated novice, someone who has conducted research previously but has not done an experiment, or has assisted with one but not conducted one of his or her own. It presumes at least one general overview course in the scientific method. Those who have some research experience but have never conducted an experiment before will not find it too challenging. For those learning from the benefit of mentors rather than an organized course, this book is meant as a reference and supplement to those excellent instructors. It also can help generate ideas for tools and strategies that one's mentors may not routinely include in their repertoire. Other readers may include academics with experience in other research methods that want to expand their abilities to explore cause and effect. In addition, professionals working in a research capacity, whether for a political candidate, advertising agency, educational institution, or other industry, will find this book helpful. I hope it inspires social science departments without a stand-alone experiments course to create one.

The chapters contain a mix of conceptual and theoretical issues as well as practical hands-on advice. It takes a step-by-step approach, walking students through writing hypotheses and research questions, designing stimuli, and writing up the methods sections. Many examples come from my own experience, allowing me to provide the backstory about why certain procedures were chosen over others, how the study evolved, and tips for responding to reviewer comments. These things frequently do not make it into published papers. I also draw from some of the excellent experiments conducted by others in various social science disciplines, although I am unable to offer inside knowledge about the choices made.

Although the chapters are presented roughly in the order in which designing an experiment might proceed, not all instructors or readers may wish to use it in the order presented. For example, after reading about deception in chapter 2, some readers may wish to skip ahead to chapter 11 where broader ethical issues are discussed in conjunction with the IRB. To make reading out of order easier, there is a Glossary at the end of the book containing each chapter's key terms, which are bolded and defined in the text. Other pedagogical tools include three types of boxed features:

- "More About . . ." boxes expand on some issue in the chapter for those who would like more detail.

- "Study Spotlight" boxes highlight a particular experiment for how it handles the topics in the chapter.

- "How To Do It" boxes give instructions and examples for executing the steps in the chapter and writing it up for a paper.

In addition, there are three other features:

- "Common Mistakes" is a short bulleted list of errors novices are especially prone to.

- "Test Your Understanding" questions at the end of each chapter is a short multiple-choice quiz so you can see how well you understood the material.

- "Application Exercises" are instructions for longer hands-on assignments that let you apply what you have learned, including a one-step-at-a-time approach for creating a research proposal for your own experiment. This is broken down into manageable pieces so that the task does not seem so daunting.

Each chapter also contains a list of suggested readings for more depth on the topics. A defining feature of every section is the practical advice and examples on everything from how to describe the stimuli and instrument to working with coauthors, submitting to journals, and responding to common questions from reviewers. There are URLs for free software to use when creating Twitter feeds or Facebook posts, online randomizers, and tutorials for conducting power analyses. Some topics are not unique to experiments, but I have tried to hone in on particular issues with this method. For example, chapter 3 explains the role of theory in experimentation, whose strength is in testing and expanding theory. It also covers how empirical evidence from the literature should be used to build a case for the hypotheses and theoretical processes being tested, and offers a "formula" for hypothesis writing that resembles diagramming a sentence.

Ethics is first introduced in chapter 2, following naturally the stories about Stanley Milgram's obedience to authority experiments and Philip Zimbardo's prison experiment, both of which raised collective consciences about the importance of ethics in experimental science. A "More About" box here delves into deception, which is more problematic with experiments than other methods. The discussion about ethics is woven throughout each chapter—for example, in chapter 7 on random assignment, some of the objections to it as unethical are discussed. The topic is revisited in greater detail in chapter 11, using IRBs as a framework considering that their standards are intertwined with ethics. Because of the step-by-step approach of this book, the IRB is discussed after the experiment is designed and researchers must apply for approval. However, the importance of ethical experiments is not an afterthought; rather, it is included in chapter 11 because IRBs are the principal means of enforcing ethical behavior, so this chapter seemed the most logical for discussing both.

What there is to know about experiments does not begin and end with this textbook; I encourage the learning process to continue by reading some of the excellent writings in the "Suggested Readings" sections, by reading experiments in one's own discipline, and by working with others. I hope you enjoy and find it helpful.

For additional teaching and learning resources that go along with this book, please visit the website at study.sagepub.com/coleman.

Instructors will find chapter-by-chapter PowerPoint® slides to assist in lecture preparation, along with a Word® test bank with multiple-choice and open-ended exam questions. Students will find the full-text version of the SAGE journal articles spotlighted throughout the book.

# ACKNOWLEDGMENTS

I would like to thank my own mentors, who infected me with the experimental bug when I was a graduate student—Esther Thorson and Glenn Leshner. Thank you for your guidance, patience, and for sharing your passion. For telling others—which got back to me—that "she always does what she says she will," which helped ensure that happened. For being the role model who measured the distance from screen to chair every time a new subject sat in it, opening my eyes to the importance of detail. And for always taking the time to hear about a new project and give advice. I also thank my longtime partner in research, Denis Wu, whom I was fortunate to meet in my first faculty position and who has stuck with me since. He always seems to be good at that which I am not, and has been my constant ally on our self-guided tour of experiments. I thank all the brilliant former graduate students I have experimented with, including but not limited to Ben Wasike, Lesa Hatley-Major, Rebecca McEntee, Lewis Knight, Carolyn Yaschur, Trent Boulter, Viorela Dan, Angela Lee, Raluca Cozma, Avery Holton, Dani Kilgo, Siobhan Smith, Kate West, Joseph Yoo, and Ji Won Kim, among others. And I thank all those who enrolled in my experimental design course, especially from other departments, opening my eyes to new theories and unique challenges in your fields, and for allowing me to experiment on you in the process of writing this book. I learn as much, if not more, from you as you do from me.

Finally, this book would not have been possible without the time and expertise of all the reviewers who gently pointed out flaws and gaps, steered me toward valuable resources, and patiently helped make this book much better. I also thank Helen Salmon, the senior editor at SAGE, who took a chance on this proposal and suggested numerous important additions; Jeremy Shermak, for creating the website for the book; and the excellent staff at SAGE who shepherded this to completion, including Chelsea Neve, Megan O'Heffernan, Eve Oettinger, Diane Wainwright, and the rest of the team in the Research Methods, Statistics, and Evaluation department.

SAGE would like to thank the following reviewers for their feedback:

Richard E. Adams, Kent State University

Francis O. Adeola, University of New Orleans

Anna Bassi, University of North Carolina

Jacqueline Craven, Delta State University

Sarah A. El Sayed, University of Texas at Arlington

Janet Reid Hector, Rutgers University

Kyle J. Holody, Coastal Carolina University

Glenn Leshner, University of Oklahoma

Ji Hoon Ryoo, University of Virginia

Gerene K. Starratt, Barry University

Michael Teneyck, University of Texas at Arlington

Geoffrey P. R. Wallace, University of Washington

## Notes

1. W. A. McCall, *How to Experiment in Education* (New York: MacMillan, 1923), Preface.
2. D. T. Campbell and J. C. Stanley, *Experimental and Quasi-Experimental Designs for Research* (Chicago: Rand McNally, 1963), 1.

# ABOUT THE AUTHOR

Rebecca Scoggin McEntee

**Renita Coleman** has a bachelor's degree in journalism from the University of Florida and a master's and PhD in journalism from the University of Missouri.

Her research focuses on ethics, framing, and agenda setting, with a special focus on visual communication. She has studied the effects of photographs on ethical reasoning, the framing and attribution of responsibility in health news, and the moral development of journalists and public relations practitioners, among other topics. She has published more than 40 peer-reviewed articles in academic journals including *Journal of Communication, Journalism and Mass Communication Quarterly, Journal of Broadcasting & Electronic Media, Journal of Mass Media Ethics, Journalism,* and *Journalism Studies.* She has coauthored two books: *Image and Emotion in Voter Decisions: The Affect Agenda* in 2015, and *The Moral Media: How Journalists Reason About Ethics* in 2005.

Before beginning her academic career, Coleman was a journalist at newspapers and magazines for fifteen years. She was a reporter, editor, and designer at the Raleigh, North Carolina, *News & Observer,* the Sarasota, Florida, *Herald-Tribune,* and the Orlando, Florida, *Sentinel,* among other news organizations.

Coleman teaches undergraduate and graduate courses in ethics, lifestyle journalism, and experimental design.

# DISCOVERING CAUSE AND EFFECT

*Life is a perpetual instruction in cause and effect.*

**—Ralph Waldo Emerson**

## LEARNING OBJECTIVES

- Explain how cause and effect work in an experiment.

- Compare the benefits of experiments to other methods.

- Identify the three basic criteria of experiments.

- Describe the elements of variation, confounds, control groups, and assignment.

- Develop a statement of the problem and answer the "so what" question for a study of your own.

This book is about experiments, the scope of which varies greatly. An experiment is a scientific test of some hypothesis or principle carried out under carefully controlled conditions in order to determine or discover something unknown. Experiments provide insights about the relationship between things where changes in one thing cause something to happen to another. We have all done informal experiments in everyday life without even knowing it, as the opening quote by Ralph Waldo Emerson illustrates. For example, if you change the amount of a certain ingredient in a recipe, does it taste better? If you drink lower-calorie beer, do you lose weight? As long as you only

change one ingredient at a time, or do not exercise more or eat lower-calorie everything, you probably assumed it was that one ingredient or that lower-calorie beer that caused the difference in taste or your weight loss.

## CAUSATION

These examples of everyday experiments illustrate the concept of cause and effect. An "effect" is what happened. Better-tasting lasagna or weight loss are the effects in the earlier examples. The "cause" is the explanation for why these things happened—more garlic in the lasagna made it taste better, the lower-calorie beer helped you lose weight. We find the word *cause* used in everyday language, such as "the cause of death" or "the cause of an accident." The meaning is no different in experiments, but you will also see the terms *causality* or **causation** used.

Of course, for the purposes of this book, we are more interested in systematic experiments than the simple, everyday ones that are described. In medicine, these are called *clinical trials* or *randomized clinical trials* (RCTs; for more about RCTs, see More About box 1.1). In web design and market research, they may also be called *A/B testing*. The language is a little different from experiments in the social sciences, but the goal is the same—to discover what treatment (or cause) works best on a particular problem. In medicine, the problem is an illness or disease, the effect being a cure or improvement. In social science, the problems for which we are seeking solutions can be TV commercials that promote brand awareness, strategies for teaching students with Down syndrome, or interventions that help accountants be more honest.

To do this, social scientists use experiments as "the basic language of proof."[6] Experiments give us evidence of cause and effect by demonstrating what happens when something is changed while everything else remains the same. In this way, we have more assurance that the thing that changed is responsible for causing the outcome or effect we have observed.

Experiments are the most common kind of research conducted in the medical field, but in social science, they can be among the least often used. In communication journals, around 12% of studies use experimental designs.[7] In international relations, it can be as low as 4%.[8] In special education, experiments are promoted as the answer to calls for increased quality and rigor in an evidence-based profession.[9] And they are growing steadily in political science,[10] among other fields. As the benefits of this method become known throughout the social sciences, software to analyze data gets easier to use, and as technology makes subjects cheaper and easier to recruit, the use of experiments should

# MORE ABOUT . . . BOX 1.1
## Randomized Clinical Trials

RCTs are basically the same things as true experiments, where subjects are randomly assigned (the R) to either a treatment or a control group and given one or more experimental procedures or drugs. They are also referred to as randomized *controlled* trials, with language purists using controlled for studies that include a **control group** where subjects receive a placebo or no treatment. When *clinical* is used, it may or may not have a control group. Presumably, the clinical usage came into being because these studies were conducted on medical patients or others in a clinical setting. The term *trial* is used because the treatment or drug being studied is being tried out—that is, it is not approved for widespread use, and the study will determine if it is safe and effective.[1]

RCTs are considered the gold standard for medical studies, just as their counterpart is in social science—the true or lab experiment.

The history of RCTs dates back to 600 BC when Daniel of Judah compared the royal Babylonian diet to a vegetarian diet.[2] Others credit James Lind, who conducted the scurvy experiments in 1747 described in chapter 2.[3] The first modern-day RCT is usually recognized as the test of streptomycin's effects on tuberculosis in 1948.[4] The study begins by explaining how the preponderance of inadequately controlled clinical trials on tuberculosis had led to "exaggerated claims" about gold as a treatment. The study presents a "full description" of the methods because of the difficulty of planning such a rigorous trial, so that others may reproduce it.[5]

only increase. Thus, knowing how to do them well is all the more important. Already, many articles discuss the increased use of experiments for both academics and professionals in disciplines such as political science[11] and information systems.[12] Others discuss the growing importance of creating organized courses in experimental methods.[13] Some go so far as to say experiments are the most important method in their discipline.[14] Experiments are central to fields that use evidence-based practice such as social work[15] and education, where the randomized clinical trial is the gold standard.[16]

# EXPERIMENTS COMPARED TO OTHER METHODS

The main benefit of the experimental method is that it offers a powerful tool to discover causation. Many other research methods, such as surveys, can identify **correlations,** or relationships, that vary together and are unlikely to have occurred by chance. This is not necessarily the same thing as causation. Experiments, by contrast, can provide insights into how changing one thing leads to changes in another. Deliberately and systematically **varying**, or changing, something allows us to see a potential causal agent.[17] Following up correlational studies with experiments is a good way to give us more confidence that the relationships we find in these studies are actually causal. **Triangulation**, or the use of different methods to study the same phenomenon, is important to scientific inquiry because it helps give us confidence that what we see using one method can be **replicated**, or reproduced, using another. Of much concern is the overreliance on surveys and observational methods that show a correlation but with no follow-up using experiments that find evidence of a causal relationship.[18]

One of the most famous illustrations of the problem with inferring causation from correlation is the long-ago pronouncement that storks brought babies. A study done in Copenhagen in the 1930s documented that the years with larger stork populations also saw more babies born—a high correlation of .85.[19] But just because these two variables are highly correlated does not mean one caused the other. Instead, there were **plausible alternative explanations**, or other possible causes, that were not studied. This was right after World War I, and all those soldiers returning home after so long led to more babies being born. In addition, people were migrating from the country to the city where the jobs were, so more people to have babies equaled more babies. As the population increased, more houses were built, which led to more places for storks to nest, leading to more storks.[20] The cycle continued.

iStock.com/zuzulicea

## BASIC CRITERIA FOR EXPERIMENTS

This example illustrates the three basic features that all experiments must have; that is, the cause must precede the effect—in this case, storks did come before the babies—but the cause must also be related to the effect, which it was not. There was no logical or theoretical reason and no empirical evidence to suggest that storks were related to babies. This is one reason why experimentalists do not test mere hunches but instead find linkages in the form of theoretical, logical, or existing evidence to test. This helps ensure that the cause is actually related to the effect. In the storks and babies example, the third feature of an experiment also was missing—there must be no other plausible alternative explanation for the effect. A real experiment must contain all three: Cause must come before the effect, be related to it, and there must not be any other plausible alternative explanations. If these three conditions are met, experiments give us a powerful way to have more

## STUDY SPOTLIGHT 1.2
Discovering Effects and Explaining Why

SAGE Journal Article:
study.sagepub.com/
coleman

**Hay, Carter, Xia Wang, Emily Ciaravolo, and Ryan C. Meldrum. 2015. "Inside the Black Box: Identifying the Variables That Mediate the Effects of an Experimental Intervention for Adolescents."** *Crime & Delinquency* 61 (2): 243–270.

This study is a good example of an experiment that not only finds effects but also explains what caused them. The authors start by reconfirming that the treatment by a particular program actually did reduce juveniles' risk for delinquency. Then they examined the mediating variables that intervene, or come between, participation in the program and reduced juvenile delinquency. They examined a total of eleven risk factors that had been suggested as the reasons why the program worked, which researchers call *causal mechanisms*. They say, "In short, if we lack insight on the precise mechanisms by which a program reduces delinquency, then efforts to build on its strengths, replicate it elsewhere, and use it to inform public policy are necessarily hindered" (p. 248).

Out of the eleven possible variables that could have explained why the program worked, the researchers found only one that was significant: "Reduced association with peers who engaged in deviance and pressured them to do so as well" (p. 263). In other words, hanging out with a bad crowd.

They explain the importance of this in terms of the time and money spent by such programs pursuing these ten other variables that, it turns out, did not actually make a difference. Put in nicer terms than the wasting of time and money, the researchers say, "Our analysis—a rare test that has considered mediating variables—suggests that many of the risk factors targeted by these programs may be unresponsive to program services" (p. 264).

confidence that one thing led to, or caused, another, not just that there is an association that was unlikely to have occurred by chance.

While being able to test cause and effect is a powerful tool, it is still merely a description; it does not explain why something occurred. For example, in the field of social work, many studies have identified programs that successfully reduce juvenile delinquency, but few have undertaken an examination of why they are effective.[21] Hay and colleagues noticed the gap and designed an experiment to discover the mechanisms that explain why participating in a program reduced delinquency rates (for more on this study, see Study Spotlight 1.2). In my own work, I hypothesized that seeing photographs would cause journalists to use better-quality ethical reasoning when making news decisions. I found the effect I was looking for,[22] but that was a description, not an explanation. That finding alone did not say anything about why it happened. To provide a causal explanation, experiments need to build in potential mechanisms that explain these effects. If photographs do improve ethical reasoning, it is important to know why. **Mediators** and **moderators** such as this will be discussed in more detail in another chapter. Suffice it to say here that good experiments should also include mechanisms for explaining why a certain effect occurred.

With this basic discussion of what experiments can do compared to other methods, next we turn to some specific elements of experiments. All of these will be elaborated in more detail in later chapters but are introduced here to provide some basic fundamental understanding of experiments.

# ELEMENTS OF EXPERIMENTS

## Variation

Varying or changing things is the first key to a good experiment. Obviously, if nothing varies, then there is nothing to study. Something has to change. In experiments, variation is achieved by **manipulating** the **independent variable**, or IV—the thing researchers think will cause a change. This is also called the *manipulation, treatment,* or *intervention.* The researcher should carefully control these. For example, many studies use professional actors to portray a political candidate rather than real politicians who may bias subjects' responses.[23] In one study, the actor was tasked with displaying positive nonverbal behaviors in one interview, negative ones in another, and neutral body language in a third. The study authors researched exactly what those looked liked—for example, crossed arms was negative, leaning forward and looking the interviewer in the eye was positive—and made sure the actor displayed those behaviors. It is not enough to merely ask an actor to behave positively or negatively but for the researchers to know exactly what that should look like and ensure that it is properly demonstrated.

Another key to good variation is that only one thing at a time can vary; otherwise, it is impossible to tell which of the several things that varied caused the outcome. Actually, many experiments do vary more than one thing at a time (more on that later), but the key is they do not allow those things to **covary**—that is, they cannot vary together. For example, one researcher noticed that studies showing negative political advertising were more powerful than positive advertising and had allowed the tone of the ads to covary with the amount of information in them.[24] There was always more information in the negative ads than in the positive ads; therefore, the more powerful effects could be due to more information, not necessarily to its negative tone. This provided a plausible alternative explanation for the effects found in these other studies. To determine if this was the case, the researcher did a study that held the amount of information **constant**—that is, there was the same amount of information in both the negative- and positive-toned ads. He found that the tone was not causing the effect at all—it was the amount of information;

negative advertising typically had more information in it than positive advertising, and that was the source of the greater levels of campaign knowledge, interest, and turnout that the other studies had documented.

In reality, cause is rarely **univariate**, or caused by one variable. Social science researchers seldom expect one thing alone to be the direct cause of another. There are usually many things that are responsible. In experiments, this is managed by holding constant other things than the one purposely being varied to make sure those things are not responsible for the effect.

## Confounds

Things that could provide plausible alternative explanations are called **confounds**. It is important that there are no confounds—that is, anything that would harm the accuracy of the experiment. Key to a successful experiment is controlling for extraneous influences that might have caused the outcome. For example, a researcher studying the effect of photographs that were placed above or below the fold in a newspaper used as stimuli a vertical photo that showed a person up close above the fold and a horizontal photo showing people far away below the fold. He used *only* the horizontal far-away photo below the fold and *only* the vertical close-up photo above the fold. The problem with this is that it could have been the vertical or horizontal format of the photo, or the close-up or far-away distance of the people in them, that was responsible for the effect he found. Those were not the variables he had deliberately varied. The pictures varied on many levels, not just the ones he was interested in, which was placement in the newspaper. This represents a confound—a plausible alternative explanation that was not controlled for.

To avoid confounds in one study designed to determine how the race of the people in photographs affected journalists' ethical judgment, the researcher took the exact same picture and digitally altered the skin tone, hair, and facial features of the people in order to manipulate their race. That way, everything was the same except race—the thing designed to vary. The backgrounds were the same, the distance from the camera, the people's attractiveness, and everything else was the same. This avoided any confounds. Researchers know, for example, that close-ups make people feel more comfortable with the people in the photographs than long-shots,[25] and that attractive people are evaluated better on a variety of characteristics than less attractive people, including trustworthiness and electability in political candidates.[26] So this study needed photographs that were exactly the same in every way except the race of the people in them.

In experiments, it is helpful to be as Type A as possible. For example, a researcher might measure the distance from the TV to the chair that subjects sit in before every new subject comes in. All subjects should be exactly the same distance from the TV because being even a little bit closer can make a difference.

Researchers discover potential confounds two ways: by using common sense and by reading other studies. The literature abounds with evidence showing, for example, that political party and ideology affect many things.[27] Thus, many experiments control for these potential confounds by creating stimuli that do not implicitly or explicitly state the political party of a fictitious candidate. This represents an **experimental control**, or carefully managing the variables in play.[28] Another example of avoiding potential confounds is not using real issues in the news at the time of an experiment held during an election.[29] When a researcher cannot control for a potentially spurious relationship between the independent and dependent variables, another approach is to measure it and **statistically control** for it—that is, take it out of the equation before examining what effect the manipulation had. Measuring people's political party and ideology, and then using them as covariates, is a form of statistical control.[i]

It is important to read the literature to discover things that need controlling. For example, in studies of moral development, researchers have found a connection between being liberal or conservative and quality of moral judgment.[30] This is not something that is intuitively obvious, so reading the literature to discover this is key. Age and education are also related to better moral judgment,[31] so experiments that use moral judgment as the outcome or **dependent variable** typically measure participants' political ideology in order to incorporate them in the statistical analyses as covariates should random assignment not have already made the groups equivalent on that variable. Covariates work by taking out the effect of the potentially confounding variable so researchers can see the true effect of whatever variable is being manipulated. It is important to know the literature in the domain being studied, because not everything one might suspect as having a potentially spurious relationship between a dependent and independent variable really does. For example, gender does not usually matter in moral judgment,[32] but it does in a great many other things. As most effects are rarely caused by simply one thing, it is important to know what else might be affecting the outcome.

It is also important to control for potential confounds that your own common sense tells you might affect the outcome. Just because you do not see something in the literature, if you think it might cause an effect, build it into the experiment so you can

---

[i]Covariates are not always necessary in experiments the way they are in observational studies because random assignment is designed to eliminate the effects of such variables. Random assignment will be discussed in more detail in chapter 7.

test it and see. Presumably you are studying a phenomenon that you know a lot about. If you are an expert, you should have some idea of what kinds of things affect the phenomenon you are studying. This is one way that knowledge is created and the literature develops.

## Control Groups

Another important requirement of experiments is not just knowing what happens to people who receive the treatment, but also knowing what would happen if they had *not* received the treatment. Having a group of people who do not get the treatment, known as the *control group*, gives us a way to infer what the outcome would be had there been no treatment. The effect is the difference between what *did* happen when people got the treatment and what *would have* happened had they not gotten it. This allows us to isolate and test the effects of one variable at a time, and provides greater certainty that the effect is due to that variable and not something else. The people who are exposed to the treatment or intervention are called the *treatment group, experimental group,* or *manipulation group.* The people who are not exposed to the treatment are the control group. This group of people who are not given the manipulation is used as a comparison for what "normal," "neutral," or "no manipulation" would be like.

In medical research, the control group is often given a placebo, which looks like a pill, injection, therapy, or some other treatment but really is only a sugar pill, saline injection, or something else that leads people to perceive they had something done to them. (See More About box 1.3 on placebos.) Because of the power of suggestion, it is not good enough to actually do nothing to the people in the control group; they must perceive that they had some sort of treatment. For social scientists, that can sometimes present a problem. For example, when testing different types of marketing messages, what constitutes a control group? No message, of course, but then what do subjects do instead? You cannot have them just come in and answer the questionnaire without having them be exposed to something or they will perceive the study as too artificial. Control groups will be discussed more in the coming chapters; the point of the discussion here is that experiments need some way to compare what happens to people who get the treatment versus what happens to people who do not.

## Assignment

Last in this discussion, but probably most important to experiments, is the topic of how people are assigned to the different interventions in an experiment. This topic is so important that it rates its own chapter (chapter 7). Briefly, the gold standard is

# MORE ABOUT . . . BOX 1.3
## Placebos

In medical research, the use of placebos is much more complicated than a simple injection of saline, a sugar pill, or the pretense of surgery to mimic an actual treatment on a group of control subjects. In fact, these inert or ineffective but harmless treatments actually have been shown to have effects. Called the *placebo effect*, people receiving them actually report improvement in whatever condition they were supposedly being treated for.

The word *placebo* is Latin for "I shall please."[33] The first controlled trial to use placebos has been traced to 1801.[34] The perception of placebos as fraudulent, deceptive, and unethical arose because up until the middle of the twentieth century, many practicing physicians would administer them to patients under the guise of actual medicine.[35] Questions about the ethicality of using placebos in research continue to this day.[36]

The first report on the placebo effect found that four out of five patients receiving the placebo reported relief of their symptoms; results were the same when they received the actual treatment.[37] The report cites the power of hope, faith, and the imagination. Ever since, research on the placebo effect has continued to show that patients improve after receiving the inert placebo to varying degrees, including equal or better results than the active drug.[38] A review of fifteen studies showed that, on average, placebos performed as well as the active treatment 35% of the time.[39] Flaws in this review have been pointed out, but research continues to show that placebos "work" about a third of the time.[40]

In 1961, Beecher conducted another review and found a placebo effect in 37% of patients.[41] The term placebo effect has been defined as the positive effects of an inert substance due to the power of suggestion,[42] or "the difference in outcome between a placebo treated group and an untreated control group in an unbiased experiment."[43]

In social science research, a placebo is akin to a control group that receives something designed to look like a treatment or manipulation[44]—for example, subjects who read stories about a new movie rather than the episodic and thematically framed crime stories that are the real focus of the study.

A placebo is the inert or fake treatment given to subjects; the placebo effect is subjects' response to it. It is different from the Hawthorne effect, described in the More About box in chapter 2, which describes how subjects' performance changes because they are being observed. In the placebo effect, subjects experience change because of their expectations, beliefs, or hopes that the treatment will work rather than the treatment itself.[45] In order to be effective, a treatment has to pass the placebo test—that is, the treatment must be significantly better on the outcome than the control group that gets the placebo.

Research in the social sciences also finds a placebo effect—for example, with products that promise better athletic performance,[46] factors that affect financial decisions,[47] drink labels and perceptions of intoxication,[48] and well-known brands.[49] Placebos are also found in daily life—for example, the buttons at intersections that lead pedestrians to feel a sense of control but don't really affect the light.[50]

**random assignment**, which is a way of placing subjects[ii] into the groups in such a way that individual differences are evenly distributed across the different groups. That feature is important to ensure that people's individual characteristics are not confounds of the study. Men and women should be evenly distributed across the groups, as should the young and old, for example. This

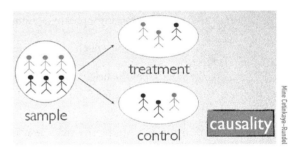

book devotes an entire chapter to assigning subjects to conditions of experiments, including discussing what to do when it is not possible to assign people this way.

## STARTING A STUDY OF YOUR OWN

Now that we have some basic understanding of what an experiment can do compared to other methods, this chapter turns to the first practical step in starting your own experiment: writing a clear and concise statement of the research problem. Clear and concise writing is important in all kinds of research but especially, in my experience, when writing up experiments. Because they can be complex, and many social scientists may not be as familiar with experimental methodology as they are with surveys or other techniques, experiments seem to be harder for readers to follow. Thus, one key focus of this book is to help readers write experiments in plain language and terms that anyone with moderate knowledge of social science can understand. That can be harder than you think. We begin with the statement of the research problem. This is more overarching than specific **hypotheses**, although they are related. Writing hypotheses will be developed in a later chapter (chapter 3). To begin a new experiment, one must come up with an idea to test. It helps to think about it in terms of cause and effect, testing if one thing causes another. For example, here are three (rather oversimplified) ideas for studies:

---

[ii]This textbook uses the term *subjects* to refer to the people studied in an experiment. The latest (6th) edition of the *Publication Manual of the American Psychological Association* (APA) says both terms, *subjects* and *participants,* are appropriate, noting that "subjects" has been in use for hundreds of years. The history of objections to "subjects" began in 1994 with the fourth edition of the APA manual, when "participants" was preferred. When the current edition appeared in 2010, subjects and participants were on equal footing. The entry on page 73 says, "Indeed, for more than 100 years the term subjects has been used within experimental psychology as a general starting point for describing a sample, and its use is appropriate." Because subjects is as appropriate as participants, this text uses subjects in order to maintain consistency with other terms in experimental design language, including *between-subjects designs, within-subjects designs,* and *human subjects* used by IRBs. For more on this topic, read the essay "What Should They Be Called" by Roddy Roediger in the APS Observer, April 2004, 17, no. 4, available at http://journal.sjdm.org/roediger.html.

1. Does seeing a photograph improve ethical reasoning?

2. Does voice pitch affect the credibility of a radio announcer?

3. Does the height of female politicians affect voters' assessments of their qualifications and the likelihood of voting for them?

In the first study, the treatment is showing subjects a photograph versus no photograph in the control condition. In the second study, the voice of a radio announcer was pitched high in one treatment condition and low in another versus normal in the control condition. In the third, pictures of short and tall women were the two treatment groups versus average-height women as the control. Of course, all three experiments ended up being more complex than this, but this simple "does A cause B" approach was the genesis of all the studies.

## Writing a Statement of the Problem

The next step is to write a clear and focused statement of the problem to be studied. A good way to start this sentence is with "The purpose of this study is . . ." or something similar. Here are some examples of good, clear, and focused statements of the problem from experiments:

- "This article investigates how media use of the microblogging tool Twitter affects perceptions of the issue covered and the credibility of the information."[51]

- "We experimentally study the common wisdom that money buys political influence."[52]

- "We assess the extent to which communication setting (i.e., face-to-face versus online chat room discussion) affects individuals' willingness to express opinions."[53]

- "A first question is whether providing general information on the welfare properties of prices and markets modify attitudes toward repugnant trades."[54]

- "... the goal of this study is to demonstrate that moral convictions and moral judgments in politics are causally affected by harm associations and moral emotions."[55]

All of these examples have three things in common: They say what the intervention, manipulation, or cause is, and what the effect or outcome is, usually in that order. And they have a verb. In the first example, Twitter is the intervention or cause, and the effect or outcomes are perceptions of the issue and credibility. In the next one, money is the cause, and political influence is the effect. In the last example, the order is reversed, with the effect—moral convictions and judgments—listed first, and the causes—harm associations and moral emotions—given last. You may also recognize these as independent variables (the cause, interventions, or manipulations) and dependent variables (the effect or outcomes). The third thing in common is that there is a verb in each of these, some word that describes the action the cause is expected to have on the outcome, or what one thing is expected to do to the other. In these examples, the verbs are "affects," "buys," "modify," and "causally affected." For experiments, it is advisable to stay away from less precise words such as "explore," "understand," and "examine," and instead to use more specific, causal language such as this. Other good words to use include "differs," "improves," and similar words. For example, a statement might say, "The purpose of this study is to test the idea that photographs *improve* ethical reasoning," or "The purpose of this study is to see if assessments of credibility *differ* with the pitch of a radio announcer's voice."

To write a clear and focused statement of the research problem for an experiment, first determine what the cause (or intervention, manipulation, independent variable) is, then say what it is expected to do (differ, affect, modify, cause—the verb) to some outcome (the effect or dependent variable). Here, I offer my fill-in-the-blanks template for writing a statement of the research problem:

*"The purpose of this study is to see how* (one thing, insert the cause, intervention, manipulation, treatment, or independent variable) (does something, insert a verb—differs, affects, modifies, causes, changes, etc.) *to* (something else, insert effect, outcome, dependent variable)."

Some of the terms in these examples, such as *harm associations*, might not be familiar if they are outside your discipline, so it helps to examine some experiments in your own field for other examples that may be more commonplace. Also notice how all of these are only one sentence long. Writing such a clear, focused, and easily understandable statement that describes the experiment in one sentence is not easy. It is not surprising to have to write, rewrite, and edit it many times. Have someone familiar with the discipline read it and see if he or she can understand it. As the project evolves, you may have to rewrite this statement, maybe even a few times.

Many experiments have more than one purpose, so two or three statements of the problem may be written. If that is the case, put them together in the paper and link them with phrases like "This study also seeks to . . ." For example: "This study tests whether photographs improve ethical reasoning. If this effect is found, this study also seeks to determine the causal mechanism for this improvement." This way, one has the primary purpose of the experiment followed by additional purposes all in one place rather than spread out around the paper. Readers will appreciate having everything the study intends to do all listed together rather than reading a slowly evolving purpose of the study, waiting for it to unfold like a murder mystery.

Once satisfied with the statement of the problem, authors will need to remind readers periodically throughout the paper what the mission is, so be sure that the statement of the problem stays consistent. One frequent problem I see when reviewing experiments for journals is how the stated goal of the study changes as the paper progresses. Finally, a good practice is to write the statement of the problem on a sticky note and paste it on your computer where you can see it as you work. This will help keep you focused and consistent.

## Answering the "So What" Question

After formulating this clear and focused statement, the next step is to articulate why this study is important. This is commonly referred to as answering the "so what" question. Some journals even have a highlighted box that is devoted to this—for example, see the "Significance" box in *Proceedings of the National Academy of Sciences*.[56] This is another area where researchers frequently think the importance of their study is obvious and should not have to point it out; in fact, this is one of the most crucial aspects of a study. For this task, I tell students they need to state the obvious. It may be abundantly clear to you, but it will not necessarily seem so to other readers. To do this, think about the reason your study is important on three different levels: (1) to other academics, (2) to professionals in the field, and (3) to society or people in general. For the first, you can point out some gap in knowledge or some obstacle that the study overcomes. It should also contribute to theory in some way or help uncover any of the mechanisms or reasons for some phenomenon. One reason that is never acceptable alone is because a study has never been done before. That is a start, but you should always go further to say why it is important that it be done beyond never having been done before; otherwise, perhaps it has never been done before for a good reason.

Frequently, one sees researchers point out the importance to other scholars but overlook the other two groups: professionals and the public. For any kind of study, being able to articulate why your findings are meaningful beyond academia is crucial to research that makes a difference. R. Barker Bausell's book *Conducting Meaningful Experiments*[57] is predicated on that premise. For the second step in considering the "so what" question, ask if your study will be of interest to those in the professional arm of your discipline. Will it help accountants, campaign managers, teachers, public relations professionals, or anyone else do their jobs better? Will the findings of the study give professionals more insight into their own subconscious decision making? Will it help them overcome some obstacle or give them evidence they need to change the way they practice their craft? Perhaps it will show them which of their efforts are paying off in the outcome they desire and which are not, whether that is more engaged citizens or more customers. Making this kind of concerted effort to solve real-world problems helps bridge the gap between scholars and the profession they serve.

Finally, being able to say why all of society will benefit results in more meaningful science. Too often, the public considers academic researchers to be "eggheads in ivory towers" writing about things that have no basis in reality in order to get another publication. There are even awards that make the news for the most wasteful research.[58] Having one's research ridiculed in this way might be avoided if studies better articulated why seemingly silly or obvious findings are important to someone other than our scholarly colleagues. This kind of attention does nothing to help advance the cause of research or increase funding for it—conducting research that is meaningful to ordinary people does. So answer the "so what" question; will it help anyone or improve any social ills? Not every study will broker world peace, but it might help lessen racial profiling, change a morally repugnant practice, or give policy makers information needed to pass a law. Not every study articulates all three, but thinking through the benefits to these different publics can help experimentalists design studies that are truly meaningful. For some examples of statements that answer the "so what" question, see How To Do It box 1.4.

---

**HOW TO DO IT 1.4**

Examples of Answers to the "So What" Question

---

**From: Neil, Nicole, and Emily A. Jones. 2015. "Studying Treatment Intensity: Lessons from Two Preliminary Studies."** *Journal of Behavioral Education* **24: 51–73.**

"There is only a recent and small literature examining treatment intensity, and the research on treatment intensity focused on specific disorders is even more limited. It may be that etiology and characteristics associated with specific etiologies impact the effects of intervention intensity. Many children with Down syndrome display poor task persistence and inconsistent motivational orientation . . . For some learners with Down syndrome, it is possible that there is an optimum moderate level of intensity, past which learners engage in greater levels of escape-motivated problem behavior and there are diminishing gains in acquisition rates."[59]

**From: Coleman, Renita. 2011. "Color Blind: Race and the Ethical Reasoning of African Americans on Journalism Dilemmas."** *Journalism and Mass Communication Quarterly* **88 (2) (Summer): 337–351.**

"This study is of value because it provides important information to evaluate one of the solutions offered to the problem of stereotypical media portrayals—hiring and promoting more minority journalists. Newsrooms across the country are staffed primarily by whites; incorporating more minority viewpoints should lead to more equal coverage of minorities, according to the argument. . . . it is important to examine whether minority journalists do in fact exhibit more tolerant attitudes toward minorities in their cognitive processing. To date, there is no empirical evidence that black journalists have more favorable perceptions of blacks in the news. . . . This study also fills that void by exploring how race influences the ethical reasoning of blacks when blacks and whites are in news stories."[60]

**From: Aday, Sean. 2006. "The Framesetting Effects of News: An Experimental Test of Advocacy Versus Objectivist Frames."** *Journalism and Mass Communication Quarterly* **83 (4) (Winter): 767–784.**

"Specifically, we still do not know enough about why effects are found in some cases and not others, and too little work has been done exploring the cognitive basis of the effect that would allow us to develop a theory for when and why some attributes would have a second-level effect and others would not."[61]

**From: Elias, Julio J., Nicola Lacetera, and Mario Macis. 2015. "Markets and Morals: An Experimental Survey Study."** *PLoS ONE* **10 (6) (June 1): 1–13. Public Library of Science.**

"Prohibiting some of these transactions has costs. Life insurance contracts, for instance, were once illegal because they were seen as gambles against God; they now create value for millions of people, and are viewed as a form of 'institutionalized altruism.' Similarly, the idea of an all-volunteer paid army was long rejected in the United States, despite arguments showing its efficiency. The prohibition of payments to people who give their organs contributes to the growing gap between organ demand and supply. Banning some trades may also lead to the formation of illegal markets, which, in turn, entail further costs such as violence . . ."[62]

**From: Grober, Jens, Ernesto Reuben, and Agnieszka Tymula. 2013. "Political Quid Pro Quo Agreements: An Experimental Study."** *American Journal of Political Science* **57 (3) (July): 582–597.**

"There are good reasons to suspect there is some truth behind the common belief that money in politics is undesirable. First, in spite of being banned, political quid pro quo can occur outside publicly observable channels. Second, for economically powerful special interests, most of which are large corporate firms, giving as an investment that increases profits is a more plausible explanation than political participation. Moreover, returned favors to such interests, such as specific tax breaks, subsidies, and regulations, can be easily concealed as an economic necessity and are therefore hard to quantify. Third, collusion between major candidates may also take the form of an agreement on a common view with regard to a given political issue . . . Finally, even if the impact of money in politics is overestimated by the public, this belief can affect the public's political trust and behavior."[63]

## Common Mistakes

- Not clearly stating the purpose of the research, and not keeping it consistent throughout the paper

- Not putting all the things the study intends to do in one place, but having the goals of the study unfold slowly through the article

- Not putting the statement of purpose up high in the paper, in the introduction and before page 3

- Failing to say why the study is important to theory, other researchers, the profession, and regular people. "Because it has never been done" is not a reason why a study is important by itself.

## Test Your Knowledge

1. Experiments need to show that the cause precedes the effect but not that it is necessarily related to it. If there is a statistically significant relationship between two things, that is all that matters.

   a. True

   b. False

2. A researcher studied the effects of attractiveness on how well students liked a teacher. The attractive teacher was twenty-five years old; the unattractive teacher was forty-five years old. The problem here is that:

a. Age is confounded with attractiveness

b. It is hard to define attractiveness

c. The cause did not precede the effect

d. The researcher did not control for political ideology

3. You assign fifteen employees to go to a one-day seminar on stress management. Another fifteen are assigned to a one-week seminar. At the end of the month, you measure each employee's perceived level of stress. What is the treatment or manipulation in this study?

a. How stressed out employees are

b. How long the seminar is

c. How you chose the thirty employees

d. The quality of the stress management teacher

4. A study measures students' arousal level before they take a test. It finds that as arousal increases, performance decreases. This finding shows:

a. Causality

b. Correlation

c. A plausible alternative explanation

d. A confound

5. Which of the following is NOT one of the three basic criteria for an experiment?

a. Cause must precede the effect

b. The effect must be unlikely to have occurred by chance

c. Cause must be related to the effect

d. There are no plausible alternative explanations for the effect

6. Variation is achieved by:

a. Holding everything constant

b. Using demographics as covariates

c. Systematically changing something

d. Having a control group

7. Things that could provide plausible alternative explanations are called:

a. Covariates

b. Confounds

c. Independent variables

d. Causal mechanisms

8. In experiments, control groups serve the purpose of:

   a. Allowing us to know what happens to people who receive the treatment

   b. Allowing us to generalize to more people

   c. Allowing us to know what would happen to subjects if they had not received the treatment

   d. Allowing us to say some effect occurred with a specific degree of certainty

9. In an experiment, "assignment" is:

   a. The task that subjects must complete

   b. How authorship order is calculated for the paper

   c. The way researchers ensure subjects believe the experiment is real

   d. How subjects are put in the different interventions or control group

10. The gold standard in experiments is to assign subjects:

   a. Representatively

   b. Purposively

   c. Randomly

   d. Haphazardly

Answers:

| | | | |
|---|---|---|---|
| 1. b | 4. b | 7. b | 9. d |
| 2. a | 5. b | 8. c | 10. c |
| 3. b | 6. c | | |

## Application Exercises

1. Use scholar.google.com or your school library's database to find studies that use experimental designs in your discipline. Include the word *experiment, experimental design,* or *controlled experiment* in the search terms. Read three of the experiments that interest you most and look for the concepts covered here. Specifically, identify the treatment group or groups. Is there a control group? If so, what is used to represent "no treatment"? Identify the statement of the problem and the answer to the "so what" question.

2. Think up three distinct studies that you would like to do with an experiment. That is, something should be manipulated or changed in order to see what effect it has on some outcome. Write a clear and focused statement of the problem. Explain why it is important to academics, the profession, and the world at large (the "so what" question). Use 250 words for each. These should not be straight replications but new ideas, or they may be replications with substantial extensions to the study you are replicating.

## Suggested Readings

The introduction and Chapters 1 and 2 of Bausell, R. B. 1994. *Conducting Meaningful Experiments: 40 Steps to Becoming a Scientist*. Thousand Oaks, CA: Sage.

Chapter 1 in Shadish, W. R., T. D. Cook, and D. T. Campbell. 2002. *Experimental and Quasi-Experimental Designs for Generalized Causal Inference*. Belmont, CA: Wadsworth Cengage Learning.

Thorson, Esther, Robert H. Wicks, and Glenn Leshner. 2012. "Experimental Methodology in Journalism and Mass Communication Research." *Journalism and Mass Communication Quarterly* 89 (1): 112–124.

## Notes

1. Markus MacGill, "What Is a Randomized Controlled Trial in Medical Research?" *Medical News Today*, http://www.medicalnewstoday.com/articles/280574.php. Accessed February 10, 2017.

2. Harald O. Stolberg, Geoffrey Norman, and Isabelle Trop, "Fundamentals of Clinical Research for Radiologists: Randomized Controlled Trials," *American Journal of Roentgenology* 183, no. 6 (2004): 1539–1544.

3. Marcia L. Meldrum, "A Brief History of the Randomized Controlled Trial: From Oranges and Lemons to the Gold Standard," *Hematology/Oncology Clinics of North America* 14, no. 4 (2000): 745–760.

4. S. Shikata et al., "Comparison of Effects in Randomized Controlled Trials with Observational Studies in Digestive Surgery," *Annals of Surgery* 244, no. 5 (2006): 668–676; Stolberg, Norman, and Trop, "Fundamentals of Clinical Research for Radiologists."

5. Streptomycin in Tuberculosis Trials Committee, "Streptomycin Treatment of Pulmonary Tuberculosis: A Medical Research Council Investigation," *British Medical Journal* 2, no. 4582 (1948): 769–782.

6. D. T. Campbell and J. C. Stanley, *Experimental and Quasi-Experimental Designs for Research* (Chicago: Rand McNally, 1963), 3.

7. Esther Thorson, Robert H. Wicks, and Glenn Leshner, "Experimental Methodology in Journalism and Mass Communication Research," *Journalism and Mass Communication Quarterly* 89, no. 1 (2012): 112–124.

8. R. McDermott, "New Directions for Experimental Work in International Relations," *International Studies Quarterly* 55, no. 2 (2011): 503–520.

9. Matthew C. Makel et al., "Replication of Special Education Research: Necessary but Far Too Rare," *Remedial and Special Education* 37, no. 3 (2016): 1–8.

10. Rebecca B. Morton and Kenneth C. Williams, *Experimental Political Science and the Study of Causality: From Nature to the Lab* (New York: Cambridge University Press, 2010): 5–6, 16–17; Gerry Stoker, "Exploring the Promise of Experimentation in Political Science: Micro-Foundational Insights and Policy Relevance," *Political Studies* 58 (2010): 300–319; Cengiz Erisen, Elif Erisen, and Binnur Ozkececi-Taner, "Research Methods in Political Psychology," *Turkish Studies* 13, no. 1 (2013): 13–33; James N. Druckman et al., "The Growth and Development of Experimental Research in Political Science," *American Political Science Review* 100, no. 4 (2006): 627–635.

11. Ulrich Hamenstädt, "Teaching Experimental Political Science: Experiences from a Seminar on Methods," *European Political Science* 11, no. 1 (2012): 114–127; Erisen, Erisen, and Ozkececi-Taner, "Research Methods in Political Psychology"; James N. Druckman and Arthur Lipia, "Experimenting with Politics," *Science* 335, no. 6 (March 9, 2012): 1177–1179; Luke Keele, Corrine McConnaughy, and Ismail White, "Strengthening the Experimenter's Toolbox: Statistical Estimation of Internal Validity," *American Journal of Political Science* 56, no. 2 (2012): 484–499; Sharon Crasnow, "Natural Experiments and Pluralism in Political Science," *Philosophy of the Social Sciences* 45, no. 4/5 (2015): 424–441.

12. Yair Levy, Timothy J. Ellis, and Eli Cohen, "A Guide for Novice Researchers on Experimental and

Quasi-Experimental Studies in Information Systems Research," *Interdisciplinary Journal of Information, Knowledge and Management* 6 (2011): 151–161.

13. Susan D. Hyde, "Experiments in International Relations: Lab, Survey, and Field," *Annual Reviews of Political Science* 18 (2015): 403–424. Hamenstädt, "Teaching Experimental Political Science."

14. Erisen, Erisen, and Ozkececi-Taner, "Research Methods in Political Psychology."

15. William J. Reid, Bonnie Davis Kenaley, and Julanne Colvin, "Do Some Interventions Work Better Than Others? A Review of Comparative Social Work Experiments," *Social Work Research* 28, no. 2 (2004): 71–81.

16. Joshua B. Plavnick and Summer J. Ferreri, "Single-Case Experimental Designs in Educational Research: A Methodology for Causal Analyses in Teaching and Learning," *Education Psychology Review* 25 (2013): 549–569.

17. William R. Shadish, Thomas D. Cook, and Donald T. Campbell, *Experimental and Quasi-Experimental Designs for Generalized Causal Inference* (Belmont, CA: Wadsworth Cengage Learning, 2002).

18. K. Imai, G. King, and E. Stuart, "Misunderstandings Between Experimentalists and Observationalists About Causal Inference," *Journal of the Royal Statistical Society* Series A 171 (2008): 481–502.

19. Gustav Fischer, "Ornithologische Monatsberichte," *Jahrgang,* 44, no. 2 (1936); Gustav Fischer, "Statistiches Jahrbuch Deutscher Gemeinden," *Jahrgang,* 48, no. 1 (1940): 27–33, http://pignottia.faculty.mjc.edu/math134/classnotes/storks.pdf

20. http://faculty.vassar.edu/lowry/ch3pt2.html

21. Carter Hay et al., "Inside the Black Box: Identifying the Variables That Mediate the Effects of an Experimental Intervention for Adolescents," *Crime & Deliquency* 61, no. 2 (2015): 243–270.

22. Renita Coleman, "The Effect of Visuals on Ethical Reasoning: What's a Photograph Worth to Journalists Making Moral Decisions?" *Journalism and Mass Communication Quarterly* 83, no. 4 (2006): 835–850.

23. H. Denis Wu and Renita Coleman, "The Affective Effect on Political Judgment: Comparing the Influences of Candidate Attributes and Issue Congruence," *Journalism and Mass Communication Quarterly* 91, no. 3 (2014): 530–543.

24. Daniel Stevens, "Tone Versus Information: Explaining the Impact of Negative Political Advertising," *Journal of Political Marketing* 11, no. 4 (2012): 322–352.

25. Arthur Asa Berger, "Semiotics and TV," in *Understanding Television: Essays on Television as a Social and Cultural Force,* ed. R. R. Adler (New York: Praeger, 1981): 91–114.

26. Zhao Na et al., "Face Attractiveness in Building Trust: Evidence From Measurement of Implicit and Explicit Responses," *Social Behavior and Personality: An International Journal* 43, no. 5 (2015): 855–866; Leslie A. Zebrowitz, Robert G. Franklin Jr., and Rocco Palumbo, "Ailing Voters Advance Attractive Congressional Candidates," *Evolutionary Psychology* 13, no. 1 (2015): 16–28.

27. Amy E. Lerman, Katherine T. McCabe, and Meredith L. Sadin, "Political Ideology, Skin Tone, and the Psychology of Candidate Evaluations," *Public Opinion Quarterly* 79, no. 1 (2015): 53–90; Sarah Reckhow, Matt Grossmann, and Benjamin C. Evans, "Policy Cues and Ideology in Attitudes toward Charter Schools," *Policy Studies Journal* 43, no. 2 (2015): 207–227; Jonathon Schuldt and Adam Pearson, "The Role of Race and Ethnicity in Climate Change Polarization: Evidence from a U.S. National Survey Experiment," *Climatic Change* 136, no. 3/4 (2016): 495–505.

28. Stoker, "Exploring the Promise of Experimentation in Political Science."

29. Kevin J. Mullinix et al., "The Generalizability of Survey Experiments," *Journal of Experimental Political Science* 2 (2015): 109–138.

30. J. R. Rest and Darcia Narvaez, eds., *Moral Development in the Professions: Psychology and Applied Ethics* (Hillsdale, NJ: Erlbaum, 1994).

31. James. R. Rest, "Morality," in *Handbook of Child Psychology, Vol. III Cognitive Development,*, ed. P. H. Mussen (New York: Wiley, 1983).

32. Stephen Thoma, "Estimating Gender Differences in the Comprehension and Preference of Moral Issues," *Developmental Review* 6, no. 2 (1986).

33. A. J. De Craen et al., "Placebos and Placebo Effects in Medicine: Historial Overview," *Journal of the Royal Society of Medicine* 92, no. 10 (1999): 511–515.

34. Ibid.

35. Ibid.; David B. Elliott, "The Placebo Effect: Is It Unethical to Use It or Unethical Not To?" *Ophthalmic & Physiological Optics* 36, no. 5 (2016): 513–518.

36. Elliott, "The Placebo Effect."

37. H. K. Beecher, "The Powerful Placebo," *JAMA* 159, no. 17 (1955): 1602–1606.

38. De Craen et al., "Placebos and Placebo Effects in Medicine."

39. Beecher, "The Powerful Placebo."

40. De Craen et al., "Placebos and Placebo Effects in Medicine."

41. H. K. Beecher, "Surgery as Placebo: A Quantitative Study of Bias," *JAMA* 176 (1961): 1102–1107.

42. Beecher, "The Powerful Placebo."

43. P. C. Goetzsche, "Is There Logic in the Placebo?" *Lancet* 344, no. 8927 (1994): 904.

44. Alan Bryman, "Placebo," in *The Sage Encyclopedia of Social Science Research Methods*, ed. Michael S. Lewis-Beck, Alan Bryman, and Tim Futing Liao (Thousand Oaks, CA: Sage, 2011): 825.

45. Ibid.

46. Aaron M. Garvey, Frank Germann, and Lisa E. Bolton, "Performance Brand Placebos: How Brands Improve Performance and Consumers Take the Credit," *Journal of Consumer Research* 42, no. 6 (2016): 931–951.

47. Michael A. Kuhn, Peter Kuhn, and Marie Claire Villeval, "Decision-Environment Effects on Intertemporal Financial Choices: How Relevant Are Resource-Depletion Models?" *Journal of Economic Behavior & Organization* 137 (2017): 72–89.

48. Yann Cornil, Pierre Chandon, and Aradhna Krishna, "Does Red Bull Give Wings to Vodka? Placebo Effects of Marketing Labels on Perceived Intoxication and Risky Attitudes and Behaviors," *Journal of Consumer Psychology (Elsevier Science)* 27, no. 4 (2017): 456–465.

49. Carlos Alberto Alves, Evandro Luiz Lopes, and José Mauro da Costa Hernandez, "It Makes Me Feel So Good: An Experimental Study of the Placebo Effect Generated by Brands," *Journal of International Consumer Marketing* 29, no. 4 (2017): 223–238.

50. Gwen Sharp, "The Placebo Effect," *The Society Pages,* March 10, 2011, https://thesocietypages.org/socimages/2011/03/10/the-placebo-effect/.

51. Mike Schmierbach and Anne Oeldorf-Hirsch, "A Little Bird Told Me, So I Didn't Believe It: Twitter, Credibility, and Issue Perceptions," *Communication Quarterly* 60, no. 3 (2012): 317–337.

52. Jens Grober, Ernesto Reuben, and Agnieszka Tymula, "Political Quid Pro Quo Agreements: An Experimental Study," *American Journal of Political Science* 57, no. 3 (2013): 582–597.

53. Shirley S. Ho and Douglas M. McLeod, "Social-Psychological Influences on Opinion Expression in Face-to-Face and Computer-Mediated Communication," *Communication Research* 35, no. 2 (2008): 190–207.

54. Julio J. Elias, Nicola Lacetera, and Mario Macis, "Markets and Morals: An Experimental Survey Study," *PLoS ONE* 10, no. 6 (2015): 1–13.

55. Pazit Ben-Nun Bloom, "Disgust, Harm and Morality in Politics," *Political Psychology* 35, no. 4 (2014): 495–513.

56. For an example, see William Minozzi et al., "Field Experiment Evidence of Substantive, Attributional, and Behavioral Persuasion by Members of Congress in Online Town Halls," *Proceedings of the National Academy of Sciences* 112, no. 13 (2015): 3937–3942.

57. R. Barker Bausell, *Conducting Meaningful Experiments: 40 Steps to Becoming a Scientist* (Thousand Oaks, CA: Sage, 1994).

58. FoxNews.com, "Senate Report Finds Billions in Waste on Science Foundation Studies," Foxnews.com, http://www.foxnews.com/politics/2011/05/26/senate-report-finds-billions-waste-science-foundation-studies/.

59. Nicole Neil and Emily A. Jones, "Studying Treatment Intensity: Lessons From Two Preliminary Studies," *Journal of Behavioral Education* 24 (2015): 51–73.

60. Renita Coleman, "Color Blind: Race and the Ethical Reasoning of African Americans on Journalism Dilemmas," *Journalism and Mass Communication Quarterly,* 88, no. 2 (Summer 2011): 337–351.

61. Sean Aday, "The Framesetting Effects of News: An Experimental Test of Advocacy Versus Objectivist Frames," *Journalism and Mass Communication Quarterly* 83, no. 4 (2006): 767–784.

62. Elias, Lacetera, and Macis, "Markets and Morals," 2.

63. Grober, Reuben, and Tymula, "Political Quid Pro Quo Agreements," 582–583.

# 2

# ETHICS AND FAMOUS EXPERIMENTS IN HISTORY

*If I have seen further than others, it is by standing upon the shoulders of giants.*

**—Isaac Newton**

This chapter briefly deviates from the practical how-to approach in order to give some context in which to understand the role of current issues, concepts, and techniques in social science experiments. This brief history will illustrate how experimental methodology has developed by using stories of some of the most famous, and infamous, experiments from the past—for example, how **randomization**, or the process of assigning subjects to groups, came about, and why experimentalists use terms like *split plots*. Some stories highlight ingenious ways to answer questions, encouraging researchers to think creatively about their own studies. Creativity is important in research not just for novelty's sake but also to help answer questions in the best way possible. Other examples show the importance of protecting participants from harm and how they helped lead to the development of Institutional Review Boards (IRBs), committees charged with ensuring researchers follow ethical guidelines. Many of these stories are quite entertaining, and some have even been made into movies for mass audiences. More important, understanding the historical roots can lead to a better grasp of contemporary practices. Other examples show how findings from experiments can affect real-world problems—for example, the famous studies that examined why good people do bad things. In this chapter are some of the stories of the "giants" from the quote by Isaac Newton upon whose shoulders experimental methodology is built.

The history of experimental design is filled with fascinating studies, often hyped as the most evil, creepy, bizarre, or ones that went horribly wrong. Studies that could never be conducted again are also a popular theme in the "mad science" category. This chapter will take a different approach; instead of dwelling on the findings or theories created by these experiments, it will highlight the development and early use of important discoveries such as random assignment, controls, and the use of confederates. Importantly, how ethical guidelines developed and IRBs came about will be included. (Chapter 11 will discuss IRBs and other ethical issues not fully addressed here in more detail.) Many of these studies are already known through popular folklore; in those cases, I try not to repeat the obvious but instead highlight aspects that are not as familiar. This chapter does not purport to be exhaustive or cover every important experiment ever conducted; of necessity, many are left out. In particular, the received history tends to leave out women and experimentalists of color. This chapter deals with some of these forgotten figures in More About . . . box 2.1, Contributions of Women. Many historians trace the development of experiments back to the ancient Greeks or others. After the introduction of one very early and important medical experiment, I devote the rest of this chapter to more modern social science experiments.

## THE SCURVY STUDIES

Some of the earliest experiments were conducted on a disease called scurvy in 1747. Rare today, it was particularly problematic on ships as it caused sailors to become weak and anemic, and also caused their skin to bleed and gums to rot.[23] A ship's surgeon, James Lind, carried out one of the first controlled experiments to find a cure.[24] He chose twelve men who all had scurvy, using only men who "were as similar as I could have them."[25] He then divided them into six groups, putting two men in each. These six

# MORE ABOUT . . . BOX 2.1
## Contributions of Women

While men are most frequently cited as early pioneers of experimental design in the social sciences, there were also many important women, including women of color. These scientists faced barriers and discrimination in their careers, including a lack of fellowships and being barred from admission to graduate programs and employment in academic positions that allowed research and publishing.[1] Some women completed doctoral work, including theses and dissertations, but were denied the degrees. Men received credit for some of the contributions of women. Some women collaborated with their husbands, and antinepotism policies prevented them from being hired. Racial discrimination placed even more burdens on minority women.[2]

What few histories include women primarily note their theoretical contributions rather than their advancements in the methodology of experimental design, which is the subject of this book.[3] Next are short profiles of three women, including one African American, who made contributions to experimental methodology.[4] More certainly deserve recognition.

**Mary Whiton Calkins** is one of the pioneers of experimental psychology, remembered for, among other things, inventing the paired-associates task, a test of memory using paired numbers and colors.[5] Despite having completed all the requirements for a doctorate, Harvard refused to grant her a degree in 1890 because she was a woman.[6] Yale and the University of Michigan offered her admission, but she turned them down because they lacked a laboratory for experiments, which Harvard had. It was easier for women to find academic positions at women's colleges, so Calkins went to work at Wellesley and established an experimental laboratory there. Despite not having a doctorate, Calkins published four books and more than 100 papers in scientific journals.[7] Her accomplishments led to Columbia University and Smith College awarding her honorary doctorates. Despite this recognition and a petition to Harvard signed by thirteen graduates who were prestigious alumni, she was again denied a degree in 1927.[8]

William Notman

Calkins crossed paths with another experimentalist in this chapter, Joseph Jastrow, who along with Charles S. Peirce helped identify the benefits of random assignment. Jastrow published a study on the kinds of words produced by men and women when asked to write them out quickly, concluding that women's words were repetitive, individual, and concrete, whereas men's words were constructive, useful, and abstract.[9] She criticized his conclusion, pointing out the confounding effects of the environment, training, and socialization of women.[10] She was an advocate for women's rights all her life, repeatedly refusing to accept a doctoral degree from Radcliffe for work she did at Harvard.

**Mamie Phipps Clark** was an African American psychologist noted for developing the Clark Doll Test for her research on race, which was used in the 1954 *Brown v. Board of Education* case that allowed African American students to attend White schools.[11] Unlike Calkins, Clark earned a doctoral degree in 1943, becoming the first African American woman to do so from

New York Post Archives/Contributor

*(Continued)*

(Continued)

Columbia University. The first African American male to earn a doctorate from Columbia was her husband and research partner, Kenneth B. Clark.[12] He always credited her with the idea for the doll test.[13]

Mamie Clark's contribution to experimental methods involved showing children two identical dolls, one Black and one White. The children were asked which doll was bad and which was good, which one the child liked to play with, and which one most looked like them. Many Black children identified the Black doll as bad, and almost half said the White doll looked most like them. This was more pronounced in children from segregated schools than integrated ones.[14] The Clarks' experiments were important evidence that segregation harmed children, and also were influential in the first mass-produced doll of a Black infant.[15] Clark never found a position in academia, instead working as a researcher and then clinical psychologist at a children's home until she and her husband opened a testing and consultation center for minority children in Harlem.[16]

**Mary Ainsworth** is remembered for an assessment technique known as the "Strange Situation."[17] Work using this method helped advance psychologists' understanding of children's attachment to their caregivers. Ainsworth's method involved researchers observing through a one-way mirror a child's behavior during eight different episodes of about three minutes each where a mother and child come to the researcher's laboratory, which is filled with toys. The different episodes involve a stranger entering the room and trying to befriend the child, the mother leaving the child alone with the stranger, returning, both mother and stranger leaving the child alone, the stranger re-entering to comfort the child, and finally, the stranger picking the child up.[18] Observations were recorded every 15 seconds on a 1 to 7 scale. The assessment had good reliability, meaning other researchers could reproduce the findings.[19] Typical for a laboratory experiment, the method was criticized as being artificial and lacking in ecological validity,[20] and also on ethical grounds for causing stress in young children.[21]

Many other women also contributed to experimental methodology by authoring or coauthoring other tests and measures, including Grace Kent-Rosanoff's Word Association Test, Florence Goodenough's Draw-a-Man Test, and Grace Fernald's character tests that preceded other tests of moral development, among many others.[22]

groups then got different treatments ranging from a quart of cider; sulphuric acid; a half pint of seawater; a mixture of garlic, mustard, and horseradish in a dose "the bigness of a nutmeg"[26]; vinegar; or two oranges and a lemon.[27] Lind had six treatment conditions for this medical study, which is considered a lot in social science today, with two to four more common.[28] He also had a very small number of subjects—only twelve, with just two in each treatment group. Small sample sizes are more typical in medical studies, where large effects are more common than in social science. Another important issue in this study was the problem of how to assign people to conditions. Lind recognized the dilemma with groups where people were dissimilar on important factors, understanding that people's inherent individual differences, such as age, weight, and general health, could affect the results. He limited his sample to men who were as similar as possible on certain requirements in order to get results of the treatment that were not confounded by these extraneous factors. Here, he used what would later be known as a **matching** strategy, pairing up men with similar characteristics. Importantly, he manipulated only these six conditions while holding everything else (that he could think of) constant. His independent variables—the six different dietary supplements—were not drawn from theory but from cures that had been proposed earlier. However, Lind did write about how the theory on scurvy was mostly conjecture by researchers who had never seen it, and advocated a mix of theory and hands-on experience. His measurement of one of the treatments' doses—the size of a nutmeg—is not very precise; today, that would be measured in grams or something similar.

James Lind

Lind's study was a huge success by any standard. After only six days, the men who were given the oranges and lemon recovered.[29] The other men also improved, but the ones who ate citrus fruit had a dramatic recovery compared to the others, which eventually led to the recognition that vitamin C was the agent at work. No statistical tests of significance were performed, but the effects at six days were obvious.

This study was important for several reasons; it recognized that people needed to be assigned to treatment groups in such a way that individual differences would not matter, which Lind accomplished by carefully selecting men who had similar characteristics. This was in 1747. By the late 1800s, assigning subjects to conditions had become a burning topic and a different solution emerged, although it was applied to the treatments rather than the subjects, as illustrated in the next story.

## THE CONTRIBUTIONS OF CHARLES PEIRCE

Charles Sanders Peirce and his student Joseph Jastrow were by some accounts the first to use random assignment.[30] The first study to use it was conducted in 1885 to see if people could judge how much something weighed just by feeling and looking at it.[31] The theoretical construct Peirce (pronounced "purse") was interested in was the source of judgment errors, resulting in concepts such as the just-noticeable difference, which business, marketing, and advertising scholars will recognize. In the first study, Peirce began the first experiment by always starting and ending with the heaviest weights. In the second study, he tried alternating the heaviest with the lightest weight. Last, he describes how he used a pack of cards

Charles Sanders Peirce

to randomly assign the order of the weights. His results were vastly different from the first two trials when the order of the weights had not been randomized, showing the importance of this technique.[32] Peirce used a deck of cards and simply shuffled them before drawing out a card that would determine which weight would come next. Today, we tend to use random number generators, but a deck of cards will still work just as well. He talked about how this method occasionally produced "long runs of one particular kind of change, which would occasionally be produced by chance," but notes that this was preferable to the subject knowing there would be no such patterns.[33]

To most people, the idea of something being "random" means it is unpredictable; but to Peirce, random meant that "in the long run any one individual of the whole lot would get taken as often as any other."[34] When smaller samples from a larger class are drawn in this way, Peirce said that the smaller group would show the same characteristics of the larger group. He called this the "rule of induction."[35] Chapter 7 will delve into random assignment in the social sciences; today, we more typically think of randomly assigning people to different treatments, but, as Peirce's and others' early work showed, it is important to randomize as much as you can, including the stimuli in an experiment.

As an aside, to illustrate the scope of Peirce's abilities, he is also known for developing a theory of semiotics, signs and symbols—one of the classic theories still in use today in critical/cultural work.[36]

# RONALD FISHER'S PLOTS AND TEA

Decades later, Ronald Aylmer Fisher revived and popularized the idea of random assignment of treatments, leading to its widespread use.[37] Fisher was an agricultural scientist outside London in the 1920s and '30s. He is credited with inventing the design of experiments, including many of the statistics, concepts, and procedures still in use today.[38] For example, Fisher developed **analysis of variance**, whose statistic, the **F test**, was named after him, and also the idea of **Latin Square**, a procedure for ordering treatments to compensate for systematic error or control unintended variation instead of randomizing (more about this in chapter 7).[i] Fisher was also credited with proposing the probability values of .05 and .01 for statistical significance, which is a scientist's way of judging whether something deviates from chance.[39] A *p* value of .05 means there is a "one in twenty chance that the result is mistaken."[40]

Fisher's job was to test various fertilizers on crops at the Rothamsted Agricultural Experimental Station in England. Because of this, many of the terms still used in experiments today have an agricultural basis, such as **split plot designs**, which actually comes from the plots in fields that were split into separate sections so that each could receive a different treatment. When Fisher arrived at the station, it had been standard to test a different fertilizer every year. But Fisher realized that each year brought inherent differences in rainfall, temperature, weed growth, drainage, and other

Ronald Fisher

factors.[41] He coined the term *confound* when he realized there was no way to separate the effects of the fertilizers from these other conditions that were out of his control.[42] To determine whether the outcome was due to the fertilizer or something else, he decided to include all of the treatments—in his case, the many different kinds of fertilizers—in the same experiment. By cutting up the fields into small plots, with the pieces divided up into different rows and each row given a different treatment, he reasoned that the yearly differences would apply to all the treatments, effectively "controlling" those confounding conditions.

In addition, Fisher also is credited with popularizing random assignment.[43] This also grew out of his efforts to control the various conditions when he realized that systematically assigning different fertilizers to the fields could not rule out confounding factors associated with the soil and fields themselves. To solve this, he randomly assigned the fields to receive different treatments. In social science today, we think of random assignment as applying to the subjects who are assigned to different treatments; for Fisher, the fields were

---

[i]As a geneticist, Fisher was also interested in evolution and eugenics—the idea that selective breeding could improve the human race. Eugenics had been discussed since early Greece and Rome, and was a respectable scientific topic in his day, supported by many including George Bernard Shaw and Alexander Graham Bell. Fisher helped found a eugenics society at Cambridge University. The idea was thoroughly discredited after being associated with the genocide policies of Nazi Germany. (Gregory Cochran and Henry Harpending, *The 10,000 Year Explosion: How Civilization Accelerated Human Evolution* [New York: Basic Books, 2009]; Encyclopedia Britannica, Sir Ronald Aylmer Fisher, https://www.britannica.com/biography/Ronald-Aylmer-Fisher, accessed March 30, 2018; Famous Scientists, https://www.famousscientists.org/ronald-fisher/, accessed March 15, 2018.)

Vanderdecken, Wikimedia Commons

his subjects. In the sense of random assignment, "random" means by a chance procedure, such as flipping a coin, and ensures that each participant has an equal chance of being assigned to any of the treatment or control groups. This helps ensure that any systematic differences are equally distributed across the different groups, so that any differences can be attributed to the treatment, not something inherently different about the people in the groups. Chapter 7 will discuss random assignment and how it is achieved in more depth.

One of Fisher's more relatable experiments that used random assignment is the now-famous Lady Tasting Tea experiment. It also illustrates the idea of a **null hypothesis**, or the supposition that there will be no difference between those who get the treatment and those who do not. As the story goes, a woman who claimed she could tell if the milk was added before or after the tea was given four cups where the tea was added first, and four cups where the milk was added first, the order of which was randomized. The null hypothesis was that she could *not* tell them apart. The chance of someone guessing all eight correctly was one in seventy; the woman in the study purportedly got all eight correct.[44] The tea experiment was supposedly a summer afternoon of fun, not a scientific investigation with published results. Fisher described it in chapter 2 of his book *The Design of Experiments*.[45] Nowhere does he say if it was actually conducted or give the results, so much of this is folklore.[46] Experiments had been done for hundreds of years before Fisher, but they were idiosyncratic, varying with each experimenter. Fisher's was the first book that systematically codified how to do experiments.

## B. F. SKINNER: SMALL SAMPLES, HIGH TECH

Fisher's principles were just becoming popular when B. F. (short for Burrhus Frederic, but friends called him Fred[47]) Skinner started studying the behavior of rats.[48] Skinner is popularly known for creating the Skinner box, a device he used to train rats to push a lever for food or to stop electric shocks that he used in developing his theory of operant conditioning.[ii] Not to belabor the details of his theory or studies here, the premise was

---

[ii] He developed another box for pigeons and one for babies; a student developed one for dogs, and much later, another student inspired by Skinner developed a human Skinner box—the study carrels of today. See Rutherford 2007, 2003.[56, 57]

that animals learned to respond to stimuli, and that reinforcing a behavior makes the animal repeat it. Although Skinner's ideas were sometimes controversial and misunderstood, his work and theory continues to inspire research today, including in human psychology, animal behavior, education, marketing, health, social work, sports training, and others.[49] The discussion here is devoted to his ideas about experimental research methodology, as that is the purpose of this book.

Skinner is credited with developing a kind of experimental research in psychology that he called the *experimental analysis of behavior*.[50] It was in contrast to the deductive approach used in most psychological experiments up to that point, which first formed a hypothesis and then tested to see if it could be falsified—the approach still most often used today. Skinner's approach was **inductive** and data-driven, characterized by

B. F. Skinner

Msanders nti, Wikimedia Commons

observing and empirically measuring behavior. He never worked with formal hypotheses, saying, "If I engaged in Experimental Design at all, it was simply to complete or extend some evidence of order already observed."[51] He published his methods in his book *The Behavior of Organisms*[52] in greater detail than normal for the time.[53]

Most of his research was done with individual cases, running one subject at a time or in small groups; four rats were used in most studies in *The Behavior of Organisms*.[54] He defended his use of small samples and described when they might be better than large samples[55]—for example, when studying populations where recruiting a large number of homogeneous subjects is difficult, such as special education students, mentally ill patients, or the disabled.[58] Today, this approach is called *single-case experimental design* and is still in use for such populations, especially in clinical work.[59]

One of the reasons why it was difficult for Skinner to study large groups was the constraint of needing a Skinner box for each subject. He only had four such boxes (which he preferred to call "operant chambers") in his lab.[60] He describes how he once got a grant to build enough boxes to measure 24 rats at the same time and aggregate the data in a single, mean performance curve. He and his colleague were able to run 95 rat subjects in one study, and Skinner wrote that "the possibility of using large groups of animals greatly improves upon the method as previously reported, since tests of significance are provided for and properties of behavior not apparent in single cases may be more easily detected."[61] But most often, he ran individual subjects or samples that were too small to perform any statistical analysis. He relied on a functional analysis to determine if the intervention worked. For example, when six out of eight pigeons performed the behavior they were trained to perform, "the resulting responses were so clearly defined that two observers could agree perfectly in counting instances."[62] He felt statistics were overemphasized when what was really needed were more rigorous controls and techniques.[63] He credits Pavlov with the insight "control your conditions and you will see order."[64]

Skinner also moved experimental methods beyond researchers' observations to more objective measuring instruments. Skinner had been an inventor since he was a boy, when he built a device to remind him to hang up his pajamas.[65] To work in conjunction with the Skinner box, he devised a "cumulative recorder" that used a pen and roll of paper to automatically record when a rat pressed a lever or pigeon pecked a key. Use of response rates was widely adopted by other researchers.[66] He went on to design what he called a "gadget" or "apparatus" for many other uses.[67] For example, the kymograph used a stopwatch to record the movement and sounds of rats running around.[68] Another device used a string on a spindle to record data in a curve. "I knew that science made great use of curves, although, so far as I could discover, very little of pips on a polygram,"[69] he wrote of his previous measures. "As it turned out the curve revealed things in the rate of responding, and in changes in that rate, which would certainly otherwise have been missed."[70] Response curves continue to be an important principle in many disciplines.[71] Another invention was his adaptation of a pharmacist's pill-making machine to make uniform rat food pellets, overcoming the problem of uncontrolled variation in the size of existing rat food. When he realized how much rat chow he would need to make to reinforce every behavior, he started reinforcing only once every minute, which set off a new program of research into "periodic reinforcement."[72]

These kinds of practical problems drove much of his research, and he came to see the problems as serendipitous rather than annoying. For example, when the rat pellet delivery device jammed, he wrote, "At first I treated this as a defect and hastened to remedy" it.[73] Then, he realized what looked like a setback actually afforded the opportunity to develop "extinction curves." "It is still no exaggeration to say that some of the most interesting and surprising results have turned up first because of similar accidents."[74]

Skinner calls science a "disorderly and accidental process" without "a well-defined beginning and end."[75] *The Behavior of Organisms*[76] illustrates the messiness of science and the role of serendipity, or finding one thing while looking for another. (For a contemporary example, see Study Spotlight 2.2 on "Messy" Research.) In Skinner's case, he was open to seeing it as such. In his own words: "Here was a first principle not formally recognized by scientific methodologists: When you run onto something interesting, drop everything else and study it."[77]

This is still good advice today.

## STUDY SPOTLIGHT 2.2
An Example of "Messy" Research

Babad, E., E. Peer, and Y. Benayoun. 2012. "Can Multiple Biases Occur in a Single Situation? Evidence From Media Bias Research." *Journal of Applied Social Psychology* 42 (6): 1486–1504.

This study is a contemporary example of the messiness of research. Such candid explanations of how research veered off course and produced unintended results and counterintuitive findings as found in this article are rare in journals. Yet it is more frequent than it would appear, and it is refreshing and reassuring to find such a frank discussion in a paper. This article also illustrates how serendipitous results can arise from studies that do not go exactly as planned.

The first sentence of this paper acknowledges that the idea emerged because of unintended outcomes of experimental research. The study concerns the cognitive and emotional biases that influence people's judgments and behavior. In these researchers' domain, that meant the unintentionally biased nonverbal (NV) behavior of television broadcasters when they interview political candidates. The problem these researchers studied arose as a function of some of the best techniques in experimental design—specifically, designing experiments that are free of interfering influences is unlike what occurs in real life. Furthermore, experimentalists' tendency to study one bias at a time is unlike what occurs in the complexity of daily life, where multiple biases operating at the same time is more likely. The authors concede that the idea did not occur to them initially, nor did published studies point to the possibility of multiple biases. They say, "We must admit that initially we did not conceive the notion of multiple biases, and the phenomenon emerged in the framework of conventional (single-bias) research on media bias in interviewers' NV behavior. This was unsettling at first, because the unplanned bias seemed to interfere with the effect magnitudes of the investigated media bias."[78]

The researchers undertook the arduous task of conducting replications of their own study with seven different samples before concluding that two different biases were at work. This paper reports the meta-analyses of them. At the conclusion of the studies, they frankly say where findings were not expected, counterintuitive, surprising, and disappointing. They admit when findings are difficult to explain. For example, "The halo effect was not really expected in this research because the experiment was not designed to create halo effects, . . . The most unexpected and counterintuitive result, perhaps with the most far-reaching conceptual and applied implications, was the independence of the two bias phenomena, as indicated by rejection of the vicarious halo effect hypothesis . . . It is not easy to explain this effect, and it is, indeed, counterintuitive."[79]

Rather than attempting to cover up and posture, these researchers reveal the struggles and messiness of experimental research that is more common than published articles lead researchers to believe.

# STANLEY MILGRAM SHOCKS THE WORLD

Stanley Milgram's studies are some of the most recognizable, known to scholars and lay people alike. Colloquially known as the "shock studies," Stanley Milgram's experiments on obedience were designed to discover the causes behind why people obey authority figures even when what they are asked goes against their own conscience. In the 1960s, the Nazi war criminals trials were being held, so interest in this question was intense. Milgram's experiments are known for the criticism they incurred from psychologists for causing psychological harm to those who participated,[80] and their deceptiveness. (For more on deception, see More About box 2.3 on Deception.) This criticism ushered in a larger discussion about ethics in social science research. These studies also are credited with helping create IRBs to ensure research did not harm the people who volunteered for them (see more about IRBs in chapter 11).

While these studies are mainly remembered as cautionary tales about ethical research, there are other aspects of the studies that lend themselves to lessons in experimental design. The main structure of all Milgram's studies was for a **naïve subject**—someone who did not know what the study was about—to "teach" another person a set of word pairs. The subject was told that the goal was to see if punishment, in the form of electric shocks, improved learning. In this case, the "learner" was an accomplice, or **confederate**, of the experimenter who knew the purpose of the study and was only pretending to be shocked. Experiments that used confederates and deception such as this were popular around this time. Milgram used a **debriefing** session at the end of each experiment, telling subjects the true purpose of the experiment, that they had not actually harmed anyone, and that their responses were normal.[81] After two articles were published and criticism had begun to appear, Milgram began reporting the steps he took to minimize harm to subjects and the poststudy surveys he conducted to understand if harm had occurred.[82] Diana Baumrind dismissed the postexperiment self-reports of Milgram that showed more than 80% of subjects of their deceptive experiments said they were glad to have participated,[83] saying they were "tacked on as an afterthought," and "After all, if self-reports could be regarded as accurate measures of the impact of experimental conditions, we could dispense entirely with experimental manipulation and behavioral measures."[84]

Confederates are out of vogue today; however, debriefings are still a best practice when experiments involve deception, although studies such as Milgram's would not likely be approved by an IRB today. Notably, however, the popularity of "experiments" in this genre continues on television shows such as ABC's hidden camera series *What Would You Do?* No IRB approval is necessary when journalists or entertainment producers are doing it.

Chapter 1 explained the concepts of cause and effect. The effect that Milgram was interested in was obedience as measured by the dependent variable of the maximum shock that a subject would give to another person, which ranged from 0 to 30.[124] The causes he was examining were a myriad of independent variables including how close the subject was to his or her victim, if the subject could hear protests and cries, had to touch the victim, the authority of the person giving the instructions to administer shocks, and more.

## MORE ABOUT . . . BOX 2.3
### Deception

While deception in social science experiments may no longer be as dramatic as Stanley Milgram's shock experiments, neither is it a thing of the past. Its use varies among disciplines; it is common in sociology and social psychology within the parameters of the major associations[85] but proscribed in economics,[86] although withholding information is not considered deceptive, so that is allowed.[87]

Deception is defined as intentionally providing false information and withholding information in order to mislead.[88] This does not prevent researchers from withholding the hypotheses, conditions of the experiment, or other aspects of the research that would cause subjects to change their behavior.[89] However, withholding such information crosses the line if the nature of it would cause subjects to not agree to participate.[90]

Deception is prohibited in studies that may cause physical pain or severe emotional distress.[91] Guidelines mandate researchers not use deception unless it is justified by the study's value or there is no other feasible way.[92] However, as Baumrind says, "It takes little to convince a researcher or a review board of his or her peers that the long-range benefits of a clever bit of deceptive manipulation outweigh the short-range costs to participants of being deceived."[93]

### Deceptive Research

Nor does the 20/20 vision of hindsight always clear things up. After his prison experiment, Philip Zimbardo wrote about considering other methods than the ones he used and employing an objective observer to monitor the study.[94] Yet in years immediately after, Zimbardo and colleagues used hypnosis to induce partial deafness that resulted in subjects experiencing paranoia, misinforming subjects about the purpose and what they would undergo.[95] Just like the prison experiment, this and another study that involved misleading subjects[96] received IRB approval. In 1977, Stanley Milgram's shock study was replicated with children as young as six.[97] This study was conducted in a country without an IRB but was approved by the department chair and other faculty, as well as the children's teachers and principals. The study reports the children who participated exhibited "loud nervous laughter, lip biting, trembling."[98] At the end of the article, the authors say, "it is indeed surprising to find that relatively few social psychologists have followed up on Milgram's pioneering work on obedience."[99] This study was published in one of the top social psychology journals then and now, which also published one of Milgram's.[100] This is not meant to imply that these researchers are unethical or even tone deaf, but that detecting issues with deception can be harder than one thinks.

Content analyses show the trajectory of deceptive research. Beginning in 1921, there was rarely any deception through the 1930s in the leading social psychology journal, *Journal of Personality and Social Psychology*. Its use grew gradually until the 1950s and then grew significantly between the 1950s and 1970s with the rise of experimental methods.[101] There was a decrease from the 1980s to 1994 when this study ended.[102] It found that computers and other bogus devices partially replaced confederates to mislead subjects. Misleading consent and false feedback to subjects fell after 1969 but rose again in 1992, and changes in topics studied explained declines in deception between 1978 and 1986.[103] Deceptive practices were found in as many as 66% of the articles examined.[104] Other

*(Continued)*

(Continued)

studies show similar results. Between 1971 and 1974, 54% of psychology experiments used deception,[105] up from 18% in 1948 and 37% in 1963.[106] More recent figures find deception in about 33% of social psychology studies.[107]

That deception can harm subjects is obvious. In addition to physical pain or psychological distress, deception harms study subjects in that it undermines their autonomy and violates their right to choose to participate.[108]

But deceptive research also has the potential to harm more than study subjects, with effects extending to the entire research profession. As many social scientists have noted, voluntary participation in research studies has been declining. This is attributable in no small part to public suspicion of research based on its history of harm, deception, and abuse of power.[109] It is not only the ability to recruit subjects that suffers, but public trust and confidence in the findings of studies can be eroded, as well as the reputation of the entire academy. Society becomes less willing to support research.[110] Furthermore, the willingness of a few experimentalists to use deception has the ability to induce others to do so as well,[111] thereby undermining the moral agency of the researchers themselves.[112] Detriments to society at large include an overall loss of trust and increasing suspicion as the social contract to tell the truth and keep promises is violated.[113]

## Using Deception Ethically

The most common reason for the use of deception includes the need to control demand characteristics, or the tendency for subjects to alter their behavior to fit with the goals of the study.[114] Baumrind contends that using deception promotes the very thing it was designed to prevent: because people know deception is routinely used in experiments, subjects are no longer naïve—that is, they do not believe the study is real.[115] At the same time, other research finds that deception does not affect the external validity of studies.[116]

The most common techniques for ethically using deception, other than avoiding it completely, include:

- Giving subjects informed consent that includes the true purpose of the study without giving away hypotheses, and describes the procedures and what they will do.[117]

- If any information is withheld, debriefing subjects immediately after the study is over.[118] Also, subjects should be asked if they agree to postpone receiving all the information until the debriefing.[119] Recognize, however, that debriefing does not undo harm.[120]

- Allow subjects to withdraw from the study at any time, including withdrawing their data after they have been debriefed.[121]

Experimentalists should realize they might be inclined to choose deceptive methods because they are easier than nondeceptive ones. Instead, researchers should consider nondeceptive methods such as natural experiments where no manipulation is involved or unobtrusive instruments where the subject is unable to alter his or her responses, such as psychological measures of heart rate, or latency response, which measures how long a person takes to respond to a stimulus. Natural experiments are covered in chapter 4, and unobtrusive instruments in chapter 10. There is more about ethics and deception in the context of IRBs in chapter 11. Other suggestions that have been made for nondeceptive experiments include having researchers be their subjects and examine their motives and behavior,[122] or using "surrogate subjects"—that is, telling people about the purposes and procedures to see if they find them acceptable.[123]

Finally, my own advice is to apply the golden rule—that is, treat others as you would like to be treated. Put yourself in the shoes of your research subjects and ask if you would have any objections to being tricked, lied to, or learning something painful about yourself. Consider the consequences, including what it would be like to have your employer, family, or friends find out about things you would prefer to keep private.

As Milgram writes, "The crux of the study is to systematically vary the factors believed to alter the degree of obedience to experimental commands."[125] In all, he conducted eighteen different experiments reported individually in original journal articles,[126] and the entire series was reported in his book *Obedience to Authority*.[127]

Chapter 1 also introduced the "so what" question, or explaining why an experiment is important. Milgram answered the "so what" question by citing practical problems his research could shed light on, from war crimes to workers obeying their bosses. He also devised a clever way to answer the criticism of research that only confirms what we already know rather than studies that reveal something new or unexpected. He built in a procedure for determining if his were obvious and intuitive findings by conducting a separate study where he invited subjects to a lecture on the topic of his study and described the experiment without disclosing the results.[128] After the lecture, subjects were asked several

Stanley Milgram

questions about what he or she would do and what they thought others would do. All 110 subjects said they would refuse to administer shocks at some point, and that virtually all the other subjects would also. That was the opposite of what had happened in the studies, with 65% of the subjects going all the way to the highest level of shocks.[129]

Thus, Milgram was able to show that his results were not intuitive and, in fact, were the reverse of what people expected would happen.

Just as Lind did with his scurvy experiments, Milgram employed a combination of theory and observation to test the causes of obedience. For example, he cited conflicting theories about women as the reason for experiment 8, where he used female subjects for the first time. Anachronistic as it is today, some theory and evidence at that time pointed to women being more obedient and less aggressive than men, which should lead them to give the shocks *more* frequently than men. Conflicting theory and evidence showed women were more empathetic than men, which predicted they would give shocks *less* frequently than men.[130] In fact, women and men performed about the same on the shock studies, but they talked about their reasons for administering the shocks in different terms in the postexperiment interviews. Chapter 3 will cover the importance of theory to experiments and how observation and experience also can drive experimental questions.

Milgram also addresses the topic of sampling and participants in his studies. He explicitly rejected the use of undergraduate students, which is fairly common today although heavily debated.[131] Noting that using students would have been far easier for him, Milgram nevertheless reasoned that students might contaminate the findings because they could have heard about the studies from others who had already participated, and were too homogeneous, being of similar age, intelligence, and familiar with psychological studies.[iii] Instead, he wanted a "wide range of individuals drawn from a broad spectrum of class backgrounds."[132] So he ran a newspaper ad to recruit participants from the surrounding community, luring them with a $4.50 cash incentive. Milgram writes about using forty subjects for each condition in all the studies but does not mention how he arrived at that number. Today, a **power analysis**, a statistical technique to determine how many subjects a particular study needs, would be used. That will be covered in chapter 8 of this book. Nor does he randomly assign subjects to condition, a feature designed to ensure equivalence that had already been discovered by others but used to order treatments rather than to assign subjects. Instead, Milgram used a matching technique similar to that employed by Lind in the scurvy studies. He writes about how it was important to balance subjects in each condition by age and occupation, so he divided them into categories of skilled and unskilled workers

---

[iii] As to the question of using students or not, after the adult citizens had been used in all the experiments, Milgram examined their results in relation to the students he had used in pilot studies and found no differences. Milgram, *Obedience to Authority: An Experimental View*, 170.

versus white collar and professionals, and also into three age groups, and assigned them based on those characteristics.[133]

The many treatment conditions, eighteen in all, were carried out one after the other, moving down to "more moderate alterations of the situation."[134] For example, in experiment 7, he started with the experimenter being physically close to the subject and gradually increased the distance between them until the experimenter was out of the room entirely, giving orders via telephone. The same thing happened in experiments 1 through 4, when the subject's proximity to the victim was systematically altered, bringing the subject and victim increasingly closer. This illustrates the principle of experiments maximizing variation by starting with the strongest manipulation first and if effects are found, moving to lower levels of the manipulation until the effect disappears. This will be covered more in chapter 9. In all the studies, Milgram also controlled for confounds by using recorded protests of the victim so they were the same for every subject and every shock level.[135]

Milgram's studies employed a variety of measurements, the subject of chapter 10. His main dependent variable was behavioral—the level of "shock" subjects administered, ranging from zero to the highest level of 30, representing a whopping 450 volts. In reality, the lowest level anyone administered was 20.[136] Using timers, he also measured **latency** of the shocks—that is, how long it took subjects to press the switch and how long subjects held down the switch.

Additional measures included **self-reports** from the subjects via **questionnaire** after the experiment about the level of conflict, tension, and nervousness they experienced during the study, and their estimation of the amount of pain felt by the victim. Milgram also used a variety of **response choices**, including **open-ended questions**, **projective tests**, and **attitude scales**.[137] All of these will be covered in detail in chapter 10. In Milgram's first four experiments, subjects also were asked how much responsibility they assigned to the experimenter, subject, and victim for a person receiving shocks against his or her will.[138] The questionnaire asked the usual demographic variables of political party, religious affiliation, education, and, in this case, length of military service, as that was common in the 1960s and deemed important to how well one followed orders.[138]

In addition, Milgram recorded the conversations between the subjects and experimenter during the study, and the researchers noted their own observations. These **qualitative measures** were used in addition to individual interviews and group discussions after the experiments, which he reported to give context to the findings, an important feature of triangulation discussed in chapter 1.

We also find in Milgram's work examples of pilot studies, one of the subjects of chapter 11, and manipulation checks, the topic of chapter 9. **Pilot studies** are used to test-drive an experiment before the real study is launched in order to work out the kinks. In his pilot studies using undergraduate students, Milgram found subjects needed practice reading the words to the learners, so he incorporated a training session where subjects read ten word pairs before the actual study began.[140] Another important lesson from the pilot studies was that of "vocal feedback."[141] Initially, Milgram had the subject shock the victim in another room with the victim remaining silent. He found no variation in how far subjects would go in delivering shocks—everyone went all the way. With no variation in the outcome—no one disobeyed—there was no way to determine the causal mechanisms of disobedience. So Milgram introduced cries and protests from the victim, and pounding on the walls, which caused subjects to stop the shocks at different points, thereby giving him the variation discussed in chapter 1.[142]

One subject of chapter 9 is how to determine whether manipulations are perceived as realistic. For example, if the experiment involves subjects reading messages written in vivid, descriptive language or in nonvivid, abstract style, it is necessary to know if subjects who got the vivid writing perceived it was more vivid than those who got the nonvivid versions.[143] For this, a **manipulation check** is used. In Milgram's case, he wanted to know if subjects believed the victims actually received painful shocks and if they believed they were the ones administering them. Only two out of the forty subjects answered those questions with "no" on the postexperiment questionnaire, so the manipulation was deemed to have worked.

Getty/Andrew H. Walker/Staff

Philip Zimbardo

# PHILIP ZIMBARDO: RAISING CONSCIENCES IN A STANFORD BASEMENT

Shortly after Stanley Milgram's shock studies, Philip Zimbardo conducted another noteworthy study in the same vein. On a personal note, Milgram and Zimbardo had met in high school in 1949 in the Bronx.[144] They reconnected in 1960 as assistant professors, with Milgram at Yale and Zimbardo at New York University. Coincidentally, Zimbardo had originally constructed the basement lab at Yale that Milgram used for his shock studies after he moved out of the "elegant interaction lab."[145] But it was a different basement across the country that was to go down in history for, among other things, the ethical questions it raised.

In the summer of 1971, Zimbardo constructed a mock prison in the basement of the Stanford University psychology building for a study funded by the Office of Naval Research, which was interested in the causes of conflict between prisoners and military guards. It was here that twenty-one college students from across the country spent six days playing the roles of either prisoners or guards. But unlike in 1961 when Milgram did his work, in the 1970s, IRBs existed. And Zimbardo and his graduate students did, in fact, get IRB approval. Zimbardo's book *The Lucifer Effect*[146] describes the steps he took to avoid harming subjects, including prohibiting physical violence. All the participants were given **informed consent**, which included the information that they were free to leave the experiment at any time. Few did. No deception was involved, unlike in Milgram's study. However, the researchers gave the guards suggestions on how they should behave rather than allowing all the behaviors to develop naturally. This study has gone down in history as one of the most harmful ever. For example, it used psychological techniques to induce boredom and take away subjects' privacy, their sense of individuation, and power. The subjects' reactions to the study were so intense, with the students playing both guards and prisoners internalizing their new identities to an alarming degree, that the experiment was stopped after six days instead of the planned two weeks because of the psychological and emotional trauma.[147] Some prisoners went into screaming, out-of-control rages and hunger strikes, while some guards exhibited sadistic behavior and even attacked prisoners with fire extinguishers. Anticipating concerns, the team did extensive debriefing of each subject immediately after the study concluded and followed each subject for a year looking for ill effects.[148] In his response to critics, Zimbardo pointed out that the only request received by the American Psychological Association to investigate the study had come from him,[149] and the research was fully cleared. A proposal for a follow-up study was turned down by the IRB, and Zimbardo apologized to the participants in the 2007 book.[150]

The prison study was a laboratory experiment, normally criticized for being highly artificial, so Zimbardo and colleagues took great pains to make it as realistic as possible, just as Milgram had. For example, they talked the Palo Alto police department into having real officers "arrest" the subjects.[iv] They outfitted the subjects who were guards in clothing similar to real prison uniforms. Inmates stayed in cells with steel bars 24 hours a day,

---

[iv]The researchers had to be creative to get the police to cooperate, using the enticement of a TV station putting it on the evening news as good publicity for the force, according to Zimbardo in *The Lucifer Effect*.

while the guards worked regular shifts. They staged visiting days with real friends and relatives, and held mock parole hearings.[151] It is hailed as a prime example of realism to this day.[152] The researchers noted that while they wanted their experiment to be as real as possible, conducting it in an actual prison was not an option because "There are too many uncontrolled variables in the real world, or in the 'field,' as social scientists call it. That's the comfort of laboratory research: The experimenter is in charge."[153] They point out that many studies had already been done in existing penal institutions, which they called **natural experiments**.[154] The differences between laboratory experiments, natural, and **field experiments** will be explored in chapter 4. Zimbardo explained, "There have been studies of actual prison life by sociologists and criminologists, but they suffer from some serious drawbacks. Those researchers are never free to observe all phases of prison life . . . They can see only what they are allowed to see."[155] They explained their choice of a realistic-as-possible lab experiment by noting that their research question could not be studied using real prisons and prisoners because it was necessary to separate the effects of the prison environment from the characteristics of its inhabitants—that is, there were confounds, described in chapter 1, in the real world. In this case, the study was undertaken because of the belief that the violence and cruelty found in prisons was due to the antisocial personalities of inmates and authoritarian characteristics of guards. Thus, they decided to construct a new prison using as guards and prisoners people who did not already possess the antisocial and sadistic personalities presumed responsible for prison conditions. The mock prison was "entirely populated by individuals who are undifferentiated in all essential dimensions from the rest of society."[156] Thus, by holding constant the situational aspects assumed to be responsible for prison conditions, the study showed that behaviors in prisons could be reliably attributed to the situation rather than just the personalities of the people in them.

To get their "normal" subjects, the research team did a combination of Milgram's purposeful selection based on specific criteria and Fisher's random assignment. They recruited subjects using a newspaper ad promising $15 a day for participation. Unlike Milgram, who thought college students would bias the study, Zimbardo chose students on purpose because they were so similar, or **homogeneous**. The seventy-five students who responded were not just from Stanford but colleges across the country that happened to be in Palo Alto for the summer. The recruits had to answer questions about their families, physical and mental health, and involvement in crime, and also be interviewed by the researchers. The researchers chose the most stable and mature subjects.[157] As with Milgram's and most other studies of the time, the subjects were male. And even though they were looking for students who were similar to the population of the United States, all but one were White.[158]

Following this careful, purposive selection procedure, the chosen subjects were then randomly assigned to be either prisoner or guard. The purpose of the random assignment to condition was to ensure that the subjects who were playing guards were not different from those playing inmates on any important characteristics. The team checked this by giving subjects a battery of psychological tests, which showed no significant differences between either group. Random assignment had worked.[159] Chapter 7 will go into more detail about how this is done.

Just as Milgram had conducted pilot studies, Zimbardo and colleagues went into this study with prior research informing it. The idea arose from a project that a student in one of Zimbardo's classes had done. Zimbardo followed that up with a "field experiment"[160] where he conducted a candid camera-type of study, putting abandoned cars in Palo Alto, CA, and Bronx, NY, and recording people vandalizing them. Ordinary citizens in the blue-collar, working-class Bronx and upper-class, white-collar Palo Alto, all White and well dressed, some encouraging their children, vandalized the cars. From these pilot studies, Zimbardo concluded that conditions that make people feel anonymous could foster antisocial behavior.[161] Chapter 11 will discuss how to conduct pilot studies.

The original research article described the prison experimental design as "relatively simple" with "a single treatment variable, the random assignment to either 'guard' or 'prisoner' condition."[162] This was slightly more sophisticated than Milgram's, where there was only one condition or level of **factor** per experiment, but much less complex than typical experimental designs today. The types of designs will be discussed in more detail in chapter 4 and factorial designs in chapter 6. The study did not even have a formal hypothesis, which the researchers explained by the "exploratory nature" of the study.[163] They do report multiple statistical tests to support the one general hypothesis offered: "That assignment to the treatment of 'guard' or 'prisoner' would result in significantly different reactions on behavioural measures of interaction, emotional measures of mood state and pathology, attitudes toward self, as well as other indices of coping and adaptation to this novel situation."[164] Milgram had not offered a hypothesis in his initial paper either.

Like Milgram's, the prison study used a plethora of measures, including video and audio recordings of the subjects' actual behavior, researchers' observations, questionnaires using self-reports, and interviews with the subjects.[165] The questionnaires included mood inventories, personality tests, scales measuring authoritarianism and Machiavellianism, and a personality scale that included trustworthiness, orderliness, conformity, activity, stability, extroversion, masculinity, and empathy.[166] Chapter 10 will go into more detail about constructing measures such as these. The researchers also triangulated their data using a combination of quantitative and qualitative techniques. For example, they used an inductive approach to categorize the data from the video and audiotapes and observations, which they converted into scores on which they performed statistical tests. They also reported findings qualitatively, including quotes from subjects. One strength of the findings was the "consistency in the pattern of relationships which emerge across a wide range of measuring instruments and different observers."[167] The findings in this paper remain a good example today of how to write this section of an experimental paper. A great deal of space is devoted to the discussion of the unique findings from the study, their meaning, and the reasons behind them. They are related to other research without the section looking like another literature review.[168] The discussion also includes limitations of the study, including the small sample size (N = 21), that the conditions in the simulated prison were minimal compared to real prisons, and **demand characteristics**, in this case, the subjects knew they were being observed and wanted to please the researchers. The paper shows how researchers overcame some of these limitations with the data they had—for example, analysis of times when the subjects did not know they were being observed but their cells were bugged. Being able to use data to show how a study's limitations do not invalidate the conclusions is a useful skill.

Finally, one of the most important things this study does is answer the "so what" question in a comprehensive and definitive way. It was hailed by the American Psychological Association as an exemplar of how psychological research could be applied to solve real-world problems and understood by nonacademics, making research relevant to ordinary citizens.[169] In response to criticisms of the unethical nature of the research, Zimbardo reported on the impact to society and listed all the ways the public had shown an interest in the work, including media stories, calls, letters, requests to speak, and changes to law and policy, among others.[170] While Zimbardo was responding to charges of unethical treatment, all experiments should present a strong rationale for the ability of the research to improve conditions in society and solve real-world problems.[171]

## CONCLUSION

All these famous experiments from the past have some things in common, including creativity. These social scientists were willing to go to great lengths to ensure their experiments found something real rather than just support a hypothesis. Philip Zimbardo enlisted the help of real police officers. B. F. Skinner invented his own measuring devices. In their quest, some ignored their duty to protect subjects, leading today's researchers to better understand the trade-offs between harm and reality. Experimentalists should still strive to make their study conditions as realistic as possible; if a study will test TV messages, then subjects should view them via TV, not in written script format, for example. But preventing harm is paramount. Chapter 11 will give more specific advice for avoiding or minimizing deception in experiments, along with other ethical issues.

Nor were these scientists afraid to try something new. Important advances in knowledge are made by knowing when to stand on the shoulders of others, and also when to strike out on one's own. Too many are afraid to deviate from what has already been done, or measure anything differently than it has already been measured. This results in studies that confirm others' findings but little else, when the purpose of science is to create new knowledge.

These historical examples also show that research is messy. It does not always proceed as neatly as the write-up in a journal makes it appear. Most of these researchers document the disorderly process in their books rather than journal articles. The books of Skinner, Milgram, and Zimbardo are good examples.

Finally, these studies show it is important not to harm subjects and to deceive them as little as possible and within ethical guidelines (see More About box 2.3 on Deception). It is essential to find valid answers to questions while balancing the duty to protect subjects. Deception should be avoided if at all possible, and when not possible, used as little as necessary. Debriefing participants after the study and offering to send them a report about the findings once concluded helps treat people with dignity and respect. These steps will also help ensure that one's own studies go down in history for all the right reasons.

## Common Mistakes

- Not making studies realistic
- Using deception when it could be avoided
- Replicating others' findings rather than creating new knowledge

## Test Your Knowledge

1. In his study on scurvy, James Lind assigned subjects to treatment conditions using _____.
   a. Random assignment
   b. A matching strategy
   c. A representative strategy
   d. A snowball strategy

2. By some accounts, one of the first experimentalists to use random assignment was _____.

   a. James Lind

   b. Isaac Newton

   c. C. S. Peirce

   d. Albert Einstein

3. Ronald Fisher's prediction that a lady would not be able to tell if the tea or milk came first is an example of _____.

   a. An alternative hypothesis

   b. A null hypothesis

   c. A duh hypothesis

   d. A theoretical hypothesis

4. B. F. Skinner was known for using _____.

   a. Small samples

   b. Large samples

   c. Random samples

   d. Purposive samples

5. When one of B. F. Skinner's devices jammed and wouldn't work, he recognized this as _____.

   a. A problem to be rectified

   b. The messiness of science and the role of serendipity

   c. Sabotage

   d. A way to control confounds

6. Stanley Milgram used latency measures, self-reports, and how subjects behaved in his obedience studies. This illustrates _____.

   a. Measurements

   b. Response choices

   c. Controlling for confounds

   d. Maximizing variation

7. Stanley Milgram also used attitude scales. This illustrates _____.

   a. Measurements

   b. Response choices

   c. Controlling for confounds

   d. Maximizing variation

8. The purpose of a pilot study is _____.

   a. To discover if the manipulations work as expected

   b. To discover if subjects think the experiment is real

   c. To test-drive the experiment to figure out what needs to be changed

   d. To ensure equivalent groups

9. In which of the following studies was deception involved?

   a. C. S. Peirce's study on weights

   b. Ronald Fisher's lady tasting tea experiment

   c. Stanley Milgram's obedience to authority experiments

   d. Philip Zimbardo's prison experiment

10. For the prison experiment, Philip Zimbardo used _____.

    a. Purposive sampling

    b. Random assignment

    c. Both a and b

    d. None of these

**Answers**

| | | | |
|---|---|---|---|
| 1. b | 4. a | 7. b | 9. c |
| 2. c | 5. b | 8. c | 10. c |
| 3. b | 6. a | | |

## Application Exercises

1. This chapter does not pretend to cover all the creative pioneers of experimental designs in the social sciences. Identify some of the others and do your own research on them—for example, Kurt Lewin, Leon Festinger, Solomon Asch, Ivan Pavlov, Paul Lazarsfeld, Muzafer and Carolyn Sherif, among many others. Especially look for women and scientists of color. Read what others have written about these experimentalists and their work, but also look up and read their *original* research papers or books written by these social scientists themselves.

2. Famous experiments in history seem to have captured the imagination of filmmakers recently. Watch one of these and write two pages on the importance of ethical research:

- *The Experimenter,* about Stanley Milgram's famous electric shock studies, 2015. Available on Netflix, Amazon, and Microsoft Movies and TV. This was a feature film at the Sundance festival in 2015. Milgram also filmed the actual experiments, and you can see real footage, with Milgram himself, on YouTube and other services by searching for "Stanley Milgram experiment video."

- *The Stanford Prison Experiment,* about Philip Zimbardo, 2015. Available on Amazon, Microsoft Movies and TV, and iTunes. Zimbardo has a website with more information on the research: http://www.prisonexp.org.

## Suggested Readings

Nothing is more enlightening than reading an original study rather than only what others say about it. Thus, I recommend the following:

- Haney, Craig, Curtis Banks, and Philip Zimbardo. 1973. "Interpersonal Dynamics in a Simulated Prison." *International Journal of Criminology and Penology* 1: 69–97.

- Milgram, Stanley. 1964. "Group Pressure and Action Against a Person." *Journal of Abnormal and Social Psychology* 69: 137–143.

- Milgram, Stanley. 1965. "Liberating Effects of Group Pressure." *Journal of Personality and Social Psychology* 1: 127–134.

- Milgram, Stanley. 1965. "Some Conditions of Obedience and Disobedience to Authority." *Human Relations* 18 (1): 57–76.

- Peirce, Charles Sanders, and Joseph Jastrow. 1885. "On Small Differences of Sensation." *Memoirs of the National Academy of Sciences* 3: 75–83.

- Skinner, B. F. 1948. "Superstition in the Pigeon." *Journal of Experimental Psychology* 38: 168–172.

For an in-depth discussion of the pros and cons of creativity in research, read:

Voosen, Paul. 2015. "For Researchers, Risk Is a Vanishing Luxury." *Chronicle of Higher Education*. www .Chronicle.com. This is a premium article, meaning there is a charge or a subscription is required. Check your college or university library for access.

For those especially interested in the history of deception, read this book:

Korn, J. H. 1997. *Illusions of Reality: A History of Deception in Social Psychology.* Albany: State University of New York Press.

For an entertaining read that shows the more human side of many of these experimentalists, read:

Slater, Lauren. 2005. *Opening Skinner's Box: Great Psychological Experiments of the 20th Century.* New York: Norton.

# Notes

1. Nancy Felipe Russo and Agnes N. O'Connell, "Models from Our Past: Psychology's Foremothers," *Psychology of Women Quarterly* 5, no. 1 (1980): 11–54.

2. Ibid.

3. Kendra Cherry, "10 Women Who Changed Psychology: A Closer Look at Women in Psychology," *VeryWellMind* https://www.verywellmind.com/women-who-changed-psychology-2795260. Accessed March 21, 2018.

4. For more biographies of women in psychology, see the special issue of *Psychology of Women Quarterly*, 1980, vol. 5, issue no. 1.

5. Agnes N. O'Connell and Nancy Felipe Russo, "Models for Achievement: Eminent Women in Psychology," *Psychology of Women Quarterly* 5, no. 1 (1980): 6–10.

6. Laurel Furumoto, "Mary Whiton Calkins (1863–1930)," *Psychology of Women Quarterly* 5, no. 1 (1980): 55–68.

7. Ibid.

8. Ibid.

9. Joseph Jastrow, "A Study in Mental Statistics," *New Review* 5 (1981): 564.

10. Mary Whiton Calkins, "Community of Ideas of Men and Women," *Psychological Review* 3 (1896): 426–430.

11. Cherry, "10 Women Who Changed Psychology."

12. "Psychologist Mamie Phipps Clark Profile: Important Contributor to the Self-Concept Among Minorities Discussion," *VeryWellMind* https://www.verywellmind.com/mamie-phipps-clark-biography-2796022. Accessed March 21, 2018.

13. L. Nyman, "Documenting History: An Interview with Kenneth Bancroft Clark," *History of Psychology* 13, no. 1 (2010): 74–88.

14. "Psychologist Mamie Phipps Clark Profile: Important Contributor to the Self-Concept among Minorities Discussion."

15. Stephen N. Butler, "Mamie Katherine Phipps Clark (1917–1983)," *The Encyclopedia of Arkansas History & Culture* http://www.encyclopediaofarkansas.net/encyclopedia/entry-detail.aspx?entryID=2938 (2016).

16. Ibid.

17. Cherry, "10 Women Who Changed Psychology."

18. M. D. Ainsworth and B. A. Wittig, "Attachment and Exploratory Behavior of One-Year-Olds in a Strange Situation," in *Determinants of Infant Behavior*, ed. B. M. Foss (London: Methuen, 1969), 113–136.

19. U. G. Wartner et al., "Attachment Patterns in South Germany," *Child Development* 65 (1994): 1014–1127.

20. M. E. Lamb, "The Development of Mother-Infant and Father-Infant Attachments in the Second Year of Life," *Developmental Psychology* 13, no. 6 (1977): 637–648.

21. M. Marrone, *Attachment and Interaction* (New York: Jessica Kingsley, 1998); E. C. Melhuish, "A Measure of Love? An Overview of the Assessment of Attachment," *ACPP Review & Newsletter* 15 (1993): 269–275.

22. Russo and O'Connell, "Models from Our Past."

23. U.S. National Library of Medicine, "Scurvy," *Medline Plus* (2016).

24. James Lind, *A Treatise on the Scurvy: In Three Parts. Containing an Inquiry into the Nature, Causes, and Cure, of That Disease. Together with a Critical and Chronological View of What Has Been Published on the Subject.* (Edinburgh: Sands, Murray, and Cochran for A. Millar, 1753).

25. Ibid., 191–192.

26. Ibid., 193.

27. Ibid.

28. R. Barker Bausell, *Conducting Meaningful Experiments: 40 Steps to Becoming a Scientist* (Thousand Oaks, CA: Sage, 1994).

29. Lind, *A Treatise on the Scurvy.*

30. Stephen M. Stigler, "Mathematical Statistics in the Early States," *The Annals of Statistics* 6, no. 2 (1978): 239–265.

31. Charles Sanders Peirce and Joseph Jastrow, "On Small Differences of Sensation," *Memoirs of the National Academy of Sciences* 3 (1885): 75–83.

32. Stephen M. Stigler, "A Historical View of Statistical Concepts in Psychology and Educational Research," *American Journal of Education* 101, no. 1 (November 1992): 60–70

33. Charles Sanders Peirce and Joseph Jastrow, "On Small Differences in Sensation," in *American Contributions to Mathematical Statistics in the Nineteenth Century*, ed. Stephen M. Stigler (New York: Arno Press, 1980/1885), 80.

34. Charles Sanders Peirce, *Essays in the Philosophy of Science* (New York: Liberal Arts Press, 1957), 217.

35. Ibid., 104.

36. Joseph Brent, *Charles Sanders Peirce: A Life*, 2nd ed. (Bloomington and Indianapolis: Indiana University Press, 1998).

37. Stigler, "Mathematical Statistics in the Early States," 249.

38. David Salsburg, *The Lady Tasting Tea: How Statistics Revolutionized Science in the Twentieth Century* (New York: W. H. Freeman, 2001).

39. Ronald A. Fisher, *Statistical Methods for Research Workers* (Edinburgh: Oliver and Boyd, 1925).

40. Diana C. Mutz and Robin Pemantle, "Standards for Experimental Research: Encouraging a Better Understanding of Experimental Methods," *Journal of Experimental Political Science* 2, no. 2 (2016): 192–215.

41. Salsburg, *The Lady Tasting Tea*.

42. Ibid.

43. Stigler, "A Historical View of Statistical."

44. Salsburg, *The Lady Tasting Tea*.

45. Ronald A. Fisher, *The Design of Experiments* (Edinburgh: Oliver and Boyd, 1937).

46. Salsburg, *The Lady Tasting Tea*, 8.

47. Robert P. Hawkins, "The Life and Contributions of Burrhus Frederick Skinner," *Education & Treatment of Children* 13, no. 3 (1990): 258.

48. B. F. Skinner, "A Case History in Scientific Method," *The American Psychologist* 11, no. 5 (1956): 221–233.

49. Joshua B. Plavnick and Summer J. Ferreri, "Single-Case Experimental Designs in Educational Research: A Methodology for Causal Analyses in Teaching and Learning," *Education Psychology Review* 25 (2013): 549–569; Denise A. Soares et al., "Effect Size for Token Economy Use in Contemporary Classroom Settings: A Meta-Analysis of Single-Case Research," *School Psychology Review* 45, no. 4 (2016): 379–399; Stephen F. Ledoux, "Behaviorism at 100," *American Scientist* 100, no. 1 (2012): 60–65; Walter R. Nord, "Beyond the Teaching Machine: The Neglected Area of Operant Conditioning in the Theory and Practice of Management," *Organizational Behavior & Human Performance* 4, no. 4 (1969): 375–401; Laura Vandeweghe et al., "Perceived Effective and Feasible Strategies to Promote Healthy Eating in Young Children: Focus Groups with Parents, Family Child Care Providers and Daycare Assistants," *BMC Public Health* 16 (2016): 1–12.

50. Ledoux, "Behaviorism at 100."

51. Skinner, "A Case History in Scientific Method," 227.

52. Skinner, *The Behavior of Organisms: An Experimental Analysis* (New York: Appleton-Century, 1938).

53. Skinner, "A Case History in Scientific Method."

54. Skinner, *The Behavior of Organisms: An Experimental Analysis*.

55. Skinner, "A Case History in Scientific Method."

56. Alexandra Rutherford, "B. F. Skinner From Laboratory to Life," in *History of Postwar Social Science Seminar Series* (London, 2007).

57. Alexandra Rutherford, "B. F. Skinner's Technology of Behavior in American Life: From Consumer Culture to Counterculture." *Journal of the History of the Behavioral Sciences* 39, no. 1 (Winter 2003): 1–23.

58. Plavnick and Ferreri, "Single-Case Experimental Designs"; T. R. Kratochwill et al., "Single-Case Designs Technical Documentation" (2010). http://ies.ed.gov/ncee/wwc/Document/229.

59. Plavnick and Ferreri, "Single-Case Experimental Designs"; Hawkins, "The Life and Contributions of Burrhus Frederick Skinner."

60. Skinner, "A Case History in Scientific Method."

61. Ibid., 227.

62. B. F. Skinner, "Superstition in the Pigeon," *Journal of Experimental Psychology* 38 (1948): 168–172.

63. Skinner, "A Case History in Scientific Method," 229.

64. Ibid., 223.

65. Hawkins, "The Life and Contributions of Burrhus Frederick Skinner."

66. Charles B. Ferster and B. F. Skinner, *Schedules of Reinforcement* (New York: Appleton-Century-Crofts, 1957).

67. Skinner, "A Case History in Scientific Method."

68. Ibid.

69. Ibid., 224.

70. Ibid., 224.

71. D. E. Blackman and R. Pellon, "The Contributions of B. F. Skinner to the Interdisciplinary Science of Behavioural Pharmacology," *British Journal of Psychology* 84, no. 1 (1993): 1.

72. Skinner, "A Case History in Scientific Method," 226.

73. Ibid., 224.

74. Ibid., 225.

75. Ibid., 232.

76. Skinner, *The Behavior of Organisms: An Experimental Analysis.*

77. Skinner, "A Case History in Scientific Method," 223.

78. Elisha Babad, Eyal Peer, and Yehonatan Benayoun, "Can Multiple Biases Occur in a Single Situation? Evidence from Media Bias Research," *Journal of Applied Social Psychology* 42, no. 6 (2012): 1486–1504.

79. Ibid., 1501–1502.

80. Diana Baumrind, "Some Thoughts on Ethics of Research: After Reading Milgram's 'Behavioral Study of Obedience'" *American Psychologist* 19, no. 6 (1964): 421–423.

81. Stanley Milgram, *Obedience to Authority: An Experimental View* (New York: Harper & Row, 1974).

82. Milgram, "Some Conditions of Obedience and Disobedience to Authority," *Human Relations* 18, no. 1 (1965): 57–76.

83. Milgram, *Obedience to Authority: An Experimental View.*

84. Diana Baumrind, "Research Using Intentional Deception: Ethical Issues Revisited," *American Psychologist* 40, no. 2 (1985): 165–174.

85. Davide Barrera and Brent Simpson, "Much Ado About Deception: Consequences of Deceiving Research Participants in the Social Sciences," *Sociological Methods & Research* 41, no. 3 (2012): 383–413

86. Ibid.; D. Geller, "Alternative to Deception: Why, What, and How?" in *The Ethics of Social Research: Surveys and Experiments*, ed. Joan E. Sieber (New York: Springer-Verlag, 1982), 38–55.

87. Barrera and Simpson, "Much Ado About Deception."

88. Karen A. Hegtvedt, "Ethics and Experiments," in *Laboratory Experiments in the Social Sciences*, ed. Murray Webster and Jane Sell (London: Elsevier, 2014): 23–51.

89. Ibid.

90. Baumrind, "Research Using Intentional Deception."

91. Immo Fritsche and Volker Linneweber, "Nonreactive (Unobtrusive) Methods," in *Handbook of Psychological Measurement—A Multimethod Perspective*, ed. M. Eid and E. Diener (Washington, DC: American Psychological Association, 2004).

92. Ibid.

93. Baumrind, "Research Using Intentional Deception," 166.

94. Philip Zimbardo, "On the Ethics of Intervention in Human Psychological Research: With Special Reference to the Stanford Prison Experiment," *Cognition* 2, no. 2 (1973): 243–256.

95. Philip G. Zimbardo, S. M. Andersen, and I. G. Kabat, "Induced Hearing Deficit Generates Experimental Paranoia," *Science* 212 (June 1981): 1529–1531.

96. G. D. Marshall and P. G. Zimbardo, "Affective Consequences of Inadequately Explained Physiological Arousal," *Journal of Personality and Social Psychology* 37 (1979): 970–988.

97. M. E. Shanab and K. A. Yahya, "A Behavioral Study of Obedience in Children," *Journal of Personality and Social Psychology* 35 (1977): 530–536.

98. Ibid., 534.

99. Ibid., 536.

100. Stanley Milgram, "Liberating Effects of Group Pressure," *Journal of Personality and Social Psychology* 1 (1965): 127–134.

101. Sandra D. Nicks, James H. Korn, and Tina Mainieri, "The Rise and Fall of Deception in Social Psychology and Personality Research, 1921 to 1994," *Ethics & Behavior* 7, no. 1 (1997): 69.

102. Ibid.

103. Ibid.

104. Ibid.

105. J. R. McNamara and K. M. Woods, "Ethical Considerations in Psychological Research: A Comparative Review," *Behavior Therapy* 8 (1977): 703–708.

106. J. Seeman, "Deception in Psychological Research," *American Psychologist* 24 (1969): 1025–1028.

107. Ralph Hertwig and Andreas Ortmann, "Experimental Practices in Economics: A Methodological Challenge for Psychologists?" *Behavioral & Brain Sciences* 24, no. 3 (2001): 383; R. Hertwig and A. Ortmann, "Deception in Experiments: Revisiting the Arguments in Its Defense," *Ethics & Behavior* 18 (2008): 59–92.

108. Hegtvedt, "Ethics and Experiments."

109. James H. Korn, *Illusions of Reality: A History of Deception in Social Psychology* (Albany, NY: University of New York Press, 1997).

110. Baumrind, "Research Using Intentional Deception."

111. Hegtvedt, "Ethics and Experiments."

112. Baumrind, "Research Using Intentional Deception."

113. Ibid.

114. Ibid.

115. Ibid.

116. Barrera and Simpson, "Much Ado About Deception"; S. Bonetti, "Experimental Economics and Deception," *Journal of Economic Psychology* 19, no. 3 (1998): 377–395.

117. Hegtvedt, "Ethics and Experiments."

118. Ibid.

119. Baumrind, "Research Using Intentional Deception."

120. Joan E. Sieber, Rebecca Iannuzzo, and Beverly Rodriguez, "Deception Methods in Psychology: Have They Changed in 23 Years?" *Ethics & Behavior* 5, no. 1 (1995): 67.

121. Baumrind, "Research Using Intentional Deception"; S. A. McLeod, "Psychology Research Ethics," *Simply Psychology* http://www.simplypsychology.org/Ethics .html.

122. Baumrind, "Research Using Intentional Deception"; McLeod, "Psychology Research Ethics."

123. Sieber, Iannuzzo, and Rodriguez, "Deception Methods in Psychology," 83.

124. Milgram, *Obedience to Authority: An Experimental View,* 23.

125. Milgram, "Behavioral Study of Obedience," *Journal of Abnormal and Social Psychology* 67, no. 4 (1963): 371–378.

126. Ibid.; Milgram, "Group Pressure and Action Against a Person," *Journal of Abnormal and Social Psychology* 69 (1964): 137–143.

127. Milgram, *Obedience to Authority: An Experimental View*; "Liberating Effects of Group Pressure"; "Some Conditions of Obedience and Disobedience to Authority."

128. Milgram, *Obedience to Authority: An Experimental View*, 27.

129. Ibid.

130. Ibid., 62.

131. Annie Lang, "The Logic of Using Inferential Statistics with Experimental Data from Nonprobability Samples: Inspired by Cooper, Dupagne, Potter, and Sparks," *Journal of Broadcasting & Electronic Media* 40, no. 3 (1996): 422–430; John A. Courtright, "Rationally Thinking About Nonprobability," *Journal of Broadcasting & Electronic Media* 40, no. 3 (1996): 414–421; Michael D. Basil, "The Use of Student Samples in Communication Research," *Journal of Broadcasting & Electronic Media* 40, no. 3 (1996): 431–440.

132. Ibid., 14.

133. Ibid., 16.

134. Ibid., 92.

135. Milgram, "Group Pressure and Action against a Person."

136. Milgram, "Behavioral Study of Obedience," 373.

137. Ibid., 374.

138. Milgram, *Obedience to Authority: An Experimental View,* 203.

139. Ibid., 205.

140. Ibid., 206.

141. Ibid., 22.

142. Ibid., 22.

143. Rebecca S. McEntee, Renita Coleman, and Carolyn Yaschur, "Comparing the Effects of Vivid Writing and Photographs on Moral Judgment in Public Relations," *Journalism and Mass Communication Quarterly* 94, no. 4 (2017): 1011–1030.

144. Philip Zimbardo, *The Lucifer Effect: Understanding How Good People Turn Evil* (New York: Random House, 2007).

145. Ibid., 508.

146. Ibid.

147. Craig Haney, Curtis Banks, and Philip Zimbardo, "Interpersonal Dynamics in a Simulated Prison," *International Journal of Criminology and Penology* 1 (1973): 69–97; Zimbardo, *The Lucifer Effect.*

148. Haney, Banks, and Zimbardo, "Interpersonal Dynamics in a Simulated Prison"; Zimbardo, "On the Ethics of Intervention in Human Psychological Research"; Zimbardo, *The Lucifer Effect.*

149. Zimbardo, "On the Ethics of Intervention in Human Psychological Research."

150. Zimbardo, *The Lucifer Effect.*

151. Zimbardo, *The Lucifer Effect.*

152. Murray Webster and Jane Sell, *Laboratory Experiments in the Social Sciences* (Amsterdam: Elsevier, 2007).

153. Zimbardo, *The Lucifer Effect*, 36.

154. Haney, Banks, and Zimbardo, "Interpersonal Dynamics in a Simulated Prison," 89.

155. Zimbardo, *The Lucifer Effect*, 32.

156. Haney, Banks, and Zimbardo, "Interpersonal Dynamics in a Simulated Prison."

157. Ibid., 21.

158. Ibid., 21.

159. Ibid.

160. Ibid., 24.

161. Zimbardo, *The Lucifer Effect*, 24.

162. Haney, Banks, and Zimbardo, "Interpersonal Dynamics in a Simulated Prison," 73.
163. Ibid., 77.
164. Ibid., 72.
165. Ibid., 69.
166. Ibid., 73.
167. Ibid., 78.
168. Ibid.
169. George A. Miller, "Giving Psychology Away in the '80s," *Psychology Today* 13 (1980): 38ff.
170. Zimbardo, "On the Ethics of Intervention in Human Psychological Research."
171. For an expanded statement of the "so what" question, see the Preface in *The Lucifer Effect*, pages x–xii.

# THEORY, LITERATURE, AND HYPOTHESES

*Full-blown successful interventions never emerge from a brainstorming session. They are always suggested by theory, previous research, or extensive clinical experience.*[1]

**—R. Barker Bausell**

To Bausell's assertion, we should add that experiments are not **exploratory** in the sense that they are used when problems are in the preliminary stage.[2] Rather, experiments presume a fair amount of well-developed theory and evidence from previous research. Thus, it is important to do the homework before starting any experiment, which involves a thorough search of the literature, including theory. This

iStock.com/baramee2554

chapter builds upon the previous one by examining the role of what researchers have discovered before us, or Isaac Newton's concept of "standing on the shoulders of giants."[3] While the information in this chapter also applies to other research methods, it is especially true that experiments are designed to create new knowledge by building upon what has been discovered previously. It also addresses two of the seven "attributes of a well-executed experiment."[4] That includes theory **explication**, or explaining the theory being tested, and clear identification of research questions and hypotheses. It looks at the literature review section of the paper from the perspective of how to explain the theory being tested, relate it to the variables used in the experiment, and link all the hypotheses to that theory. Hypotheses are particularly powerful analytic tools in experiments, so knowing how to write a literature review and the hypotheses that arise from it is especially important for this method.

As covered in chapter 1, the first step in designing an experiment is to formulate an idea of what causal relationships are to be tested and clearly articulate that in the statement of purpose. But these relationships should not be based merely on hunches or curiosity. Preferably, the idea of what to test should grow out of an understanding of the domain and the literature and theories within it. Measuring causality requires thinking theoretically; otherwise, experiments would be a haphazard process of trial and error.[5] (For more about theory, see More About box 3.1.)

One common pathway by which social scientific knowledge can develop is by starting with exploratory work using methods such as observations, interviews, and ethnography, among others. These types of qualitative methods are explicitly designed to be descriptive and generate theories.[14] They reveal **latent** meaning—that is, not readily apparent on the surface—or help us understand the nature of phenomena and predict the conditions under which they occur.[15] But because of their inherent qualities (small samples, not randomly drawn, lack of control, etc.), they are not well suited for testing or refining the theories they generate. That is one of the main purposes of experiments.[16] After theory is generated by qualitative or other means, research then can progress to methods that test them. Surveys are good for eliciting opinions, attitudes, and self-reports about behavior. Content analyses can uncover the characteristics of various types of messages, text, or visuals. While these methods produce research that adds knew knowledge and expands theory, they also suggest causes and provide correlational evidence that lays the ground-work for experimental work. Experimental studies are then able to determine if the phenomenon observed in a natural setting can be reproduced in a controlled environment,

## MORE ABOUT . . . BOX 3.1
### Theory

Theory is a generalized explanation for some particular phenomenon, or "an organized body of concepts and principles."[6] This is an academic way of saying that theory is about things that actually occur in the real world. To invoke Kurt Lewin, the father of gatekeeping, "There is nothing more practical than a good theory."[7] Although theory can seem mysterious and hard to comprehend, it really is nothing more than a tool for understanding what happens in life. Theories evolve when hypotheses are continually supported.[8] A good theory should do more than describe; it should also explain and allow predictions about the phenomenon. For example, one aspect of framing theory describes how news stories are constructed as discrete episodes—a story about a crime, for example—or more generally as themes that add context—a story about crimes, not just one in particular. It explains how people perceive these types of frames and also allows us to predict how people will react to them—for example, by holding individuals responsible when events are framed episodically but placing blame on social factors when events are framed thematically.[9] Experiments build theory by testing assumptions and expanding upon our existing understanding.

However, there has been some discussion of "exploratory experimentation" in biology and related disciplines.[10] What these researchers mean by an exploratory experiment is not an atheoretical, aimless data-gathering project. Rather, an exploratory experiment is one that is *directed* or *informed* by theory but does not necessarily *test* it via formal hypotheses.[11] These studies have a theoretical background, not a lack of theoretical framework altogether.[12] Theory is still "crucial to the success of exploratory experiments."[13] It is never appropriate to justify a lack of theory, low power, subjects not randomly assigned, uncontrolled variables, or other weaknesses by labeling the experiment as "exploratory." In these cases, the researchers should consider it to be a pilot study, take what they learned, and mount another experiment that improves upon the weaknesses rather than attempt to publish it as an exploratory work.

where all the many variables that could confound results or be responsible for plausible alternative explanations in the real world can be ruled out. Having arrived at the place where an experiment is the next logical method, the first step is to conduct a thorough search of the literature and particular theory.

All this is not to say that researchers can never come up with ideas for experiments by other means, such as by observing and becoming curious about why a particular phenomenon happens, as James Lind did for his study of scurvy. Ideas generated this way can certainly be tested with experiments. But there also should be some reason for testing them based on theory or evidence. When pursuing research questions generated from observations, it is important to find empirical evidence and theories that can help guide and refine them. This purpose can be served by correlational studies that link two variables, as can experiments that use a different population or different dependent variable (DV). For example, in a study to see if journalists' moral judgment could be improved by showing them photographs,[17] no work had been done using moral judgment as the DV and photographs as the independent variable (IV). However, photographs had been shown to improve other cognitive processes such as elaboration, empathy, and involvement.[18] All of these DVs are related to moral judgment, as shown by other studies.[19] These theoretical and empirical rationales provided links to the independent and outcome variables, albeit indirectly. This idea came about as a result of much speculation in essays and other nonempirical works about how journalists' ethical reasoning improved when photographs were involved.[20]

# THE LITERATURE REVIEW

The explanation of the theory being used and how it relates to the variables of the study is achieved in the literature review section of the paper. A well-done literature review provides a strong foundation for the entire experiment, yet Bausell says the "single rule most often violated by beginning researchers" is not knowing the relevant literature thoroughly enough.[21] Seasoned researchers may not feel the need to write a formal literature review in advance of running an experiment because they keep abreast of the latest findings and also work with theories they know well. But for others, before forming any testable hypothesis, a thorough search of pertinent literature and familiarization with relevant theories should be undertaken. The first step in this process is to perform a search of the literature, and the second is writing it up in the literature review section of the paper, which is the subject of this chapter.

Reading others' research can be a great source of ideas for experiments. First, reading existing studies will show whether the idea has been done already, so the study is not just a simple replication.[i] It will also reveal gaps in what has been done and what still needs to be done to flesh out a theory. The statements of "limitations" and "future studies" at the end of every research article can provide even more ideas. This includes ideas for studies that need replicating and for extending and improving upon a theory. Reading literature also provides methodological help, including information about how others have measured the variables, how many subjects might be needed, and ideas for novel procedures.

---

[i]In some disciplines, replications that do not extend theory or empirical knowledge in some relevant way are frowned upon.

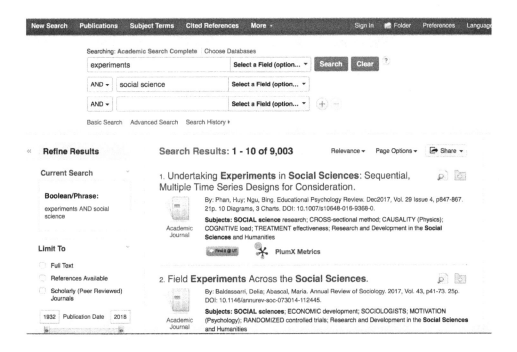

This book presumes that readers are familiar with how to conduct a literature search and write a review, perhaps even having conducted and written one or more already. Because an experiment is so much work on the front end of designing it, and it cannot be changed once the data have been collected, it is especially important that the literature search for an experiment be performed thoroughly. I recommend actually writing a draft of the literature review before proceeding to collect data no matter how familiar you are with the topic. I have found that the act of writing slows me down and gives me time to think about the literature in a way I would not if I had just been reading it. It also forces me to synthesize the many different findings, which helps me better analyze the meaning and find gaps that may need filling. Making a chart or table can help show things more clearly, and sometimes these figures end up in the published study—for example, table 3.1.

With experiments, it is necessary to isolate or control all things that could possibly affect the outcome or DV except for the one thing being manipulated, so it is especially crucial to know what all those things are. They can then be controlled, or used as mediators, moderators, or covariates. If a researcher does not know what they are and fails to measure or control them, the validity of the findings for the entire experiment is put in jeopardy.

There are many good books and articles on how to perform a literature search and write a literature review, so those will not be described in detail here. Instead, next is advice for avoiding some of the most common problems with literature reviews in

| TABLE 3.1 ● INDICATORS OF IMAGINATIVE CAPACITIES (LIAO ET AL., 2016) | | |
|---|---|---|
| **Indicator** | **Definition** | **References** |
| Novelty | The ability to generate unique ideas | Beaney (2005) and Vygotsky (2014/1967) |
| Productivity | The ability to produce thoughts using the extensive application of free association | Folkmann (2010) and Gaut (2005) |
| Concentration | The ability to formulate thoughts through focus and immersion | Csikszentmihalyi (1996) and Folkmann (2010) |
| Sensibility | The ability to evoke feelings during the creative process | Ricoeur (1978) and Scheffler (1986) |
| Intuition | The ability to generate immediate associations with a goal | Reichling (1990) and Townsend (2003) |
| Effectiveness | The ability to generate relevant and profound thoughts to attain a goal | Gilbert and Reiner (2000) and Shin (1994) |
| Dialectics | The ability to seek improvement by logically analyzing possibilities and alternatives | Cartwright and Noone (2006) and Reiner and Gilbert (2000) |
| Exploration | The ability to inquire about the unknown | Coiello (2007) and Thomas (2004) |
| Crystallization | The ability to visualize abstract concepts by using concrete examples | DeVries (1988) and Vygotsky (2004/1967) |
| Transformation | The ability to perform tasks by applying information acquired across multiple fields of knowledge | Kunzendorf (1982) and Liu and Noppe-Brandon (2009) |

From: Liao, Kai-Hung, Chi-Chen Chang, Chao-Tung Liang, and Chaoyun Liang. 2016. "In Search of the Journalistic Imagination." *Thinking Skills and Creativity* 19: 9–20.

experimental designs. These tips are not exclusive to this method, but the problems they address occur often enough in experiments that they are worth mentioning.

## Tips on Writing the Literature Review for Experiments

### It Is Not a Book Report

It is important to analyze and synthesize the findings of the various studies found in the literature search. Too often, literature reviews read like book reports. They are summaries of the findings of previous studies, but there is no analysis of those findings that shows the connections among or between them and the study about to be conducted. Do not assume that readers will be familiar with the topic; therefore, how the studies reviewed connect to each other and to the current study will not be as obvious to them as to you. Spell it out. Furthermore, experiments test hypotheses, which are proposed based on previous findings; therefore, an analysis of those findings is especially important for this method.

Rather than stringing together summaries of the abstracts (Smith and Jones found . . . ; White, Brown, Green, and Black showed . . . ; Tinker and Taylor studied . . .), a good literature review is a critical analysis of the studies, synthesizing the findings, and coming up with new ideas of your own. This approach also avoids what can look like shameless name-dropping or an attempt to bump up an author's citations or a journal's **impact factor**—a measure of how important it is.

As an example of analyzing and synthesizing, I relate a story of a colleague and I who were doing an agenda-setting study to discover whether issues in the news or attributes of candidates had more powerful effects on voters. We conducted a literature search and noticed that the correlations between the media's agenda and the public's agenda (the basic premise of agenda-setting theory) were consistently higher for attributes than for issues. That was the foundation for the resulting hypothesis, which predicted that attribute agenda setting would be more powerful than issue agenda setting.[22] This was not something we found already written about but discovered by thinking critically about the theory and comparing the findings of all the studies.

### Do Not Be Wikipedia

Too many literature reviews read like Wikipedia entries. Instead of reviewing everything ever written about a topic, a good review covers only the literature related to the study. For example, if the experiment is on second-level agenda setting, it might be important to briefly mention what first-level agenda setting is and say how it differs from second level, but it is not necessary to explain it in detail, summarize every study on it, and describe all the mediators, moderators, or **contingent conditions**—that is, when it works and does not. Instead, mention it and say how it differs from what this experiment will test, and move on. In other words, only focus on B if the study is about B, even if there is also an A. Do be sure to cover all the *relevant* literature; some authors go too far in the opposite direction and leave out important work. Key is finding balance—cover just the right amount and do not leave out any of the truly **seminal studies**, or the classics.

This also applies to the theories written about in the literature review. There are many theories that overlap and can be used to inform an experiment, but a study should

## STUDY SPOTLIGHT 3.2

**Shoemaker, P., J. Tankard, and D. Lasorsa. 2003.** *How to Build Social Science Theories.* **Thousand Oaks, CA: Sage.**

Novice researchers frequently have a difficult time understanding not only what theory is but especially how to build it. It is not uncommon for journal reviewers to ask authors: "What is your theoretical contribution?" "What theoretical statements does this study offer?" and "What does this study do to build theory?" Finding ways to answer these concerns keeps many a budding social scientist up at night. When this book on how to build theory in the social sciences came out, it spoke directly to my inner experimentalist in its logical, step-by-step approach. It delivered on its promise to teach "the challenging activity of theory building with the minimum amount of difficulty."[25] This book begins by assuring readers that they are not alone and that there is no shame in admitting a lack of understanding of how to build theory and provide theoretical contributions.

The chapters build logically, beginning by describing hypothesis writing. It then explains theoretical concepts, which it calls "the building blocks of theory."[26] It illustrates ways to combine concepts into theoretical statements, which broadly describe relationships among variables. It shows how to synthesize disparate parts and make linkages, both theoretical and operational. Then it shows how to describe and explain the relationships among concepts in ways that offer explanatory power. Chapters deal with how to relate two variables, three, four, and more, and how to build models in advance of a full-blown theory.

The book offers examples that social science scholars can relate to. The development of cultivation theory by George Gerbner and colleagues is one, showing how it began as a way of explaining the effects of television on viewers.[27] One hypothesis proposed that watching television shapes viewers' beliefs, ideologies, and worldviews. As studies were conducted and the hypothesis supported, it grew to include other concepts with labels such as "resonance" and "mainstreaming," which specified the conditions necessary for the effect to occur. More research resulted in more revisions and additions to the theory, including first- and second-order effects that delineated perceptions based in reality and beliefs.

*How to Build Social Science Theories* stresses the importance of creativity to building theory, an idea that is also important in this book. It offers concrete, practical ways to make contributions to theory. How to develop theory never really "clicked" for me until I read it.

typically use only one or two. For example, there are at least ten theories that can be used to explain aggression from watching television.[23] In studies using other methods, reviewing many similar theories may be more appropriate than in an experiment designed to test a specific theory. Find the one theory that is best suited to what the experiment is trying to do, and write a solid rationale for why it is used and not others rather than reviewing every possible theory. Sometimes, two theories will lead to opposite predictions, and so those can be juxtaposed in a single study.[24] In this process, a compelling link should be made between independent, dependent, and **intervening variables**, or those that come between the treatment and the outcome.

## Make a Theoretical Contribution

Far too many studies of all kinds will summarize a theory and then go on to do whatever the authors intend to do but never circle back to the theory at the end. They often fail to explicitly say what the study intends to do to contribute to that theory or theories. With experiments, this is an especially egregious oversight given that one of the main reasons for doing an experiment is to develop, test, refine, or otherwise contribute to theory. It is never enough to lay out a theory as the foundation and then abandon it. It should be explicitly stated what this experiment will do for the theory or theories, and that should be expanded on in the discussion and conclusion of the paper. (For a synopsis of a book on how to build theory, see Study Spotlight 3.2.)

Toward this end, it is important to link all the variables—dependent, independent, causal mechanisms, and individual difference variables—clearly explicating the relationships among them.[28] Start by stating how the IV will affect the DV, and then explain through what theoretical processes this will occur. If it helps, make a figure that models this and use it to visualize the process (for an example, see table 3.1). As an example, the study on photographs' effects on moral judgment[29] mentioned earlier was interested in establishing a causal relationship between journalists who were exposed to photographs and their levels of moral judgment compared to journalists who were not exposed to photographs. The study theorized this would occur because photographs had been shown to increase empathy, which intensifies involvement and also encourages central route processing, all of which were found to increase moral judgment. The theoretical contribution was not only that photographs had the ability to improve moral judgment—an intervention that had not been tested previously—but also the demonstration of the theoretical explanation for *why* photographs worked.

## Connect the Dots

Finally, another important feature of a good literature review is to relate other studies to your own, what I call connecting the dots. After reviewing every batch of studies on a common topic, explicitly say how they are related to the study to be conducted. Will it be measured the same way? Do they contain gaps that this one will fill? What connections in these studies will this experiment build upon? Always relate the findings of other studies to your study, locating it within the context of the larger body of work. A reader should never have to go more than a paragraph or two to find out why specific studies are being reviewed and how they are connected to the current one. For example, in the study mentioned earlier that examined the correlations from various agenda-setting studies, the paper explained how they were relevant to the current study by saying, "All these second level correlations are similar to the highest

## HOW TO DO IT 3.3

### Examples of Connector Sentences

In a literature review, it is important to relate studies to each other and to your own, locating your work in the context of others. I offer here some examples of how various researchers have made this explicit in their experiments.

- After reviewing the three sequences in the Hierarchy of Effects Model, this study said, "We are not particularly concerned with the sequence but rather with the strength of the first two components of these models—knowledge and attitudes—on the behavioral outcome, voting. In other words, we seek to determine not which came first, but which has a stronger effect: cognition about issues (first level) or feelings about attributes (second level).[31]

- After reviewing celebrities' Twitter use and source credibility, the authors say, "Acknowledging the aforementioned novelty and importance of celebrity-generated messages embedded in social media, this research tested the effects of celebrities' Twitter-based electronic word-of-mouth on consumers' perceptions of source credibility, intention to spread electronic word-of-mouth, brand-related outcomes, online bridging social capital, and social identification with celebrities."[32]

- Before reviewing attribution styles, this study said, "This study delves into the role of consumers' different attribution style, specifically how different attribution styles lead to the differential impacts in evaluation of the negative celebrity information."[33]

- In a study of math learning, the authors reviewed the literature and summarized the findings, and then tied it to the question this study was designed to answer this way: "Simply put, as math anxiety increases, math achievement declines. A possible inherent relationship between anxiety and achievement poses an obvious question, however: Is a poor performance on a math assessment/problem due to math anxiety or due to lack of mastery of the content?"[34]

- After reviewing studies on different methods that were effective in helping students learn English, this study summed it up this way: "An examination of the salient characteristics and benefits of a technology-enriched curriculum for English Language Learners underscores the pivotal role Computer Assisted Language Learning can play in second language teaching and learning."[35]

- Before summarizing literature, the authors of a study testing businesses that drop out of overcrowded markets note the similarities among the studies and point out the gap their work fills: "Although wars of attrition have an important place in the game theoretic literature, there are surprisingly few experimental studies directly relating to them."[36]

correlations at the first level; none reaches the lowest levels or even the mean level of .53 in meta-analysis of the first level effects."[30] That is an example of a sentence that connects all the studies just reviewed to the current one.

These connections can never be too obvious. Good connecting sentences include: "This is relevant to our study because . . ." "We use this finding in our study by incorporating it as a mediator . . ." "These studies raise questions about . . . , which is the purpose of this research," and similar phrases. Many good examples of connector sentences exist; some are presented in How To Do It box 3.3. As you read other studies, look for them and adapt to your own work.

## Conceptual Definitions vs. Operationalizations

The literature review is also where all the important concepts and variables in a study are conceptually defined. A **conceptual definition** is an abstract, theoretical description of something using general qualitative terms. Students often confuse conceptual definitions with **operational definitions**, or operationalizations, which take a concept and define it in the specific, concrete ways it is measured. A **concept** is a general idea about something that has many specific characteristics. For example, credibility was conceptually defined as "the public perception of news quality"[37] in one study, and then it was operationalized with thirteen specific characteristics that included how fair, complete, accurate, believable, credible, informative, interesting, likeable, in-depth, important, and well written a news story was, plus how trustworthy the sources and information were. These are two different kinds of definitions, which appear in two separate sections of a paper. It is not adequate to provide a list of terms to be used to measure the concept as the conceptual definition. The conceptual definition should instead describe and explain the concept based on theory. Another example is the conceptual definition of moral judgment as the reasons "that people use to decide that a course of action is ethically right or wrong."[38] The operationalization given in the methods section is a list of twelve statements about things that were important to the subject when deciding what to do about a particular dilemma (for examples, see the footnote[ii]).

---

[ii]The twelve statements vary according to each dilemma, but an example is: (1) A chance like this photo comes only a few times in a career; (2) The kids will grow up having this horrible, graphic reminder of what happened; (3) This is a family newspaper, children might see this photo at the breakfast table; (4) You'll probably get a lot of angry calls and people will cancel their subscriptions; (5) How these people and their families will feel when they see this; (6) Your competition is working on a similar story. If you don't run the photo, your competition will just run something similar; (7) Publishing this photo would help your paper's reputation for investigative reporting; (8) Whether it is our duty as journalists to show all the news, regardless of the circumstances; (9) Whether the public has a right to know all the facts about drug use and its effects on people, especially children; (10) What would best serve society; (11) Photos that are painful to some have to be shown so others will benefit; (12) If I don't run this photo, I may prevent these children from being taken from their parents, but the conditions leading to situations like theirs will persist.

The credibility study cited previously also provides a good example of a concept that has been defined differently by various researchers, including as "attitude toward a source of communication," "global evaluation of the believability of the message source," a combination of trustworthiness, expertise, and goodwill, and as the combined public perceptions of media's approach to "quality, profit making, privacy, community well-being and trustworthiness."[39] It is not uncommon to find a lack of consensus about the conceptual definition of some concept. When that is the case, it is important to acknowledge that in the literature section, review the different conceptual definitions, and then defend your choice of definition and explain why it is best suited for your study. To repeat: Every variable used in a study must appear in three places:

- conceptually defined in the literature review,

- incorporated in the hypothesis or research questions, and

- operationalized in the methods section.

Trace each variable throughout the paper and be sure that each one appears in all three places. There should be no orphan concepts or variables.

A good way to make sure that all bases are covered is to think of the literature review in terms of an outline that lists all the DVs, IVs, intervening variables (mediators, moderators, causal mechanisms), and covariates, if any. Use subheads that mirror the outline to help clarify it for readers and also to help organize the writing. This ensures that everything is defined, the empirical evidence is covered, and all the discussion about one variable is in the same place. Experienced readers expect to find all the information about a particular concept together and can become annoyed when something pops up in different places throughout the paper.

## Literature Reviews With Multiple Experiments

Many researchers report more than one experiment in a single article for reasons that range from replicating a finding to ruling out plausible alternative explanations. Sometimes this is planned beforehand, and other times the need arises only after the first study results are known. This phenomenon will be explored in chapter 5 on validity. When multiple experiments are reported in one paper, there may be one section that covers all the literature for both studies, or there may be two literature reviews, the first one the longest and the second that includes only new literature that pertains just to the second study. Usually, these will be labeled "Study 1" and "Study 2," or more if there are more experiments. The general pattern is to report the literature for the first study, followed by the methods for it under a subhead such as "Study 1," then the results and discussion of it. The second study will follow under a subhead "Study 2" or "Experiment 2," starting with a description of it and a small literature review if necessary to explicate any new variables. For example, if new IVs, mediators, or moderators were introduced in order to rule out confounds or plausible alternative explanations that may have arisen in the first study, they obviously were not covered in the first literature review. It is not necessary to repeat all the previous information from the main literature review, only to add the new concepts and put them into context with the previous literature and theory. A good illustration comes from a study of cognitive processing in agenda setting.[40] The second experiment was conceived of after the first one showed the effects the authors expected on some subjects but not others. They speculate this could have been affected by the content of the stories they used, and write: "We decided to conduct a follow-up study to test the assumption that people who process information more centrally than others could be influenced by content aspects of the articles such as journalistic evaluations of an issue's importance."[41] They follow with the subhead "Study 2" and begin with a one-page literature review just of studies that deal with content of news stories.

Finally, a few miscellaneous but still important points for the literature review:

- *Include current sources.* In addition to the seminal or classic studies, be sure to include up-to-date works. This is especially important if a study was started some time ago. Go back and see what has been done recently and include it.

- *Use different search methods.* Searches using key words in databases do not always uncover all the important literature, even when using multiple databases. To avoid missing important studies, go through the last two or three years of journals that are likely to publish articles on the topic to see if anything has been missed. Include the journal you plan to submit to in this process.

- *Include conflicting findings.* Very few programs of research always produce consistent findings. Look for studies that *did not* work as expected. Not only is it important to be honest, it is important to know what might cause your experiment to not work as planned so you can control for it as much as possible. Review the studies with findings that do not support your predictions and explain why they might have come out this way.

- *Use quotes sparingly.* Quoting others at great length or too often raises red flags for readers because it can appear as if you did not understand what the author was trying to say. Paraphrasing someone else's writing also affords the opportunity to write it in a clearer way. Make it a habit not to use direct quotes unless there is absolutely no better, clearer, more concise way to say it. There are very few sentences in academic papers that meet this criterion. When direct quotes are used, cite them appropriately with page numbers.

- *Be careful not to plagiarize.* See preceding point. Much plagiarism results from careless practices rather than bad intentions—for example, taking notes by copying and pasting from the original article and then forgetting whether these were already rewritten in your own words. Repeating your own writing from a different article is also a form of plagiarism. Develop a system to know what is paraphrased and what is not, for example, by highlighting, using quotes, or putting them in a different type font.

- *Always read the paper.* It can be time consuming to trace back and read the original papers cited in others' literature reviews, but relying on another author's interpretation of a paper rather than reading it yourself can be perilous. Scholars have been known to uncritically report the same summary of a study over and over, perhaps even wrongly.[42] I find this to be the case particularly when books or articles are written in another language and not translated.

## HYPOTHESES AND RESEARCH QUESTIONS

The literature review is also where the hypotheses and research questions are typically incorporated. One approach is to list all hypotheses at the end of the literature review. This style involves a block of hypotheses before the methods section, like this:

"Hypothesis 1 (H1): Individual donors will donate less when they know that a nonprofit receives some amount of government funding. (Categorical crowding-out hypothesis)

Hypothesis 2 (H2): Individual donors will donate less if a nonprofit receives a greater share of its funding from government. (Continuous crowding-out hypothesis)

Hypothesis 3 (H3): Knowing that government funding comes from a competitive merit-based program will increase individuals' willingness to donate. (Crowding-in hypothesis)"[43]

For the purpose of illustration, in these hypotheses I have slightly edited the second one to keep the wording parallel; the original paper uses "give" in H2, while the other hypotheses use the term "donate." As "give" and "donate" could conceivably be defined differently, it is important not to use synonyms in writing hypotheses. Instead, use parallel wording for hypotheses whenever possible.

To keep readers from having to refer many pages back in the literature review in order to recall the evidence leading up to each hypothesis, some journals use a short summary of the literature that led to each prediction just prior to or after the hypothesis. As it can be inefficient to have the full description of studies in the literature review section and then to repeat a summary of it at the end of the literature review with the hypotheses, another style embeds hypotheses into the literature review at the point where the topic of each hypothesis is covered. So, for example, literature on topic A is followed by a hypothesis related to A; literature on topic B is followed by a hypothesis related to B. That approach allows the empirical evidence to be fresh in readers' minds. For example, in a study on the climate of opinion judgments comparing the relative weight of explicit cues to implicit cues,[44] the authors first reviewed the literature on explicit cues and gave this hypothesis:

> "**H1**: Surveys, as explicit media cues, influence recipients' judgments of the climate of opinion in the direction of the survey results."[45]

They next reviewed implicit cues and predicted:

> "**H2**: If arguments in a media report support (oppose) a certain opinion, the perceived public agreement to this opinion increases (decreases)."[46]

They then reviewed literature on persuasive effects of both kinds of cues in media and gave this hypothesis:

> "**H3a**: If survey information on an unknown issue is presented, recipients tend to follow the majority opinion."[47]

There were several more hypotheses, with it all visually summarized in a model (see figure 3.1).

It can be a challenge not to introduce a concept in a hypothesis before having explicated it in the literature review. So, for example, do not introduce hypotheses that include the

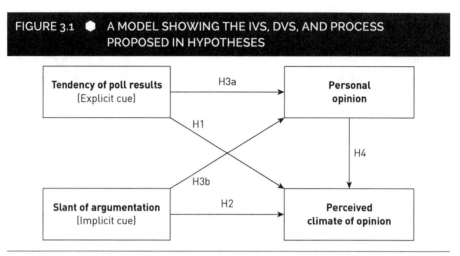

**FIGURE 3.1  ●  A MODEL SHOWING THE IVS, DVS, AND PROCESS PROPOSED IN HYPOTHESES**

Source: Zerback, Thomas, Thomas Koch, and Benjamin Kramer. 2015. "Thinking of Others: Effects of Implicit and Explicit Media Cues on Climate of Opinion Perceptions." *Journalism and Mass Communication Quarterly* 92 (2): 421–443.

current or future state of something until the empirical evidence on that has been covered. Organizing the literature in such a way that it flows naturally and does not assume reader knowledge of concepts before they are explicated is tricky. This makes it tempting to plop all the hypotheses in at the end, but then readers may have trouble recalling what was said about the concepts in H1 by the time they get to it. Instead, breaking hypotheses down into smaller statements, one IV at a time, in the order that the process occurs, is key.

The hypotheses in the previous examples are formally phrased and given the designation "H" plus a number (H1, H2, H3, etc.). The lower-case letters (H5a, H5b, H5c) indicate a subset of related hypotheses. But it is also quite common to see hypotheses phrased in a narrative style. For example, in a study of whether authoritarian governments are willing to include citizen preferences in the policies they enact, scholars in China posed their hypotheses this way:

> Thus, based on previous research as well as statements by the CCP, we have reason to believe that when state–society relations are harmonious, leaders may be equally receptive to opinions expressed on the Internet and to those expressed through formal channels. However, when leaders believe that antagonism exists between the state and citizens, we expect that they will be less receptive to both formal and Internet channels.[48]

Hypotheses should be written in future tense (e.g., "will have," "may be") rather than present tense (e.g., "is") because they have yet to be tested; the present tense can sound like it is already a fact.

*How many hypotheses are needed?* Students often ask this question, but I am unable to give anything but the Goldilocks answer: Not too many, but not too few—just the right amount. One hypothesis may indicate a too-small study or the need to break a too-large hypothesis down into smaller bites. Hypotheses that run into the double digits may indicate a study that attempts to do too much and should be split into two publications. Let theory, logic, and reader attention decide. Have colleagues read the literature review to see if they can follow it clearly without getting lost or bored.

More important than how many hypotheses there are is how clearly they are written. If a process is specified, the hypotheses should build logically upon each other. Sometimes, experiments explore causal mechanisms that involve multiple steps in complex theoretical processes. When this is the case, it makes sense to break things down into a series of specific hypotheses that build upon each other in a cohesive model. For example, in the study of how photographs elevate moral judgment, the process was broken down into three hypotheses:

> "H1: Participants who see photographs will have significantly higher levels of elaboration about stakeholders than those who do not.
>
> H2: More elaboration about stakeholders will be significantly associated with higher ethical reasoning.
>
> H3: Ethical reasoning will be significantly higher for participants who see photographs than for those who do not."[49]

The third hypothesis was what the study was most interested in, but it occurred last in the causal chain of events.[iii]

Mutz offered a similar set of hypotheses, in narrative fashion, in a study of close-up camera perspectives and uncivil TV discourse (they are broken into separate paragraphs for easier reading here):

> "The first hypothesis is that close-up camera perspectives and incivility will both increase levels of emotional arousal.
>
> A second hypothesis following from the first is that heightened arousal will increase levels of recall."[50]

---

[iii]This study also predicted an interaction of photographs and involvement, but I leave the discussion of main effects and interactions for later.

In this example, the first prediction involved close-up camera perspective and incivility leading to emotional arousal. The second prediction takes arousal from the first hypothesis and connects it to recall. The order is not chosen randomly; the researcher proposed them in this order because it was posited that they occurred in this order. With more involved processes, these pathways can be diagrammed out in figures to make it easier to visualize.

## Hypothesis Basics

### Null vs. Alternative

Before explaining how to write a hypothesis, this is a good place to review the concepts of null and **alternative hypotheses**, where a null hypothesis says there is no difference or direction, and the alternative hypothesis says there is. These were invented in order to reduce experimenter bias, or the tendency to find evidence that supports our ideas. A long time ago, scientists came up with the idea of basically arguing against your own position—that is, researchers should not try to show that a treatment causes effects but to *disprove* that it does not. In other words, to try to show that there is no relationship between two things, or no difference between two groups. The null hypothesis is written $H_0$ and the alternative $H_a$ or $H_1$. By rejecting the null, we say we have reason to think that there *is* a relationship or a difference, thus we can say there is a likelihood that our hypothesis is correct. This is technically the alternative hypothesis. In other words, we start from the position that the null (no difference, or no relationship) is true until evidence shows otherwise. If the null hypothesis is rejected, we say we have found support for our hypothesis. We never use the term *prove* because that cannot technically be done. Instead, the proper language to use is to *support* our hypothesis or *reject* the null; to reject the hypothesis or have it "*fail to be rejected*"; or to say that the hypothesis was "*not disconfirmed.*"[51] This is rarely stated explicitly in research papers but is the thought process underlying them all.

A hypothesis is a prediction of how independent and dependent variables are related.[52] They can be thought of as "if . . . then . . ." statements—for example, "If journalists see photographs, then they will use higher levels of moral judgment." Hypotheses should be stated in terms of concepts rather than operationalizations.[53] For example, in business, there is a concept called managerial trustworthiness, abbreviated MTW, and conceptually defined as "the trustworthiness attributed to supervisors."[54] It is measured with nine items including capable, competent, concerned, and a strong sense of justice, among others. The hypotheses refer to managerial trustworthiness, not competence, justice, etc. For example:

> "H1: Emphasis on internal management that relates to setting challenging but feasible goals has a positive effect on an individual's perception of MTW."[55]

### Difference vs. Direction

Hypotheses come in two flavors: those that predict a causal direction—for example, which of two variables will have larger effects than the other—and those that merely predict a difference but do not propose which variable will have a greater impact than the other. These are also called *nondirectional hypotheses*. An example of a hypothesis that predicts a difference is:

> H: Journalists who see photographs will use significantly *different* levels of moral judgment than journalists who do not see photographs.

It predicts a difference between seeing and not seeing photographs, but it does not specify whether the outcome will be higher or lower. By this account, seeing photographs could result in moral judgment that is either better or worse. By contrast, this version of the hypothesis predicts a direction:

> H: Journalists who see photographs will use significantly *higher* levels of moral judgment than journalists who do not see photographs.

The second hypothesis goes further than the first to say specifically what the difference between the two conditions—seeing photographs or not—will be.

Another example of a directional hypothesis is from the previous example of a study on managerial trustworthiness:

> "H1: Emphasis on internal management that relates to setting challenging but feasible goals will have a positive effect on an individual's perception of MTW."[56]

This hypothesis predicts a causal direction with the use of the word *positive*; the researchers expect *higher* levels of MTW in the goal-setting condition. A nondirectional way to state this hypothesis would be to say that goal setting would have an effect on MTW that was different from the other conditions, but not to specify whether that effect would be positive or negative.

Whether to make a hypothesis that predicts a direction or a difference depends on the theory and empirical evidence available; if there is enough to suggest a causal direction, then it is appropriate to make that prediction. If there is not enough evidence, or theory does not suggest a direction, then it is more appropriate to predict a difference but not specify a direction. For example, the first time the effects of photographs on moral judgment were tested, there were theoretical reasons to believe that photographs could either improve or worsen moral judgment. In that case, it is appropriate to propose that seeing photographs will cause subjects to behave differently without predicting whether their moral judgment would be better or worse than those who did not see photographs. After a study finds effects in a certain direction, from then on it is appropriate to use directional hypotheses.

If theory and prior evidence is in such short supply as to prevent a researcher from making a prediction at all, then a **research question** should be used. A research question represents a more preliminary state of affairs concerning theory and evidence.[iv] So continuing the previous example, if there was even less theory and evidence to make the prediction that photographs would have some effect on moral judgment, it is appropriate to ask, "Does seeing photographs affect journalists' moral judgment?" As a rule of thumb, it is always best to make the most specific prediction possible with the available evidence and theory, as that provides us with more powerful analytical tools.[57]

Whether a researcher makes a prediction of direction or not is important in how hypotheses are tested statistically. What follows may not make sense to readers who have not taken an introductory statistics course; for them, the point is that the type of hypothesis used matters later in the data analysis phase. For those who are familiar with basic statistics, a one-tailed test is appropriate for testing a directional hypothesis. For a nondirectional hypothesis, a two-tailed test is used. (For simplicity, these examples assume two groups—one treatment and one control.) The graphic illustration of that is found in the normal distribution. A nondirectional or hypothesis of differences is tested with a two-tailed $t$ test. Because no direction was specified, the hypothesis is supported if the $t$ value

falls in either end of the normal distribution, marked by the blue shaded areas in figure 3.2.

A directional hypothesis is only supported if the $t$ value falls in the end of the normal distribution that is specified in the hypothesis. In this example, the hypothesis is that photographs would lead to *higher* levels of moral judgment, so the $t$ value must fall in the blue shaded area to be significant, represented in figure 3.3. Practically speaking, if significance exists, it is easier to find it with a directional hypothesis; however, if the direction predicted is wrong, then a

---

[iv]Other uses of research questions will be covered later in this chapter.

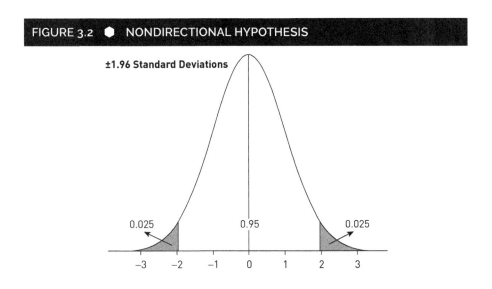

FIGURE 3.2 ● NONDIRECTIONAL HYPOTHESIS

±1.96 Standard Deviations

0.025    0.95    0.025

−3  −2  −1  0  1  2  3

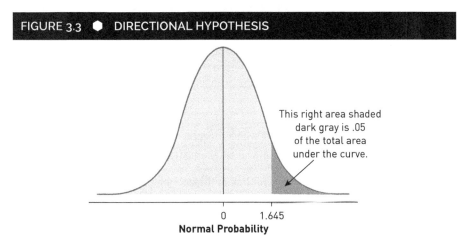

FIGURE 3.3 ● DIRECTIONAL HYPOTHESIS

This right area shaded dark gray is .05 of the total area under the curve.

0    1.645
**Normal Probability**

statistical test may find significance but in the opposite direction that was predicted, in which case the hypothesis is not supported.

## Hypothesis Writing Formula

Now that this textbook has covered when and why to propose a hypothesis that specifies a direction or not, I offer a basic formula to write clear and focused hypotheses. For each hypothesis, the formula includes:

- Prediction of either a statistically significant difference or direction of that difference (shown in <u>underlines</u> as follows).

- The independent variable (shown in **bold**).

- The dependent variable, stated in conceptual terms (shown in <u><u>double underline</u></u>).

For experiments that use two groups, a treatment and control, hypotheses use the term *between*. Future tense is also preferred. Written out as if we were filling in the blanks, this looks like:

- There will be a significant <u>difference</u> in <u>credibility</u> ratings (the DV) between subjects who see the story on **Twitter** and those who see it on a **website** (the IV).[58]

- There will be a significant <u>difference</u> in <u>importance</u> ratings (the DV) between subjects who see **long or short stories** (the IV).[59]

- Audiences exposed to the **advocacy frame** (IV) will rank crime as significantly <u>different</u> in <u>importance</u> (DV) than those exposed to the **objective stories** (IV).[60]

These are all nondirectional hypotheses, as they specify a difference but do not say whether that difference will be higher or lower, large or small. They could be written directionally, for example:

- <u>Credibility</u> ratings (the DV) will be significantly <u>higher</u> for subjects who see the story on **Twitter** than for those who see it on a **website** (the IV).

- <u>Importance</u> ratings (the DV) will be significantly <u>lower</u> for subjects who see a **short story** than for those who see a **long story** (the IV).

- Audiences exposed to the **advocacy frame** (IV) will rank crime as significantly <u>more</u> <u>important</u> (DV) than those exposed to the **objective frame** (IV).

If an experiment involves three or more groups—for example, two treatments and a control group—the term *among* is used instead of between, like this:

- There will be a significant <u>difference</u> in <u>credibility</u> ratings (the DV) among subjects who see the story on **Twitter**, a **website**, or in a **newspaper** (the IV).

Notice this one has simply changed the IV to include three conditions—Twitter, a website, and a newspaper—instead of two.

In all these examples of basic hypotheses, each is precisely worded. They use clear, simple, single cause-and-effect predictions. The same words are used throughout rather than synonymous terms. These should be the same terms used in the literature review. Each predicts a clear causal relationship between specific IVs and DVs. Directional hypotheses are preferred if they can be supported by theory and/or prior evidence.

If an experiment includes covariates or statistical controls for individual differences that have been shown to affect the DV but are not equivalently distributed during random assignment, the phrase *controlling for age, education, and gender*, or whatever the variables are, is added to the end of the hypothesis:

> H1: There will be a statistically significant difference in credibility ratings among subjects who see the story on Twitter, a website, or a newspaper, controlling for age, education, and gender.

## Hypotheses With More Than One IV

So far in this book, we have talked about manipulating one independent variable at a time—for example, the format of the message in the preceding hypothesis is whether subjects see it on Twitter, a website, or in a newspaper. In the previous example, the independent variable is the frame: advocacy or objective. These are known as *single-factor designs* and will be explained in detail in a later chapter. In reality, many experiments manipulate more than one independent variable at a time—for example, the format of the message *and* its frame, in the same study. When more than one independent variable, or **factor**, is manipulated, separate hypotheses should be written for each factor, also called a *main effect*, and for the **interaction** of the two factors or the effects of the two factors considered together. So, for example, in an experiment that manipulates the message format (Twitter, website) and the frame (advocacy, objective), there should be two hypotheses, one for each independent variable or factor's main effect:

> H1: Credibility scores will be significantly higher for subjects who read stories on Twitter than on a website.

> H2: Credibility scores will be significantly higher for subjects who read objectively framed stories than advocacy framed stories.

Finally, there should be either a hypothesis or a research question about the interaction between the format and the frame, such as:

H3: Credibility scores will be higher for subjects who read objectively framed stories on a website than for any of the other combinations of message format and frame;

OR

RQ1: Is there an interaction between message format and frame?

Naturally, the choice of whether to make a prediction or ask a research question depends on theory and evidence; use a hypothesis whenever possible. This next example of an interaction hypothesis shows the two experimental manipulations or IVs—disgust and harm—interacting with subjects' preexisting political views. The author predicts different effects of the IVs depending on whether the subject supports or opposes a political practice:

> "H4: Incidental disgust and harm associations will increase moral conviction and lead to a harsher moral judgment among opponents of a political practice but lead to the opposite effect among supporters."[61]

These hypotheses for studies with more than one independent variable, or factor, also build in a logical progression, from one IV to another, then to the interaction of the two IVs. If intervening variables are proposed, then they too are taken one at a time in a logical order. To think more clearly about these more complicated hypotheses, it may help to create a table listing the independent variables or factors and their levels, the intervening variables, and dependent variables. Use these to visualize the hypotheses, as shown in How To Do It box 3.4.

Here is an example of a hypothesis that includes an intervening variable: the concept of powerfulness. This experiment studies spokespeople who respond to an organizational crisis of contaminated food. The IV in this experiment is voice pitch, with the two levels being high pitch or low pitch. The intervening variable is powerfulness, which has been perceived in low-pitched voices. Thus, the hypothesis says:

> "A lowered voice pitch will result in greater perceptions of competence compared to a raised voice pitch due to an intermediate effect of perceived powerfulness (H2)."[62]

There are many more variations on hypotheses in published journal articles; this is meant to introduce the beginner to the basics of hypothesis writing. As you read published experiments and conduct your own, adapt your hypothesis writing to the needs of each study.

## HOW TO DO IT 3.4

### Hypothesis Writing Table

To more easily diagram out the steps for writing hypotheses, it may be helpful to visualize the variables with a table, as follows. List the independent variables or factors in a column on the left, with the levels of each. List the dependent variables in the column on the right. If there are any intervening variables or causal mechanisms, list them in the middle column. Then, draw lines to demonstrate the process and predictions that will become the hypotheses. The tables that follow are simplified but can be expanded to accommodate as many factors, intervening variables, and dependent variables as needed.

**For an Interaction Effect When There Are Two or More Factors**

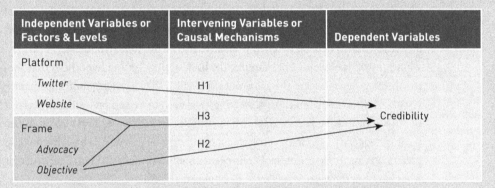

| Independent Variables or Factors & Levels | Intervening Variables or Causal Mechanisms | Dependent Variables |
|---|---|---|
| Platform | | |
| *Twitter* | H1 | |
| *Website* | H3 | Credibility |
| Frame | | |
| *Advocacy* | H2 | |
| *Objective* | | |

H1: Subjects who read stories on Twitter will have significantly higher credibility scores than subjects who read stories on a website. (Main effect of Platform factor.)

H2: Subjects who read objectively framed stories will have significantly higher credibility scores than subjects who read advocacy framed stories. (Main effect of Frame factor.)

H3: Credibility scores will be higher for subjects who read objectively framed stories on a website than for any of the other combinations of message format and frame. (Interaction of Platform and Frame factors.)

**For Hypotheses With Causal Mechanisms That Build on Each Other**

| Independent Variables or Factors & Levels | Intervening Variables or Causal Mechanisms | Dependent Variables |
|---|---|---|
| Photographs    H1 | H2 | Ethical |
| *See* | Elaboration about | |
| *Do Not See* | Stakeholders    H3 | Reasoning |

*(Continued)*

(Continued)

H1: Participants who see photographs will have significantly higher levels of elaboration about stakeholders than those who do not. (Factor leads to causal mechanism.)

H2: More elaboration about stakeholders will be significantly associated with higher ethical reasoning. (Causal mechanism leads to DV.)

H3: Ethical reasoning will be significantly higher for participants who see photographs than for those who do not. (Factor leads to DV.)

One final piece of advice on writing hypotheses is to think about the importance of each one. Ask if the hypotheses are interesting, meaningful, or important. Are they self-evident or already well tested? Try not to propose what I call "duh hypotheses"—that is, those whose answer is obvious. For example, the basic agenda-setting hypothesis that the issues the media cover most are the same ones that the public says are most important is well tested. There is simply no earth-shattering revelation to be had by testing this as if it were the first time anyone had asked it. Many agenda-setting studies never ask it. When they do, it is frequently used to establish that a media agenda existed as a basis for more specific predictions, or to see if untested contingent conditions make the outcome different than what has been shown repeatedly for forty-plus years.

Also, ask what it would mean if one of these three things happened:

- What would it mean if the hypothesis was supported?

- What would it mean if it was not? (No significance)

- For directional hypotheses, what would it mean if significance was found in the opposite direction than predicted?

This exercise is designed to help you think about all the possible outcomes and what it would mean if each occurred. This will help you think about the meaningfulness of your study and also how you might explain the results in the discussion section. If you cannot imagine the conclusions under any of these situations, or they seem obvious or unimportant, it is time to rethink the study. Also, think about what might be included in the study as evidence to back up the explanations. For example, if data fail to support the hypothesis or find significance in the opposite direction than predicted, why might that have happened? This exercise also addresses a phenomenon I find frequently among novice experimentalists—feeling they have "failed" if their hypotheses are not supported. Even in studies that fail to support the hypotheses, something valuable has been learned. In some cases, not supporting a hypothesis is more interesting than supporting it. This, after all, is the purpose of conducting research in the first place, not merely to support all hypotheses. As Campbell and Stanley say, "The task of theory-testing . . . is therefore predominantly one of rejecting inadequate hypotheses."[63] Rest assured, failing to support the hypotheses does not make a study unpublishable.

## Research Questions

In addition to being used to probe interactions between two independent variables, research questions are sometimes found for main effects. These are made when there is not enough evidence or theory to support a prediction, and also when models are being tested. Writing research questions for experiments is no different than for other methods. In addition to the formal research question style shown earlier, research questions can also be written in narrative style, for example:

> In sum, there are four primary questions addressed by this study. First, do the two teaching interventions differ in their overall effectiveness with respect to CVS learning? Second, do the two teaching interventions differ in the degree to which learning transfers to new domains? Third, do students learn different things from the two interventions? Specifically, do they develop a better understanding of the need to control irrelevant variables from the intervention based on invalid designs? Fourth, do the two teaching interventions differ in their relative effectiveness for students in different learning environments (i.e., higher vs. lower achieving schools)?[64]

The process of designing an experiment does not necessarily work in the same order as the chapters in this book. Sometimes, researchers need to revisit something they have already done. Writing good, clear hypotheses is one of those things. In addition, it is usually necessary to write, rewrite, edit, rewrite, edit, and rewrite again before being satisfied with the precision and clarity of the hypotheses.

The next chapter will discuss experimental designs, including the classic versions of the true laboratory experiments this book focuses on, as well as quasi, natural, and field experiments. As with hypothesis writing, once you have thought through your design, it might be necessary to go back and rework the hypotheses and research questions. This is normal, and research is messy.

## Common Mistakes

- Not knowing the relevant literature thoroughly enough

- Orphan Variables—not having all the variables conceptually defined in the hypotheses or research questions, and operationally defined in the methods sections

- Not explaining the posited relations among variables and how they relate to theory

## Test Your Knowledge

1. Which of these is an example of a conceptual definition?

    a. Authoritarianism is defined as a personality trait strongly related to aversion to uncertainty and threat sensitivity.

    b. Authoritarianism is measured by valuing respect for elders, having good manners, being obedient, and being well behaved.

    c. Authoritarianism is measured on a 7-point scale.

    d. Authoritarianism is defined differently by various researchers.

2. Which type of hypothesis does the following represent?

    "Sources with high levels of expertise will positively affect perceptions of credibility."

    a. Directional hypothesis

    b. Nondirectional hypothesis

    c. Interaction hypothesis

    d. Null hypothesis

3. Whether you make a directional or nondirectional hypothesis is determined by how much risk you are willing to take that your hypothesis will be supported or not.

    a. True

    b. False

4. When you have more than one hypothesis, always start with the one that represents the final outcome of the process you are testing.

    a. True

    b. False

5.  The purpose of a literature review is to _____.

a.  Develop theoretical contributions

b.  Explain how variables are measured

c.  Provide enough detail that other researchers can replicate the study

d.  Build upon what has been discovered previously

6.  The idea for an experiment should come from:

a.  Hunches and conventional wisdom

b.  A process of trial and error

c.  Theory and existing evidence

d.  None of these

7.  Hypotheses should _____.

a.  Be described as proven or not

b.  Be stated in terms of operationalizations

c.  Go in the methods section

d.  Build logically upon each other

8.  Research questions should be used instead of hypotheses when there is not enough evidence to make a prediction

a.  True

b.  False

9.  "Journalists who see photographs will use significantly different levels of moral judgment than journalists who do not see photographs." This statement represents which of the following?

a.  A directional hypothesis

b.  A nondirectional hypothesis

c.  A research question

d.  A null hypothesis

10.  Whether to make a directional or nondirectional hypothesis depends upon _____.

a.  Theory

b.  Evidence

c.  The statistical test being used

d.  Both A and B

Answers:

| | | | | | | | |
|---|---|---|---|---|---|---|---|
| 1. a | | 4. b | | 7. d | | 9. b |
| 2. a | | 5. d | | 8. a | | 10. d |
| 3. b | | 6. c | | | | |

## Application Exercises

1.  Choose one of your three ideas from the assignments in chapter 1 and add to it at least five pages that review the theory it will develop, test, or extend, and the literature related to it. Use at least twenty-five articles. Be sure to analyze and synthesize the literature, not just summarize it, and to connect the literature to your study.

2.  Write two to three clear and concise hypotheses to go with the experiment you are developing. Use the formula in this chapter. If you have more than one factor (IV) in your experiment, write a hypothesis for the main effect of each factor and a hypothesis for the interaction effect. Have two colleagues read it to see if it is clear.

## Suggested Readings

From the University of Washington's Psychology Writing Center, this white paper on how to write a literature review:

https://depts.washington.edu/psych/files/writing_center/litrev.pdf

Shoemaker, P., J. Tankard, and D. Lasorsa. 2003. *How to Build Social Science Theories.* Thousand Oaks, CA: Sage.

Chapter 2, "Manuscript Structure and Content," in the *Publication Manual of the American Psychological Association,* 6th ed. (2010). Washington, DC: American Psychological Association.

Chapters 2, 3, and 4 in Bausell, R. Barker. 1994. *Conducting Meaningful Experiments: 40 Steps to Becoming a Scientist.* Thousand Oaks, CA: Sage.

## Notes

1.  R. Barker Bausell, *Conducting Meaningful Experiments: 40 Steps to Becoming a Scientist* (Thousand Oaks, CA: Sage, 1994), 32.

2.  Thomas S. Kuhn, *The Structure of Scientific Revolutions*, 3rd. ed. (Chicago: University of Chicago Press, 1996); Earl Babbie, *The Practice of*

*Social Research*, 11th ed. (Belmont, CA: Thompson-Wadsworth, 2007).

3. H. W. Turnbull, ed. *The Correspondence of Isaac Newton: 1661–1675, Volume 1* (London: The Royal Society at the University Press, 1959).

4. Esther Thorson, Robert H. Wicks, and Glenn Leshner, "Experimental Methodology in Journalism and Mass Communication Research," *Journalism and Mass Communication Quarterly* 89, no. 1 (2012): 112–124.

5. Rebecca B. Morton and Kenneth C. Williams, *Experimental Political Science and the Study of Causality: From Nature to the Lab* (New York: Cambridge University Press, 2010).

6. Paul D. Leedy and Jeanne Ellis Ormrod, *Practical Research: Planning and Design* (Boston: Pearson Education Inc., 2010), 5.

7. Kurt Lewin, *Field Theory in Social Science: Selected Theoretical Papers by Kurt Lewin* (London: Tavistock, 1952), 169.

8. Leedy and Ormrod, *Practical Research*.

9. S. Iyengar, *Is Anyone Responsible?: How Television Frames Political Issues* (Chicago: University of Chicago Press, 1991).

10. L. R. Franklin, "Exploratory Experiments," *Philosophy of Science* 72, no. 5 (2005): 888–899; C. Kenneth Waters, "The Nature and Context of Exploratory Experimentation: An Introduction to Three Case Studies of Exploratory Research," *History and Philosophy of the Life Sciences* 29, no. 3 (2007): 275–284.

11. Franklin, "Exploratory Experiments"; Waters, "The Nature and Context of Exploratory Experimentation."

12. Franklin, "Exploratory Experiments."

13. Ibid.

14. Babbie, *The Practice of Social Research*.

15. Bausell, *Conducting Meaningful Experiments*.

16. Ibid.

17. Renita Coleman, "The Effect of Visuals on Ethical Reasoning: What's a Photograph Worth to Journalists Making Moral Decisions?" *Journalism and Mass Communication Quarterly* 83, no. 4 (2006): 835–850.

18. H. B. Brosius, "The Effects of Emotional Pictures in Television News," *Communication Research* 20, no. 1 (1993): 105–124; David Domke, David Perlmutter, and Meg Spratt, "The Primes of Our Times? An Examination of the 'Power' of Visual Images,"

*Journalism* 3, no. 2 (2002): 131–159; A. Friedman, "Framing Pictures: The Role of Knowledge in Automatized Encoding and Memory for Gist," *Journal of Experimental Psychology: General* 108 (1979): 316–335; Doris Graber, "Seeing in Remembering: How Visuals Contribute to Learning From Television News," *Journal of Communication* 40, no. 3 (Summer 1990): 134–155; George E. Marcus, W. Russell Neuman, and Michael MacKuen, *Affective Intelligence and Political Judgment* (Chicago: University of Chicago Press, 2000); Richard E. Petty and John T. Cacioppo, *Communication and Persuasion: Central and Peripheral Routes to Attitude Change* (New York: Springer-Verlag, 1986).

19. Elinor Amit and Joshua D. Greene, "You See, the Ends Don't Justify the Means: Visual Imagery and Moral Judgment," *Psychological Science* 23, no. 8 (2012): 861–868; J. D. Greene et al., "The Neural Bases of Cognitive Conflict and Control in Moral Judgment," *Neuron* 44 (2004): 389–400; J. D. Greene et al., "An fMRI Investigation of Emotional Engagement in Moral Judgment," *Science* 293 (2001): 2105–2108; Joshua Greene and Jonathan Haidt, "How (and Where) Does Moral Judgment Work?" *Trends in Cognitive Sciences* 6, no. 12 (2002): 517–523; D. Kahneman and S. Fredrick, "Representativeness Revisited: Attribute Substitution in Intuitive Judgment," in *Heuristics and Biases*, ed. T. Gilovich, D. Griffin, and D. Kahneman (New York: Cambridge University Press, 2002), 49–81; Emma Rodero, "See It on a Radio Story: Sound Effects and Shots to Evoked Imagery and Attention on Audio Fiction," *Communication Research* 39, no. 4 (2012): 458–479; Adam B. Moore, Brian A. Clark, and Michael J. Kane, "Who Shalt Not Kill? Individual Differences in Working Memory Capacity, Executive Control, and Moral Judgment," *Psychological Science (0956-7976)* 19, no. 6 (2008): 549–557.

20. Vicki Goldberg, *The Power of Photography: How Photographs Changed Our Lives* (New York: Abbeville, 1991).

21. Bausell, *Conducting Meaningful Experiments,* 21.

22. H. Denis Wu and Renita Coleman, "Advancing Agenda-Setting Theory: The Comparative Strength and New Contingent Conditions of the Two Levels of Agenda-Setting Effects," *Journalism and Mass*

*Communication Quarterly* 86, no. 4 (Winter 2009): 775–789.

23. James Potter, *On Media Violence* (Thousand Oaks, CA: Sage, 1999).

24. Thorson, Wicks, and Leshner, "Experimental Methodology."

25. Pamela Shoemaker, James W. Tankard, and Dominick Lasorsa, *How to Build Social Science Theories* (Thousand Oaks, CA: Sage, 2003), 11.

26. Ibid., 11.

27. George Gerbner et al., "Living with Television: The Dynamics of the Cultivation Process," in *Perspectives on Media Effects*, ed. Jennings Bryant and C. Zillmann (Hillsdale, NJ: Erlbaum, 1986), 17–40; George Gerbner et al., "Growing Up with Television: The Cultivation Perspective," in *Media Effects: Advances in Theory and Research*, ed. J. Bryant and C. Zillmann (Hillsdale, NJ: Erlbaum, 1994), 7–14.

28. Ibid.

29. Coleman, "The Effect of Visuals on Ethical Reasoning."

30. Wu and Coleman, "Advancing Agenda-Setting Theory," 778.

31. Ibid., 777.

32. Seung-A Annie Jin and Joe Phua, "Following Celebrities' Tweets About Brands: The Impact of Twitter-Based Electronic Word-of-Mouth on Consumers' Source Credibility Perception, Buying Intention, and Social Identification with Celebrities," *Journal of Advertising* 43, no. 2 (2014): 183.

33. Nan-Hyun Um and Wei-Na Lee, "Does Culture Influence How Consumers Process Negative Celebrity Information? Impact of Culture in Evaluation of Negative Celebrity Information," *Asian Journal of Communication* 25, no. 3 (2015): 329.

34. Elena Novak and Janet Tassell, "Using Video Game Play to Improve Education-Majors' Mathematical Performance: An Experimental Study," *Computers in Human Behavior* 53 (2015): 125.

35. Horacio Alvarez-Marinelli et al., "Computer Assisted English Language Learning in Costa Rican Elementary Schools: An Experimental Study," *Computer Assisted Language Learning* 29, no. 1 (2016): 105.

36. Ryan Oprea, Bart J. Wilson, and Arthur Zillante, "War of Attrition: Evidence from a Laboratory Experiment on Market Exit," *Economic Inquiry* 51, no. 4 (2013): 2019.

37. Miglena Mantcheva Sternadori and Esther Thorson, "Anonymous Sources Harm Credibility of All Stories," *Newspaper Research Journal* 30, no. 4 (2009): 56.

38. James R. Rest, Lynne Edwards, and Stephen J. Thoma, "Designing and Validating a Measure of Moral Judgment: Stage Preference and Stage Consistency Approaches," *Journal of Educational Psychology* 89, no. 1 (March 1997): 5–28.

39. Sternadori and Thorson, "Anonymous Sources Harm Credibility of All Stories," 56.

40. Kristin Bulkow, Juliane Urban, and Wolfgang Schweiger, "The Duality of Agenda-Setting: The Role of Information Processing," *International Journal of Public Opinion Research* 25, no. 1 (Spring 2013): 43–63.

41. Ibid., 52.

42. Tara Halle, "A Cautionary Tale: Have You Checked That Citation?" *Covering Health* (2017); Lisa Marriott, "Using Student Subjects in Experimental Research: A Challenge to the Practice of Using Students as a Proxy for Taxpayers," *International Journal of Social Research Methodology* 17, no. 5 (2014): 503–525.

43. Mirae Kim and Gregg G. Van Ryzin, "Impact of Government Funding on Donations to Arts Organizations: A Survey Experiment," *Nonprofit and Voluntary Sector Quarterly* 43, no. 5 (2014): 913.

44. Thomas Zerback, Thomas Koch, and Benjamin Kramer, "Thinking of Others: Effects of Implicit and Explicit Media Cues on Climate of Opinion Perceptions," *Journalism and Mass Communication Quarterly* 92, no. 2 (2015): 421–443.

45. Ibid., 423.

46. Ibid., 424.

47. Ibid., 425.

48. Tianguang Meng, Jennifer Pan, and Ping Yang, "Conditional Receptivity to Citizen Participation," *Comparative Political Studies* (2014): 8.

49. Coleman, "The Effect of Visuals on Ethical Reasoning," 839.

50. Diana C. Mutz, "Effects of 'In-Your-Face' Television Discourse on Perceptions of a Legitimate Opposition," *American Political Science Review* 101, no. 4 (2007): 624.

51. D. T. Campbell and J. C. Stanley, *Experimental and Quasi-Experimental Designs for Research*. (Chicago: Rand McNally, 1963), 35.

52. Thorson, Wicks, and Leshner, "Experimental Methodology."

53. Ibid.

54. Y. J. Cho and E. J. Ringquist, "Managerial Trustworthiness and Organizational Outcomes," *Journal of Public Administration Research and Theory* 21 (2011): 53–54.

55. Mogens Jin Pedersen and Justin M. Stritch, "Internal Management and Perceived Managerial Trustworthiness," *American Review of Public Administration* (2016): 5.

56. Ibid.

57. Thorson, Wicks, and Leshner, "Experimental Methodology."

58. Adapted from Mike Schmierbach and Anne Oeldorf-Hirsch, "A Little Bird Told Me, So I Didn't Believe It: Twitter, Credibility, and Issue Perceptions," *Communication Quarterly* 60, no. 3 (July-August 2012): 317–337.

59. Ibid.

60. Adapted from Sean Aday, "The Framesetting Effects of News: An Experimental Test of Advocacy Versus Objectivist Frames," *Journalism and Mass Communication Quarterly* 83, no. 4 (Winter 2006): 767–784.

61. Pazit Ben-Nun Bloom, "Disgust, Harm and Morality in Politics," *Political Psychology* 35, no. 4 (2014): 500.

62. An-Sofie Claeys and Verolien Cauberghe, "Keeping Control: The Importance of Nonverbal Expressions of Power by Organizational Spokespersons in Time of Crisis," *Journal of Communication* 64 (2014): 1162.

63. Campbell and Stanley, *Experimental and Quasi-Experimental Designs for Research,* 35.

64. Robert F. Lorch et al., "Using Valid and Invalid Experimental Designs to Teach the Control of Variables Strategy in Higher and Lower Achieving Classrooms," *Journal of Educational Psychology* 106, no. 1 (February 2014): 18–35.

# TYPES OF EXPERIMENTS

*Truth has nothing to do with the conclusion, and everything to do with the methodology.*

**—Stefan Molyneux**

## LEARNING OBJECTIVES

- Summarize the different types of experiments using Campbell and Stanley's typology.

- Recommend when to use each of the three true experimental designs.

- Critique the strengths and weaknesses of designs with pretests.

- Describe quasi, natural, and field experiments.

- Explain how quasi, natural, and field experiments differ from each other and from true experiments.

With the literature review written or at least in draft form, as discussed in the previous chapter, the next step is to decide what basic type of experiment to conduct[i]—that is, the methodology or system of the experiment itself referred to in this chapter's opening quote. One authoritative word on this topic is the classic *Experimental and Quasi-Experimental Designs for Research* by Donald T. Campbell and Julian C. Stanley.[1]

---

[i]Normally, experiments are not designed in such a linear fashion. Typically, researchers think about all the issues covered in this book simultaneously.

This work is only seventy-one pages long without the references. It started life as a chapter in a research handbook in 1963 but is so popular that it continues to be published as a monograph. It describes sixteen different ways to do an experiment, all still valid today, although some designs are more popular than others. It was written for the teaching field, so examples are from education research. Next is a summary of Campbell and Stanley's typology of experimental designs, highlighting six designs popular in social science along with a critique of each. Most experiments actually conducted today are slight variations of the designs described here. In addition to these designs in Campbell and Stanley's typology, this chapter will also briefly describe quasi experiments, natural experiments, and field experiments.

# CAMPBELL AND STANLEY'S TYPOLOGY OF EXPERIMENTS

Campbell and Stanley use graphic shorthand to describe experiments that should be familiar to football fans but have different meanings here.

X = an exposure, treatment, manipulation, or intervention. Usually an independent variable (IV).

O = an observation or measurement of an outcome variable. Usually a dependent variable (DV). These are the data that are recorded, either by the researcher, with technical instruments such as a heart rate monitor, or a self-report by the subject. If observations are made or data recorded more than once, that is indicated by a subscript—$O_1$, $O_2$—meaning the first and second observation.

If there is a space (____) and no X or O, that means no treatment was given or no observation made.

R = random assignment of subjects to conditions. This will be discussed more in chapter 7. Basically, this is the element that qualifies an experiment as a "true" experiment versus a "quasi" experiment.

The first three design types are classified as "pre-experimental designs" and are "of almost no scientific value," according to Campbell and Stanley.[2] These designs tend to be reported as "exploratory" in articles I review, but "pre-experimental" is a more accurate term. They also qualify as quasi experimental designs because of the lack of random assignment. Here, I briefly review them but recommend using other designs as described.

## Three Pre-Experimental Designs

### The One-Shot Case Study

This can sometimes be seen reported in news stories when someone wants to attribute a cause to some effect—for example, how school absentee rates went down compared to previous years after some intervention. It might be something like a school that implemented a text messaging system that pinged students in time to get them to school by 9 a.m. This is graphically represented as:

$$\text{—} \quad X \quad O$$

The text messaging system was the intervention (X) and absentee rates the observation (O). There are several problems with this, however—among them that the students who were observed were not randomly sampled, there is no control group of students who did not get the text messages to compare against, and there were no controls in place that would rule out alternative explanations. For example, some students' parents could have started making waffles for breakfast, new construction outside others' windows woke them up early, some could have gotten new cars and were excited to get to school to show them off, and maybe others saw a presentation on the importance of college and suddenly figured they needed to get to school in order to be able to support themselves. All these things—uncontrolled confounds—could have explained the lower absentee rates, not just the text messaging system. Because of these problems, the one-shot case study is not a good design for a true social science experiment.

### One-Group Pretest–Posttest Design

Slightly better than the one-shot case study is when an observation or measurement is added before the treatment is given, called a **pretest**. The same observation or measurement is given after the intervention (the posttest), so researchers have a baseline measure to compare any changes against.

$$O_1 \quad X \quad O_2$$

For example, researchers might measure how much math a student knows in the pretest, then give the intervention, such as computer-aided tutoring, and then test the students again to see how much they learned. The difference between the pretest and posttest scores represents the effect. Sometimes, however, adding a pretest does not necessarily make things better, because people tend to learn how to do better on a test after they have taken it once or when they realize they are being watched. For example, those who take IQ tests more than once have been shown to get smarter on the second try.[3] In research, this effect of testing is called "test, retest gain."[4] There could be other explanations as well. Reactivity is the idea that measuring something changes it; just by knowing they are being observed, people tend to do better[5] (see More About box 4.1).

# MORE ABOUT . . . BOX 4.1
## The Hawthorne Effect

Western Electric Company

Hawthorne, Illinois, Works of the Western Electric Company, 1925

The Hawthorne effect is a specific type of reactivity, the idea that people react to being observed and change what they do. It is important in research because some people will not give true answers if they know they are participating in a study. This effect is not necessarily intentional; sometimes, people simply change without realizing it. The Hawthorne effect is the popular, although some say inappropriate, name for a demand characteristic that arises when subjects of study change their behavior because they know they are being observed.[6]

It developed from studies of worker productivity commissioned by the Hawthorne Works, a Western Electric factory outside Chicago from 1924 to 1932.[7] They are also known as the illumination studies because higher and lower levels of lighting were tested for changes in worker productivity; in reality, many other variables were also studied, including work hours, break times, the cleanliness of floors and work stations, among others.[8] The truncated version of the study results is that when the researchers changed the workers' lighting and break times, their productivity improved. In spite of the changes that led to improvements staying in place, worker productivity fell when the study was over. The original conclusion that paying attention to workers would result in greater productivity was later reinterpreted to say that people change their behavior when they know they are being observed.[9]

Not all studies show a Hawthorne effect,[10] and research still investigates it today,[11] especially in the health sciences, human relations, and organizational behavior.[12] The illumination studies, for there were many over several years, are more complex than usually presented. For example, it is a myth that improvement was continuous, and there were potential confounding variables such as learning, feedback, and incentive pay. Thus, the term *Hawthorne effect* to describe reactivity is diminishing in use.[13]

A similar phenomenon is known as the **demand effect**, or demand characteristics—the idea that some people change their answers or behavior in order to please an experimenter.[14] In studying the experimental situation, Martin Orne discovered that study subjects tried to guess the purpose and altered their behavior to fit their interpretations.[15] Similar phenomena include the *halo effect* or *social desirability effect*, where study participants try to portray themselves in a positive light.[16]

The Hawthorne studies make another important contribution to experimental design in that they show the importance of manipulation checks,[17] which will be covered in chapter 9. In the Hawthorne studies, it was not so much the manipulations that had an effect but the workers' interpretation of them, and understanding subjects' interpretations is the purpose of a manipulation check.

There could also be a change in the measurement standards if observers are recording the data. There is also a phenomenon known as *regression to the mean*, whereby those who score extremely well or poorly tend to go back toward the middle the next time they are tested.[18] Moreover, if there is a time gap between the first and second observation, something else could have happened. For example, if the observation being recorded is a person's level of fear about flying, and if an airplane crashes and is reported in the news between $O_1$ and $O_2$, that could change the outcome.

### Static Group Comparison

In this type of design, a second group that has not received the treatment has been added ($O_2$).

$$X \quad O_1$$
$$\text{---} \quad O_2$$

An example would be comparing people who saw the presidential candidates' debate versus those who did not, or comparing students who got antibullying training to those who did not. There are also problems with this, including that there is no way to tell if the people in the two groups are the same on important individual characteristics—for example, perhaps there were more Republicans in the debate-watching group than the nonwatching group, or more aggressive students in one group than the other. This will be discussed in greater detail in chapter 7 on random assignment. People's political identification and students' innate aggressive tendencies could affect the outcome.

As I do not recommend these three designs, they will not be discussed in detail regarding their strengths and weaknesses. Instead, this chapter will concentrate on the next three, which are true experimental designs that I do recommend.

## Three True Experimental Designs

### Pretest–Posttest Control Group

This design is one of the most used in social science. It adds the crucial feature of randomly assigning subjects to either the treatment or control conditions, thus making sure the groups are equal on important characteristics that could otherwise cause any changes.

$$R \quad O_1 \quad X \quad O_2$$
$$R \quad O_3 \quad \text{---} \quad O_4$$

The drawback of this design is the same as in the one-group pretest–posttest design—that is, being observed or measured twice may cause changes in the subjects' performance, attitudes, or whatever else the outcome is. Because this threat has been shown to be so prevalent, the popularity of pretests has been declining, and pretests are actually not essential to true experimental designs.[19]

### Solomon Four-Group Design

It is common for the Solomon four-group design to be described as the gold standard. And it is. It eliminates all the drawbacks described earlier, plus the researcher can actually tell if there are any effects of testing by having groups where no pretest is given.

$$R \quad O_1 \quad X \quad O_2$$
$$R \quad O_3 \quad - \quad O_4$$
$$R \quad - \quad X \quad O_5$$
$$R \quad - \quad - \quad O_6$$

But it is also time consuming, costly, difficult, and has statistical issues, so relatively few studies actually use it.[20] Bausell even calls it "wasteful."[21] In this design, there are four groups, with subjects randomly assigned to all of them. There are two control groups consisting of subjects who do not get the treatment or manipulation; they serve as the baseline for comparison with the groups that did get the treatment. One of the treatment groups is given a pretest and one is not, and one of the control groups is given a pretest and the other is not. This allows the researcher to compare not only the differences before and after the treatment, but also to see if the pretest affected the results. This provides what Levy and Ellis call a "defensible response to most rival hypotheses."[22] It also requires many, many more subjects to participate in the experiment, the costs of which sometimes outweigh the benefits. (See Study Spotlight 4.2 for an example of a Solomon four-group design.)

### Posttest-Only Control Group Design

The final design in the Campbell and Stanley typology is one that includes no pretests and is the one I use most often. It is also the one that is now most recommended.[23]

$$R \quad X \quad O$$
$$R \quad - \quad O$$

# STUDY SPOTLIGHT 4.2

## A Study Using the Solomon Four-Group Design

SAGE Journal Article:
study.sagepub.com/
coleman

Genç, M. 2016. "An Evaluation of the Cooperative Learning Process by Sixth-Grade Students." *Research in Education* 95 (1): 19–32.

This study used a Solomon design to assess the effects of a particular teaching strategy on sixth graders' science knowledge. The teaching strategy, called cooperative learning, has teachers organize students into groups who do research on their own to learn information and solve problems together. Cooperative learning classrooms were the manipulation or treatment group; classrooms as they were organized already, with teachers presenting information to the students in the traditional way, were used as the control groups.

In this Solomon four-group design, two groups of students got the cooperative learning treatment, and two did not, making them the control groups. Pretests were used for one control group and one treatment group; the other groups did not get pretests. The author says that the reason the Solomon design was used was to be able to know if use of pretests caused effects because students could have learned simply by taking the test twice. Students were randomly assigned to all four groups. Here is how it is described:

"The Solomon four-group design is an attempt to eliminate the possible effect of a pretest. It involves random assignment of subjects to four groups, with two of the groups being pretested and two, not. One of the pretested groups and one of the unpretested groups is exposed to the experimental treatment. All four groups are then posttested. Although each group is put through post-experimental evaluation, the pre-experimental evaluations are performed in only two groups, one being an experimental group and the other being a control group. The first two groups are treated as the pretest–posttest control group design, and the other two groups are treated as the posttest–control group design" (p. 22).

The study does not go into whether the pretest affected the outcome; however, it can be seen from the mean scores that the groups that received pretests did score higher on the posttests than those that did not get the pretests. No significance tests are reported in this study to determine if the pretest alone had a significant effect, however. The mean posttest scores for those given the pretests were 27.70 (treatment) and 22.50 (control) versus 26.74 (treatment) and 21.91 (control) for students who were not given the pretest. I have reworked the author's tables into the one that follows in order to illustrate the design and also facilitate comparison between posttest scores for the pretested groups compared to the non-pretested groups.

It should be noted that alternative forms of the tests were used for pre- and posttesting rather than identical tests for both occasions, which helps guard against learning from taking the test twice.

The cooperative learning treatment worked, as both pretested and unpretested students in the cooperative learning classrooms performed significantly better on the science tests given at the end of the experiment.

Some social science disciplines use the Solomon design more than others, so it is important to know where your colleagues stand on this.

*(Continued)*

(Continued)

## Means and Standard Deviations for a Solomon Four-Group Design Experiment

| Group | Pretest | Instruction type | Posttest Scores M (SD) |
|---|---|---|---|
| Treatment 1 | X | Cooperative learning | 27.70 (2.531) |
| Treatment 2 | | Cooperative learning | 26.74 (1.797) |
| Control 1 | X | Regular curriculum | 22.50 (2.219) |
| Control 2 | | Regular curriculum | 21.91 (2.327) |

In a study comparing the pretest–posttest and posttest-only designs, Gorard[24] found the results of the posttest-only design to be "less misleading." Even Campbell and Stanley[25] say that pretests are not essential to true experimental designs and explain that they are misunderstood. When the purpose of a pretest is to ensure equivalence of subjects assigned to conditions, random assignment is an adequate precaution, so pretests are not needed. They point out that almost all of Ronald Fisher's agriculture experiments had no pretests. Pretesting is still preferred in some disciplines but not all; it is important to know the standard in the field. The interaction of a pretest with the treatment is not large in most cases, but in education, psychology, and sociology in particular, the effects are larger and should not be ignored.[26] Some studies straddle the line, so to speak, for example by conducting a pilot study that uses a pretest, and if the effects of testing are ruled out, conduct the actual experiment without a pretest.[27] (See How To Do It box 4.3 for examples of how to describe a posttest-only control group design.)

These designs represent a basic structure; actual experiments may use slight variations and still be acceptable. So far, this chapter has reviewed three experimental designs that are classified as "true" experiments and three that are "pre-experimental" from Campbell and Stanley's typology. Campbell and Stanley go on to describe ten other designs they term "quasi experimental." This book will not go into them in detail but will instead summarize the essential features of a quasi experiment and refer readers to the Campbell and Stanley book for more details.

## QUASI EXPERIMENTS

The key difference between true and quasi experiments is that in quasi experiments, subjects are not randomly assigned to conditions, the groups may not necessarily be

## HOW TO DO IT 4.3

### Describing a Posttest-Only Control Group Design

As the most used and recommended of all the Campbell and Stanley true experiment types, the posttest-only control group design is likely one you will use often. Unlike experiments that use the Solomon four-group design, most studies that use this ubiquitous design do not announce themselves formally. Rather, you can determine they use this typology by looking for mention of a control group and random assignment, and no mention of a pretest.

Here are two examples; in the first, it does specify it is a posttest-only design, followed by the second, which does not.

**Coleman, Renita, Paul Lieber, Andrew Mendelson, and David Kurpius. 2008. "Public Life and the Internet: If You Build a Better Website, Will Citizens Become Engaged?"** *New Media & Society* **10 (2): 179–201.**

"This study used a post-test, control group experimental design. The experimental stimulus for this study was a website on the topic of the state budget created by mass communication students in a class in website development . . ." (p. 188). "The control group website was the official state government website on the state budget. It was created without usability tests or knowledge of any of the issues described above, which guided the creation of the experimental website. It was important that the control site was on the same topic as the experimental site in order to rule out the possibility of effects due to the subject matter rather than content, appearance or navigation . . ." (p. 189). "The 60 participants were randomly assigned to view either the control website or the experimental website" (p. 190).

**Bennion, Elizabeth A., and David W. Nickerson. 2011. "The Cost of Convenience: An Experiment Showing E-Mail Outreach Decreases Voter Registration."** *Political Research Quarterly* **64 (4): 858–869.**

"The design of the e-mail experiment itself was straightforward. Students were randomly assigned to one of three conditions: (1) a control group receiving no e-mail, (2) a treatment group receiving three e-mails from an administrator such as the university president or dean of students, or (3) a treatment group receiving three e-mails from a student leader—usually the student body president. The e-mails were brief, explaining why registration is important and providing a link to the Rock the Vote online registration tool" (p. 862).

independent—that is, some of the same people may be in more than one group—and, finally, that quasi experiments cannot control for all the extraneous factors that true experiments do. These features of random assignment, independence, and control are not always possible. When that is the case, a quasi experiment is considered a viable option, and even preferable in some cases. Some things simply cannot be "assigned." For example, researchers cannot ethically assign someone to smoke and someone else to not smoke in order to have randomly assigned treatment and control groups. Experiments in business and education settings especially make it difficult to have complete control over the research.[28] Businesses involved in a study may want to handpick participants for

When students in intact classrooms are used in experiments, these are known as *quasi experiments* because the subjects are not randomly assigned.

some reason, or want everyone to be treated the same and not appear to be showing favoritism. In other cases, participants unwittingly self-select the group they are in. For example, education research frequently works with intact classrooms rather than classes whose students were randomly assigned. Educators may assign students to classes because they want diversity or a mix of boys and girls, do not want twins in the same class, or want to keep two children together. At the college level, it is obvious that there is something individually different about people who sign up for a class in experimental design than those who register for ethnographic methods. Students might choose one course over another because they heard a certain teacher is good. Or it might be a timing issue—some students do not like getting up early in the morning, have part-time jobs on Wednesday afternoons, or want to leave town on Fridays. Whatever is at work to create these individual differences could compromise the validity of an experiment.

Only random assignment is an antidote to such individual differences affecting results. Research can still uncover important knowledge from quasi experiments, but they bring different threats to validity than do true experiments, and these must be addressed and documented. It is important to say in the final paper that subjects could not be randomly assigned and to give the reasons why. The paper also should explain what was done to minimize any issues with systematic differences—for example, were key variables measured and then used as covariates? Were statistical tests run to see if groups were equivalent on important variables? It is important to make a credible claim for being able to infer causality, or to generalize beyond the one case studied. Finally, quasi experiments cannot control all the extraneous factors that may cause an outcome the way true experiments can. Without random assignment, a quasi experiment cannot eliminate the possibility of uncontrolled variables confounding the results and impairing the ability to make causal claims. However, researchers should always attempt to measure possible confounding variables, then control for them statistically by using covariates. Every study has its weaknesses, including true experiments (see more about these in chapter 5). Limitations do not necessarily invalidate the importance of the findings, especially if this is the only way to study a particular phenomenon. Quasi experiments can feel less artificial than true experiments and are usually easier to conduct longitudinally than controlled experiments—all benefits. It is better to know what the study found than to not know anything, but readers should always be told about the limitations.

Triangulation, or confirming what has been found using one method with another, is also important. If different methods confirm the same finding—for example, if what is found in a true experiment in an artificial setting dovetails with what happens in the real world of a quasi experiment—then we can have more confidence that the findings represent something real.

One example of best practices in a quasi experiment in social work education used two similar classes to study whether online or face-to-face teaching would result in greater learning.[29] In this quasi experiment, the researchers used intact classrooms and so were unable to randomly assign students to classes with different teaching styles. To attempt to control as much as possible for individual student differences, they used as covariates the students' ages and grade point averages adjusted for grade inflation. They say some of the limitations are the unaccounted for extraneous variables and the lack of generalizability.

In a business study, the researcher examined how formal mentoring affected workers' ability to build interpersonal networks.[30] Those who were mentored represented the treatment group; those who were not mentored were the control group. In that study, participants were not randomly assigned; rather, the management of the company chose the employees who would be mentored based on their perceived potential for advancement within the organization. This represents a serious threat to group equivalence, considering one group was chosen specifically because they were perceived as superior to the other, but the company would not agree to random assignment. To decrease the uncertainty, the researcher used a "matched pairs" design, where every worker in the treatment group was paired with a worker in the control group who was as similar as possible on important characteristics—they had the same salary, performance rating in the prior year, length of time with the company, and were in the same office. The author of that study provides statistical evidence that matching was successful, showing that there were no significant differences between the treatment and control groups on other characteristics, including age, education, and the number of networking contacts each group made before mentoring began. More network contacts was one of the outcome goals of the program, so this assured that people in the treatment group were not more likely to network to begin with. Still, the workers in the treatment and control groups could have differed in other unknown ways that could have caused differences in outcomes that were supposed to be attributed to the mentoring treatment, so various other strategies were used to help overcome the lack of random assignment. However, because we can never think of all the other confounding variables, we can never be assured these were as successful as simple random assignment; more uncertainty always remains.

Another example of a quasi experiment is the study of an intervention where investigators interviewed abused and neglected children about their mental health and quality of life.[31]

This type of research typically only interviewed adults, as it was thought children were unreliable sources and did not need to be upset by these kinds of questions. In this study, the cases where only adults were interviewed represented the control group; the cases where both children and adults were interviewed represented the intervention. Random assignment to treatment or control group was not possible because the Dutch Medical Ethics Committee refused to approve it out of concern that the adult-only interview group might receive inferior care. The researchers were able to have treatment and control groups, but the participants could not be randomly assigned to them. The article notes the possibility of selection bias.

Beyond the pre-experimental, true, and quasi experimental designs in Campbell and Stanley's typology, researchers also employ natural or field experiments. These are briefly covered next, and there are many good books that treat these topics in depth (see the "Suggested Readings" section). Instead, this is offered as an introduction as food for thought about whether your topic is best suited for a true experiment, a quasi experiment, a natural or a field experiment.

## NATURAL EXPERIMENTS

Natural experiments are a subset of quasi experiments in that researchers do not randomly assign subjects to conditions or create the manipulation. Instead, natural experiments take advantage of some naturally occurring phenomenon that creates treatment and control groups. One group of people was exposed to something, and another group was not, in a natural setting. This is seen as approximating randomization as far as possible, what some researchers call *near random* or *as-if random*.[32] Nature or society creates the treatment or exposure, and researchers discover it after it has already occurred, then conceive of it as an experiment. Crasnow says it is really more of an observational study.[33] Because researchers did not design the treatment or intervention, they cannot control all other possible factors that could have caused the observed outcome. This could lead to plausible alternative explanations, which need to be explained and accounted for as much as possible.

Evaluations of programs designed to improve some condition in society are frequently conducted as natural experiments. One example is a study evaluating a program developed by the Maryland Network Against Domestic Violence that provided social service advocates for victims.[34] In this study, the police and social service organizations designed their own intervention—providing advocacy, safety planning, and referral services to women. The researchers came in afterward to study the efficacy of it.

At other times, researchers simply notice an "intervention" that takes place naturally and study it. For example, researchers compared criminal offenders who moved against those who did not to see if the locations of their crimes changed to be closer to their new homes.[35] The researchers did not design the intervention—assigning people to move—it just happened naturally. The researchers used a host of covariates to help keep the plausible alternative explanations to a minimum, including type of crime, time between crimes, where previous crimes were committed, and where previous homes were. Despite these precautions, a number of other plausible explanations are discussed, as they should be.

This is a good place to note that researchers sometimes use terms such as quasi experiment and natural experiment interchangeably; for precision of language, this book uses *quasi experiment* for studies where researchers design the intervention and *natural experiment* for studies that take advantage of some naturally occurring intervention. Neither of these uses random assignment. Articles that report true experiments or **laboratory experiments** with random assignment do not typically use the terms *true* or *laboratory* but are just called experiments, and refer to anything not conducted in its natural setting that uses random assignment.

Another example of a natural experiment, a classic in the field of communication, is the study of three Canadian towns: one that had no TV, one that had one TV channel, and another that had four channels. This was back in the days when television signals were broadcast over the airwaves through antennas, and small towns were the last to receive television. All three towns in the study were revisited three years after the no-TV town had gotten TV. This research added longitudinal knowledge about the short- and long-term nature of television's effects on children's aggressive behavior, reading skills, cognitive development, leisure activities, use of other media, sex-role attitudes, and other personality traits and attitudes.[36] In these experiments, people were assigned to conditions by forces other than researchers—that is, whatever led them to live in those towns. There is some treatment or exposure to something; in this example, it was exposure to television in varying levels—no TV, one TV channel, four channels—that leads to the ability to say that TV exposure caused any differences in outcomes. Because it was not a randomly assigned, in-laboratory experiment, there are many other things that could have caused the differences or confounded the outcomes,[37] but the researchers did everything they could think of to control for these.

Natural experiments are becoming increasingly popular in many different disciplines.[38] Researchers can take advantage of changes in the world to conduct natural experiments. For example, when business scholars studied the changes in Peru's soft-drink market before and after the country entered into a free trade agreement with the United States, they used as a control group the country of Bolivia, which has no such agreement.[39] They selected the control country by matching important characteristics such as demographics, income growth, population, and economic trade indicators. While the comparison countries are not exact, they are as close as the researchers could get. The authors discuss the limitations and include suggestions for future studies that would include more controls for wage rates, economic and political stability, and using more than one country as a comparison.

Another study in London looked at public health before and after the introduction of free bus rides for young people.[40] Potential confounds included the fact that other policies designed to change people's choice of transportation had also been introduced recently (e.g., higher charges for driving during congested times), a change in cultural attitudes in general (e.g., walking to prevent obesity increased), and that there was no control group (all people under eighteen were given free bus passes). They list other limitations of a natural experiment as including a weaker ability to make causal claims than true experiments and difficulty generalizing beyond the single case being studied. The paper explains well the trade-offs between a realistic setting and internal validity, and offers some solutions that include mixing designs and data collection. They say the results are "good enough" evidence and "as robust an evaluation as possible."[41]

Advance planning allows researchers to obtain approval to study human subjects from their **Institutional Review Boards** (IRBs; more on this in chapter 11). Not all situations that are ripe for natural experiments come with advance warning, however—for example, the study of how re-incarceration rates changed after Hurricane Katrina, forcing parolees to spread out around the state rather than be concentrated in particular neighborhoods,[42] or how attitudes toward welfare recipients changed before and after riots.[43] These studies can only be done if researchers use data collected before the event, receive approval after the fact, or are in the enviable position of having already obtained IRB approval for a study on a similar topic before the event happens and can quickly get approval for an amendment. Some even make a distinction between natural experiments and "nature's experiments," but this book will not go into that.[44] It is never a bad thing to keep an eye open for opportunities such as this.

## FIELD EXPERIMENTS

While natural experiments typically do not have the benefit of random assignment because people are exposed to the experimental or control conditions based on natural factors outside the control of researchers, there is another type of experiment, the field experiment, that takes advantage of real-world settings but also employs random assignment to treatment and control groups.[45]

The term *field experiment* makes the distinction between experiments conducted in natural settings versus laboratory settings, even though not many "lab" experiments are conducted in actual laboratories anymore. For example, experiments that use survey software (covered in chapter 7) can be conducted in the subjects' own homes. Field experimentalists consider any setting other than the environment under which something would naturally occur to be a lab. Anything conducted on a college campus is a lab experiment, unless the actual context is a college setting—for example, a study of cheating on tests. Another example would be having participants look at TV commercials on their home computer and evaluate them to be considered a lab experiment. Even though the subjects are in their own homes, they are not looking at the ads on TV and they know that they are doing so for a research study. That is another key distinction for field experimentalists; subjects should not be aware of being studied. Field experiments "strive to be as realistic and unobtrusive as possible."[46] The focus on realism and subjects being unaware of being studied stems from concerns about misleading results due to people behaving differently when they are being watched, known as the Hawthorne effect, and reactivity, or participants wanting to give the "right answer" or the answer the experimenter wants. Whether these are serious problems with lab experiments is unclear, as few studies replicate experiments in both field and lab conditions in order to estimate treatment effects.[47] Field experimentalists also note that what works in a lab setting might not work in the real world.[48] Some effects can be immediate and strong, so they show up in a lab experiment but decay over time and would show up weaker in a field experiment.

Another objection field experimentalists have to lab experiments is the potential lack of realism in the messages or stimuli created by researchers. These are all important concerns, and lab experimentalists should be careful to see that their stimuli are as realistic as possible, having practitioners in their field create or review the interventions. This is a topic of chapter 9 on creating stimuli.

Field experiments should be authentic on four dimensions: the participants, treatment, context, and outcome measures.[49] Participants should be real voters, not students pretending to be, for example. The treatment should be a real political debate, not one fielded by actors. The context should have voters watching TV in their living rooms, not with a group of strangers in a university classroom. And the outcome measures should be their votes or donations to the candidate, not self-reports of their intentions to vote or donate.

Field experiments can be more expensive and difficult than traditional lab experiments, and also ethically challenged given that one hallmark is that subjects do not know they are participating in an experiment (see chapter 11 on ethics). Gerber and Green discuss in detail three of the most common challenges:[50] Briefly, noncompliance is when subjects that were assigned to one treatment actually got something else; attrition is when outcome measures are not obtained for every subject; and interference occurs when subjects talk to each other, compare notes, or remember treatments. These issues are minimized or nonexistent in the environment of a lab experiment.

Whereas lab experiments are commonly employed to test theoretical propositions, where tightly controlled conditions are important, field experiments are better for applied studies—for example, evaluations of a program's effectiveness.[51]

A few examples of field experiments:

To see if interacting directly with a politician could persuade people to change their attitudes about issues, their assessments of the politicians' qualities, and how they vote, researchers used online town hall meetings, noting that the only studies up to that point had used laboratory settings that simulated only a few of the characteristics of personal interactions.[52] Previous research was equivocal about whether real-life results were the same as those from hypothetical settings. So the researchers recruited U.S. senators and members of the U.S. House of Representatives to interact with their constituents in a real-time online forum. The intervention in this field experiment was created by the researchers but was more true-to-life than a mock town hall with an actor playing a politician. Citizens who participated were randomly assigned either to participate in the online discussion with the politician or to the control group, which only received reading material with background about the issues. Those in the treatment group got the same reading material but also participated in the online session. You can see some of the same kinds of effort exhibited here as Philip Zimbardo did in recruiting the Palo Alto police to "arrest" his prison experiment subjects.

Other researchers did a randomized field experiment in the Netherlands on the effectiveness of an extended day program on elementary students' math and language learning.[53] They noted that the research on program effects in education rarely used randomized experiments and that quasi experiments that did not have proper controls were the norm. In this study, the researchers randomly selected students and offered them the chance to participate in the program rather than allowing them or their teachers to select who participated. Like studies before them that used randomized experiments and found small to nonexistent effects, this one did not find any effects. It is important to know when different methods generate opposite results; for example, on this topic, quasi experiments without random assignment were likely to show effects, but more rigorous randomized true experiments were not. In this case, the field experiment, using random assignment, helped educators know which results to have more confidence in.

As with the terms quasi experiment and natural experiment, researchers also use the term *field experiment* to mean different things. In this book, I advocate the use of the term field experiment to mean an experiment that is conducted in a natural or real-life setting and also uses random assignment. I use quasi and natural experiments when subjects are not randomly assigned to treatment and control conditions.

This book is devoted primarily to true experiments, also called lab experiments, although the concepts covered here are applicable to other types of experiments as well. Those conducting a quasi, natural, or field experiment should also consult texts that address the specific issues associated with those designs.

In summary, there is no perfect experiment. One cannot usually have the benefit of a real-world setting and also have random assignment. The best researchers can do to understand a particular phenomenon is conduct many different studies of varying designs that have at least one of these features, using different contexts. Replication under different conditions affords more confidence that what has been found is real. In fact, being bold enough to understand when an opportunity presents itself to study something by an unconventional method is one of the hallmarks of a creative researcher.

This chapter is not an exhaustive compilation of all the many different experimental designs available. Many other options exist, and the creative experimentalist will be open to discovering new and better ways to study important causes and effects. The next chapter begins this textbook's sole focus on true or laboratory experiments, starting with issues of internal and external validity.

## Common Mistakes

- Using pretests when they are not truly necessary

- Reporting an experiment as "exploratory" because it contains flaws

- Failing to randomly assign subjects to conditions. Studies that aspire to be true experiments but fail to use randomization are rarely published.

# Test Your Knowledge

1. From Campbell and Stanley's typology of experimental designs, which one is considered the gold standard?

   a. Pretest–posttest control group design

   b. Solomon four-group design

   c. Posttest-only control group design

   d. Static group comparison design

2. From Campbell and Stanley's typology of experimental designs, which one is most recommended today?

   a. Pretest–posttest control group design

   b. Solomon four-group design

   c. Posttest-only control group design

   d. Static group comparison design

3. A pretest is essential for an experiment to be considered a true experiment.

   a. True

   b. False

4. What is the *main* reason for using random assignment?

   a. To make sure subjects in treatment and control groups are equivalent on important characteristics.

   b. To make sure the same number of subjects are in the treatment and control groups.

   c. To ensure that the same people are not in more than one group.

   d. To make it fair to all subjects.

5. Which type of experiment uses random assignment in a naturally occurring setting?

   a. Lab experiment

   b. Quasi experiment

   c. Natural experiment

   d. Field experiment

6. Which of the following designs is recommended when a pretest would NOT threaten to change subjects' performance?

   a. Static group comparison

   b. Pretest–posttest control group

   c. One-group pretest–posttest design

   d. Quasi experiment

7. Which of the following is a strength of designs with pretests?

   a. It gives a baseline measure to compare any changes against.

   b. Being observed or measured twice may cause changes in the subjects' performance.

   c. Pretests are essential to true experimental designs.

   d. It ensures the groups are equal on important characteristics that could otherwise cause any changes.

8. A study used two similar intact classes to see whether online or face-to-face teaching would result in greater learning. This is an example of:

   a. A natural experiment

   b. A field experiment

   c. A laboratory experiment

   d. A quasi experiment

9. An experiment that is conducted in a natural or real-life setting and also uses random assignment is:

   a. A quasi experiment

   b. A natural experiment

   c. A field experiment

   d. A true experiment

10. Which of the following allows the researcher to compare the differences before and after treatment, and also to tell if there were any effects of a pretest?

   a. Static group comparison

   b. Solomon four-group design

   c. Pretest–posttest control group

   d. One-group pretest–posttest design

Answers

| | | | |
|---|---|---|---|
| 1. b | 4. a | 7. a | 9. c |
| 2. c | 5. d | 8. d | 10. b |
| 3. b | 6. b | | |

## Application Exercises

1. Use Googlescholar.com or your school library's database to find studies that use experimental designs in your discipline. Read three of the experiments that interest you most and identify the design of the experiment; is it a true or laboratory experiment, quasi experiment, natural or field experiment? Is it a pretest–posttest control group design, Solomon four-group design, or something else? What are some of the limitations, and how did the authors address them?

2. Examine the literature about your topic for the methodologies used. A grid-type chart will help you see which methods have been most used. Of the twenty-five-plus articles you read for the literature review assignment in chapter 3, categorize them by method, including critical essay, focus group, interviews, ethnography, content analysis, survey, and experiment, among others. Which method has been most used? Is it appropriate for an experiment to be conducted now that establishes cause and effect?

## Suggested Readings

Campbell, Donald T., and J. C. Stanley. 1963. *Experimental and Quasi-Experimental Designs for Research.* Chicago: Rand McNally.

Crasnow, S. 2015. "Natural Experiments and Pluralism in Political Science." *Philosophy of the Social Sciences* 45 (4/5): 424–441.

Gerber, Alan S., and Donald P. Green. 2012. *Field Experiments: Design, Analysis, and Interpretation.* New York: Norton.

Levy, Y., T. J. Ellis, and T. Cohen. 2011. "A Guide for Novice Researchers on Experimental and Quasi-Experimental Studies in Information Systems Research." *Interdisciplinary Journal of Information, Knowledge and Management* 6: 151–161.

## Notes

1. D. T. Campbell and J. C. Stanley, *Experimental and Quasi-Experimental Designs for Research.* (Chicago: Rand McNally, 1963).
2. Ibid., 6.
3. David W. Catron and Claudia C. Thompson, "Test-Retest Gains in WAIS Scores after Four Retest Intervals," *Journal of Clinical Psychology* 35, no. 2 (1979): 352–357.
4. Ibid.
5. Brendon R. Barnes, "The Hawthorne Effect in Community Trials in Developing Countries," *International Journal of Social Research Methodology* 13, no. 4 (2010): 357–370.
6. John G. Adair, "The Hawthorne Effect: A Reconsideration of the Methodological Artifact," *Journal of Applied Psychology* 69, no. 2 (1984); 334–345; Ryan Olson et al., "What We Teach Students About the Hawthorne Studies: A Review of Content Within

a Sample of Introductory I-O and OB Textbooks," *The Industrial Organization Psychologist* 41 (2004): 23–39.

7. E. Mayo, 1933; Chen-Bo Zhong and Julian House, "Hawthorne Revisited: Organizational Implications of the Physical Work Environment," *Research in Organizational Behavior* 32 (2012): 3–22.

8. Olson et al., "What We Teach Students."

9. Henry A. Landsberger, *Hawthorne Revisited. Management and the Worker: Its Critics, and Developments in Human Relations in Industry* (Ithaca, NY: Cornell University, 1958).

10. J. G. Adair, D. Sharpe, and C. Huynh, "Hawthorne Control Procedures in Educational Experiments: A Reconsideration of Their Use and Effectiveness," *Review of Educational Research* 59, no. 2 (1989): 215–227.

11. Barnes, "The Hawthorne Effect in Community Trials"; Zhong and House, "Hawthorne Revisited."

12. Baptiste Leurent et al., "Monitoring Patient Care through Health Facility Exit Interviews: An Assessment of the Hawthorne Effect in a Trial of Adherence to Malaria Treatment Guidelines in Tanzania," *BMC Infectious Diseases* 16 (2016): 1–9; Jim McCambridge, John Witton, and Diana R. Elbourne, "Systematic Review of the Hawthorne Effect: New Concepts Are Needed to Study Research Participation Effects," *Journal of Clinical Epidemiology* 67, no. 3 (2014): 267–277; Magnus Hansson and Rune Wigblad, "Recontextualizing the Hawthorne Effect," *Scandinavian Journal of Management* 22, no. 2 (2006): 120–137.

13. Olson et al., "What We Teach Students."

14. Martin T. Orne, "Demand Characteristics and the Concept of Quasi Controls," in *Artifacts in Behavioral Research: Robert Rosenthal and Ralph L. Rosnow's Classic Books*, ed. Robert Rosenthal and Ralph L. Rosnow (Oxford: Oxford University Press, 2009): 110–137; D. Steele-Johnson et al., "Goal Orientation and Task Demand Effects on Motivation, Affect, and Performance," *Journal of Applied Psychology* 85, no. 5 (2000): 724–738.

15. Martin T. Orne, "On the Social Psychology of the Psychological Experiment: With Particular Reference to Demand Characteristics and Their Implications," *American Psychologist* 17 (1962): 776–783; "Demand Characteristics and the Concept of Quasi-Controls,"

in *Artifact in Behavioral Research*, ed. R. Rosenthal and R. Rosnow (New York: Academic Press, 1969), 143–179.

16. Barnes, "The Hawthorne Effect in Community Trials."

17. Adair, "The Hawthorne Effect."

18. David Salsburg, *The Lady Tasting Tea: How Statistics Revolutionized Science in the Twentieth Century* (New York: W. H. Freeman, 2001).

19. Campbell and Stanley, *Experimental and Quasi-Experimental Designs.*

20. Kaanan Butor-Bhavsar, John Witton, and Diana Elbourne, "Can Research Assessments Themselves Cause Bias in Behaviour Change Trials? A Systematic Review of Evidence from Solomon 4-Group Studies," *PLoS ONE* 6, no. 10 (2011): 1–9; Campbell and Stanley, *Experimental and Quasi-Experimental Designs*; Shlomo Sawilowsky and D. Lynn Kelley, "Meta-Analysis and the Solomon Four-Group Design," *Journal of Experimental Education* 62, no. 4 (Summer 1994): 361.

21. R. Barker Bausell, *Conducting Meaningful Experiments: 40 Steps to Becoming a Scientist* (Thousand Oaks, CA: Sage, 1994), 90.

22. Yair Levy, Timothy J. Ellis, and Eli Cohen, "A Guide for Novice Researchers on Experimental and Quasi-Experimental Studies in Information Systems Research," *Interdisciplinary Journal of Information, Knowledge & Management* 6 (2011): 154.

23. Stephen Gorard, "The Propagation of Errors in Experimental Data Analysis: A Comparison of Pre- and Post-Test Designs," *International Journal of Research & Method in Education* 36, no. 4 (2013): 372–385.

24. Ibid., 372.

25. Campbell and Stanley, *Experimental and Quasi-Experimental Designs.*

26. V. L. Willson and R. R. Putnam, "A Meta-Analysis of Pretest Sensitization Effects in Experimental Design," *American Educational Research Journal* 19 (1982): 249–258.

27. For an example of this, see Charles Boy Kromann, Morten L. Jensen, and Charlotte Ringsted, "The Effect of Testing on Skills Learning," *Medical Education* 43, no. 1 (2009): 21–27.

28. Levy, Ellis, and Cohen; J. W. Creswell, *Educational Research: Planning, Conducting, and Evaluating*

*Quantitative and Qualitative Research*, 2nd ed. (Upper Saddle River, NJ: Pearson, 2005).

29. Ralph Woehle and Andrew Quinn, "An Experiment Comparing HBSE Graduate Social Work Classes: Face-to-Face and at a Distance," *Journal of Teaching in Social Work* 29, no. 4 (2009): 418–430.

30. Sameer B. Srivastava, "Network Intervention: Assessing the Effects of Formal Mentoring on Workplace Networks," *Social Forces* 94, no. 1 (September 2015): 427–452.

31. Froukje Snoeren et al., "Design of a Quasi-Experiment on the Effectiveness and Cost-Effectiveness of Using the Child-Interview Intervention During the Investigation Following a Report of Child Abuse and/or Neglect," *BMC Public Health* 13, no. 1 (2013): 1–16.

32. Sharon Crasnow, "Natural Experiments and Pluralism in Political Science," *Philosophy of the Social Sciences* 45, no. 4/5 (2015): 429.

33. Ibid.

34. Jill Theresa Messing et al., "The Oklahoma Lethality Assessment Study: A Quasi-Experimental Evaluation of the Lethality Assessment Program," *Social Service Review* 89, no. 3 (2015): 499–530.

35 Andrew Wheeler, "The Moving Home Effect: A Quasi Experiment Assessing Effect of Home Location on the Offence Location," *Journal of Quantitative Criminology* 28, no. 4 (2012): 587–606.

36. Tannis MacBeth Williams, *The Impact of Television: A Natural Experiment in Three Communities*, ed. Tannis MacBeth Williams (Orlando, FL: Academic Press, 1986).

37. Campbell and Stanley, *Experimental and Quasi-Experimental Designs.*

38. Crasnow, "Natural Experiments and Pluralism."

39. Phillip Baker et al., "Trade and Investment Liberalization, Food Systems Change and Highly Processed Food Consumption: A Natural Experiment Contrasting the Soft-Drink Markets of Peru and Bolivia," *Globalization and Health* 12 (2016): 1–13.

40. Judith Green et al., "Integrating Quasi-Experimental and Inductive Designs in Evaluation: A Case Study of the Impact of Free Bus Travel on Public Health," *Evaluation* 21, no. 4 (2015): 391–406.

41. Ibid., 395–396.

42. David S. Kirk, "A Natural Experiment of the Consequences of Concentrating Former Prisoners in the Same Neighborhoods," *Proceedings of the National Academy of Sciences of the United States of America* 112, no. 22 (2015): 6943–6948.

43. Aaron Reeves and Robert de Vries, "Does Media Coverage Influence Public Attitudes Towards Welfare Recipients? The Impact of the 2011 English Riots," *British Journal of Sociology* 67, no. 2 (2016): 281–306.

44. Mary S. Morgan, "Nature's Experiments and Natural Experiments in the Social Sciences," *Philosophy of the Social Sciences* 43, no. 3 (2013): 341–357.

45. Alan S. Gerber and Donald P. Green, *Field Experiments: Design, Analysis, and Interpretation* (New York: W. W. Norton, 2012).

46. Ibid., 9.

47. Ibid.

48. Ibid.

49. Ibid.

50. Ibid.

51. Ibid.

52. William Minozzi et al., "Field Experiment Evidence of Substantive, Attributional, and Behavioral Persuasion by Members of Congress in Online Town Halls," *Proceedings of the National Academy of Sciences* 112, no. 13 (2015): 3937–3942.

53. Erik Meyer and Chris Van Klaveren, "The Effectiveness of Extended Day Programs: Evidence from a Randomized Field Experiment in the Netherlands," *Economics of Education Review* 36 (2013): 1–11.

# INTERNAL AND EXTERNAL VALIDITY

*No issue . . . has a longer half-life or recurs with more regularity than the argument over the validity and generalizability of findings obtained from social scientific experiments.*[1]

**—John A. Courtright**

---

## LEARNING OBJECTIVES

- Illustrate internal and external validity and the trade-offs.

- Identify how generalizability is achieved in experiments.

- Compare logical inference versus statistical inference.

- Discuss the role of replication in experimentation.

- Explain how random assignment provides internal validity.

- Identify the seven classes of extraneous variables that jeopardize internal validity.

---

The previous chapter looked at different kinds of experiments—lab or true, quasi, natural, and field—and concluded there is no perfect experiment. As in life, experiments involve trade-offs, and that is especially true of the two sides of **validity**—external and internal. Like children on a seesaw, one type of validity tends to go up as the other goes down. In social science experiments, the goal is to maximize both, but that is usually difficult to achieve.[2] As the opening quote shows, this debate can continue for a very long time. To be "valid" means something is well founded, accurate, or authoritative. In the case of science, it is especially important that the conclusions of research be valid or true, at least with an acceptable level of probability. The topic of validity is especially important for experiments, which are most often lauded for one type—**internal validity**—and criticized for their lack of the other—**external validity**. Internal validity refers to the extent to which the effects of an experiment are actually due to the treatment, whereas external validity concerns the ability of a study to generalize beyond the subjects, settings, and treatments in that particular study—that is, to the idea that effects from the experiment also would be found in real life. Because external validity can be as big of a threat to experiments as internal validity is to observational studies,[3] this chapter begins with a discussion of external validity.

## ECOLOGICAL AND EXTERNAL VALIDITY

In broad strokes, external validity is the extent to which the results of an experiment can be generalized to other people, settings, and treatments. One of the concerns that affects external validity is how realistic (or artificial) the experiment is, called **ecological validity**. When an experiment reflects real-life circumstances or mimics the environment, providing subjects with an experience that is akin to what really happens, it is said to be ecologically valid.[4] Creating as much of a natural situation as possible enhances the chances of subjects responding as they normally would.[5] Quasi, natural, and field experiments are higher in ecological validity than are true or lab experiments. The challenge for lab experimenters is to maximize realism while still maintaining control. From chapter 2, we saw that Stanley Milgram and Philip Zimbardo worked hard to do just that. Without going so far as to construct a mock prison or shock-generating machine, today's experimentalists still can achieve some degree of realism with a little extra effort and imagination. For example, running a political science experiment in an actual polling place, using real polling equipment and registered voters, helps enhance ecological validity.[6] Having subjects interact with a real teacher is more realistic than asking them to imagine an interaction from reading about it. Researchers in some disciplines find it easier to approximate real life than others. For example, studying whether getting a raise improves performance by bringing people into a lab, creating jobs, manipulating the reward, and then observing or measuring performance seems improbable for a business experiment. But a real-life setting affords no control, and people obviously cannot be randomly assigned to get raises. Having subjects read about a job, imagine themselves in that situation, and answer questions about what they might do may be the best available option. This is an example of the trade-offs. Experimental economics has long had concerns over the artificiality of laboratory experiments, not only for setting and tasks that are unlike those in the real world but also for reactivity and demand effects, which were covered in chapter 2.[7] Researchers should understand the thinking in their particular field.

Creating realism often requires more work and creativity on the researcher's part but can be worth it in the results. I found this out firsthand when, as a graduate student, I helped conduct an experiment to determine if news stories that were framed differently would cause people to attribute blame for problems to society or individuals and to endorse different solutions. In the first attempt, my professor and I used real news stories but presented them to the subjects typed up on 8.5 x 11-inch paper. Beyond having a headline and byline, they did not look much like stories in a real newspaper. We found no effects. After some debate over what could have gone wrong, we decided to present the stories more realistically; instead of giving the stories to subjects on pieces of typing paper, we generated mock broadsheet newspapers with the manipulated stories embedded alongside other real news stories, photos, a nameplate, and page numbers. We printed them out on an oversized copy machine on paper that was 22-inches long and 13-inches wide, the same size as broadsheet newspapers. The same stories that produced no differences previously now showed the effects that theory had predicted.[8] All we did was change the appearance to be more realistic. It cost more and took longer, but the realism of the mock newspaper pages seemed to have been key. We did not make everything realistic; for example, our subjects were still reading the mock newspapers in a university classroom rather than at their breakfast tables, and it was a fictional newspaper name rather than a real one. But that one change seemed to be enough. A cheaper and easier compromise to the 13 x 22-inch broadsheet, I discovered, is what newspaper journalists call a "clip"—that is, a story that looks like it is cut out of a newspaper. I also find effects with clips, and they are easier to make. Today, researchers are more likely to have to create web pages or tweets. (Chapter 9 will discuss creating realistic stimuli.)

# GENERALIZABILITY

Realism is one of the keys to **generalizability**, or how well the effects of highly artificial experiments translate to real life.[9] In addition to how real it seems, external validity is also about whether results from a specific experiment will translate to other people, in other settings, at different times, and for different treatments.[10] When results generalize beyond the specifics of the study, they are said to be "**robust**."[11] Most experiments do not randomly sample from a population[12] the way surveys and other quantitative

**Here is An Example of A Newspaper Story With Low Ecological Validity (Top), Versus The Same Story, Presented As A "Clip," With High Ecological Validity (Bottom).**

### Diabetes class promotes social support

*Communities help diabetics maintain happy, healthy lives, says class*

**By Tyler Daniels**
DAILY RECORD STAFF

Angela Mitchell doesn't have end-stage renal disease or an inoperable brain tumor. Her disease is more manageable. In fact, tens of millions of American are just like Angela. They are diabetic.

Mitchell joined a diabetes education class offered through West Anderson Community Hospital and discovered the number of Americans with diabetes or pre-diabetes now reaches 75 million.

Diabetics and pre-diabetics represent 25% of the American population. The number of people with diabetes in the United States is projected to reach 39 million by the year 2050.

But Mitchell, a 40-year-old San Bernardino mother of three with Type II diabetes, is taking small steps toward living a healthier life - eating better, exercising and testing her blood glucose levels. She's also getting help from her community, according to those teaching the class.

Many of the fast food restaurants in town have stopped promoting the "super-sized" fast food options that can worsen diabetes. Snack machine vendors are even replacing much of the sugary sodas and snacks with water and fruit. Schools in the community have banished soda machines entirely. Coincidentally or not, the rise of obesity and Type II diabetes in the United States parallels the increase in sugar-sweetened soft drink consumption.

Even the federal government is waking up to the need to make changes, perhaps because diabetes costs the United States nearly $132 billion each year. The U.S. Department of Agriculture is considering redefining its guidelines for sugar consumption, especially in soft drinks.

More and more communities are realizing that diabetes isn't caused entirely by individuals. Social factors such as lack of free and safe places to exercise also contribute to diabetes and other diseases. Other environmental factors that influence the number of diabetics in America include lack of access to health insurance that makes it harder for some people to manage their diabetes, said Gladys Knight, the singer and celebrity spokesperson for the American Diabetes Association. Uninsured adults with diabetes are far less likely to receive needed care and effectively manage their disease.

Access to health insurance is more difficult for diabetics. In most states, people with diabetes are considered "uninsurable" and are often denied coverage. Diabetics face similar obstacles with Medicaid or Medicare.

However, quality medical care is essential for diabetics. The risk for death is twice as high for people with diabetes compared to people of similar ages without the disease.

# Health & Science

| Monday, June 15, 2007 | The Daily Record | Section D |

## Diabetes class promotes social support

**Communities help diabetics maintain happy, healthy lives, says class**

**By Tyler Daniels**
DAILY RECORD STAFF

Angela Mitchell doesn't have end-stage renal disease or an inoperable brain tumor. Her disease is more manageable. In fact, tens of millions of Americans are just like Angela. They are diabetic.

Mitchell joined a diabetes education class offered through West Anderson Community Hospital and discovered the number of Americans with diabetes or pre-diabetes now reaches 75 million.

Diabetics and pre-diabetics represent 25% of the American population. The number of people with diabetes in the United States is projected to reach 39 million by the year 2050.

But Mitchell, a 40-year-old San Bernadino mother of three with Type II diabetes, is taking small steps toward living a healthier life – eating better, exercising, and testing her blood glucose levels. She's also getting help from her community, according to those teaching the class.

Many of the fast food restaurants in town have stopped promoting the "super-sized" fast food options that can worsen diabetes. Snack machine vendors are even replacing much of the sugary sodas and snacks with water and fruit. Schools in the community have banished soda machines entirely. Coincidentally or not, the rise of obesity and Type II diabetes in the United States parallels the increase in sugar-sweetened soft drink consumption.

Even the federal government is waking up to the need to make changes, perhaps because diabetes costs the United States nearly $132 billion each year. The U.S. Department of Agriculture is considering redefining its guidelines for sugar consumption, especially in soft drinks.

More and more communities are realizing that diabetes isn't caused entirely by individuals; social factors such as lack of free and safe places to exercise also contribute to diabetes and other diseases. Other environmental factors that influence the number of diabetics in America include lack of access to health insurance that makes it harder for some people to manage their diabetes, said Gladys Knight, the singer and celebrity spokesperson for the American Diabetes Association. Uninsured adults with diabetes are far less likely to receive needed care and effectively manage their disease.

Access to health insurance is more difficult for diabetics. In most states, people with diabetes are considered "uninsurable" and are often denied coverage. Diabetics face similar obstacles with Medicaid or Medicare.

However, quality medical care is essential for diabetics. The risk for death is twice as high for people with diabetes compared to people of similar ages without the disease.

Knight is working with the California government to help change that. Already, several drug stores in the state offer free or low-cost medical care and supplies to monitor and control blood glucose levels. Normally, these supplies and services are expensive, and can be complicated for uninsured diabetics to get.

Knight recommended that ensuring access to and delivering high-quality care for all people with diabetes should be a national priority and that policymakers must act to make health insurance available, affordable, and adequate for people with diabetes. This will also help offset medical costs that are covered by tax dollars.

"This is a public health issue. Yes, we have newer medications and treatment methods, but that's not stopping the rise in cases," said Knight.

methods do. Random sampling, which allows every person in a population an equal chance of being chosen, results in a sample that affords the researcher the ability to say that the findings apply to the larger population with a certain level of probability. Most experiments do not randomly sample subjects, but there are other ways they achieve generalizability, including using people as close as possible as those to be generalized to. For example, experiments using twenty-year-old college students may not generalize to people on probation and parole. Findings about volunteers may not translate to people who do not volunteer.[13] What causes someone to donate to a health-related charity may be different for patrons of the arts.[14] Results from an experiment using accountants may not generalize to factory workers, and so on. The possibility that a treatment only works on the unique population used in the experiment is one concern of external validity.[15] One of the most serious limits to experiments is when they cannot be generalized beyond the specific people studied.[16] Campbell and Stanley give an example of a hypothetical researcher who tries to recruit ten different schools to participate in an experiment and is turned down by nine, saying, "This tenth almost certainly differs from the other nine, and from the universe of schools to which we would like to generalize, in many specific ways. It is, thus, nonrepresentative."[17] Something about that school that led them to agree to be in the experiment might also cause the treatment to be effective, such as better teacher morale, for example. If the effects found apply only to one group of people, they cannot be generalized to a larger group that was not included in the study.[18] This leads to the obvious conclusion that researchers should use samples that are as similar as possible to the people or other units such as businesses, schools, or organizations the researcher intends to study—for example, using registered voters rather than those not registered, citizens from throughout the country rather than just one state, or accountants instead of students, if those first groups are the target populations to be generalized. This argues against what has become the rather routine use of students in subject pools; if the purpose of an experiment is to study decision making by military leaders or the type of public service announcements that best encourage parents to have their children vaccinated, then the use of sophomore advertising majors in the departmental subject pool is not a good choice. When subjects do not represent the population to which the results are supposed to apply, then external validity is low and the credibility of the results comes into question. If the population to which the research is aimed is advertising students, or even advertising professionals, for example, then the subject pool is more defensible, considering that advertising students will likely soon be advertising practitioners.[19] It may be easier to use students from the subject pool, but if those students do not approximate the population the experiment is designed to generalize results to, then it can be advantageous to expend more effort to find more representative subjects. Chapter 8 goes into more detail about the mechanics of selecting samples, and students in particular.

Campbell and Stanley describe twelve factors that jeopardize validity.[20] This chapter will not go into detail about all of them but will instead focus on a few of the more popular ways to combat low external validity. Occasionally, experimentalists will find that their experiments are being evaluated by journal reviewers who are experts in the topic but unfamiliar with experimental methods. This sometimes results in feedback that says the study should not be considered valid if the subjects were not randomly sampled, and should not be published. In those cases, it is helpful to be prepared with a knowledgeable, respectful response. This section is designed to help create experiments that avoid such criticism in the first place, and also to respond should it be given.

Recently, research has tackled the problem of generalizability in experiments and come up with ways to address the problem or at least estimate how likely the results are to accurately represent a particular population beyond the study subjects.[21] Some include different methods for selecting subjects, while others create measures from outcome variables or covariates to estimate how representative of the population the experimental sample is.[22] Some of these techniques can be used when selecting samples, and others are used after data are collected.[23] These are fairly advanced techniques, which this textbook will not discuss in detail; rather, this chapter covers the basic issues and solutions.

## Random Sampling

Just as random assignment is the gold standard for achieving equivalent groups in experiments, the gold standard for achieving generalizability is random sampling.[24] As we have known since 1936 when *Literary Digest* magazine predicted the wrong winner of the U.S. presidential election while George Gallup's polling organization predicted it correctly,[25] random sampling is the most efficient and effective way to estimate some characteristic of an entire population from a smaller sample of it. But you rarely see it used in experiments.[26]

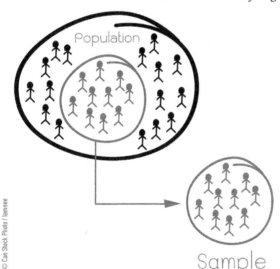

First, we should make clear the difference between random *assignment* and random *sampling*. Random sampling is the process of selecting subjects for a study so that they adequately represent a larger population. It ensures that each person, site, or other unit from a population has an equal chance of being chosen, and is cheaper and easier than measuring a whole population, especially when it would be impossible to do so. Random assignment, by contrast, is the act of deciding which subjects get a particular experimental treatment or are put into a particular group. Random assignment is typically done with **convenience samples**, or those subjects who are easily available, rather than with subjects who are randomly sampled. The purposes of each are quite different. "Random assignment . . . facilitates causal inference by making samples randomly similar to *each other*, whereas random sampling makes a sample similar to *a population*."[27] In the case of experiments, it is not as important that the subjects look like the people who are not in the study, but that the subjects in the different groups of the study look like each other.

## Two-Step Randomization

If each of these kinds of randomization is the gold standard, then the use of both in combination surely should be platinum. In fact, some experiments do use a **two-step randomization model**, where subjects are first randomly sampled from a population and then randomly assigned to a treatment group,[28] but that is rare. One of the most obvious reasons is that researchers would need a complete and up-to-date list of all the members of a population in order to randomly sample from. The larger the population, the less likely this is to exist. For example, no complete list exists of all parents of school-age children in the United States, including those enrolled in private schools or being homeschooled. And while there are lists of registered voters, there are not lists of *un*registered ones. Constraining the population to be generalized makes random sampling more feasible in some cases; for example, it would be possible to obtain a list of all school students in a certain school district, but the narrowing of the sample raises the same questions as before—do effects from one school district generalize to others? If a researcher could draw a random sample from across the United States, it would be difficult, if not impossible, to administer some of the treatments experimentalists use to all these people scattered all across the country. Researchers would have to travel around the country or bring the subjects to the lab, both of which are expensive, or rely on others to give the manipulation, which jeopardizes internal validity because subjects respond differently to different experimenters who may even deliver the stimuli in a different way. Besides these logistic considerations, there are budget realities. For example, a database of all working U.S. journalists *is* available commercially, but it costs thousands of dollars. That is understandable when considering how much time and effort it takes to compile such information. Most researchers do not have this kind of time or money. Researchers should weigh the benefits against the costs.

## Nonresponse Bias

In situations where a population list is easier to acquire, experimentalists then run into the same kinds of problems that survey researchers do when recruiting people. To estimate a population requires a lot more participants than it does to find an effect; for example, 400 might be needed for generalizing instead of the forty that is more common to experiments that are only looking for effects.[29] Therefore, if an experimenter also wants to generalize, more subjects are needed, which costs more. Also, not everyone who is randomly chosen will agree to be in a study; poll and survey researchers deal with this in one of their biggest external validity concerns—**nonresponse bias**, which happens when people do not answer a question or refuse to participate. People who do not respond can be very different in unknown ways from those who do, such as the schools that refused to participate in Campbell and Stanley's fictional example. Nonresponse bias carries threats to generalizability, and response rates have been dipping into the teens and below for years. There also is the worry about **attrition**, or subjects who drop out before completing a study. It does not make sense for an experimental researcher to go to all the time, expense, and trouble to obtain a list of a population to randomly sample from, only to discover that not enough people will agree to participate to ensure generalizability anyway. When it *is* possible to obtain a list of all units in the study, such as Malesky and colleagues[30] did with firms in Vietnam for an online experiment of bribery, and then randomly sample them before randomly assigning them to conditions, response rates must be calculated and reported, and a discussion of response bias presented (see Study Spotlight 5.1, Generalizability and Representativeness). As that study showed, random sampling did not make the generalizability question disappear. The authors provided a table comparing the characteristics of their sample to those of the population

These issues make random sampling "an inadequate solution" to the problem of generalization from experiments.[32] In addition, some businesses, government agencies, or other organizations will not allow their employees or members to be randomly sampled; they may feel it is unfair to give some an opportunity that others do not have, among other reasons. If researchers are offering a career development seminar as the manipulation, for example, employers may be reluctant to tell some employees they cannot participate and invite charges of favoritism and discrimination. Because random sampling requires "a high level of resources and a degree of logistical control that is rarely feasible,"[33] most experimentalists use other sampling methods that are accepted throughout all fields of scientific experimentation. These sampling methods are the topic of chapter 8. Instead, to give us more confidence in the generalizability of experiments, researchers use other approaches, described next.

## Representativeness

The goal of random sampling from a larger population is to ensure that the smaller sample looks like the larger population—that is, that it is representative. In the absence of

# STUDY SPOTLIGHT 5.1
## Generalizability and Representativeness

Next is an example of a discussion of generalizability of the experiment. The authors included a table comparing the sample to the population for representativeness.

**Malesky, Edmund J., Dimitar D. Gueorguiev, and Nathan M. Jensen. 2015. "Monopoly Money: Foreign Investment and Bribery in Vietnam, a Survey Experiment."** *American Journal of Political Science* **59 (2): 419–439.**

Appendix 4: Characteristics of Provincial Competitiveness Index Sample and Census Data in 2010

| Foreign invested (3,888) | | | Domestic enterprises (19,363) | | |
|---|---|---|---|---|---|
| **Legal form of investment** | **Weighted PCI** | **GSO** | **Legal form of investment** | **Weighted PCI** | **Tax** |
| 100% Foreign-directed enterprise | 84.35% | 82.95% | Sole proprietorship | 16.2% | 19.4% |
| Joint venture with a Vietnamese private | 4.84% | 16.36% | Limited liability | 54.5% | 59.1% |
| Joint venture with a Vietnamese SOE | 4.55% | | Joint stock | 27.6% | 21.4% |
| Registered as a domestic company | 2.52% | 0.46% | Joint stock with shared listed on stock exchange | 1.1% | NA |
| Domestic company w/overseas VN capital | 0.61% | | Partnership and other | 0.7% | 0.0% |
| Other | 3.13% | 0.23% | | | |
| **Sector** | **Weighted PCI** | **GSO** | **Sector** | **Weighted PCI** | **Tax** |
| Industry/manufacturing | 64.59% | 59.44% | Industry/manufacturing | 30.2% | 34.5% |
| Construction/infrastructure investment | 4.09% | 4.72% | Construction/infrastructure investment* | | |
| Service/commerce/finance | 29.33% | 28.94% | Service/commerce/finance | 64.6% | 62.2% |
| Agriculture/forestry/aquaculture | 2.36% | 5.87% | Agriculture/forestry/aquaculture | 4.0% | 1.9% |
| Mining/natural resource exploitation | 0.86% | 1.03% | Mining/natural resource exploitation | 1.2% | 1.4% |
| **Size of labor force** | **Weighted PCI** | **GSO** | **Size of labor force** | **Weighted PCI** | **GSO** |
| Less than 5 | 2.92% | 4.18% | Under 5 | 12.1% | 23.36% |
| 5 to 9 | 5.99% | 6.79% | 5 to 9 | 24.1% | 35.63% |
| 10 to 49 | 31.79% | 29.67% | 10 to 49 | 41.9% | 33.22% |
| 50 to 299 | 31.35% | 30.95% | 50 to 200 | 14.9% | 6.11% |
| 300 to 399 | 6.38% | 7.64% | Over 200 | 7.1% | 1.7% |
| 400 to 499 | 7.26% | 7.09% | | | |
| 500 to 999 | 7.17% | 6.88% | | | |
| 1000 and over | 7.13% | 7.81% | | | |
| **Licensed investment size** | **Weighted PCI** | **GSO** | **Licensed investment size (Total assets, BVND)** | **Weighted PCI** | **GSO** |
| Under 0.5 BVND ($25,000 USD) | 2.52% | 2.25% | Under 0.5 BVND ($25,000 USD) | 10.9% | 8.9% |
| From 0.5 to under 1 BVND ($50,000 USD) | 1.39% | 2.17% | From 0.5 to under 1 BVND ($50,000 USD) | 17.0% | 13.5% |
| From 1 to under 5 BVND ($250,000 USD) | 15.85% | 12.75% | From 1 to under 5 BVND ($250,000 USD) | 42.8% | 49.6% |
| From 5 to under 10 BVND ($500,000 USD) | 8.75% | 11.71% | From 5 to under 10 BVND ($500,000 USD) | 12.7% | 13.4% |
| From 10 to under 50 BVND ($2.5 Million USD) | 35.14% | 36.04% | From 10 to under 50 BVND ($2.5 Million USD) | 11.9% | 11.5% |
| From 50 to under 200 BVND ($10 Million USD) | 23.13% | 22.83% | From 50 to under 200 BVND ($10 Million USD) | 4.8% | 3.2% |
| From 200 to under 500 BVND ($25 Million USD) | 7.62% | 7.29% | From 200 to under 500 BVND ($25 Million USD) | | |
| Above 500 BVND ($25 Million USD) | 5.61% | 4.97% | Above 500 BVND ($25 Million USD) | | |
| **Major customer** | **Weighted PCI** | **GSO** | **Major customer** | **Weighted PCI** | **GSO** |
| Export directly or indirectly | 55.00% | 66.8% | Export directly or indirectly | 11.7% | NA |
| Foreign individuals or companies in Vietnam | 24.51% | 16.2% | Foreign individuals or companies in Vietnam | 9.9% | NA |
| Sold domestically to SOE | 3.52% | 2.8% | Sold domestically to SOE | 14.8% | NA |
| Sold domestically to state agency | 1.42% | 0.9% | Sold domestically to state agency | 20.3% | NA |
| Sold domestically to private individuals | 15.55% | 13.0% | Sold domestically to private individuals | 43.4% | NA |

Note: This table compares data on the nationally weighted sample of domestic and foreign firms from the PCI to the data collected from the National Tax Authority (Tax) and General Statistical Office (GSO) Enterprise Census. Weighted PCI is the PCI survey sample, but weighted by provincial share of enterprises to create a nationally representative sample. General Statistical Office (GSO) Data available at (www.gso.gov.vn) and GSO Enterprise Census (2009) available at (http://www.gso.gov.vn/default_en.aspx?tabid=515&idmid=5&ItemID=9775). NA = Not Available for 2010. *Tax Authority data does not disaggregate construction firm from manufacturing. The PCI data records 15 percent construction.

PCI = Provincial Competitiveness Index

BVND = Billion Vietnamese Dollars

SOE = state-owned enterprise

VN = Vietnamese

Source: Survey data from Vietnam PCI 2010 Report (www.pcivietnam.org); and GSO Enterprise Census 2009 (www.gso.gov.vn)

*(Continued)*

(Continued)

"Our final sample is composed of 19,363 domestic firms and 3,888 FIEs, which registered after 2000 and are located throughout the country's 63 provinces. In all three years, the sample frame for selection was the list of registered domestic firms and FIEs in the General Tax Authority database of registered operations. The survey response rate was about 30% for domestic operations and 25% for FIEs, much higher than rates commonly reported in the international business literature (White and Luo 2006), but still small enough to create concerns about reliability (Dillman et al. 2002). As a result, it is reasonable to ask whether nonresponse creates selection bias that might affect our conclusions (Jensen, Li, and Rahman 2010). In Appendix 4 in the supporting information, we compare the PCI data to available information from the General Statistical Office's Enterprise Census and Tax Authority Databases in 2012, showing that PCI data in a given year reflect observable characteristics of the national population and therefore offer a highly accurate depiction of foreign and domestic investors in Vietnam."[31]

the ability to randomly sample, taking precautions to ensure that the sample adequately represents the rest of the population is one step that gives us more confidence in the external validity of the results of experiments.[35] Shadish, Cook, and Campbell discuss the various ways that the term *representative sampling* has been used in experiments, including as a miniature of the population, saying this is used to "describe samples that are representative in a purposive sense."[36] The goal is to know the key characteristics of the population and ensure that the sample adequately represents as many of these key characteristics as possible. Many experiments take pains to compare their sample's characteristics to those of the target population—for example, a national census.[37] It is also important to point out where samples differ from the population.[38] It is acceptable for the sample not to be in the exact proportions of the population on some demographics, as similarity to some variables but not all of the key characteristics are all that is required.[39] For example, Klaiman and colleagues' sample mirrored the census in gender, age, income, and rural and urban regions, but was slightly more educated than the population.[40] Researchers should be especially concerned about variables that affect the outcome variable.

Regardless of how good the fit, this type of generalizing is never backed up by statistical logic yet remains widely used in experiments.[41] Verschoor et al.'s[42] study of economic risk taking specifically tests the question of how well experiments reflect real-world behavior. In this study of farmers in Uganda, the researchers use a representative sample and bill their study as "a test of the external validity of the experimental method,"[43] finding that indeed, this experiment that used a representative population was externally valid if enough care was taken with sampling methods and other validity concerns, such as minimizing confounding variables.

# MORE ABOUT . . . BOX 5.2
## Experiments With Random
## Sampling and Random Assignment

True experiments that use both random sampling and random assignment are rare. While it is not recommended as the only way to generalize to a population, Shadish, Cook, and Campbell do say, "We unambiguously advocate it when it is feasible."[34]

"Feasible" usually means a population that is constrained to a manageable level, such as residents of one city or state, or when a list of an entire population exists, such as for members of a licensed profession. Random sampling is also facilitated when databases are publicly available, researchers enlist the aid of officials with access to information about a population, or can purchase databases; for example, the company Cision tracks all print, broadcast, and online journalists in the United States, and also top social media influencers (http://www.cision.com/us/pr-software/media-database/).

Two examples of experiments that use two-step randomization are summarized next:

**Lu, Fangwen, Jinan Zhang, and Jeffrey M. Perloff. 2016. "General and Specific Information in Deterring Traffic Violations: Evidence From a Randomized Experiment."** *Journal of Economic Behavior & Organization* **123: 97–107.**

This experiment conducted in Tsingtao, China, used the city's database of registered vehicles, which also listed cell phone numbers of the owners. This resulted in a census of 85,448 car owners. The researchers enlisted the cooperation of the Tsingtao Police Department to provide the data. The study also randomly assigned the registered vehicle owners to one of several treatment conditions where they were sent text messages with varying content about traffic violations they had received, a general safety message, or a control group that received no message. They then tracked to see which safety message resulted in drivers incurring fewer violations in the future.

**Shi, Ying. 2016. "Cross-Cutting Messages and Voter Turnout: Evidence From a Same-Sex Marriage Amendment."** *Political Communication* **33 (3): 433–459.**

This study used publicly available databases of voter registration and voting history from the state of North Carolina as the population, and then drew a random sample of registered Democrats and Republicans who then received direct-mail postcards with messages either for or against their party's position on same-sex marriage to see if cross-cutting views stimulate or discourage political participation, measured by whether they voted in the election after receiving the postcards.

There are various ways to increase the chances of a sample being representative—for example, oversampling of certain hard-to-obtain populations and use of multiple sites, which should add diversity.[44] The use of online survey methods to conduct experiments, frequently called **survey experiments**, also has increased the ability of experiments to use representative samples,[45] as has the use of panels of survey respondents recruited by sampling firms.[46] These will be discussed in more detail in chapter 8.

When experimental samples do not accurately represent populations, the paper's discussion section should include an acknowledgment of this limitation and an explanation of why this is not problematic or should not invalidate the findings.[47] (See How To Do It box 5.3 for examples of how some experimentalists have handled this.) A good practice is to always say something like "findings should be interpreted with caution" if the sample is not representative of the population, and to be careful to talk about findings from "these subjects" or "the people in this sample," "our subjects," or similar language that does not imply extrapolating beyond those in the sample.

# CAUSE AND EFFECT

It can also be a good idea to point out in the article the fact that experiments are not designed to be generalizable but are intended to find effects if they exist. In most experiments,

---

**HOW TO DO IT 5.3**

## What to Say When It Is Not Representative

When samples are not representative of the target population, experimentalists are up front about it but defend the results on various other grounds. Here are some excerpts of such discussions from a few studies:

**Kim, Mirae, and Gregg G. Van Ryzin. 2014. "Impact of Government Funding on Donations to Arts Organizations: A Survey Experiment."** *Nonprofit and Voluntary Sector Quarterly* **43 (5): 910–925.**
  "Compared to the U.S. population, there are relatively high proportions of females and Whites in the panel, a feature that Berrens, Bohara, Jenkins-Smith, Sliva, and Weimer (2003) find to be common in other voluntary online panels in the United States. Although this limits the external validity of studies using online panels, there is some evidence to suggest that, at least for some topics, this type of voluntary panel can approximate survey results based on probability sampling of the U.S. population. Although not representative of the general population, the participants in our study clearly appear interested and supportive of the arts and thus perhaps more closely resemble the potential donor community for many U.S. arts nonprofits" (pp. 916–917).

**Dunlop, Claire A., and Claudio M. Radaelli. 2016. "Teaching Regulatory Humility: Experimenting with Student Practitioners."** *Politics* **36 (1): 79–94.**
  "Neither of the groups are representative samples of public sector administrators or MPA students. This is not problematic, however, given that our purpose is to illustrate the utility of experiments in the classroom in helping student-practitioners critically reflect rather than make any empirical contribution to the illusion of control literature. The utility of data gathered is pedagogic rather than research-oriented" (p. 82).

representing a larger population is not the goal.[48] Rather, experiments are good for studying theoretically important relationships. This is a fundamental misunderstanding about experimental research that the public, media, and researchers using other methods occasionally make.[49] Researchers can get caught up in issues such as generalizability and lose sight of the fact that the purpose of an experiment is to establish causality—that is, to discover if some treatment variable is the cause of some outcome or effect. The purpose of laboratory experiments is not to generalize to a particular population.[50] And in this regard, the issue of random assignment is far more crucial; more about that in chapter 7.

Surveys, content analyses, and other methods have the opposite problem that experiments have; if sampled correctly, they can generalize to the population, but they cannot infer the cause of the relationships they find.[51] These kinds of studies should be careful to talk about "associations" or "relationships" rather than declaring or implying "cause." Generalizability is more important for survey researchers, who are interested in obtaining the attitudes and opinions of people. It is more reasonable to ask if those attitudes and opinions are widely held by others. But for experiments, aimed at determining cause and effect, that question takes a backseat to whether the outcome was confounded by something other than the manipulation or treatment.

## LOGICAL INFERENCE

There can also be a misunderstanding about the kind of inferring that experiments attempt. Rather than making a **statistical inference**, which means that a confidence level or interval can be mathematically calculated to determine the fit between the sample and larger population, experimentalists rely on **logical inference**, the idea that reasonable conclusions can be drawn on the basis of common sense. For example, if an experiment tests some function that is relatively unaffected by race, gender, or where one lives, among other things[52]—for example, the cognitive process of opinion formation—then it is appropriate to draw inferences to others not in the sample. Basil gives an example of hardwired physiological responses to photographs taken from a close range versus photographs that show something or someone farther away, saying arousal to such images should be the same regardless of who is in the sample.[53] It is reasonable to assume that such processes should be similar for others not in the sample if there is no evidence to the contrary. For example, if college students were more afraid of scary close-up shots than scary far-away shots, why would we not expect the same response among noncollege students? Similarly, media effects such as agenda setting, priming, and framing have been shown to work the same way with a variety of populations all around the country and even the world.[54] If, however, what is being studied changes with various conditions—for example, in cultures that have state-run media—we would not generalize to them from conclusions made in different conditions, such as in free-press societies. Unless a phenomenon is different for different people, the findings should hold for everyone. The real concern for experiments is whether the sample is appropriate to what is being studied, not as much as how it was drawn.[55]

Finally, to dismiss experiments based on the generalizability of the samples used would be to reject findings in medicine, psychology, chemistry, and physics, among other disciplines, that have made valuable contributions to science and everyday life based largely on nonrepresentative samples.

# REPLICATION

Rather than concentrating so much on how samples are drawn or how well they mimic a larger population, experiments rely primarily on **replication** to make generalizations about their conclusions.[56] Replication is the ability to repeat findings from an experiment with different subjects, under different conditions, at different times and places, with different issues, variables, etc. If consistent effects are found in different studies, then there is more confidence that those findings represent something real and generalizable rather than being caused by chance, bias, or error.[57] Replications are "purposeful duplications of the methods used that specifically assess the veracity of previous research results."[58] Some professions that rely on evidence-based practices are especially concerned with replication to make sure results are reproducible before instituting costly changes in practice.[59] Political science began a replication movement in the 1990s,[60] and social psychology has recently renewed its own, begun in the 1970s.[61] Unfortunately, replication is not as prevalent as calls for more of it; for example, in special education, only 0.5% of articles sought to replicate previous findings,[62] up from 0.13% in education in general.[63] Psychology journals are among the highest, at 1.07%,[64] which still seems pretty low.

Social scientists working in every method have often heard that a single study never proves anything; this is equally true of experiments. Researchers also advise caution with language—the "p" word (proves) should not be used even with results that are replicated; rather, good phrases include things like "this increases our confidence in the ability to generalize," or "with replication, we are in a stronger position to make generalizations or causal inferences."

## Self-Replication

Researchers can strengthen the generalizability of their own findings by replicating their own work, called **self-replication**. In some fields, this is required to demonstrate the results were not due to some quirk. Replicating one's own study with a second study in the same article is one way replication is achieved. The number of experiments in one article was up to three by 1998 for one social psychology journal.[65] This also fits into a systematic program of work that is encouraged by academic departments. For example, a program of work on moral judgment in journalism started with an experiment that manipulated whether journalists saw photographs or not when making ethical decisions and found that the photographs improved the quality of their moral judgment.[66] The main results were replicated in a second experiment in the same paper. Those experiments raised more questions about the process of journalists' moral decision making, so research continued to explore that topic, following it with three studies of whether race made a difference,[67] and another one that used audiences rather than journalists.[68] All these experiments tested whether photographs improved moral judgment and found that they did. Consistent results across five studies using students, professionals, and audiences of different races, in different parts of the country, at different times, gives us confidence to make a more firm assertion about the ability of photographs to elevate the quality of reasons used to make ethical decisions.

## Exact vs. Conceptual Replication

One important thing to note is that none of these follow-up studies were **exact** or **direct replications** of the first one—that is, they did not duplicate the original methods and procedures exactly. That type of replication is not as valued or recommended in the social sciences as it is in other fields such as medicine.[69] Exact replications can even be impossible in social science, as *something* must be different, such as the subjects.[70] Rather, replications are expected to also *extend* a study in some theoretically meaningful way. These are called **conceptual replications**,[71] or reproductions,[72] with key features deliberately varied, such as the setting, subjects, variables, or interventions. Conceptual replications test the theory of a study, while direct or exact replications test its operationalization. Conceptual replications extend an experiment's generalizability,[73] thus, the kind this chapter focuses on. In the previous example, examining how race communicated via photographs affected moral judgment of journalism students was a first step in extending the findings about effects of photographs. The study after that did the same but by investigating in-group/out-group processes using Black journalism students, because race was expected to work differently for minorities, which it did. The next one extended it from journalism students to professional journalists of three different races, and also examined the mediating role of empathy. The last one moved away from journalists to news audiences and examined how cognitive elaboration worked. These studies represent a systematic progression of replication by logically expanding beyond one type of subject and also incorporating different concepts theorized to be causal mechanisms in the process of moral judgment when photographs are involved. Causal mechanisms are the variables or pathways through which some outcome occurs; they are what links some cause to an effect. In this case, race, empathy, and elaboration were the causal mechanisms that led to better moral judgment (the outcome or effect) from seeing photographs (the cause). Recall in chapter 1 the discussion of explanations for why some effect occurs. A good example of replication by systematic extension of findings to different populations, in different settings at different times, and the incorporation of different theoretical concepts as causal mechanisms is found in Stanley Milgram's book about his series of experiments on obedience to authority, which was covered in chapter 2.[74]

## Multiple Experiments

Many social science experiments are reported as single studies, but some disciplines are more apt to report multiple experiments in one article. For example, social psychology is moving toward multiple studies in one paper as a means of evidence of replicability.[75] Multiple experiments are also becoming more common in communication, with successive experiments systematically eliminating alternative explanations.[76] Fiske recommends researchers publish multiple studies in one paper.[77] And while it may seem more helpful to one's career trajectory to publish more articles by splitting up studies into one per paper, it aids the cause of generalizability to report multiple experiments in one paper, as consistent findings provide stronger reinforcement for conclusions. One example is an article by Schweizer,[78] who reports in one paper the results of two experiments designed to assess the effectiveness of teaching students a skill that promotes idea generation and discussion. The second experiment replicated the first one's results and extended them by determining how many classroom sessions were necessary for students to learn the technique.

It also makes sense to report more than one experiment in a single paper when one study raises questions or plausible alternative explanations for the results and a second experiment is needed to answer those questions or rule out the alternative explanations. By itself, the paper may not pass muster with journal reviewers without the additional experiment to explain findings and answer questions. An example of multiple experiments in one article is a paper that reports two experiments on the effects of harm and disgust on moral judgment in politics.[79] The second experiment was devised to test alternative explanations that arose in the first, in addition to replicating those results. It also introduced new political issues and so replicated results for three different issues. For more examples of replications, see More About box 5.4.

## External Replication

Replicating one's own work does help with making it generalizable, but it is also desirable to have results replicated by independent researchers—that is, by someone other than yourself, your coauthors, or even others at your own institution. This is known as **external replication**. Confidence is increased if an experiment can be replicated by outside researchers, independent of the first set, as it helps confirm that the previous results were not the result of a mistake, poor-quality work, or even outright fraud.[80] Some studies have found that when one or more of the authors on a replication were also involved in the original study, they were significantly more likely to reproduce the original findings than when outside researchers attempted replications.[81] Of course, there are plenty of reasons for this that do not point to nefarious activity. Nor does one failed replication necessarily mean the effect was false or the study a fraud. Rather, results are considered holistically, and when multiple replications show similar patterns or are close to the original study's results, they are considered successful.[82] When an external replication fails to reproduce the original's results, it could be because of too small a sample size, bad measures, experimenter effects, execution, or many other reasons. Rather than spelling doom, it encourages more study. This may be a sign that something new or interesting has been found; for example, if a political strategy has consistently worked but is suddenly not, this could be a sign that strategy should be updated rather than a sign that the experiment was flawed. Nonstatistically significant finds are still meaningful and should be reported.[i] It is too long to report here, but to see how researchers responded when external researchers failed to replicate their original findings, read Ebersole et al. (2017).[83]

In fact, it is common for results not to be replicated or to reproduce some results but not others. Some studies have found replication rates of 50% or lower.[84] In the example of research on photographs' ability to improve moral judgment, after five successful conceptual replications, one did not show the same thing.[85] That paper proposed theoretical reasons, backed up by empirical evidence, for why this happened. One thing that is *not* ethical to do is to fail to report or not attempt to publish failed replications. Such a lack of transparency or attempt to cover up unwanted results can result in the end of a promising research career, as some have taken it upon themselves to police the profession.[86]

Scientific knowledge is cumulative; it accrues over time across related studies. Thus, conceptual replication is important not just to generalizability but also to advance our understanding of important human phenomena. Social science research is about discovering as much as possible about human processes, not about supporting one's hypotheses at all costs.

---

[i] I would like to thank an anonymous reviewer for suggesting the addition of these last two observations.

# MORE ABOUT . . . BOX 5.4
## Examples of Replication Studies

**Krupnikov, Yanna, and Spencer Piston. 2015. "Accentuating the Negative: Candidate Race and Campaign Strategy."** *Political Communication* 32 (1): 152–173.

This study experimentally manipulated race and tone to see how voters responded to Black and White candidates' negative campaign ads. It reproduced the results of previous work and extended it by studying the interaction of race and negativity; the two had been considered independently in previous studies. The authors did a second experiment to test alternative explanations that arose in the first study and replicated their own results as well. This experiment used a nationally representative sample embedded in a survey.

**Camerer, Colin F., Anna Dreber, Eskil Forsell, Ho Teck-Hua, Jürgen Huber, Magnus Johannesson, Michael Kirchler, Johan Almenberg, Adam Altmejd, Taizan Chan, Emma Heikensten, Felix Holzmeister, Taisuke Imai, Siri Isaksson, Gideon Nave, Thomas Pfeiffer, Michael Razen, and Hang Wu. 2016. "Evaluating Replicability of Laboratory Experiments in Economics.** *Science* 351 (6280): 1433–1436.

The reason why this article has so many authors will be apparent once you learn that this study replicated the most important finding from eighteen different laboratory experiments in economics. They were able to reproduce findings of eleven of them (61%). They note the limitations include a smaller number of studies to be replicated than many other reproducibility projects. Details of all eighteen studies are not in the article but on a companion website.

**Nazarian, Deborah, and Joshua M. Smyth. 2010. "Context Moderates the Effects of an Expressive Writing Intervention: A Randomized Two-Study Replication and Extension."** *Journal of Social and Clinical Psychology* 29 (8): 903–929.

The two experiments reported in this article tested the effects of expressive writing by changing where subjects wrote—at home or in a lab—and the authority of the experimenter via how formally he or she was dressed. This study also speaks to the issue of ecological validity, or generalizability outside the laboratory, as it found that students did better when writing in a lab and adults did better when writing at home. The use of students in one experiment and adults in the other also aided the cause of generalizability to different populations.

One of the main goals of a well-written methods section is so others may replicate the study. Methods sections are like the recipe for an experiment, with enough detail that others should be able to reproduce a study without having to contact the original author. When methods and protocols are clear, complete, and precise, it is more likely that other researchers will be able to successfully replicate results because they will have all the necessary elements exactly the same. Another movement currently in progress is to make freely available one's data and the coding used to analyze it so that others may easily check the work. It has always been an ethical tenet that researchers make their data available to others who request it. The web is making this practice more widespread, as researchers can simply download the data rather than make requests of other researchers. More and more journals are encouraging authors to include not only the datasets and code but also stimuli and other components on their supplemental materials website. Some researchers even include them on their own websites or on academic social media sites like Researchgate.net and Academia.edu. While a few journals require it, most are still voluntary. Similarly, a few journals are including regular sections devoted to replications.[87]

## Triangulation

Another means of establishing the validity of some finding is by using both qualitative and quantitative methods. This is also important to generalizability. If findings from a lab experiment are also the conclusions of interviews, ethnographies, and other methods, that can have important implications for real-world relevance.[88] Fiske and others recommend field experiments as replications of lab experiments because of their high external validity.[89]

A final word on external validity concerns the use of pretests, a discussion started in chapter 4 that will be revisited later. In addition to the pros and cons outlined previously, experimental designs without pretests are preferred for reasons of external validity.[90] Because of the interaction of testing and treatment, exposing subjects to the test twice may sensitize them to the topic or have the opposite effect and diminish their sensitivity to it, reducing a treatment's effectiveness. Thus, results with subjects who have been tested more than once may not generalize to subjects who have not had multiple tests.[91]

This is not a complete list of all threats to external validity. Others expand on these basic threats with, for example, lack of message variance and message repetition, which involves giving subjects more than one version of a stimulus for each treatment level. By using just one stimulus, the only conclusion that can be reached is that exact stimulus had an effect, not that all stimuli of that type have an effect.[92] This will be discussed in more detail in chapter 9.

# INTERNAL VALIDITY

All the concerns about generalizability and ecological validity discussed thus far are of no consequence if the findings from an experiment are not accurate because of a problem with internal validity. Campbell and Stanley call it the "basic minimum" requirement for any experiment.[93] Internal validity is the primary strength of true experiments; no other method offers researchers as high a degree of internal control—that is, control over the causal mechanisms between conditions.[94] Internal validity goes to the heart of the cause and effect relationship—that what the experiment found to be the cause is actually responsible for the outcome rather than something else. In the trade-off between external and internal validity, experimenters usually choose internal validity.

## Three Basic Criteria

The three basic criteria for an experiment covered in chapter 1 speak directly to internal validity, as reviewed briefly: (1) that the cause comes before the effect, (2) that the cause and effect are related, and (3) that there are no other plausible alternative explanations for the effect. The first two are barely ever discussed in laboratory experiments; which came first is more a concern of field and natural experiments. For example, whether unemployment causes inflation or inflation causes unemployment is a chicken-and-egg-like question. If you cannot definitively say which came first, it is not internally valid. This is mostly a concern with Campbell and Stanley's three pre-experimental designs, quasi or natural experiments. But in laboratory or true experiments, researchers should ensure that subjects get the treatment or manipulation before measuring the outcome. The second criteria for internal validity, that the cause and effect be related, is illustrated by the example in chapter 1 about whether storks bring babies. Except perhaps to those living in Denmark in the 1930s, a relationship between storks and babies is obviously not logical, nor is it supported by any theory.[95] This is also why experimenters do not test hunches but must first conduct a literature review and establish theoretical and empirical links between any proposed cause and effect. Performing that task, detailed in chapter 3 on theory and literature, should quickly disabuse a researcher of spurious notions about cause and effect. Rather, it is the third criterion that occupies much of experimentalists' time: ensuring there are no confounding factors or plausible alternative explanations that account for the effect. Internal validity in experiments is achieved when there is tight management of all possible confounds and alternative plausible explanations, minimal bias and error, and strong controls in place. This is the key task that experimentalists will encounter related to internal validity.

While there are an unlimited number of confounds and other plausible explanations for an outcome in experimental studies, there is, unfortunately, no comprehensive list of them. Reviewers are expert at pointing out what they are, though. The trick is to identify them ahead of time, which is accomplished by thoroughly reviewing the literature and also by applying one's own expertise and common sense. One example of a possible confound in the studies on photographs' effect on moral judgment[96] was whether the people in the photographs were close up or far away. A thorough review of the literature resulted in evidence from the study of proxemics in nonverbal behavior, which showed that being close to others makes people believe they are more persuasive, credible, and sociable than does being farther away.[97] Had the studies not controlled for proximal distance by using pictures that were the same in terms of shot distance, the real cause of the bump in moral judgment could have been due to how close or far away people in the photographs were rather than what was being manipulated. Another example of this is in experiments that control for message length; we know that giving people more information can affect their knowledge levels, attitudes, and other outcome variables, so it is standard practice to keep the length of manipulated messages as similar as possible to control for this confound.[98]

## Random Assignment

The gold standard of random assignment also aids the cause of internal validity by making comparison groups as similar as possible. Thus, there should not be anything inherently different about one group that caused a treatment to work on one group and not the other. Therefore, we can assume that it was the treatment that caused the outcome. The benefits of random assignment cannot be stressed enough, and this will get its own chapter in chapter 7.

## Confounds

When possible confounds are only raised after a study has been conducted, this provides fodder for replications that extend a study, as described earlier in the external validity section. Such conceptual replications mainly for purposes of external validity also aid the cause of internal validity by ruling out confounding variables as plausible explanations. When a possible confound is identified, it is sometimes possible to rule out the plausible alternative explanation by doing additional analyses with the data the researcher already has. For example, a reviewer once questioned the way religiosity was measured when it was made up of three questions. The reviewer disagreed that one of the questions was a true measure of the concept and suggested it might have confounded the results. To see if this concern was indeed serious, the authors reanalyzed the data, eliminating the offending question and using only a two-item measure of religiosity. The results were the same. This satisfied the reviewer and the article was published. Another time, a reviewer was concerned that subjects had tried only to support their preexisting ethical decisions rather than seriously grapple with other points of view to come to a considered judgment as was proposed. The concerns were addressed by going back through the open-ended responses subjects had given and demonstrating that, indeed, they had considered arguments opposite to their own by counting the self-supporting and counterfactual arguments and reporting this, with examples. For the explanation that ended up in print, see How To Do It box 5.5.

**HOW TO DO IT 5.5**

Explaining Experimental Validity and Confounds

In the review process for this study, reviewers suggested the results might have been confounded by variables such as different degrees of violence in the images, the emotions they created in the viewers, or the seriousness of the crime depicted. In the response, the authors invoked both the controlled nature of experiments and also previous empirical evidence. Here is what ended up in the article:

"Because this was a controlled experiment, we can be sure that this effect was due to the only thing that was altered—the format of the visual. We can say for certain that it was not emotion, violent images, seriousness of the crime or some other variable because those were the same for all the subjects—all subjects saw all three stories. The videos were the same, with the only difference being in how many times subjects saw them, or if they saw a still image taken directly from each video."[99]

Later, the article addressed it again:

"We did not measure audiences' emotional responses to the stories because emotion has repeatedly been shown not to be a causal agent in moral judgment (Blanchette, Gavigan, & Johnston, 2014; Hauser, 2006)."

"Attribution of responsibility, crime severity, and other factors should be examined in future studies concerned with idiosyncrasies of issues; however, we note again that these or any other differences among the stories do not affect our main finding, which is the ability of still photographs over one-time video to improve moral judgment. We can be assured that still photographs caused higher levels of moral judgment compared with one-time video because that was the only thing that changed. All subjects received all three stories, so any differences due to the stories themselves were controlled because all subjects in the different conditions got all the exact same stories."[100]

**Meader, Aimee, Lewis Knight, Renita Coleman, and Lee Wilkins. 2015. "Ethics in the Digital Age: A Comparison of the Effects of Moving Images and Photographs on Moral Judgment."** *Journal of Media Ethics* **30 (4): 234–251.**

The most extensive list of threats to internal validity is outlined in Campbell and Stanley's little book and includes seven different classes of extraneous variables relevant to internal validity in true experiments.[ii] They are briefly described here, along with some practical applications.

## History

This refers to what happens in between the time a treatment is given to a subject and the outcome is measured. For example, if researchers are testing interventions designed to reduce fear of flying and a plane crashes during the study, participants might have more anxiety about flying; the intervention might have worked, but the plane crash

---

[ii]There is an eighth, which is related to quasi experimental designs. As true experiments are the focus of this book, this chapter reviews the seven related to true experiments.

compromised the validity of the experiment. History also becomes a concern when long-term effects are an important consideration, and the outcome may need to be measured more than once. For example, newly formed attitudes tend to decrease over time, and under some conditions, time lapses actually *increase* persuasive effects.[101] Studies interested in long-lasting persuasion and attitude formation find it important to measure effects after a delay, in which case events out of a researcher's control could threaten the validity of results. The longer the time lapse, the greater the threat.

In other cases, what happens preceding a treatment may influence the outcome. For example, an experiment that looks at how Muslims are framed in manipulated news stories may produce different results if a radicalized individual attacks a nightclub right before the experiment is conducted. Changes in attitudes may be due to the terrorist attack rather than the treatment.

Threats due to history can be controlled with the pretest–posttest control group design, as whatever events might cause a change in the treatment group would produce the same change in the control group. All groups should be run simultaneously so that whatever happens to one, happens to all. In addition, simultaneous sessions help control for differences due to time of day, day of the week, season, and other changes.[102] In many social science disciplines, history is not much of a problem, as researchers can control threats by exposing subjects to the manipulation and then immediately measuring their responses—for example, showing journalists photographs and immediately asking them to solve an ethical dilemma;[103] this fits with what would normally occur in newsrooms on tight deadlines. No delay occurred, so history could not have been a threat to internal validity.

## Maturation

This also is related to the passage of time but is specifically concerned with what happens to the *subject* over time, such as getting older, wiser, hungrier, more tired or bored, etc. Experiments on effective teaching methods can be spread out over weeks, months, semesters, or even a year. During this time, biological and psychological changes can occur in subjects, and that can be the cause of the outcome rather than the treatment. Even a study that takes too long to complete can result in subjects getting bored or fatigued, which may change their responses. Campbell and Stanley give examples of the cumulative effects of learning and pressure of the experience as being the cause of improvements rather than the educational intervention.[104]

## Testing

This refers to the problem discussed earlier about pretests, which are not only a threat to external validity but also to internal validity. When subjects are tested more than once, they tend to do better or worse, for reasons such as they learned how to take the test or grew bored, among other things. People routinely do better the second time they take personality, achievement, and intelligence tests[105] but show more prejudice on stereotyping tests.[106] All this can occur without any intervention whatsoever. Avoiding the use of pretests unless necessary is one way to circumvent this threat. When a pretest is necessary, using alternate but equivalent forms of the test for pre- and postsessions can help alleviate this concern.[107] Another way to lessen the threat of testing is by using **nonreactive or unobtrusive measures**, which are those that leave subjects unaware that they are being studied, unsuspecting of what is being measured, or unable to alter their responses, such as with measures of sweating, heart rate, or how long they spend looking at something as measured by eye tracking devices or web screen recording software. When subjects are aware that they are being studied and are able to guess the hypothesis, demand characteristics and social desirability come into play. Unobtrusive measures also can be devised so that while subjects know they are being studied, they do not know what the "right" answers are or the specific hypotheses of the study. In moral judgment research, for example, subjects know they are taking an "ethics test" but do not know the "right" answers unless they also know Kohlberg's moral development theory.[108] Subjects think the important question is what action they would take, whereas the important measure actually is how many statements they choose that represent higher levels of moral judgment. Many more examples of unobtrusive measures will be given in chapter 10. Observing subjects is probably the most popular unobtrusive measure—for example, recording which magazines subjects read while in a waiting room after receiving some treatment. Festinger and Carlsmith's[109] measure of cognitive dissonance was whether the subjects tried to convince others that the experiment was fun, interesting, and worthwhile, or whether they told the truth that it was boring and worthless. Another observation measure could be whether a subject puts a plastic cup in a recycling bin after receiving some message about the environment.

## Instrumentation

This threat involves issues with the actual instruments, such as galvanic skin response machines that measure the sweat on a subject's skin, often used to indicate psychological or physiological arousal. When machines break down or need to be recalibrated, this threatens internal validity because it may produce changes in the scores recorded. Another form of instrumentation is human—when people are used to observe behavior, score, or code something, they can vary in their judgment or standards can change. They can also get better with practice or tired over time. Campbell and Stanley[110] recommend randomly assigning observers and using each one for both experimental and control groups as well as **double blinding** them—that is, not letting either the subjects or the observers know who is getting the treatment so as not to bias the observers' ratings. There are also techniques to determine if standards are different for different scorers, or if standards have changed over the time the scoring is being done, called **interrater reliability**, which is explained in chapter 10. If observed outcomes can be unobtrusively recorded—for example with a video camera or web tracking software—then how similarly the two scorers are measuring things can be assessed.

### Statistical Regression

Also called **regression to the mean**, it represents a threat when extreme scores tend to revert to the mean of the group—for example, when the smartest students appear to be getting duller while the dullest students appear to be getting smarter. This occurs with the very highest and lowest scores, so researchers are advised not to select subjects for a study *because* they are particularly good or poor at something; they likely will be more average when tested again. So, for example, a teaching intervention that uses only students with the worst test scores will likely show a pseudo effect of the intervention rather than a real effect.[111] When subjects are chosen that represent the full range, the effects of regression to the mean by extreme scorers can be controlled by random assignment. Extreme scorers should be equally assigned to both treatment and control groups so that each group regresses to the mean equally.[112]

### Selection

Selection of subjects that results in biases also is controlled by random assignment; whatever differences there are should be equally distributed among the groups.[113] When random assignment is not possible—for example, when students self-select to be in a certain class—the study becomes a quasi experiment, and readers should refer to one of the many good books on this topic for advice on how to lessen this threat.

### Attrition

Also known as mortality, this is when subjects drop out of studies or do not answer all the questions. When the attrition rate is different for treatment and comparison groups, it can compromise validity. When there is systematic attrition—for example, if subjects drop out of the treatment group in higher rates than the control group—then any effects may be due to group differences rather than the treatment. Even if the groups had been equal before the study, dropouts can make them unequal. For example, subjects may drop out of an educational intervention because they do not think it is working for them, or out of an exercise program because they think it is too hard. A poststudy analysis of group equality will uncover this if it is a problem. Shortening the length of the study can help alleviate attrition concerns.

In summary, the most effective way to control for internal validity is by using randomization and designs with a control group.[114] Randomization includes not only randomly assigning subjects to condition but also randomly assigning as many other elements as possible—for example, randomizing the order of experimental sessions or which experimenters run which session if all groups cannot be tested at the same time. These will be discussed in more depth in chapter 7. Control groups have everything happen to them that the treatment groups have except the treatment; they are subject to the same threats of history, maturation, regression, testing, instrumentation, and attrition. If researchers can control these threats to internal validity, then an experimental design is said to be **rigorous,** meaning the most accurate, precise, or valid that one can design.

Readers will also no doubt realize some contradictions in this chapter—for example, that pretests present a threat to internal validity via testing effects but are one way to alleviate concerns about threats from history. As with all decisions regarding the design of an experiment, researchers must weigh the pros and cons, and carefully consider which issues represent the greatest threat to the validity of a particular experiment, and a well-articulated discussion of the trade-offs should be presented in the paper.

There are other more specific types of internal validity, such as construct validity, face validity, internal consistency and reliability, which will be dealt with in chapter 10. Next, this book turns to more specific decisions to be made on the type of design for an experiment—specifically, how many independent variables will be manipulated and how many each subject will get.

## Common Mistakes

- Designing experiments that are not as realistic as possible
- Not using subjects that are similar to those one intends to make logical inferences about
- Replicating others' findings without extending them in some theoretical way
- Failing to control confounding variables

## Test Your Knowledge

1. Lab experiments are usually weaker in _____ validity than in _____ validity.

   a. External, internal

   b. Internal, external

   c. Ecological, external

   d. Logical, statistical

2. Typically, lab experiments use random sampling in order to be generalizable.

   a. True

   b. False

3. The idea that reasonable conclusions can be drawn based on common sense without a mathematical calculation of the fit between a sample and a population is referred to as _____.

   a. Statistical inference

   b. Logical inference

   c. Nonsensical inference

   d. Replication

4. Repeating a study to test the theory while also extending it in some theoretically meaningful way is known as _____.

   a. Self-replication

   b. Direct replication

   c. External replication

   d. Conceptual replication

5. Basic criteria for internal validity are _____.

   a. The cause must precede the effect

   b. The cause and effect must be related

   c. There are no other plausible explanations for the effect

   d. All of these

6. Of the seven classes of extraneous variables that threaten internal validity, which one describes when people who are recording observations differ in their judgments or change their standards?

   a. Selection

   b. Attrition

   c. Regression to the mean

   d. Instrumentation

7. How does random assignment provide internal validity?

   a. By making samples randomly similar to each other.

   b. By sampling from the population to be generalized.

   c. By ensuring that each person or unit from a population has an equal chance of being chosen.

   d. By ensuring representativeness.

8. Of the seven classes of extraneous variables that threaten internal validity, which one describes when the smartest students appear to be getting duller, while the dullest students appear to be getting smarter?

   a. Selection

   b. Attrition

   c. Regression to the mean

   d. Instrumentation

9. Of the seven classes of extraneous variables that threaten internal validity, which one describes when subjects drop out of studies or do not answer all the questions?

   a. Selection

   b. Attrition

   c. Regression to the mean

   d. Instrumentation

10. Of the seven classes of extraneous variables that threaten internal validity, which one describes when students choose to be in a certain class?

   a. Selection

   b. Attrition

   c. Regression to the mean

   d. Instrumentation

**Answers**

| | | | |
|---|---|---|---|
| 1. a | 4. d | 7. a | 9. b |
| 2. b | 5. d | 8. c | 10. a |
| 3. b | 6. d | | |

## Application Exercises

1. Continue to develop your experiment by writing about how you will ensure external and internal validity in your study. Write one or two pages on how you will increase external validity by making your study more realistic and generalizable. Use the topics in this chapter as a guide. Write one or two more pages on how you will minimize threats to internal validity, specifically considering the seven threats described in the chapter. Also include a discussion of the trade-offs, as you can rarely have perfect internal and external validity. Which is more important, and what would you give up; why? Imagine reviewers have challenged you on these issues and respond to their concerns.

2. Find three published experiments in your field and write a one-page critique of each on how the authors addressed issues of internal and external validity. What trade-offs did they make? Was it convincing? Are there other arguments you would have used? Are there other threats they did not consider but should have?

## Suggested Readings

Chapter 2, "Statistical Conclusion Validity and Internal Validity," and part of chapter 3, "External Validity," pp. 83–102, in Shadish, W. R., T. D. Cook, and D. T. Campbell. 2002. *Experimental and Quasi-Experimental Designs for Generalized Causal Inference.* Belmont, CA: Wadsworth. You do not need to read the Construct Validity section yet; that will come in the next chapter.

For a good example of experimental realism, read Iyengar, Shanto, and Donald R. Kinder. 1987. *News That Matters: Television and American opinion.* Chicago: University of Chicago Press. These studies simulate actual national news broadcasts as much as possible.

Stoker, Gerry. 2010. "Exploring the Promise of Experimentation in Political Science: Micro-Foundational Insights and Policy Relevance." *Political Studies* 58: 300–319. This paper discusses issues of validity in arguing for more experimentation in political science, but the arguments are applicable to all of social science.

## Notes

1. John A. Courtright, "Rationally Thinking About Nonprobability," *Journal of Broadcasting & Electronic Media* 40, no. 3 (1996): 414.

2. D. T. Campbell and J. C. Stanley, *Experimental and Quasi-Experimental Designs for Research.* (Chicago: Rand McNally, 1963).

3. E. A. Stuart et al., "Estimates of External Validity Bias When Impact Evaluations Select Sites Purposively." Paper presented at the Proceedings from the Society for Research on Annual Effectiveness (Washington, DC, Spring 2012).

4. Rebecca B. Morton and Kenneth C. Williams, *Experimental Political Science and the Study of*

*Causality: From Nature to the Lab* (New York: Cambridge University Press, 2010).

5. Murray Webster and Jane Sell, *Laboratory Experiments in the Social Sciences* (Amsterdam: Elsevier, 2007).

6. Morton and Williams, *Experimental Political Science.*

7. Maria Jimenez-Buedo and Francesco Guala, "Artificiality, Reactivity, and Demand Effects in Experimental Economics," *Philosophy of the Social Sciences* 46, no. 1 (2016): 3–23.

8. Renita Coleman and Esther Thorson, "The Effects of News Stories That Put Crime and Violence into Context: Testing the Public Health Model of Reporting," *Journal of Health Communication* 7, no. 4 (2002): 401–426.

9. Campbell and Stanley, *Experimental and Quasi-Experimental Designs,* 17.

10. Morton and Williams, *Experimental Political Science*; Campbell and Stanley, *Experimental and Quasi-Experimental Designs.*

11. Morton and Williams, *Experimental Political Science*, 253.

12. Elizabeth Tipton, "How Generalizable Is Your Experiment? An Index for Comparing Experimental Samples and Populations," *Journal of Educational and Behavioral Statistics* 39, no. 6 (2014): 478–501.

13. Roger Kirk, *Experimental Design: Procedures for the Behavioral Sciences,* 4th ed. (Thousand Oaks, CA: Sage, 2013).

14. Mirae Kim and Gregg G. Van Ryzin, "Impact of Government Funding on Donations to Arts Organizations: A Survey Experiment," *Nonprofit and Voluntary Sector Quarterly* 43, no. 5 (2014): 910–925.

15. Campbell and Stanley, *Experimental and Quasi-Experimental Designs.*

16. Morton and Williams, *Experimental Political Science.*

17. Campbell and Stanley, *Experimental and Quasi-Experimental Designs*, 19.

18. Ibid.

19. Annie Lang, "The Logic of Using Inferential Statistics with Experimental Data From Nonprobability Samples: Inspired by Cooper, Dupagne, Potter, and Sparks," *Journal of Broadcasting and Electronic Media* 40, no. 3 (Summer 1996): 422–430; Courtright, "Rationally Thinking About Nonprobability"; Michael D. Basil, "The Use of Student Samples in Communication Research," *Journal of Broadcasting and Electronic Media* 40, no. 3 (Summer 1996): 431–440.

20. Campbell and Stanley, *Experimental and Quasi-Experimental Designs.*

21. Tipton, "How Generalizable Is Your Experiment?"

22. For example, see Elizabeth Tipton, "Stratified Sampling Using Cluster Analysis: A Balanced-Sampling Strategy for Improved Generalizations from Experiments," *Evaluation Review* 37 (2014): 109–139; E. A. Stuart, "Matching Methods for Causal Inference: A Review and a Look Forward," *Statistical Science* 25 (2010): 1–21; Stuart et al., "Estimates of External Validity Bias."

23. L. V. Hedges and C. A. O'Muircheartaigh, "Improving Generalizations from Designed Experiments," (Evanston, IL: Northwestern University, 2011). Quoted in Tipton, 2014.

24. Tipton, "How Generalizable Is Your Experiment?"

25. David Freedman, Robert Pisani, and Roger Purves, *Statistics*, 4th ed. (New York: Norton, 2007), 335.

26. William R. Shadish, Thomas D. Cook, and Donald T. Campbell, *Experimental and Quasi-Experimental Designs for Generalized Causal Inference* (Belmont, CA: Wadsworth Cengage Learning, 2002), 342.

27. Ibid., 248.

28. For example, see Edmund J. Malesky, Dimitar D. Gueorguiev, and Nathan M. Jensen, "Monopoly Money: Foreign Investment and Bribery in Vietnam, a Survey Experiment," *American Journal of Political Science* 59, no. 2 (2015): 419–439.

29. Lang, "The Logic of Using Inferential Statistics."

30. Malesky, Gueorguiev, and Jensen, "Monopoly Money."

31. Ibid., 426–427.

32. Shadish, Cook, and Campbell, *Experimental and Quasi-Experimental Designs,* 373.

33. Ibid., 23.

34. Ibid., 348.

35. P. Rossi, M. Lipsey, and H. Freeman, *Evaluation: A Systematic Approach,* 7th ed. (Thousand Oaks, CA: Sage, 2004).

36. Shadish, Cook, and Campbell, *Experimental and Quasi-Experimental Designs,* 355.

37. Eric Kramon, "Where Is Vote Buying Effective? Evidence from a List Experiment in Kenya," *Electoral Studies* 44 (2016): 397–408.

38. For examples, see Arnstein Øvrum and Elling Bere, "Evaluating Free School Fruit: Results from a Natural Experiment in Norway with Representative Data," *Public Health Nutrition* 17, no. 6 (2014): 1224–1231.

39. Shadish, Cook, and Campbell, *Experimental and Quasi-Experimental Designs*.

40. Kimberly Klaiman, David L. Ortega, and Cloé Garnache, "Perceived Barriers to Food Packaging Recycling: Evidence from a Choice Experiment of US Consumers," *Food Control* 73 (2017): 291–299.

41. Shadish, Cook, and Campbell, *Experimental and Quasi-Experimental Designs*.

42. Arjan Verschoor, Ben D'Exelle, and Borja Perez-Viana, "Lab and Life: Does Risky Choice Behaviour Observed in Experiments Reflect That in the Real World?" *Journal of Economic Behavior & Organization* 128 (2016): 134–148.

43. Ibid., 136.

44. Alese Wooditch, Lincoln B. Sloas, and Faye S. Taxman, "A Multiside Randomized Block Experiment on the Seamless System of Care Model for Drug-Involved Probationers," *Journal of Drug Issues* 47, no. 1 (2017): 50–73.

45. For example, see Malcolm Fairbrother, "Geoengineering, Moral Hazard, and Trust in Climate Science: Evidence from a Survey Experiment in Britain," *Climatic Change* 139, no. 3/4 (2016): 477–489; Mogens Jin Pedersen and Justin M. Stritch, "Internal Management and Perceived Managerial Trustworthiness," *The American Review of Public Administration* (2016): 1–20.

46. For example, see Øvrum and Bere, "Evaluating Free School Fruit"; Rosie Campbell and Philip Cowley, "What Voters Want: Reactions to Candidate Characteristics in a Survey Experiment," *Political Studies* 62, no. 4 (2013): 745–765; Tianguang Meng, Jennifer Pan, and Ping Yang, "Conditional Receptivity to Citizen Participation," *Comparative Political Studies* (2014): 1–35; Klaiman, Ortega, and Garnache, "Perceived Barriers to Food Packaging"; M. L. Loureiro and W. J. Umberger, "A Choice Experiment Model for Beef: What U.S. Consumer Responses Tell Us About Relative Preferences for Food Safety, Country-of-Origin Labeling and Traceability," *Food Policy* 32, no. 4 (2007): 496–514.

47. For examples, see Claire A. Dunlop and Claudio M. Radaelli, "Teaching Regulatory Humility:

Experimenting with Student Practitioners," *Politics* 36, no. 1 (2016): 79–94; Jin Huang et al., "Individual Development Accounts and Homeownership Among Low-Income Adults With Disabilities: Evidence From a Randomized Experiment," *Journal of Applied Social Science* 10, no. 1 (2016): 55–66; Wooditch, Sloas, and Taxman, "A Multiside Randomized Block Experiment."

48. Lang, "The Logic of Using Inferential Statistics."

49. Ibid.

50. Courtright, "Rationally Thinking About Nonprobability."

51. Lang, "The Logic of Using Inferential Statistics."

52. Ibid.

53. Basil, "The Use of Student Samples."

54. Joanne M. Miller, "Examining the Mediators of Agenda Setting: A New Experimental Paradigm Reveals the Role of Emotions," *Political Psychology* 28, no. 6 (2007): 689–717.

55. Basil, "The Use of Student Samples."

56. Shadish, Cook, and Campbell, *Experimental and Quasi-Experimental Designs*.

57. B. G. Cook, M. Tankersley, and T. J. Landrum, "Determining Evidence-Based Practices in Special Education," *Exceptional Children* 75 (2009): 365–383.

58. S. Schmidt, "Shall We Really Do It Again? The Powerful Concept of Replication Is Neglected in the Social Sciences," *Review of General Psychology* 13 (2009): 7.

59. Matthew C. Makel et al., "Replication of Special Education Research: Necessary But Far Too Rare," *Remedial and Special Education* 37, no. 3 (2016): 1–8; ibid.

60. Gary King, "Replication, Replication," *PS: Political Science and Politics* 28, no. 4 (1995): 444–452.

61. Susan T. Fiske, "How to Publish Rigorous Experiments in the 21st Century," *Journal of Experimental Social Psychology* 66 (2016): 145–147.

62. Makel et al., "Replication of Special Education Research."

63. Matthew C. Makel and Jonathan A. Plucker, "Facts Are More Important Than Novelty: Replication in the Education Sciences," *Educational Researcher* 43 (2014): 304–316.

64. Matthew C. Makel, Jonathan A. Plucker, and B. Hegarty, "Replications in Psychology Research: How Often

Do They Really Occur?" *Perspectives on Psychological Science* 7 (2012): 537–542.

65. S. A. Haslam and C. McGarty, "100 Years of Certitude? School Psychology, the Experimental Method, and the Management of Scientific Uncertainty," *British Journal of Social Psychology* 40 (2001): 1–21.

66. Renita Coleman, "The Effect of Visuals on Ethical Reasoning: What's a Photograph Worth to Journalists Making Moral Decisions?" *Journalism and Mass Communication Quarterly* 83, no. 4 (Winter 2006): 835–850. I use examples from my own work not because they are paragons of excellence in experimental design but because I know the backstory and reasoning process behind them and can explain it from a firsthand perspective.

67. Renita Coleman, "Race and Ethical Reasoning: The Importance of Race to Journalistic Decision Making," *Journalism and Mass Communication Quarterly* 80, no. 2 (2003): 295–310; Renita Coleman, "Color Blind: Race and the Ethical Reasoning of African Americans on Journalism Dilemmas," *Journalism and Mass Communication Quarterly,* 88, no. 2 (Summer 2011): 337–351; Renita Coleman, "The Moral Judgment of Minority Journalists: Evidence from Asian American, Black, and Hispanic Professional Journalists," *Mass Communication and Society* 14, no. 5 (September-October2011): 578–599.

68. Aimee Meader et al., "Ethics in the Digital Age: A Comparison of the Effects of Moving Images and photographs on Moral Judgment," *Journal of Media Ethics* 30, no. 4 (2015): 234–251.

69. Shadish, Cook, and Campbell, *Experimental and Quasi-Experimental Designs,* 342; Makel et al., "Replication of Special Education Research"; Fiske, "How to Publish Rigorous Experiments."

70. Christian S. Crandall and Jeffrey W. Sherman, "On the Scientific Superiority of Conceptual Replications for Scientific Progress," *Journal of Experimental Social Psychology* 66 (2016): 93–99.

71. Ibid.; Makel et al., "Replication of Special Education Research"; Makel et al., "Facts Are More Important Than Novelty"; Makel et al., "Replications in Psychology Research."

72. B. D. McCullough, Kerry Anne McGeary, and Teresa D. Harrison, "Lessons from the JMCB Archive,"

*Journal of Money, Credit, and Banking* 38, no. 4 (2006): 1093–1107.

73. Crandall and Sherman, "On the Scientific Superiority."

74. Stanley Milgram, *Obedience to Authority: An Experimental View* (New York: Harper & Row, 1974).

75. Fiske, "How to Publish Rigorous Experiments."

76. Esther Thorson, Robert H. Wicks, and Glenn Leshner, "Experimental Methodology in Journalism and Mass Communication Research," *Journalism and Mass Communication Quarterly* 89, no. 1 (2012): 112–124.

77. Fiske, "How to Publish Rigorous Experiments."

78. Tim Schweizer, "Introducing Idea Mapping into the Business Curriculum: Results from Two Experiments," *The International Journal of Technology, Knowledge and Society* 7, no. 1 (2011): 190–200.

79. Pazit Ben-Nun Bloom, "Disgust, Harm and Morality in Politics," *Political Psychology* 35, no. 4 (2014): 495–513.

80. Makel et al., "Replication of Special Education Research"; Makel et al., "Facts Are More Important Than Novelty"; Makel et al., "Replications in Psychology Research."

81. Ibid.

82. Crandall and Sherman, "On the Scientific Superiority."

83. Charles R. Ebersole et al., "Observe, Hypothesize, Test, Repeat: Luttrell, Petty and Xu (2017) Demonstrate Good Science," *Journal of Experimental Social Psychology* 69 (2017): 184–186.

84. J. P. A. Ioannidis, "Why Most Published Research Findings Are False," *PLoS Medicine* 2 (2005): 696–701; Paul H. P. Hanel and Katia C. Vione, "Do Student Samples Provide an Accurate Estimate of the General Public?" *PLoS ONE* 11, no. 12 (2016): 1–10.

85. Rebecca S. McEntee, Renita Coleman, and Carolyn Yaschur, "Comparing the Effects of Vivid Writing and Photographs on Moral Judgment in Public Relations," *Journalism and Mass Communication Quarterly* 94 no. 4 (2017): 1011–1030.

86. Fiske, "How to Publish Rigorous Experiments."

87. McCullough, McGeary, and Harrison, "Lessons from the JMCB Archive."

88. Eric M. Camburn et al., "Benefits, Limitations, and Challenges of Conducting Randomized Experiments

with Principals," *Educational Administration Quarterly* 52, no. 2 (2016): 187–220; J. A. Maxwell, "Causal Explanation, Qualitative Research, and Scientific Inquiry in Education," *Educational Researcher* 33, no. 2 (2004): 3–11.

89. J. K. Maner, "Into the Wild: Field Studies Can Increase Both Replicability and Real-World Impact," *Journal of Experimental Social Psychology* 66 (2016): 100–106; Fiske, "How to Publish Rigorous Experiments"; Camburn et al., "Benefits, Limitations, and Challenges."

90. Campbell and Stanley, *Experimental and Quasi-Experimental Designs.*

91. Kirk, *Experimental Design: Procedures for the Behavioral Sciences.*

92. Thorson, Wicks, and Leshner, "Experimental Methodology in Journalism."

93. Campbell and Stanley, *Experimental and Quasi-Experimental Designs*, 5.

94. Cengiz Erisen, Elif Erisen, and Binnur Ozkececi-Taner, "Research Methods in Political Psychology," *Turkish Studies* 13, no. 1 (2013): 13–33.

95. Gustav Fischer, "Ornithologische Monatsberichte," *Jahrgang* 44, no. 2 (1936).

96. Coleman: "Race and Ethical Reasoning"; "Color Blind: Race and the Ethical Reasoning of African Americans on Journalism Dilemmas"; "The Moral Judgment of Minority Journalists: Evidence from Asian American, Black, and Hispanic Professional Journalists."

97. Paul Ekman, Wallace V. Friesen, and Phoebe Ellsworth, *Emotion in the Human Face* (New York: Pergamon, 1972); A. Mehrabian: "Inference of Attitudes from the Posture, Orientation, and Distance of a Communicator," *Journal of Consulting and Clinical Psychology* 32, no. 3 (June 1968): 296–308; "Some Referents and Measures of Nonverbal Behavior," *Behavioral Research Methods and Instrumentation* 1 (1969): 213–217; *Silent Messages* (Belmont, CA: Wadsworth, 1971); *Nonverbal Communication* (Chicago: Aldine/Atherton, 1972); J. K. Burgoon, T. Birk, and M. Pfau, "Nonverbal Behaviors, Persuasion, and Credibility," *Human Communication Research* 17, no. 1 (Fall 1990): 140–169.

98. Thorson, Wicks, and Leshner, "Experimental Methodology in Journalism."

99. Meader et al., "Ethics in the Digital Age," 245.

100. Ibid., 247.

101. Alice H. Eagly and Shelly Chaiken, *The Psychology of Attitudes* (Fort Worth, TX: Harcourt Brace Jovanovich, 1993).

102. Campbell and Stanley, *Experimental and Quasi-Experimental Designs.*

103. Coleman, "The Effect of Visuals on Ethical Reasoning."

104. Campbell and Stanley, *Experimental and Quasi-Experimental Designs*, 8–9.

105. Anne Anastasi, *Differential Psychology*, 3rd ed. (New York: Macmillan, 1958); V. R. Cane and A. W. Heim, "The Effects of Repeated Testing: III. Further Experiments and General Conclusions," *Quarterly Journal of Experimental Psychology* 2 (1950): 182–195; C. Windle, "Test-Retest Effect on Personality Questionnaires," *Educational Psychology Measurement* 14 (1954): 617–633.

106. R. E. Rankin and D. T. Campbell, "Galvanic Skin Response to Negro and White Experimenters," *Journal of Abnormal and Social Psychology* 51 (1955): 30–33.

107. Campbell and Stanley, *Experimental and Quasi-Experimental Designs.*

108. Lawrence Kohlberg, *The Philosophy of Moral Development: Moral Stages and the Idea of Justice* (Cambridge, MA: Harper & Row, 1981); *The Psychology of Moral Development: The Nature and Validity of Moral Stages* (San Francisco: Harper & Row, 1984).

109. L. Festinger and J. M. Carlsmith, "Cognitive Consequences of Forced Compliance," *Journal of Abnormal and Social Psychology* 58, no. 2 (1959): 203–210.

110. Campbell and Stanley, *Experimental and Quasi-Experimental Designs.*

111. Ibid.

112. Ibid.

113. Ibid.

114. Ibid.

# FACTORIAL DESIGNS

*Needless complexity seldom makes for better experimental research.*[1]

**—Diana Mutz**

## LEARNING OBJECTIVES

- Identify single-factor and factorial designs.

- Diagram an experiment using factorial notation and design tables.

- Explain the differences among between- and within-subjects designs, mixed and incomplete factorials.

- Create an experiment and explain the use of factors and how subjects are assigned.

- Plan how to implement a control group.

In chapter 4, this text discussed the different kinds of experiments in broad strokes, including natural and field experiments, true and quasi experiments, and the typologies such as the pretest–posttest control group design and Solomon four-group design. This chapter hones in on one type of experiment—the true or laboratory experiment—and drills down into more specific decisions about designing it. Specifically, this chapter looks at the number of factors in an experiment, how subjects are used in different designs, and control groups. When reading this chapter, keep in mind the advice in the opening quote, as things can get complicated quickly.

# SINGLE-FACTOR DESIGNS

*Factor* is another word for the independent variable that is manipulated—that is, the treatment of interest, or the thing deliberately changed in a true experiment. So far, this book has stressed the importance of manipulating one thing that is the independent variable of interest, whatever is hypothesized to cause a change in some outcome or have an effect on some dependent variable. When there is only one factor in an experiment, it is called a **single-factor**, **one-factor**, or **one-way design**.[2] For example, in a study of news stories, the factor to be manipulated might be how stories are framed or the angle that they use. In an interpersonal communication study, the factor of interest might be lying. In a psychology study, researchers could be interested in people's feelings of insecurity. In a political science experiment, the factor may be political position. Framing, lying, political position, and insecurity are the theoretical concepts considered to be the factors.

For any factor, there must be two or more **levels**, or different discrete values of each.[3] In a study of news frames, one researcher[4] studied two levels: objective and advocacy frames. He defined advocacy frames as one-sided stories that gave the perception of consensus, and objective frames as stories written as two-sided, detached news stories that did not give a perception of consensus. In a study of insecurity, researchers used two levels of the factor—high or none—by having subjects either write about their financial futures (creating high insecurity) or write about listening to music, a neutral topic not expected to create any feelings of insecurity.[5] A political science study used two levels of political position by labeling one position as liberal and another as conservative.[6]

Three and even four levels of a factor are also common. For instance, in a study of lying, researchers used three levels: lying by omission, truthful statements that were misleading, and the truth.[7] It is unusual to see more than this because too many can make a study unwieldy. It is more common to conduct another experiment if more than a few factors with many levels are investigated.

# FACTORIAL DESIGNS

The single-factor experiment is one of the simplest designs and is a good way to begin learning to do experiments. In reality, however, most experiments manipulate more than one independent variable at a time, making it a **factorial design**. Factorial designs look at the effect of more than one variable at the same time but still independently of each other. This is a more efficient method of testing hypotheses, as two or more things can be studied at one time instead of having to conduct multiple separate experiments.[8] Most experiments were single-factor designs up until Ronald Fisher started arguing for multiple factors being more economical, coining the term *factorial* in his book *Design of Experiments*.[9] Campbell and Stanley call the one-variable-at-a-time approach ineffective and a "blunt tool."[10] The value added by a factorial design is that it not only allows researchers to see what happens when each of the factors is changed independently but also allows them to see what happens when the factors are combined. This ability to look at how phenomena depend on the joint actions of two or more variables represents the complex world more realistically, as many outcomes are produced by several factors at a time.[11]

For example, when people see a public service announcement (PSA) on TV, they typically are influenced by a variety of characteristics of the PSA. In a study on PSAs about HIV/AIDS, researchers examined three of those things, represented by the following factors: (1) the quality of the argument in the ad, with the levels being a strong or weak argument; (2) how personally relevant the subject of HIV/AIDS was to each subject (high/low); and (3) two different types of ad formats, one that used a narrative storyline and one that relied on statistical data.[12] The results showed that strong arguments were significantly better than weak ones in changing people's attitudes toward and intentions to use condoms, but that ad format did not matter; the narrative and statistical formats worked about the same. Also, subjects who said HIV/AIDS was more relevant to them personally were more likely to intend to use condoms. These three findings are the **main effects**—that is, the ability for the different levels in one factor alone to cause a change in the outcome variables.[13] It represents the difference between *levels* of one factor and has nothing to say about any other factor. In the prior example, strong arguments produced changes in subjects' attitudes and intention when weak arguments did not; thus, there was a main effect of argument strength. There was also a main effect of personal relevance, with high relevance being more effective than low relevance. But there was no main effect of ad format; regardless of whether the ad was in narrative or statistical format, the effect on the outcome was the same.

The study in this example used three factors, also called a three-way design. Experiments with two factors are called two-way designs and are the simplest version of a factorial experiment, containing two factors with two levels each. Terms for the number of factors in an experiment are intuitive—four-way for four factors, etc. However, four-way designs and higher are rare and more complicated to analyze and interpret, so they are not found as often.

## Main Effects and Interactions

Several outcomes are possible with a factorial design: the main effect of each of the factors by itself, described previously, and the effect of the two or more factors in tandem—that is, if the effect of one factor *changes* depending on the other.[14] When the outcome of one factor depends on another, this is known as an **interaction effect**. In other words, the effects of two factors acting in combination could not be predicted from knowing the effects of each one separately.[15] An interaction is between factors, not levels, the way a main effect is. An easy way to think about this is with diet and exercise being two factors that affect your weight. If changing your diet alone affects your weight, that is a main effect; if changing your exercise program alone affects your weight, that is a main effect. When both diet and exercise are changed at the same time, there can be an interaction—for example, if you only lose weight when you eat a low-fat diet and also exercise for three more days a week. In the study of HIV/AIDS messages described earlier, there was an interaction effect where strong arguments and low personal relevance together had an effect. To report an interaction, you first say which of the factors interacted with each other and then go on to describe the levels of each factor that produced the effect. For example, the HIV/AIDS study would say something like, "The factors of argument strength and personal relevance interacted. For subjects who found HIV/AIDS to be of little personal relevance, strong arguments were significantly better at encouraging them to use condoms."[16] This study shows the benefits of studying three factors in one experiment; the researchers would not have known that strong arguments work for people with low personal relevance had they studied argument strength in one study and relevance in another.

A factorial design can result in different combinations of outcomes:

- Significant main effects for all the factors but no interaction effect

- Significant main effects for one or some of the factors but not all of them, with either a significant or nonsignificant interaction

- A significant interaction but no main effects[17]

Campbell and Stanley[18] give an example of a hypothetical study of three different teacher personality types as one factor, and three different teaching methods as the other factor. If all three personalities and methods are equally effective, there would be no main effects for any of them; that is, none of the different levels of the factors are significantly better than any others within that factor. But the teaching method and teacher personalities could interact so that, for example, the spontaneous teachers do better with group discussion than with tutorials.

In many studies, the interaction effect is really what researchers are interested in. For example, in a health communication study, researchers point out that framing messages differently has little effect,[19] saying that this may be because people's assessments of risk need to be considered along with framing effects. This study is specifically designed to examine the interaction of framing and risk assessment, and is less interested in the main effects of either factor, primarily because the main effects are already known.[20]

When conducting a factorial design, hypotheses should be predicted for each factor independently (the main effects), and either a hypothesis or a research question (RQ) posed for each of the possible interactions. For example, a study with two factors such as the teaching method and teacher personality study will have two hypotheses that predict main effects—one for teacher personality and one for teaching methods. It will also have a third hypothesis or RQ about the interaction between the two factors—that teacher personality and teaching method will interact. If there is not enough evidence to make a prediction for possible interaction effects, researchers typically ask an RQ; here is an example of one phrased in narrative instead of a formal RQ. It is from a study that looked at whether different types of warnings could prevent people from buying accessories like wireless speakers that were incompatible with their electronic devices like cell phones; in this field, warning messages are called a "nudge":

> The study also tested for interaction effects between the socio-demographic variables (age and education) and the experimental treatments (warning message . . .). In other words, if there were an effect of age and education on the purchase of incompatible products, would this effect be the same in all experimental conditions? Or could it be that this effect is increased (or reduced) in the presence of a given type of nudge? Since it is difficult to predict the direction and magnitude of these interaction effects, this part of the investigation was exploratory and not guided by specific hypotheses.[21]

Alternately, a formal RQ could be written:

> RQ: Is there an interaction between sociodemographics (age and education) and warning message style (traditional, emotive, no warning)?

In another example, using a study of framing health messages and the level of risk people had for contracting the human papillomavirus (HPV), researchers were mainly interested in how risk and framing depended on each other, so they proposed two hypotheses that only predicted interactions; there were no predictions of main effects.[22] They also had enough evidence to make predictions of direction for the interaction effects. The italicized words (mine) represent the level of each factor predicted to interact.

"H1: When parents perceive their children to be at *low risk* of contracting HPV infections, a *loss-framed* (vs. gain-framed) message will induce greater intentions to vaccinate their children (a) free of cost and (b) with cost."

"H2: When parents perceive their children to be at *high risk* of contracting HPV infections, a *gain-framed* (vs. loss-framed) message will induce greater intentions to vaccinate their children (a) free of cost and (b) with cost."[23]

To put it another way, low-risk people are expected to have greater intentions to vaccinate when they see loss-framed messages, and high-risk people when they see gain-framed messages.

I recommend not getting carried away with too many factors or too many levels of each factor, because the experiment can become so complex that it gets unwieldy on a number of fronts. For example, the number of interactions goes up exponentially with each factor. In an experiment with two factors, there is one possible interaction (Factor 1 with 2). But add a third factor and there is a possibility of four interactions (Factor 1 with 2; Factor 1 with 3; Factor 2 with 3; and between all three, Factors 1, 2, and 3). Experiments with ten factors at two levels produces $2^{10} = 1,024$ combinations! And it can get tricky to interpret the meaning of interactions where there are more than two factors.[24] It is better to control all other variables that might affect the outcome and manipulate them in different studies.

In addition to the number of interactions, designs with multiple factors and multiple levels of each require creating more **stimuli**, which are the way treatments are conveyed—for example, through messages, advertisements, or teaching technique. In one political communication study, the researcher had to write 256 press releases because the study used five factors with two to four levels for each.[25] Fortunately, the press releases were short.

Not only are the number of stimuli an issue, the number of subjects needed also increases, which will be covered in a later chapter. Interactions may call for larger sample sizes because they are harder to detect than main effects.[26] Factorial designs can require fewer subjects than separate single-factor studies if each subject is exposed to both factors,[27] but the benefits decrease at a certain point because of the need to perform multiple statistical tests, making it harder to find significance unless even more subjects are added.[28] In short, it can be better to design several sequential experiments instead of trying to examine too much in one study. Two, three, or four factors are the most commonly used factorial designs.[29]

## Factorial Notation

When a factorial design is used, it is standard practice to refer to it using **factorial notation**—for example, as a 2 x 2 design, a 3 x 3 design, or a 2 x 2 x 3, with the "x" pronounced "by" as in "two by two." Each number refers to a factor, so the number of

# MORE ABOUT . . . BOX 6.1
## Factorial Notation

In factorial notation, the number of numbers tells how many factors or variables are in the experiment. The value of the numbers tells how many levels of the factor there are. Table 6.1 explains some of the most common factorial designs.

| Design notation | The number of numbers tells how many factors | The first number tells how many levels of the first factor | The second number tells how many levels of the second factor | The third number tells how many levels of the third factor | Multiplying gives the number of cells |
|---|---|---|---|---|---|
| 2 x 2 | 2 numbers = 2 factors or IVs | The first factor/IV has 2 levels | The second factor/IV has 2 levels | N/A—there is no 3rd number | 2 x 2 = 4 cells |
| 2 x 3 | 2 numbers = 2 factors or IVs | The first factor/IV has 2 levels | The second factor/IV has 3 levels | N/A—there is no 3rd number | 2 x 3 = 6 cells |
| 3 x 3 | 2 numbers = 2 factors or IVs | The first factor/IV has 3 levels | The second factor/IV has 3 levels | N/A—there is no 3rd number | 3 x 3 = 9 cells |
| 2 x 2 x 2 | 3 numbers = 3 factors or IVs | The first factor/IV has 2 levels | The second factor/IV has 2 levels | The third factor/IV has 2 levels | 2 x 2 x 2 = 8 cells |
| 2 x 2 x 3 | 3 numbers = 3 factors or IVs | The first factor/IV has 2 levels | The second factor/IV has 2 levels | The third factor/IV has 3 levels | 2 x 2 x 3 = 12 |

**TABLE 6.1 ● COMMON FACTORIAL DESIGNS**

numbers tells how many factors there are. The value of each number refers to the number of levels of that factor. A 2 x 2 means there are two factors, and each factor has two levels. A 3 x 3 means there are two factors because there are only two numbers. Each of the two factors has three levels. A 2 x 2 x 3 means there are three factors, as indicated by the presence of three numbers, with the first and second factor having two levels each and the third factor having three levels. (See More About box 6.1, Factorial Notation.)

I know of no rules about the order in which the factors are represented in the notation; some researchers put the factors with more levels first, and others put the most important factors first. The beginning of an experiment's methods section should describe the design using this notation, usually incorporating the names of the factors and the levels in parentheses, like this:

- "We employed a 2 (argument quality: strong/weak) x 2 (personal relevance: high/low) x 2 (evidence: narrative/statistical) mixed factorial design."[30]

- "The second study used a 2 (crisis stage: during the crisis vs. postcrisis) x 2 (visual nonverbal cues: powerless vs. powerful) between-subjects factorial design."[31]

A single factor design can be reported like this:

- "Study 1 used a single-factor design in order to examine the impact of lowered and raised voice pitch on the perceptions of an organizational spokesperson."[32] In this example, the two levels of the single factor "voice pitch" are raised and lowered.

For more examples of how to report factorial designs, see How To Do It box 6.2.

---

## HOW TO DO IT 6.2

### Reporting Factorial Design

The portion of the methods section that describes the factorial design, levels of each, and the control group comes at the beginning of the methods section and is usually very brief, ranging from one or two sentences to a paragraph. It should include all of the following:

- Whether it is a single-factor or factorial design

- The number of factors and levels of each using factorial notation. If it is an incomplete factorial, that should be noted here.

- A short description of each level contained within parentheses immediately after the notation

- A description of how subjects are assigned—between-subjects, within-subjects, or as a mixed design

- Whether it has a control group or not and if so, what it is

- Also note the use of random assignment, the subject of the next chapter.

Not all studies follow this exact approach, with some describing these features in a more narrative style. However, it is always safe to do it this way.

Next are examples of how to describe the design, adapted from real studies in order to ensure that they include all of the previous points.

## Single-Factor Design 1

This was a single-factor, between-subjects experiment reflecting the five levels of internal management reviewed previously (goal, commitment, participation, feedback, reward). Each of the subjects was randomly assigned to one of five treatment groups or a control condition. Respondents in the treatment groups received the exact same information as those in the control groups. In addition, subjects in the treatment group were provided one line of text describing the managerial activities.

Adapted from: Pedersen, Mogens Jin, and Justin M. Stritch. 2016. "Internal Management and Perceived Managerial Trustworthiness: Evidence From a Survey Experiment." *The American Review of Public Administration* 48 (1): 67–81. https://doi.org/10.1177%2F0275074016657179.

## Single-Factor Design 2

We use a single-factor, between-subjects experiment with subjects randomly assigned to either two levels of the treatment of source of suggestions for citizen participation (formal institutions/Internet) or a control group. The control group received identical information with the exception of a treatment item concerning suggestions of residents from either formal institutions or the Internet.

Adapted from: Meng, Tianguang, Jennifer Pan, and Ping Yang. 2014. "Conditional Receptivity to Citizen Participation: Evidence From a Survey Experiment in China." *Comparative Political Studies* 50 (4): 399–433. https://doi.org/10.1177%2F0010414014556212.

## Between-Subjects Factorial 1

This experiment had a 3 (reminder frequency: no reminder, monthly, or weekly reminders) x 2 (method of donation: standing order or one-off donation) factorial design resulting in a total of six treatments. Subjects were randomly assigned to one of the six conditions.

(Note: This study did not specify a control group, but the no-reminder condition represents a baseline for that factor.)

Adapted from: Sonntag, Axel, and Daniel John Zizzo. 2015. "On Reminder Effects, Drop-Outs and Dominance: Evidence from an Online Experiment on Charitable Giving." *PLoS ONE* 10, no. 8 (August 7): 1–17.

## Between-Subjects Factorial 2

This study was a 2 x 3 between-subjects design with the first factor being school level of achievement (High vs. Low) with subjects randomly assigned to be instructed with valid experimental designs only (Valid) or with a mixture of confounded and valid designs (Invalid), and teaching only after the posttest (Control condition).

Adapted from: Lorch, Robert F. Jr., Elizabeth P. Lorch, Benjamin Dunhan Freer, Emily E. Dunlap, Emily C. Hodell, and William J. Calderhead. 2014. "Using Valid and Invalid Experimental Designs to Teach the Control of Variables Strategy in Higher and Lower Achieving Classrooms." *Journal of Educational Psychology* 106, no. 1 (February): 18–35.

*(Continued)*

(Continued)

## Within-Subjects Factorial

There were three within-subjects factors, each with two levels. The gaze cue factor manipulated the cue face's gaze direction; in the cued condition, the cue face looked toward the target face, while in the uncued condition the cue face looked away from the target face, toward the empty side of the screen. The emotion factor was the manipulation of the cue face's emotional expression (either positive or negative). The number of cues factor was the single or multiple cue face manipulation. There was one cue face in the single cue face condition. All three cue faces were presented in the multiple cue face condition.

(Note: Obviously, when all conditions are within-subjects, participants are assigned to all groups, and designating that they were "randomly assigned" is unnecessary. Also, no control group is designated, as this is one of those situations where a face cannot have no gaze direction. In this study, the groups are compared to each other rather than to a control group that got no treatment.)

From: Landes, Todd Larson, Yoshihisa Kashima, and Piers D. L. Howe. 2016. "Investigating the Effect of Gaze Cues and Emotional Expressions on the Affective Evaluations of Unfamiliar Faces." *PLoS ONE* 11, no. 9: 1–24.

## Mixed Factorial

This was a 4 x 2 x 2 mixed factorial design. The first within-subjects factor was issue (prostitution, drugs, elder abuse, domestic violence). All participants received all four dilemmas. The second within-subjects factor was decision type (run the photograph or use anonymous sources); all participants received two dilemmas that asked whether they should run a photograph after someone associated with the subject requested it not run, and two dilemmas that asked whether a story should run when there are many sources but none who would allow their names to be used. The between-subjects factor was photograph condition (with photograph/without photograph). Subjects were randomly assigned to either the treatment group, where they saw photographs with all four dilemmas, or the control group, where they did not see photographs.

*Adapted from:* Coleman, Renita. 2006. "The Effect of Visuals on Ethical Reasoning: What's a Photograph Worth to Journalists Making Moral Decisions?" *Journalism and Mass Communication Quarterly* 83, no. 4 (Winter): 835–50.

## Design Tables

Another way to represent a factorial design is with a **design table**. These are used to help in planning an experiment and do not seem to be reported in journal articles very often. Tables are also used to determine the characteristics of the stimuli and the number of subjects in each condition, represented by the "cells," or individual boxes. Table 6.2 represents a hypothetical 2 x 2 factorial design in which one factor is whether a person in a photograph is smiling or not, and the other is whether the camera distance is close-up or far away in what is known as a long shot. (The dependent variable, which is not

**TABLE 6.2 ● EXAMPLE OF A 2 X 2 FACTORIAL DESIGN TABLE**

| | | SMILING FACTOR | |
|---|---|---|---|
| | | Smiling | Not Smiling |
| CAMERA DISTANCE FACTOR | Close-Up | $n = 40$ | $n = 40$ |
| | Long Shot | $n = 40$ | $n = 40$ |

N = 160

shown in a table, could be something like how caring and compassionate subjects rate the person after seeing the photograph.) The rows and columns represent the factors; the cells represent one of the four distinct conditions, and this is described in the text of the article as: Smiling/Close-up; Smiling/Long shot; Not Smiling/Close-up; Not Smiling/Long shot. Inside the cells is the number of subjects in each condition, represented by the symbol $n$. The large N refers to the total number of subjects, the sum of all the cell $n$s. How to determine the number of subjects is covered in chapter 8. The number of conditions is formed by combinations of the levels of the independent variables and is found by multiplying the numbers of levels. In a $2 \times 2$ design, there are four conditions; in a $3 \times 2$ design, there are 6.

The cells of design tables can include other information, such as the marginal means of the groups once the study is conducted. Design tables can include as many levels of the two factors as needed simply by adding to the columns or rows, as shown in table 6.2. However, it can only accommodate a design with two factors because it is obviously two-dimensional; a three-dimensional table would be needed for three or more factors. It makes it easy to visualize how the number of subjects and stimuli increase as more levels are added.

**TABLE 6.3 ● EXAMPLE OF A 2 X 3 FACTORIAL DESIGN TABLE**

| | | SMILING FACTOR | |
|---|---|---|---|
| | | Smiling | Not Smiling |
| CAMERA DISTANCE FACTOR | Close-Up | $n = 40$ | $n = 40$ |
| | Medium Shot | $n = 40$ | $n = 40$ |
| | Long Shot | $n = 40$ | $n = 40$ |

N = 240

## Choosing a Design

There is nothing about a factorial design that makes it inherently better or more theoretical than a single-factor design. However, if the topic being studied is likely to be influenced by two or more factors at a time, and if those factors are likely to interact, then a factorial design is a better choice. Factorial designs are more common than single-factor designs in journals, and the advantages of being more economical as well as being able to test interactions makes them more compelling. Bausell[33] points out that the more treatment groups there are, the more subjects are needed and the lower the probability of reaching significance when multiple statistical tests are performed. He says, "I would always counsel beginning with a two-group design."[34] He then goes on to say that if the resources are available, more than two groups can add to theory by teasing out causal agents.

Researchers make decisions about which type of design to use based on evidence and what theory predicts about the concepts used as the dependent variable. Experiments that test two competing theories, or predictions that contradict each other, call for factorial designs. For example, in a study of how people learn about foreign nations from the media, two competing ideas about the causal mechanism of this type of influence were explored.[35] Logic can also dictate whether a study is a single-factor or factorial design. For example, a dissertation looked at a serious problem working journalists face in the current media environment: whether it is better to report a story quickly but with some inaccuracies, or to have it be accurate but lag behind all the other news organizations.[36] The speed vs. accuracy question lent itself to a single-factor design with two levels: fast with some inaccuracies, or slow but accurate. The reason for not splitting speed into two levels of speed (fast, slow) and accuracy (accurate, inaccurate) into separate levels is because the combinations of fast and accurate or slow and inaccurate are simply not realistic. Fast and accurate is obviously the ideal; if journalists could always produce this combination, there would be no problem. Slow and inaccurate is also an unlikely combination in the real world. If journalists are producing a story slowly, there is no excuse for inaccuracies; they have plenty of time to make sure information is right. Two of the four conditions that would result from a 2 x 2 factorial design simply did not make sense. Shadish, Cook, and Campbell call it a waste of resources "to test treatment combinations that are of no theoretical interest or unlikely to be implemented in policy."[37] This illustrates the decision-making process; articles do not always explain why the researcher chose a single-factor or factorial design. However, the choice should always be made for good practical or theoretical reasons that can be explained to readers. In addition, the number of subjects rises with every additional factor and level, raising the study's cost and time to conduct. Astronomical costs are a legitimate reason to limit factors. Practical things such as number of subjects, costs, study duration, and dropout rates, among others, are important to consider when choosing a design.[38] Because experiments are designed to answer very specific questions raised by theory, narrowly focused studies can do a better job at developing theory than including "everything but the kitchen sink." Common parlance is to say that including concepts X, Y, and Z were "beyond the scope of this study."

---

# STUDY SPOTLIGHT 6.3
## Example of a Single-Factor and Factorial Design in One Study

This study from organizational communication looked at how nonverbal expressions by spokespersons in times of crisis affect the public's perceptions of the company. The authors did two experiments, one using a single-factor design and the other a factorial design.

In the first study, the single factor was voice pitch of the spokesperson, which the researchers manipulated to be either high or low. Subjects were assigned to only one condition—that is, they heard either the high-pitched voice or the low-pitched voice, not both—making this a between-subjects design.

In the second experiment, the researchers manipulate a different form of nonverbal communication than the verbal cues of the first study—visual cues—and they add a second factor, the stage of the crisis. This was a 2 x 2 factorial design with the first factor being the crisis stage and the two levels being during the crisis and after the crisis. The second factor was nonverbal visual cues, with the two levels being powerful or powerless. Read the study to see how power was manipulated in three nonverbal expressions. This resulted in four treatment conditions, diagrammed in this design table:

| TABLE 6.4  ● CRISIS STAGE FACTOR | | | |
|---|---|---|---|
| | **Crisis Stage Factor** | | |
| Nonverbal Visual Cue Factor | | During | After |
| | Powerful | $n = 29$ | $n = 30$ |
| | Powerless | $n = 30$ | $n = 29$ |

Note: The study does not say how many subjects were in each group, only that there were 118 total, so this is a guesstimate of the cell $n$s.

Subjects were randomly assigned to one of the four conditions, making this a between-subjects design. The literature review established that visual cues alone are known to have an impact on perceptions of the person's competence, so this second experiment was not interested in the main effects of the two factors so much as the interaction of them. It found a significant interaction, showing that during a crisis, looking powerful leads to being perceived as competent, but that after the crisis, visual cues of power had no effect on perceptions. The study also tests perceptions of sincerity and other hypotheses but has been simplified here to illustrate the use of single-factor and factorial designs.

---

*From:* Claeys, An-Sofie, and Verolien Cauberghe. 2014. "Keeping Control: The Importance of Nonverbal Expressions of Power by Organizational Spokespersons in Time of Crisis." *Journal of Communication* 64: 1160–1180.

# HOW SUBJECTS ARE USED IN DESIGNS

Another aspect of designing a true experiment is determining how many levels of a factor subjects will be exposed to. Described next, these also affect how many subjects are needed, how many stimuli must be created, and other concerns.

## Between-Subjects Designs

A **between-subjects design** is probably the easiest to conceptualize and one of the most commonly used. In this design, each subject is assigned to receive one and only one type of treatment, represented by one cell in the design table. Each subject is part of one group, not multiple groups. Morton and Williams call it being "in one state of the world."[39] It is sometimes referred to as a "nested design" because subjects are nested within the levels of the condition.[40] The simplest between-subjects experiment is a single-factor design with two groups: a treatment and a control. A hypothetical example would be an education study with a treatment group that learned math using self-paced computer tutorials and a control group that learned from a teacher lecturing to a class, the usual way math is taught. In this case, a between-subjects design is necessary in order to avoid **carry-over effects**—that is, if subjects are likely to react to receiving the second condition because they have already received the first. Students can only be put in either the computer tutorial or lecture group because they would obviously learn the information, which would carry over to contaminate the outcome of being in the other group. Once they have learned the math, they cannot "unlearn" it. A completely different set of people is needed for each of the groups. Unmeasured variables that could possibly confound the results are controlled for with random assignment in a between-subjects design.

Between-subjects factors are also used when the condition is something the researcher cannot manipulate, like gender—a subject can only be in one gender. If the researcher in the hypothetical example thought that boys learned math differently from girls, for example, then gender might be another between-subjects factor. In one study, researchers measured adolescents' prior drug use and used that as a factor, albeit one they could not manipulate.[41] Age, ethnicity, political ideology, and education, among others, are commonly used in experiments as between-subjects factors. These nonmanipulated factors are also called "measured factors."

One drawback of the between-subjects design is the number of subjects necessary. If a power analysis shows the two groups in the math study need forty subjects in each cell, then eighty different subjects are needed. If a second type of treatment such as group learning is added, then another forty subjects are needed for a total of 120.

And this is just for a single-factor design. For a 2 x 2 factorial design that calls for forty subjects in each cell, that would mean a total of 160 subjects. A 2 x 3 design would require 200 subjects, and so on. The more complicated the design, the more subjects needed.

## Within-Subjects Designs

One way to get around the exponentially increasing number of subjects is to use a **within-subjects design**. If carry-over effects, such as doing better because of practice, are not an issue, this is the most economical type of design because the same subject can be part of all the treatment groups. Using the earlier example of a study[42] of news frames with two levels—objective and advocacy—there is no reason to think that reading an advocacy framed story would carry over to contaminate the response to reading an objective framed story or vice versa (as long as the stories are different), so a within-subjects design would allow the forty people to be included in both groups, whereas a between-subjects design would need eighty people, forty for each group. Morton and Williams call this being in "two states of the world simultaneously."[43] It is sometimes called a crossed design because subjects are crossed with condition.[44] The same exponential increase is found when adding factors or levels. For example, in the hypothetical study of smiling and camera distance, a 2 x 2 design, each person could get all four types of photographs—one of a smiling close-up photo, one of a smiling long-distance photo, one of a not-smiling close-up photo, and one of a long-distance not-smiling photo. Because each person is represented in all four cells, a within-subjects design only needs forty people total rather than 120 for a between-subjects design. Essentially, each person "counts" as four subjects. It is sometimes called a "repeated measures" design. A system of randomly rotating the order the stimuli will be presented in should be employed to reduce potential carry-over effects; for example, a quarter of the subjects are randomly assigned to get smiling close-up photos first, a quarter to get smiling long-distance photos first, a quarter to get nonsmiling close-ups first, and a quarter to get nonsmiling long-distance photos first. This helps "wash out" any carry-over effects across the entire sample and will be covered in chapter 7.

The trade-off for within-subjects designs is that the researcher needs to create more stimuli. For example, in the study of objective and advocacy framed stories, the researcher could not use the exact same story written both ways. The researcher would need to write equivalent stories but have them be different enough so that subjects would not perceive they were reading the same thing twice. Where there is savings in subjects, there is more time spent creating stimuli.

The primary reason for not using a within-subjects design is to avoid carry-over effects—that is, if subjects are likely to react to the other conditions because of receiving the first one.

The easiest-to-understand example of this is if the "treatment" is really something that can cure a person. So if a factor is the type of headache medicine with three levels—aspirin, ibuprofen, and NSAIDs—then a researcher can only assign subjects with headaches to one cell or treatment because after taking the medicine their headache might be cured. Another way to think about it is if a subject cannot be returned to the way they were originally, then a within-subjects design is not appropriate.[45]

As a social science example, a study examined people's belief in the ability of humans to have a free will to see how it would affect their charitable giving.[46] The free-will factor was manipulated by having subjects read an article from a science journal that argued against free will; the control group read an article on sustainable energy from the same science journal with no free-will messages. The dependent variable was how much subjects would give to charity, with those reading the article arguing against free will hypothesized to give less. This was a between-subjects design because once a participant read the article saying humans did not have free will, there was no way that could *not* affect their giving decisions. They could not be restored to their previous state where they did not know what the arguments were against humans having free will. They had been permanently changed. In other words, there is no going back from some treatments. The researchers could not have made this a within-subjects design without contaminating the treatments and confounding the results. Another example comes from a business study where the treatments were a company that voluntarily recalled a defective product versus a company that did not issue a recall. Subjects read about the companies and then rated them on integrity, trust, and benevolence.[47] Subjects could only be exposed to the voluntary recall or no recall condition, not both, as being exposed to the treatment in one would have an effect on the other.

Researchers also use between-subjects designs when they are concerned that subjects may "catch on" to the hypotheses. For example, after reading about recalls more than once in the business study, subjects may begin to suspect that researchers expect whether a company recalls a product to make a difference in how they view the company. We know from demand characteristics (see chapter 4) that subjects like to please researchers and may rate the recalling company better because they think that is what researchers want them to do. If it makes sense that subjects are assigned to only one kind of treatment, then a between-subjects design is called for. Another reason not to do a within-subjects design is if doing multiple tests takes a long time, subjects may become fatigued and not give the same amount of effort and attention to the later tests. However, if there is no reason to believe that subjects cannot receive more than one treatment without it affecting their responses, then the greater efficiency of within-subjects designs makes them preferable to between-subjects designs.

Another benefit of within-subjects designs is that each subject acts as his or her own control. That is, whatever individual differences the person has that may affect their response will be the same for both treatments. For example, in the advocacy vs. objective framing study,[48] having a college education might make a person think critically about all messages more than people who do not have a college degree. In that case, the college-educated subject is exposed to both advocacy and objective framed messages, which controls for education because each subject is acting as a control for him- or herself by getting both types of messages. In a between-subjects design, random assignment is used to help control for individual differences by helping ensure that experimental groups are equivalent in terms of things like education, age, gender, race, and other characteristics that might make a difference—for example, political ideology or even psychological characteristics such as fundamentalism or authoritarian personalities. But equivalence of groups using random assignment is never as good as equivalence achieved by having exactly the same subject in each group. This will be covered in more detail in chapter 7.

## Mixed Factorial Designs

Some studies use a combination of between- and within-subjects designs in the same experiment. When there are two or more factors, and one or more is not prone to carry-over effects, fatigue, or hypothesis guessing but the other is, then a **mixed factorial design** is appropriate. In these designs, one independent variable is given as a between-subjects factor so that subjects get only one level of that treatment, and the other is given as a within-subjects factor so that subjects get all levels of that treatment. For example, in one study that used a mixed design,[49] subjects read four ethical dilemmas that journalists might face and then made a decision about what they would do. The within-subjects factor was the type of decision they had to make, with the two levels being whether they should run a photograph or not and whether they should run a story with anonymous sources or not. All subjects got two dilemmas where they made decisions about running photographs and two dilemmas where they made decisions about using anonymous sources. The between-subjects factor was whether subjects got photographs with the dilemmas or not. For this factor, half of the subjects saw photographs with all four dilemmas, and the other half got all four dilemmas without any photographs. This was done because making a decision about running photographs was not expected to have any effect on subjects' decision to use anonymous sources or not, and vice versa; however, there was concern that seeing photographs for some dilemmas might color the way subjects reacted to other dilemmas where they did not see photographs. It made sense for subjects to receive only one of the levels of the photograph factor; they either received photographs or did not receive photographs. In this between-subjects factor, each subject got one kind of treatment, not both. It also made sense for them to receive both kinds of decisions, using photographs or anonymous sources. In this within-subjects factor, each subject got both treatments.

At first, it may be hard to remember which type of design has subjects in only one group and which has them in both. Try this mnemonic phrase: "Choose *between* the two; you can only have one." Thus, a between-subjects design has subjects in only one group.

The paper should report which type of subjects' design was used—between, within, or mixed—along with the factorial notation. Here are examples, with the type of subject design underlined:

- "We employed a 2 (argument quality: strong/weak) x 2 (personal relevance: high/low) x 2 (evidence: narrative/statistical) <u>mixed factorial design</u>."[50]

- "The second study used a 2 (crisis stage: during the crisis vs. postcrisis) x 2 (visual nonverbal cues: powerless vs. powerful) <u>between-subjects factorial design</u>."[51]

For more examples of how to report experimental designs in the paper, see How To Do It box 6.2, Reporting Factorial Design.

## Incomplete Factorials

All the designs described previously are what are called **fully crossed factorial designs**, sometimes shortened to just **full factorials** or **complete factorials**. In these, all combinations of the levels and factors are assigned subjects. But some designs leave one or more of the cells in the design table empty; these are called **incomplete factorial designs** or **fractional factorial** designs. As we discussed earlier, some of the combinations might not make sense. Shadish, Cook, and Campbell give an example of a research design that did not assign subjects to eight cells that were either too politically unpopular or expensive to be able to implement in a government policy on poverty.[52] When there is no practical or theoretical reason to study some cell combinations, it is more economical to leave those cells empty and not assign any subjects to them; then it is reported as an incomplete factorial design. Another reason to use an incomplete factorial is to allow for a control group that receives no treatment. If a control group does not fit into any of the cell combinations, it is considered to be its own cell. It would look like the design in table 6.5. The hypothetical study in the figure has three levels of the "visual type" factor, where subjects see either a still photograph, watch a video shown one time the way it is on TV, or watch a video shown three times, the way one could watch it on the Internet. The second factor represents the camera distance from the people in the images, either a close-up, medium, or a long shot. The control group got no pictures or video, only the story that all the other subjects got with

| TABLE 6.5 ● EXAMPLE OF A 3 X 3 INCOMPLETE FACTORIAL DESIGN WITH A CONTROL GROUP | | | | |
|---|---|---|---|---|
| | | **VISUAL TYPE FACTOR** | | |
| | | **Still Photo** | **TV Video (1x)** | **Internet Video (3x)** |
| **CAMERA DISTANCE FACTOR** | Close-up | $n = 45$ | $n = 45$ | $n = 45$ |
| | Medium shot | $n = 45$ | $n = 45$ | $n = 45$ |
| | Long shot | $n = 45$ | $n = 45$ | $n = 45$ |

Control Group (no image treatment/stories only)

| |
|---|
| n = 15 |

their visuals. There was no way to "fit" this into the design table because both factors in the table were a feature of photographs or video. Thus, the control group gets its own cell, outside the table. This kind of experiment is more economical because the control group can have fewer subjects than the treatment groups. At least a 3:1 ratio is recommended,[53] meaning that up to three times as many subjects can be in the treatment groups as the control.

## CONTROL GROUPS

One of the advantages of a factorial design, whether it is complete or incomplete, is for control in the form of a comparison to a group that does not receive a treatment.[54] In complete factorials, one of the levels of the factors can represent the control condition[55]—for example, a study[56] that was a 4 x 3 mixed factorial with one factor called Social Issue, represented by three different stories, one about a flood victim, one about teenage girls beating another girl, and one about a prostitution sting. The second factor was visual type, the same as in the hypothetical example—still photo, TV video, Internet video—but with a control group: No Image. Control group subjects read the same stories about the three different social issues but saw no pictures or video. That design table looked like table 6.6.

As we see from Campbell and Stanley's[57] typology of experimental designs covered in chapter 4, a control group is essential to all three of the "true experiments." The pretest–posttest control group design and the posttest-only control group design both have one control group, while the Solomon four-group design has two. A control group is crucial in ensuring that different groups are reacting under controlled conditions.[58]

| TABLE 6.6 ⬡ EXAMPLE OF A 4 X 3 FACTORIAL DESIGN WITH A CONTROL GROUP | | | | | |
|---|---|---|---|---|---|
| | | VISUAL TYPE FACTOR | | | |
| | | Still Photo | TV Video (1x) | Internet Video (3x) | No Image (Control Group) |
| SOCIAL ISSUE FACTOR | Beating | $n = 33$ | $n = 45$ | $n = 38$ | $n = 29$ |
| | Flood | $n = 33$ | $n = 45$ | $n = 38$ | $n = 29$ |
| | Sting | $n = 33$ | $n = 45$ | $n = 38$ | $n = 29$ |

"Well, I guess we're the control group."

Another way to look at a control group is as a baseline measure of something that has not yet had a treatment or intervention,[59] or as a neutral situation.[60] If the experimental group receives the treatment and changes, and if the control group does not receive the treatment and changes, then we know the treatment did not cause the change. But if the experimental group receives the treatment and changes, while the control group that does not receive the treatment does not change, then we know the treatment did cause the change.[i]

After random assignment, having a control group is the most important thing one can do when conducting a true experiment. It is the way experimenters compare what happens to people who get the treatment against people who do not. The control group is another way of ensuring that any effects observed are due to the treatment variable and not something else. As pointed out in chapter 1, medical researchers typically give their control group subjects a placebo such as a sugar pill, injection of saline, or something else that leads people to believe they got some "treatment" even if it was inert or not expected to have any beneficial effects. Because of the power of suggestion, people need to think they have gotten some treatment or had something done to them in order to accurately represent a control group. As Campbell and Stanley[61] point out, thinking of a control group as "the comparison of X with *no X* is an oversimplification. The comparison is actually with the specific activities of the control group which have filled the time period corresponding to that in which the experimental group receives the X."[62] An adequate control group is not a group of people who are measured on some outcome variable without having received something that they perceive to be a treatment. For social scientists, there is no "sugar pill." Next, this chapter discusses some ways that these researchers create social science placebos.

## The No-Treatment Control Group

The classic example of a control group is one that gets the absence of the manipulation in the treatment group. For example, researchers in one study used stories that explicitly called an issue "important" for one treatment group and stories that implicitly labeled an issue as important by presenting its consequences for the other treatment group. The control group saw the exact same stories without the evaluation of the issue as being important or any discussion about consequences.[63] In the insecurity study example discussed earlier, the treatment group wrote essays about their financial futures, creating feelings of high insecurity. The control group wrote essays about music, which was not expected to

---

[i] I would like to thank an anonymous reviewer for suggesting this clear and simple way of describing control groups.

create any feelings of insecurity.[64] Key to the idea of control is that subjects in the control or "no treatment" group get a manipulation that is as similar to the treatment group as possible without affecting the outcome.

## Creativity in Control Groups

Sometimes, it takes a little creative thinking to determine what subjects should do instead of doing nothing. For example, researchers studying cooking practices used three types of marketing messages as their treatment: messages about health benefits, messages about time and money savings, and messages about both.[65] No message was the obvious control group, but then what would they have subjects do instead? The researchers solved that problem by using a discussion group as the control condition, having subjects talk with others about common cooking practices instead of being exposed to a marketing message. In a journalism study that compared advocacy to objective stories about crime, the control group read stories about topics other than crime so they would not experience the same emotions, such as fear, that crime stories engender.[66] They still read stories, just not crime stories. In both of these studies, instead of having the control group subjects do nothing, they did something—participate in a group discussion instead of seeing a marketing message, or read a newspaper story on a topic completely unrelated to the topic of the treatment groups' stories. What Bausell calls "jazzing up the control group to receive interesting but irrelevant activities"[67] means that giving control subjects something that appears to be the same as the treatment subjects is much better than having them come in, fill out the questionnaire, and then leave, without getting anything as a treatment. Control group subjects must perform some task that makes them think they have received a legitimate treatment. They need to perceive that something happened.

## The Status Quo Control Group

In other cases, researchers will define the control group as what is most normal, common, or typical.[68] In these experiments, a different group that represents the status quo but is not identified as a control group may be used. For example, in one experiment of how to best teach English to Costa Rican third-graders, two treatment groups used different computer-assisted learning software while a control group got English instruction by a teacher, the way the schools normally taught it.[69] The teacher-instructed group served as the control group. Journalism studies frequently use stories written in the detached, two-sided manner that is common in mainstream news organizations as the control condition because it represents what audiences normally read.[70]

## No Control Group

Not all experiments have control groups, and in some cases one may not be necessary.[71] In some studies, it is extremely difficult to provide a control treatment that is similar to the manipulation. For example, in the study of HIV messages, what would be the control for the story frame factor?[72] There is no such thing as a story that does not have some sort of frame. Or in the study of voice pitch, where the two levels were raised and lowered voice pitch[73]—there is no such thing as no voice pitch. In many studies that compare two or more treatments, what is defined as the control group is ambiguous.[74] In these studies, a control group may not be necessary because they are comparing the treatment groups to each other,[75] not against some group that gets the absence of voice pitch or a story with no frame.

Whether a study has a classic control group or some other kind, there should always be careful control in the management of variables.[76] Refer to the threats to validity outlined in chapter 5 when designing an experiment and put every element under a microscope.[77] Groups should differ only with respect to the intervention. Even something as simple as running one group in the morning and the other in the afternoon, or in dissimilar rooms, or with different experimenters, can confound the outcome.[78]

There are, of course, more types of factorial designs than the ones outlined here, notably split plot designs, fractional replications, and randomized blocks, among others—what Campbell and Stanley call "some of the traumatizing mysteries of factorial design."[79] As this is an introductory text, it will not delve into the mysteries of each but instead refer readers to more advanced texts.

The next chapter will take on the single most important thing that must be done to qualify as a true experiment—random assignment.

## Common Mistakes

- Designing a study that is too complicated
- Not using a control group when possible
- Not giving the control group something to do

## Test Your Knowledge

1. An experiment that has two independent variables with two or more levels of each is called a _____.

   a. Single-factor design

   b. One-way design

   c. Factorial design

   d. Three-way design

2. What factorial notation would be used for this hypothetical experiment?: A researcher manipulates the tone of an ad campaign (positive/negative/neutral) and the medium that carries it (TV/print/Internet).

   a. 2 x 2

   b. 2 x 3

   c. 3 x 3

   d. 2 x 3 x 3

3. A factorial design can have which of the following outcomes?

   a. Significant main effects for all the factors but no interaction effect

   b. Significant main effects for one or some of the factors but not all of them, with either a significant or nonsignificant interaction

   c. A significant interaction but no main effects

   d. All of these

4. If subjects are likely to do better on something because of practice, then it is best to use a(n) _____.

   a. Between-subjects design

   b. Within-subjects design

   c. Mixed design

   d. Incomplete design

5. Identify the control group in a study of the best way to remind drivers to pay a traffic ticket:

   a. Reminders sent via text message

   b. Reminders sent by e-mail

   c. Reminders sent by mail, the way they are normally sent

   d. Reminders sent by phone call

6. In a study on PSAs about HIV/AIDS, researchers examined the quality of the argument in the ad with the levels being a strong or weak argument, how personally relevant the subject of HIV/AIDS was to each subject, and two different types of ad formats, one that used a narrative storyline and one that relied on statistical data. This was a _____ design.

   a. Single-factor

   b. Factorial

   c. Between-subjects

   d. Within-subjects

7. The ability for the different levels in one factor alone to cause a change in the outcome variables is called a(n) _____.

   a. Confound

   b. Plausible alternative explanation

   c. Main effect

   d. Interaction effect

8. When the outcome of one factor depends on another, this is known as a(n) _____.

   a. Confound

   b. Plausible alternative explanation

   c. Main effect

   d. Interaction effect

9. In a study of cooking practices where the three conditions were messages about health benefits, messages about time and money savings, messages about both, and a discussion group, which represented the control group?

   a. Messages about health benefits

   b. Messages about time savings

   c. Messages about money savings

   d. A discussion group

10. In an education study that compared computer-assisted learning software to instruction by a teacher, the way the schools normally taught it, which kind of control group was used?

   a. No control group

   b. Status quo control group

   c. Comparison of two treatments

   d. Internal control group

Answers:

| | | | |
|---|---|---|---|
| 1. c | 4. a | 7. c | 9. d |
| 2. c | 5. c | 8. d | 10. b |
| 3. d | 6. b | | |

## Application Exercises

1. Take one of the ideas for an experiment that you came up with in chapter 1 and wrote a literature review and hypotheses for in chapter 3, and draw a design table to help you visualize the factors, levels, and the combinations of each. Translate that into factorial notation. Include the type of design, your factors, and levels. See the How To Do It box.

2. Write one page that explains your choice of between- or within-subjects designs. Defend your decision (e.g., why there will be no carry-over effects). Imagine a reviewer has challenged your choice, suggesting that the opposite would be better. What would you say?

3. Write one page on your type of control group and what the subjects will do instead of receiving the treatment. Explain your choices and defend your decisions.

## Suggested Readings

Chapter 6, "Designing Experimental Studies to Achieve Statistical Significance," in R. Barker Bausell (1994). *Conducting Meaningful Experiments: 40 Steps to Becoming a Scientist.* Thousand Oaks, CA: Sage Publications.

Chapter 10, "Complex Experimental Designs," in Paul C. Cozby (2009). *Methods in Behavioral Research*, 10th Edition. Boston: McGraw-Hill.

## Notes

1. Diana Mutz, *Population-Based Survey Experiments* (Princeton, NJ: Princeton University Press, 2011), 125.

2. Graeme D. Ruxton and Nick Colegrave, *Experimental Design for the Life Sciences*, 3rd ed. (Oxford, UK: Oxford University Press, 2011).

3. William R. Shadish, Thomas D. Cook, and Donald T. Campbell, *Experimental and Quasi-Experimental Designs for Generalized Causal Inference* (Belmont, CA: Wadsworth Cengage Learning, 2002), 263.

4. Sean Aday, "The Framesetting Effects of News: An Experimental Test of Advocacy Versus Objectivist Frames," *Journalism and Mass Communication Quarterly* 83, no. 4 (Winter 2006): 767–784.

5. Tim Kasser and Kennon M. Sheldon, "Of Wealth and Death: Materialism, Mortality Salience, and Consumption Behavior," *Psychological Science* 11, no. 4 (July 2000): 348–351.

6. Christopher D. Johnston and Julie Wronski, "Personality Dispositions and Political Preferences Across Hard and Easy Issues," *Political Psychology* 36, no. 1 (2015): 35–53.

7. T. Rogers et al., "Artful Paltering: The Risks and Rewards of Using Truthful Statements to Mislead Others," *Journal of Personality and Social Psychology* 112 (3), 456–473.

8. Shadish, Cook, and Campbell, *Experimental and Quasi-Experimental Designs.*

9. Ronald A. Fisher, *The Design of Experiments* (Edinburgh: Oliver and Boyd, 1937).

10. D. T. Campbell and J. C. Stanley, *Experimental and Quasi-Experimental Designs for Research.* (Chicago: Rand McNally, 1963), 3.

11. Ibid.

12. Jueman Zhang et al., "Persuasiveness of HIV/AIDS Public Service Announcements as a Function of Argument Quality, Personal Relevance, and Evidence Form," *Social Behavior and Personality: An International Journal* 42, no. 10 (2014): 1603–1612.

13. Ruxton and Colegrave, *Experimental Design for the Life Sciences*, 3rd ed.

14. Campbell and Stanley, *Experimental and Quasi-Experimental Designs,* 29.

15. Ruxton and Colegrave, *Experimental Design for the Life Sciences*, 3rd ed.

16. Zhang et al., "Persuasiveness of HIV/AIDS Public Service Announcements."

17. Campbell and Stanley, *Experimental and Quasi-Experimental Designs,* 29.

18. Ibid.

19. Xiaoli Nan et al., "Message Framing, Perceived Susceptibility, and Intentions to Vaccinate Children Against HPV Among African-American Parents," *Health Communication* 31, no. 7 (2016): 798–805.

20. Ibid.

21. Gabriele Esposito et al., "Nudging to Prevent the Purchase of Incompatible Digital Products Online: An Experimental Study," *PLoS ONE* 12, no. 3 (2017): 1–15.

22. Nan et al., "Message Framing, Perceived Susceptibility."

23. Ibid., 800.

24. Ruxton and Colegrave, *Experimental Design for the Life Sciences*, 3rd ed.

25. Debby Vos, "How Ordinary MPs Can Make It Into the News: A Factorial Survey Experiment with Political Journalists to Explain the Newsworthiness of MPs," *Mass Communication and Society* 19, no. 6 (2016): 738–757.

26. Shadish, Cook, and Campbell, *Experimental and Quasi-Experimental Designs*, 265.

27. Ibid.

28. R. Barker Bausell, *Conducting Meaningful Experiments: 40 Steps to Becoming a Scientist* (Thousand Oaks, CA: Sage, 1994).

29. Murray R. Selwyn, *Principles of Experimental Design for the Life Sciences* (Boca Raton, FL: CRC Press, 1996), 55.

30. Zhang et al., "Persuasiveness of HIV/AIDS Public Service Announcements," 1606.

31. An-Sofie Claeys and Verolien Cauberghe, "Keeping Control: The Importance of Nonverbal Expressions of Power by Organizational Spokespersons in Time of Crisis," *Journal of Communication* 64 (2014): 1160–1180.

32. Ibid., 1162.

33. Bausell, *Conducting Meaningful Experiments.*

34. Ibid., 97.

35. Paul R. Brewer, Joseph Graf, and Lars Willnat, "Priming or Framing," *Gazette: International Journal for Communication Studies* 65, no. 6 (2003): 493–508.

36. Angela Min-Chia Lee, "How Fast Is Too Fast? Examining the Impact of Speed-Driven Journalism on News Production and Audience Reception" (unpublished dissertation, University of Texas, 2014); Angela M. Lee, "The Faster the Better? Examining the Effect of Live-Blogging on Audience Reception," *Journal of Applied Journalism and Media Studies* 8, no. 1 (in press).

37. Shadish, Cook, and Campbell, *Experimental and Quasi-Experimental Designs,* 265.

38. Selwyn, *Principles of Experimental Design,* 53.

39. Rebecca B. Morton and Kenneth C. Williams, *Experimental Political Science and the Study of Causality: From Nature to the Lab* (New York: Cambridge University Press, 2010), 86.

40. Charles M. Judd, Jacob Westfall, and David A. Kenny, "Experiments with More Than One Random Factor: Designs, Analytic Models, and Statistical Power," *Annual Review of Psychology* 68, no. 1 (2017): 601–625.

41. H. Cho and F. J. Boster, "Effects of Gain Versus Loss Frame Antidrug Ads on Adolescents," *Journal of Communication* 58, no. 3 (2008): 428–446.

42. Aday, "The Framesetting Effects of News."

43. Morton and Williams, *Experimental Political Science,* 86.

44. Judd, Westfall, and Kenny, "Experiments with More Than One Random Factor."

45. Ruxton and Colegrave, *Experimental Design for the Life Sciences*, 3rd ed.

46. Job Harms et al., "Free to Help? An Experiment on Free Will Belief and Altruism," *PLoS ONE* 12, no. 3 (2017): 1–15.

47. Luiza Venzke Bortoli and Valeria Freundt, "Effects of Voluntary Product Recall on Consumer's Trust," *Brazilian Business Review* 14, no. 2 (2017): 204–224.

48. Aday, "The Framesetting Effects of News."

49. Renita Coleman, "The Effect of Visuals on Ethical Reasoning: What's a Photograph Worth to Journalists Making Moral Decisions?" *Journalism and Mass*

*Communication Quarterly* 83, no. 4 (Winter 2006): 835–850.

50. Zhang et al., "Persuasiveness of HIV/AIDS Public Service Announcements," 1606.

51. Claeys and Cauberghe, "Keeping Control," 1167.

52. Shadish, Cook, and Campbell, *Experimental and Quasi-Experimental Designs,* 265.

53. Bausell, *Conducting Meaningful Experiments.*

54. Shadish, Cook, and Campbell, *Experimental and Quasi-Experimental Designs.*

55. Ibid.

56. Aimee Meader et al., "Ethics in the Digital Age: A Comparison of the Effects of Moving Images and Photogaphs on Moral Judgment," *Journal of Media Ethics* 30, no. 4 (2015): 234–251.

57. Campbell and Stanley, *Experimental and Quasi-Experimental Designs.*

58. Gerry Stoker, "Exploring the Promise of Experimentation in Political Science: Micro-Foundational Insights and Policy Relevance," *Political Studies* 58 (2010): 300–319.

59. Morton and Williams, *Experimental Political Science.*

60. Cengiz Erisen, Elif Erisen, and Binnur Ozkececi-Taner, "Research Methods in Political Psychology," *Turkish Studies* 13, no. 1 (2013): 13–33.

61. Campbell and Stanley, *Experimental and Quasi-Experimental Designs.*

62. Ibid., 13.

63. Kristin Bulkow, Juliane Urban, and Wolfgang Schweiger, "The Duality of Agenda-Setting: The Role of Information Processing," *International Journal of Public Opinion Research* 25, no. 1 (2013): 43–63.

64. Kasser and Sheldon, "Of Wealth and Death."

65. Theresa Beltramo et al., "The Effect of Marketing Messages and Payment Over Time on Willingness to Pay for Fuel-Efficient Cookstoves," *Journal of Economic Behavior & Organization* 118 (2015): 333–345.

66. Aday, "The Framesetting Effects of News."

67. Bausell, *Conducting Meaningful Experiments,* 74.

68. Ibid.

69. Horacio Alvarez-Marinelli et al., "Computer Assisted English Language Learning in Costa Rican Elementary Schools: An Experimental Study," *Computer Assisted Language Learning* 29, no. 1 (2016): 103–126.

70. Aday, "The Framesetting Effects of News."

71. Ruxton and Colegrave, *Experimental Design for the Life Sciences,* 3rd ed.

72. Nan et al., "Message Framing, Perceived Susceptibility."

73. Claeys and Cauberghe, "Keeping Control."

74. Morton and Williams, *Experimental Political Science.*

75. Ruxton and Colegrave, *Experimental Design for the Life Sciences,* 3rd ed.

76. Stoker, 304.

77. Bausell, *Conducting Meaningful Experiments.*

78. Ibid.

79. Campbell and Stanley, *Experimental and Quasi-Experimental Designs,* 27.

# RANDOM ASSIGNMENT

*Just as representativeness can be secured by the method of chance . . . so equivalence may be secured by chance.*[1]

**—W. A. McCall**

## LEARNING OBJECTIVES

- Understand what random assignment does and how it works.

- Produce a valid randomization process for an experiment and describe it.

- Critique simple random assignment, blocking, matched pairs, and stratified random assignment.

- Explain the importance of counterbalancing.

- Describe a Latin square design.

Just as the mantra in real estate is "location, location, location," the motto in experimental design is "random assignment, random assignment, random assignment." This book has discussed random assignment all throughout. It bears repeating that random assignment is the *single* most important thing a researcher can do in an experiment. Everything else pales in comparison to having done this correctly.[2] Random assignment is what distinguishes a true experiment from a quasi, natural, or pre-experimental design. In chapter 1, experiments were referred to as the gold standard. Without successful random assignment, however, they can quickly become "the bronze standard."[3] This chapter will review some of the advantages of random assignment, discuss the details of how to do it, and explore related issues of counterbalancing.

## THE PURPOSE OF RANDOM ASSIGNMENT

People vary. That is, they are different. Were this not so, there would be no reason to study them. Everyone would be the same, reacting the same way to different teaching techniques, advertisements, health interventions, and political messages. There would be no need to conduct experiments. The fact that people vary provides social scientists with a reason for doing research, and also with their biggest challenge. When people vary on things that are not of interest to the experiment, it is called **random variation** or **noise**.[4] These things that are not the focus of a study can still be responsible for some of the changes in the outcome of experimental treatments. That is, they can confound the results. One major focus of experimentalists is to control for confounds, removing or reducing the noise from random variation. That way, the effects the study is concerned with can be seen more clearly. Randomization is arguably the greatest weapon a scientist has because it helps ensure that subjects in different treatment and control groups are virtually the same on variables that create noise.

Random assignment is a technique for placing subjects into the different treatment and control groups in a true experiment for the purpose of ensuring that subjects in each group will have similar characteristics—that is, that they will be **equivalent**. By equivalent, we mean equal on average, or probabilistically equal, not identical. The purpose of equivalence is to "level the playing field," helping ensure that the only systematic differences between the two groups are the treatments they receive in the experiment. It helps ensure that subjects in one group are not better on the outcome variable to begin with, and that one group is not filled with subjects who are more likely to change regardless of treatment.[5] This allows researchers to have more confidence that any changes observed are because of the treatment the subjects received and not because of inherent differences in the subjects themselves. Groups that are systematically different in one or more ways can invalidate an experiment. For example, if one group contained only men and the other only women, it would be confounded; there would be no way to tell if the results were due to the treatment or to gender. One way random assignment helps achieve equivalence is by avoiding **selection bias,** which occurs when people self-select the groups to be in, or researchers select subjects for some subjective reason or to improve the chances of supporting a hypothesis, even if done subconsciously.[6]

For example, an education study would be invalid if the treatment group gets mostly subjects who are better at math to begin with and the control group gets subjects who are poor at math. If the treatment is the way math is taught, then it might appear as if the treatment is working, but it really could be the fact that those who were taught the new way were better at math to begin with. On the other hand, if students who are poor at math are assigned to the treatment group by educators who want to be sure that students who need math help the most get it, then the treatment group is stacked with poor-math students and the control group with good-math students. The new teaching strategy could actually work, but might look like it was not if it only raised the treatment group up to the level of the controls; in other words, there is no significant difference between the groups after treatment.

Another example is that some people are simply more prone to change than others. If the treatment group got more subjects who changed more easily than the control group, then a study designed to influence people's positions on public policy could show spurious results—the treatment did not really change people's minds; they were more likely to change their minds to begin with. Giving the same treatment to harder-to-change people might have no effect at all.

## Avoiding Confounds

The beauty of random assignment is that the researcher does not have to predetermine every characteristic of every subject that could possibly confound the study. It might be easy to anticipate that prior math knowledge would influence math learning, for example, and pretest subjects on math and assign equivalent numbers of high-math knowledge and low-math knowledge subjects to each group. But it might be more difficult for a researcher to anticipate a penchant for changing one's mind as a confounding variable. With random assignment, no pretests for math ability or mind changing are necessary because equivalent numbers of easy-changers and hard-changers are in each group; or equivalent numbers of good-at-math and poor-at-math students are in each group. Because humans, including researchers, are notoriously bad at anticipating every little thing that might affect something else, and because some things are unknowable, random assignment is of tremendous benefit. Also, recall the drawbacks of pretesting from chapter 4; random assignment can eliminate the need for pretests and their accompanying threats to validity.

Random assignment, while not perfect, is the best way we currently know of to ensure that systematic variation among subjects does not confound the results of an experiment. It helps eliminate spurious variables, including those a researcher might not have thought of.

When it is impossible for the same people to simultaneously have the treatment and not have it, covered in chapter 6, researchers use random assignment to try to make sure that individual differences are assigned equivalently to each group.

## What Is Random?

Random assignment works because of chance. To assign subjects randomly, everyone in the study must have an equal chance of being in the control or treatment groups. Chapter 2 recounted the story of how random assignment was discovered. When Charles Sanders Peirce and Joseph Jastrow conducted a study of how accurately people could judge the weight of something just by feeling and looking at it,[7] they started by presenting the heavy weights first. Then they presented the heavy weights last. They also alternated the heavy and light weights. Finally, they shuffled a deck of cards and assigned the weights at random based on the cards. They got vastly different results when the weights were presented in any of the systematic patterns than when they were presented in a random order. Having subjects who could not guess the weight based on a pattern produced more valid results.

Random does *not* mean haphazard, and researchers must be careful to use appropriate random methods.[8] What is not random is anything that has some kind of pattern, purpose, or system to it. In my first experiment, I apparently did not understand exactly what random meant, but I was concerned with having equal numbers of subjects in each group. I assigned the first person to come into the lab to the first group, the second person to the second group, then the third person back to the first group, etc. Basically, they were assigned like this: 1, 2, 1, 2, 1, 2, 1, 2 . . . . When I told my professor, her eyes got wide and she said, "That's NOT random." I ended up throwing away all that data and starting over again.

As Gueron says, "It does not help to be a little bit random."[9]

## MORE ABOUT . . . BOX 7.1
### Random Assignment Threats to Internal Validity

When subjects and/or the experimenters that assign subjects to condition are not "blind" to the group they are being assigned to, random assignment itself, and violations of it, can result in threats to internal validity. The four types are:[13]

- *Diffusion of treatment*—This occurs when subjects in different groups communicate with each other and learn information not intended for them. For example, if subjects in the treatment and control group talk to each other, they may learn material intended only for the treatment group; the outcomes may not be different and will not truly reflect the treatment benefits.

- *Compensatory equalization*—This occurs when experimenters or those providing the treatment attempt to give some of the advantages that the treatment group has to those in the control group.

- *Compensatory rivalry*—This refers to when members of the control group try to gain some of the benefits of the treatment group.

- *Resentful demoralization*—This refers to the control group subjects underperforming because they resent being denied the treatment.

In some studies, subjects in the treatment group feel demoralized or stigmatized—for example, as being in the class for "dummies."[14] Thus, it is important that subjects be blind to which group they are in whenever possible.[15]

Researchers should be careful not to portray one intervention group as better or newer than another in recruitment materials.[16] If it is not possible to keep subjects from knowing which group they are in, researchers should measure subjects' preferences for assignment to a particular group and statistically control for it.[17]

Another threat to internal validity occurs when there is an imbalance of subjects who have a greater preference for their assignment in one group than in the other.[18] For example, if 60% of subjects in both groups are pleased with the group they are in and 40% are not, then preference is equivalent across all conditions. However, if one group has 60% pleased and the other has only 40% pleased, the outcomes could be confounded.[19] As long as both groups have the same percentage of pleased and displeased subjects, no threat occurs.[20] For example, in a business study, 89% of those asked to be in the treatment group agreed to participate, whereas only 45% of those asked to be in the control group agreed.[21]

True randomization is a process that is either done correctly or not.[10] In order for random assignment to work, the researcher cannot choose which group a subject is in for any reason, nor can a subject choose his or her own group. The subjects must be **blind,** or unaware, as to whether they are receiving the treatment or not. It is important that subjects remain in the dark so they do not try to give researchers what they think they want,[11] or so their disappointment at not getting the treatment does not bias the results.[12] It is also a good idea to have the researcher be unaware of which treatment or control groups subjects are in, which is then termed a *double-blind* study. For more about threats to internal validity when subjects and/or researchers know which group they are assigned to, see More About box 7.1.

# OPERATIONALIZING RANDOM ASSIGNMENT

There are many ways to "do" random assignment. In 1883, Peirce and Jastrow used a special deck of cards to determine random assignment, and that is still a valid method today. Other methods include rolling dice, flipping a coin, drawing numbers out of a hat, or using a book of random numbers. For details on how to do these manual methods, see How To Do It box 7.2.

## Computerized Randomization

Today, it is more likely that researchers will use random number generators found online or in spreadsheet or statistical software. For example, free online randomizers allow a researcher to specify the number of subjects and number of groups, and quickly return a list showing which subjects go to which groups, as shown in figures 7.1 and 7.2 (see pp. 180–181). Simply search the Internet for "random assignment generator" to find these.

To use QuickCalcs by GraphPad, in the first box labeled "Assign," put in the total number of subjects. Put the number of groups in the second box. Leave "Repeat" at 1. Click "Do it!"

It will return a list of subjects, numbered 1 to your final number, with the group labeled A, B, C, etc., beside the subject number.

This applet is specifically designed by a group of academic researchers for factorial experiments. In the first box, "Number of Participants, $N$" put the total number of subjects for the entire study. In the second box, "Number of Conditions, $C$," put the number of groups. Click "Compute."

It will return a list of groups to assign participants to, in order; it lacks the subject number of the QuickCalcs randomizer, but it is not hard to see that the first subject is assigned to the first group number, the second subject to the group number listed next, etc.

## HOW TO DO IT 7.2

### Randomizing Subjects

*Coin flipping* works when there are two groups. If the coin lands heads up, assign the subject to the treatment group; if it lands tails up, assign the subject to the control group. Or vice versa.

A *lottery* works with any number of groups. On slips of paper, write a number for each of the groups (1, 2, 3, 4, for example). Make as many slips of paper as subjects you intend to have, with equal amounts of group numbers. For example, if you need 160 subjects, with forty in each group, make forty slips of paper with the number 1, forty with number 2, etc.

*Decks of cards and dice* will need to use cards and die with only the number of groups on them. For example, get rid of all cards that are not 1, 2, 3, or 4 if you have four groups. You might need multiple decks. Shuffle the cards and then draw them one at a time each time a subject arrives. The subject is assigned to the group represented on the card drawn. For dice, use only dice that have the same number on them as your groups. Or roll again if a number comes up that is greater than your number of groups. Once the maximum number of subjects in a group is reached, ignore that number when it comes up on a card or die.

*Book of random numbers.* These are obsolete today, replaced by online random number generators. They consisted of page after page of numbers, randomly ordered. Believe it or not, a researcher decided where to start by closing his or her eyes and pointing to a starting place on the table. Then, the researcher would assign subjects to the group that the numbers correspond to, skipping over numbers that are outside the range. For example, if the numbers are: 3, 2, 5, 3, 7, 4, 1, etc., and the study has three groups, subjects would be assigned to groups 3, 2, 3, 1, etc., skipping over 5 and 7 because there are not five or seven groups. Once the maximum number of subjects in a group has been reached, that group's number is skipped over as well. Stop assigning subjects to a group after a group reaches the maximum, but continue on until all the other groups have been filled. My favorite book of random numbers was *A Million Random Digits With 100,000 Normal Deviates* (RAND). Your library might still have it if you are curious or a history buff.

*Excel.* For a tutorial on how to draw random numbers in Excel, see https://exceljet.net/formula/randomly-assign-data-to-groups.

*SAS and SPSS.* Shadish, Cook, and Campbell[22] give directions on random number generation in these popular statistical software packages on pages 311–313.

For other statistical software, such as *Stata* and *R*, consult the tutorials.

For pencil-and-paper studies, an online randomizer can be used to arrange the printed questionnaires in the specified random order before going to the lab or site where subjects will take the study. Questionnaires can then be handed out from the top of the stack without needing to refer to the output of random numbers each time a subject arrives.[i]

---

[i]Be sure to make a notation on the paper questionnaire or use another method to keep track of which group, treatment, or control the subject was in if it is not obvious.

---

FIGURE 7.1    ⬡    GRAPHPAD

---

**GraphPad**
Software

Scientific Software    Data Analysi

# QuickCalcs

1. Select category    2. Choose calculator    **3. Enter data**    4. View results

## Randomly assign subjects to treatment groups

Randomly choose a group for each subject

Assign  100    ⬍ subjects to each of  2  ⬍ groups. Repeat  1  ⬍ times.

[ Do it! ]

---

**GraphPad**
Software

# QuickCalcs

1. Select category    2. Choose calculator

## Assign subjects to groups

| Subject # | Group Assigned |
|---|---|
| 1 | A |
| 2 | A |
| 3 | B |
| 4 | B |
| 5 | B |
| 6 | A |
| 7 | B |
| 8 | B |
| 9 | A |
| 10 | A |
| 11 | B |
| 12 | A |
| 13 | A |
| 14 | B |
| 15 | A |
| 16 | A |
| 17 | B |
| 18 | A |
| 19 | B |
| 20 | A |
| 21 | B |
| 22 | B |
| 23 | A |
| 24 | B |
| 25 | A |
| 26 | A |
| 27 | B |
| 28 | A |
| 29 | A |
| 30 | A |

---

Source: http://www.graphpad.com/quickcalcs/randomize1.cfm

**FIGURE 7.2  ⬡  RANDOM ASSIGNMENT GENERATOR**

**Random Assignment Generator for a Factorial Experiment with Many Conditions**

| Description | Generate list of random numbers for assignment |
|---|---|
| This applet provides a list of random numbers that can be used to assign participants to conditions in an experiment with many conditions, such as a factorial experiment. (Read more about factorial experiments.)<br><br>Enter the number of participants $N$, and the number of conditions $C$, for the experiment you are planning. This applet will then provide a random number for each participant. This will be a number from 1 to $C$. For example, if the 4th number in the list is 7, the 4th subject is randomly assigned to experiment condition 7. Random numbers will be generated so that the experiment is approximately balanced. | Number of Participants, $N$ :  100<br><br>Number of Conditions, $C$:    2<br><br>Compute |

# Random Selection

Return to Sample Size Calculator

Download: CSV | Excel

Number of Participants, N : 100

Number of Condition, C: 2

## Assignments:

2
1
1
2
2
1
2
1
1
2
1
2
2
1
1
2
2
1
2
1
1
2
2
1
1

Source: http://www.methodologymedia.psu.edu/most/rannumgenerator

Online randomizers will automatically assign equal numbers of subjects to each group if the maximum number of subjects is divisible by the number of groups; for example, for three groups with forty subjects in each, set the total number of subjects at 120, not 125.

## Survey Experiments

One of the newest techniques revolutionizing the way experimental subjects are randomly assigned is with software designed to administer surveys online, such as Qualtrics and SurveyMonkey, among others. These **survey experiments**, also frequently described as an "experiment embedded in a survey,"[23] use a randomizer function to randomly assign subjects to treatment and control conditions without the researcher having to do anything other than set the randomizer before launching the survey. Computer-Assisted Telephone Interviewing software can also randomly assign subjects to conditions, similar to the survey software, with subjects taking the study over the phone instead of online.

Some researchers reserve the term *survey experiment* for studies that randomly sample from a population and also randomly assign subjects to conditions,[24] while others use the term when random sampling is not used[25] but random assignment is. Erisen[26] and colleagues make a distinction between survey experiments and lab experiments, explaining that lab experiments are conducted in a controlled environment where factors such as room temperature, time of day, or other things that could contaminate results can be controlled, whereas survey experiments can be taken by subjects in their own homes and with external factors out of the control of researchers, such as whether the subject takes a break to answer the door, go to the bathroom, or take a phone call. This is especially important when measuring things like the time a subject takes to complete the study, knowledge questions where subjects could look up the answers online,[27] or group decision studies where subjects may not believe they are interacting with real people over the Internet.[28] In cases where this kind of internal validity needs to be assured, survey software can be used with subjects in a lab, providing researchers with both control and the convenience of random assignment and data collection by computer. In a study of politicians' decision making,[29] the researchers had subjects do the study online using survey software, but in order to maintain control, they performed the study in the presence of a researcher. Other researchers have explored ways to discourage cheating on knowledge questions by looking up answers so that online experiments are less prone to this kind of error.[30]

There has been much debate and research on the subject of whether survey experiments that use random samples are better because they are generalizable, or if convenience samples produce similar results. Many studies show little to no differences.[31] That issue was covered extensively in this book in the section on external validity in chapter 5. The point in this chapter is that whether it is called a survey experiment or lab experiment, the defining feature of all true experiments is that subjects must be randomly assigned to treatment and control groups.

### In-Person Randomizing

Having subjects participate in an experiment via computer makes random assignment easier on many levels. But sometimes an experiment is best conducted with paper and pencil. In-person studies require different random assignment strategies. For example, political scientists might conduct an experiment using voters as they exit polling stations to ensure that subjects actually voted. If a message in a pamphlet or newspaper is the message being tested, then using a printed version is more realistic than one shown online. Most studies on moral judgment are conducted in person because of the complexity of the topic.[32] Moral judgment experiments with journalists may be conducted in the newsrooms with the researcher providing lunch and having subjects take the study while they eat; this generates more participation from busy working professionals.[33] Other experiments may be conducted at professional association conferences, giving the study with paper and pencil at tables in the lobby.[34] For some studies, an old-fashioned paper-and-pencil test conducted in a classroom or library might provide faster data collection.[35] In these cases, random assignment needs to be conducted by online randomizers or old-fashioned methods described earlier.

## REPORTING RANDOM ASSIGNMENT

Regardless of how random assignment is achieved, it should always be reported in the research paper as having been done, and preferably the procedure used. No great amount of detail on the specifics is usually necessary, but the report should at least say that subjects were randomly assigned to conditions lest readers think otherwise. Here are two actual published examples:

> "Participants were randomly assigned to a condition."[36]

> "Participants were then randomly given a booklet, which contained instructions for the research, a test pamphlet, and a response questionnaire. The test pamphlet was one of the four versions of a health pamphlet about HPV and genital warts. Thus participants were randomly assigned to one of the experimental conditions."[37]

The best practice is to provide a description of the randomization mechanism—for example, whether it was done with a deck of cards or die, or the randomizer function in a particular piece of software—and whether it was pregenerated or produced on site.[38]

## BALANCED AND UNBALANCED DESIGNS

Random assignment can raise concerns about unequal numbers of subjects in groups, as it did for me in my first experiment. This is called an **unbalanced design**. Very unequal sample sizes can affect group equivalence. It is not crucial to have exactly the same number of subjects in each group; as long as the numbers in each group are close, it will be approximately balanced.[39] However, balanced designs, where the exact same numbers of subjects are in each group, give a study more statistical power (the subject of chapter 8).

There may be very practical and unavoidable reasons for an unbalanced design, such as some subjects dropping out or being purged. For example, in moral judgment studies, there is a built-in check for subjects who are trying to fake a better score.[40] When faking is detected, these subjects are eliminated from the data set, usually resulting in unequal numbers of subjects in groups. Sometimes, researchers lose subjects who did not complete enough questions for their data to be useful, or when subjects systematically drop out of a study, which is called **attrition**. Concerns about unequal numbers of subjects in groups should never be a reason to deviate from randomization, as failing to properly randomize is a far greater threat than unbalanced groups. As was pointed out in the discussion of control groups in chapter 6, having up to a third fewer subjects in the control group of an incomplete factorial is acceptable.[41] When treatments are expensive or difficult to run, having fewer subjects in the groups that are of less interest is also acceptable. In addition, when a treatment is desirable, people may be reluctant to participate if they think they may be denied it by being assigned to the control group. Having more subjects randomly assigned to the treatment group can help overcome these objections.[42]

It is also important to report attrition rates, as was done in a business experiment of a mentoring program. In that study, 52% of subjects dropped out of the study; the researcher compared the dropouts to those who remained in the study and found no statistical differences on the observable characteristics.[43] Rules of thumb for attrition rates say between 5% and 20% may be a source of bias.[44]

Many good statistics books explain ways of analyzing data from unbalanced designs. Statistical techniques such as Levene's test[45] can be used to determine if the unequal number of subjects results in unequal variance. When the Levene's test is significant, indicating the variance is not homogeneous, the researcher then uses more stringent tests of differences that do not assume equal variances. This is a subject for a statistics class or text. Suffice it to say that there are better ways to deal with unbalanced groups than by going off course with the randomization mechanism.

## CHECKING THAT RANDOM ASSIGNMENT WAS EFFECTIVE

Even though random assignment is the best method researchers have for getting equivalent groups, and randomization failure is rare,[46] some are skeptical. That is when a random assignment or balance check, which is a comparison of the groups' equivalence, is in order. It is not necessary for *all* variables to be equally distributed among groups; those that are highly related to the outcome or dependent variables are of most concern. A rule of thumb for when something is "highly related" is that if a variable correlates with the dependent variable at .45 or greater, that variable must be equivalently distributed among groups.[47] It is a common misunderstanding that random assignment must result in equivalence on every variable known to mankind; that is not the case.[ii]

## Aggregate Level Random Assignment

Random assignment checks are more important when assignment is done at aggregate levels rather than with individuals; for example, businesses, families, polling precincts, or classrooms can be randomly assigned as units.[48] Aggregate level assignment[iii] is usually done when it is difficult or impossible to randomly assign individuals, but this is less preferable than individual random assignment, as people within a group or organization may differ systematically. For example, a start-up business may have younger workers than an established firm. An intact classroom may have group dynamics that create different motivation levels. Polling precincts may have voters who vary systematically because of the neighborhood they can afford to live in. It is more important to test equivalence when groups, such as classes or whole schools rather than individuals, are randomly assigned. This is because the sample size is usually lower when using aggregate groups than when using individuals.[49] For example, one study[50] assigned forty-one schools to three conditions, giving each group thirteen to fourteen schools. This is well below the suggested size of twenty.[51]

## Reporting Random Assignment Results

Not all journal articles will report the results of a random assignment check, but the practice is growing more common, although not without controversy.[iv] The field of political science has developed guidelines that require reporting whether random assignment was employed, as well as the unit that was randomized, and tables or text showing baseline means and standard

---

[ii]For a detailed discussion of this, see Mutz and Pemantle.

[iii]It is also important that the unit of *assignment* be the same as the unit of *analysis* in statistical tests. For example, if schools or classrooms are assigned as aggregate units to receive a treatment, then statistical analysis should be based on the aggregate level, not the individual level. In a hypothetical study of 2,500 students at thirty schools, fifteen of which are assigned to treatment and fifteen to control conditions, the total sample size is thirty, not 2,500. Otherwise, the precision of results will be overstated due to the overinflated N.

[iv]To get a sense of the controversy, read Gerber et al., (2014), the challenge to it by Mutz and Pemantle (2016), and Gerber et al.'s response (2016): Alan Gerber et al., "Reporting Guidelines for Experimental Research: A Report from the Experimental Research Section Standards Committee," *Journal of Experimental Political Science* 1, no. 1 (2014): 81–98; Alan S. Gerber et al., "Reporting Balance Tables, Response Rates and Manipulation Checks in Experimental Research: A Reply from the Committee That Prepared the Reporting Guidelines," ibid. 2, no. 2 (2016): 216–29; Diana C. Mutz and Robin Pemantle, "Standards for Experimental Research: Encouraging a Better Understanding of Experimental Methods," ibid.

deviations for certain variables.[52] To monitor the results of random assignment, researchers can test the equivalence of the groups on important variables with means and standard deviations or statistics designed to detect differences such a *t* tests, chi-square, and analysis of variance (ANOVA). These are then reported in a table. For example, if gender is important to the outcome variable, it will be checked to see that the groups have equivalent numbers of men and women; this is one time where finding no significant difference is a good thing. Only basic information is necessary for most randomization reports. For example, here is how one study reported it in an experiment testing the vividness effect on health messages:

> Two-way ANOVA crossing the two manipulated variables ("message vividness" and "argument strength") were performed on participants' gender, age, sex behavior, and so forth. Results showed that the participants in the four experimental conditions were not significantly different from each other (p > .05). Therefore, randomization appears to be effective.[53]

Some authors go further. For example, one study[54] included a table showing the descriptive statistics for various independent variables by group but no significance tests (see figure 7.3). Here is the narrative that was included in that study, and also the table:

> The means of the independent variables in each of the experimental conditions are reported in table 1. As shown in table 1, there were no substantial differences between the means and standard deviations of all the independent variables. The gender proportions in both conditions were also equivalent. Since the independent variables were asked before the manipulation, this shows that the random assignment indeed resulted in equal groups.[55]

Ho and McLeod included this table illustrating that random assignment resulted in equivalent groups on various variables.

Here is another example from a study on tutoring that did include the results of significance tests of random assignment and also included a table:

> In order to test whether the students were distributed randomly in terms of these background measures, group means were calculated and t-tests were run to test for significant differences between the treatment and control groups. Tests of significance indicated that, for all background measures but one, there were no statistically significant differences between the treatment and control groups: the randomisation had worked to create pre-treatment equivalence.[56]

It is important to report randomization checks after a study has been completed if there has been considerable attrition, or subjects dropping out. This is to ensure that the dropouts did

| FIGURE 7.3 ● TABLE OF RANDOM ASSIGNMENT | | | | |
|---|---|---|---|---|
| | **FTF (n = 192)** | | **CMC (n = 160)** | |
| | *M* | *SD* | *M* | *SD* |
| Gender | Females (71.9%) | — | Females (69.1%) | — |
| Print news use | 4.73 | 2.07 | 4.49 | 2.11 |
| Television news use | 5.02 | 1.96 | 4.98 | 2.04 |
| Fear of isolation | 2.98 | 1.10 | 3.26 | 1.10 |
| Communication apprehension | 3.00 | 1.23 | 3.03 | 1.26 |
| Current opinion congruency | .09 | .24 | .09 | .25 |
| Future opinion congruency | .32 | .50 | .30 | .49 |

From: Ho, Shirley S., and Douglas M. McLeod. 2008. "Social-Psychological Influences on Opinion Expression in Face-to-Face and Computer-Mediated Communication." *Communication Research* 35 (2) (April): 190–207.

not differ significantly from the subjects who stayed in the study. Sometimes, the treatment itself is the reason. It may be too long, boring, or difficult, so subjects quit. Experiments that are conducted over a long period of time are especially prone to this problem.

## When Random Assignment Fails

Random assignment is the best available method for achieving equivalence among experimental groups, but it does not guarantee that groups will be perfectly matched on every individual difference variable.[57] It minimizes, rather than prevents, confounding.[58] Differences still may occur due to chance. It is not necessary to have equivalent groups on every possible variable; it is most important on variables that are correlated with the outcome variable.[59] For example, in moral judgment studies, age and education are highly correlated with moral judgment, but gender is not.[60] So it is more important to have groups be equivalent on age and education, and not worry so much about having equivalent numbers of men and women. When groups are not equivalent on important characteristics, internal validity decreases and researchers run the risk of making erroneous inferences.[61] However, failure to achieve equivalence with a proper randomization mechanism is rare.[62] Furthermore, the alpha level of significance testing already takes into account the fact that some variables will be spread unevenly across groups due to chance.[63] There is no way to "fix" a true failure of random assignment other than to start from scratch and redo the randomization properly.[64]

| FIGURE 7.4 ● RANDOM ASSIGNMENT REPORTING | | | | |
|---|---|---|---|---|
| | **FTF (n = 192)** | | **CMC (n = 160)** | |
| | *M* | *SD* | *M* | *SD* |
| Gender | Females (71.9%) | — | Females (69.1%) | — |
| Print news use | 4.73 | 2.07 | 4.49 | 2.11 |
| Television news use | 5.02 | 1.96 | 4.98 | 2.04 |
| Fear of isolation | 2.98 | 1.10 | 3.26 | 1.10 |
| Communication apprehension | 3.00 | 1.23 | 3.03 | 1.26 |
| Current opinion congruency | .09 | .24 | .09 | .25 |
| Future opinion congruency | .32 | .50 | .30 | .49 |

From: Ritter, Gary W., and Rebecca A. Maynard. 2008. "Using the Right Design to Get the 'Wrong' Answer? Results of a Random Assignment Evaluation of a Volunteer Tutoring Programme." *Journal of Children's Services* 3 (2): 4–16.

Here are some tips for achieving equivalence:

- If it is possible to include all subjects in all the groups without carry-over effects—that is, using a within-subjects design—then equivalence is a nonissue because the exact same people are in each group.

- Groups are considered nonequivalent if twice as many subjects in one group have some nuisance variable compared to the other group[65]—for example, if there are twice as many men as women in one group where gender is related to the outcome; ten men and five women in a group is considered nonequivalent.

- Start by ensuring there are enough subjects in each group. A power analysis, explained in chapter 8, will do this. The more subjects, the greater the chance that equivalence will be achieved.[66] In studies that employ multiple runs, more subjects can be recruited and randomly assigned, and the experiment conducted again to reach equivalence.[67]

- A good rule of thumb for achieving equivalence is to have at least twenty subjects in each group.[68] But even then, groups with fewer than twenty subjects actually are protected from erroneous conclusions of nonequivalence because statistics tests have a harder time detecting spurious differences with small numbers.[69]

- The random assignment process can be redone until equivalence is achieved.[70] Obviously, this only works if random assignment can be checked before the treatments are given.

- If nonequivalence can only be detected after the study is conducted, one widespread strategy is to use the nonequivalent variable as a covariate in the statistical analysis using analysis of covariance.[71] This will help reduce the influence of that variable before testing differences between the groups. For example, if there are twice as many men in the treatment group as the control group, and gender is expected to affect the outcome, using gender as a covariate will help level the playing field. That is, it helps remove unexplained variability due to the effects of gender before testing the effects of the treatment, which leads to more precise estimates.[72] This approach should be used conservatively, however, as covariates should only be used if planned in advance (a topic of the next chapter), as this will not "control" for the lack of true random assignment. And the growing tendency to include numerous covariates defeats the purpose of a well-designed, controlled experiment.[73]

One thing researchers should *not* do is purposively recruit more subjects with the needed characteristic and assign them just to the group low on that variable.[74] That is not random. Nor should a researcher try to rebalance the groups by moving subjects around to even out the groups before giving the treatment.[75] That also is not random.

Finally, it is somewhat reassuring to know that if groups are not equivalent on some variables, the differences will represent random error, not systematic error, and are unlikely to produce incorrect inferences.[76] Additionally, replication helps correct for any erroneous conclusions from a study threatened by nonequivalence; for more on that, refer to chapter 5. Over multiple studies, the truth tends to prevail.[77]

In fields where equivalence can be prone to problems, such as in education, social work, criminology, and program evaluations, a significant amount of time may need to be devoted to achieving equivalent groups. For example, in a study of a drug program in schools,[78] after random assignment was completed and checked for equivalence, two schools dropped out, making the groups nonequivalent. The researchers had to draw new schools, randomly assign them, and recheck equivalence.

# BLOCKING, MATCHING, AND OTHER STRATEGIES

One way to reduce the chances of unequal groups is with a **matched pairs** strategy and **blocking**. This involves matching subjects on important variables and then assigning them to treatment and control groups as a pair or block.[79] This is used to help ensure that an extraneous or nuisance[80] variable related to the outcome variable does not confound the results. Groups are created based on subjects with the same level of the blocking variable. For example, if gender is the blocking variable, subjects would be randomly paired by gender—a man with a woman—and then each pair randomly assigned to the treatment or control group.[81]

In a business study on the effectiveness of a mentoring program, the researcher was not allowed to randomly assign subjects to condition by the employers, who wanted to select employees with the highest potential for promotion to the program.[82] Instead, the study used a matched pairs design, selecting control group employees who were similar to treatment group employees based on five characteristics such as similarity of salary, performance rating, tenure in the organization, working in the same office, and not previously participating in a mentoring program. The study reports statistical tests showing no differences between treatment and control group subjects on these variables, while also noting "the treatment and matched control groups may have varied on unobserved characteristics."[83]

Experimenters must anticipate and be able to measure the variable before conducting the study, so matching is no help for confounding variables that are not known; simple random assignment is still preferable for this reason.

Blocking also can be done with more than two levels of variables. For example, if age is the variable one wanted to ensure is equivalent across groups, then blocks of different age groups could be created; for example, four blocks for the age groups eighteen to thirty-four years old, thirty-five to fifty-four years old, fifty-five to sixty-four years old, and sixty-five years and older. After these blocks are created, the subjects in each are randomly assigned to treatment and control groups so that an equal number of subjects from each age block are in each group. Now, age cannot be the cause of any differences between the experimental groups.

Blocking is not preferable to straightforward random assignment but is useful when very few potential subjects are available or small sample sizes are likely—for example, when groups such as schools are the units. Matching strategies are frequently used in education studies, where schools are matched on important characteristics and then randomly assigned one to each condition.[84] Another example comes from a study on the effects of having grown up with friends of a different ethnicity on stereotyping.[85] The researcher anticipated it would be hard to find subjects who had grown up in integrated neighborhoods, so he pretested experimental volunteers, measuring their level of personal contact with minorities, and then matched high-contact subjects with low-contact subjects before randomly assigning them to the treatment or control group.

Blocking and matching strategies also can be useful when random assignment is not likely to be implemented correctly—for example, in program evaluations where the researcher is not in control of assignment.[86]

## Blocking vs. Simple Random Assignment

Matching strategies are *not* preferable to simple randomization,[87] although they can be misleading in their intuitive appeal.[88] For one thing, statistical tests lose power when blocking factors do not have much influence on the outcome variable.[89] Blocking is more common in the life sciences when studying plants and animals.[90] Another drawback is that blocking requires a two-step process, first measuring subjects on the blocking factor, then randomly assigning them to groups, administering the treatment, and measuring the outcome. Social science experts agree that simple random assignment is preferable to other methods for achieving comparable groups.[91] Even the harshest critics of random assignment do not argue for an alternative.[92] Campbell and Stanley are particularly critical of the "widespread and mistaken preference . . . for equation through matching,"[93] saying, "matching is no real help when used to overcome initial group differences." When confounding variables are unknown, and so uncontrollable (sometimes called *lurking variables*), random assignment is the best strategy, as it automatically balances these.[94]

### Stratified Random Assignment

One technique that makes it easier to assess equivalence on many variables is **stratified random assignment**, where numerous variables are combined into a single variable, similar to a factor created by factor analysis.[95] This does not block or match up subjects or units using any particular variables, but rather combines numerous related variables into one overarching factor that can be measured for equivalence after subjects are randomly assigned. In other words, it allows researchers to measure equivalence on one global factor instead of worrying about numerous discrete variables. For example, one study[96] used seven key variables such as the type of community a school was in, number of grades in the school, percentage of White students, enrollment per grade, and rural or urban setting. It then used a statistical technique to arrive at one composite stratifying variable. This was done to find a combination of variables that were closely related within these schools, which the authors called "rurality," explaining that rural schools often were similar on these characteristics. After random assignment, equivalence was checked by the single composite factor rather than on seven individual variables. The actual process was more complicated than described here.[97] The authors found equivalence using ANOVA tests of differences and reported it in a table (see figure 7.6). This stratifying procedure has the advantage of having unknown or unmeasured variables be randomly distributed across groups, whereas blocking and matching strategies do not.[98] As with achieving equivalence, this strategy is reserved for variables that are likely to be highly correlated with the outcome variable, not for every variable.[99] This technique, like blocking, is more common in some disciplines than others, so it is important to know the standard in your field.

## RANDOM ASSIGNMENT OF OTHER THINGS

So far, this chapter has focused on randomly assigning individual subjects to conditions. But random assignment applies to more than simply how subjects are assigned to groups. In fact, experts advise randomly assigning as many of a study's procedures as possible.[101]

**FIGURE 7.5 ● RANDOM ASSIGNMENT CHECK**

The text explaining the random assignment equivalence check said, "First, we verified that the assignment procedure worked to provide group equivalence on the school-level variables relating to CIS score. We conducted a simple ANOVA (SAS Proc GLM), with Program (Rural, Classic, Control) listed as a class variable. Table 3 presents the results for the overall F test. As expected, program group membership was unrelated to the CIS score, the two factors making up the CIS score, and the seven items making up the factors."[100]

| | Tutored students | Control students | Total sample |
|---|---|---|---|
| Average reading grade, 1997-98 year-end (A = 4.0) | 1.65 | 1.61 | 1.63 |
| Average math grade, 1997-98 year-end (A = 4.0) | 1.79 | 1.85 | 1.82 |
| Average SAT-9 reading open-ended national percentile score, 1998 | 23.1 | 23.2 | 23.2 |
| Average SAT-9 math open-ended national percentile score, 1998 | 16.7 | 18.6 | 17.6 |
| Full year attendance rate, 1997-98 | 91.8 | 90.6 | 91.2 |
| % of students not promoted, 1997-98 | 9.2 | 9.0 | 9.1 |
| % of students African American | 95.9 | 96.8 | 96.4 |
| % in home receiving welfare assistance (TANF) | 63.3 | 60.9 | 62.1 |
| % with guardian with a high school degree or more | 68.6 | 74.5 | 71.5 |
| % with guardian currently working for pay | 57.2 | 51.9 | 54.6 |
| % with guardian reporting health problem that limits activity | 19.5 | 23.2 | 21.3 |
| % in home with both mother and father | 37.4 | 31.1 | 34.4 |
| % reporting that someone helps with homework | 73.2 | 78.4 | 75.7 |
| % reporting that someone at home reads with them | 67.0 | 69.5 | 68.2 |
| Average number of children in household | 3.39 | 3.02 | 3.20 |
| **Total study sample** | **196** | **189** | **385** |

1. The welfare assistance data were derived from the School District of Philadelphia student information system.
2. The background data related to student guardians and the numbers of children per household were derived from the baseline survey completed by the guardians who gave parental consent for the student to participate in the tutoring programme (September 1998).
3. The figures on household composition and help with reading and homework were derived from the tutee follow-up survey administered to tutees at programme completion in May 1999.

Shadish, Cook, and Campbell deliberately refer to random assignment of "units" so as not to imply that only people should be randomized.[102] Anything that could introduce systematic bias should be randomly assigned. For example, if more than one experimenter

| Variable | F(2,38) | p |
|---|---|---|
| CIS | 0.25 | .78 |
| Factor 1 | 1.05 | .36 |
| Factor 2 | 0.08 | .93 |
| Rurality | 0.45 | .64 |
| Npergrade | 1.62 | .21 |
| Numgrades | 0.41 | .67 |
| Pctwhite | 1.60 | .21 |
| Pctlunch | 0.10 | .90 |
| Scores | 0.22 | .81 |
| Rdrugs | 0.80 | .46 |

FIGURE 7.6 ● TESTING FOR RANDOM ASSIGNMENT TABLE

Note: Post hoc tests with the Duncan test showed no significant differences ($p<.10$) for any individual comparisons.

will administer the study, the experimenters should be randomly assigned to the sessions and conditions he or she will supervise.[103] An experimenter who observes and measures subjects might become better after practice or, conversely, grow tired and get worse at measuring. It is important that the experimenter not be assigned to observe all subjects in the control group first and the treatment group last (or vice versa) in order to avoid introducing systematic differences between the groups. Instead, experimenters should be randomly assigned to each group as well as to session.

Typically, when there is more than one stimulus—advertisements, news stories, and health messages, for example—these should be presented to subjects in a random order. In a study of politicians' decision making, the researchers randomized many things.[104] In addition to randomly assigning subjects to condition, they randomized the three types of tasks and also the thirteen decisions within each type of task that subjects had to make. The study also gave subjects an incentive in the form of a donation to a charity, and the way that was offered was also randomized; here is the explanation:

> To make each decision that includes a monetary payoff relevant, but simultaneously ensure that tasks do not influence each other, we randomly selected one task that determined how much money was donated to the charity on behalf of the participant. Specifically, we randomly selected either the lottery-choice or the lottery-valuation part of the experiment, and then we randomly selected one task from this part. This avoided that participants' choices were influenced by so-called portfolio effects (e.g., some safe and some risky choices for a balanced portfolio) or by previous earnings.[105]

This study used a within-subjects design, but because the scenarios in the two conditions (gain frames, loss frames) were similar, the researchers did not want subjects to read each scenario in both conditions, so they randomly assigned each participant to read half the scenarios in each condition. They explain it like this:

> For each scenario, it was randomly determined whether a participant was presented with the loss or the gain frame, so it was possible that a participant would get the gain frame for one scenario and a loss frame for another scenario. We also randomly determined the order of the scenarios.[106]

Clearly, these researchers followed Bausell's advice: "When in doubt—randomize."[107]

## Counterbalancing

The reasons for randomly assigning or rotating the order of something, or **counterbalancing**, is to avoid carry-over effects. These were described in chapter 6 as effects due to learning, practice, fatigue, or the subjects changing. Carry-over effects happen when receiving one treatment affects a subject's response to the next treatment. One specific kind of carry-over effect arises from the order in which things are presented, known as **order effects**. Order effects have been well documented under the study of **primacy** and **recency**, the ideas that we remember best what we are exposed to first and last. This is a special concern for within-subjects designs where every subject gets all the different treatments, as they are especially prone to fatigue, practice effects, carry-over, and order effects.[108] Counterbalancing is helpful because often the carry-over effect in one direction will cancel out the effect in the other direction. For example, some subjects may do better on the last treatment (recency effect) and others on the first (primacy effect). When the data are aggregated, these two effects cancel each other out. The same applies to everything that is randomly assigned; for example, if more than one experimenter will supervise multiple runs of a study, the different experimenters should not only be randomly assigned to the treatment or control conditions, they should also be rotated, or counterbalanced, among sessions.[109] The goal of counterbalancing is to make order effects equivalent across the conditions. And, as with all things equivalent, failing to counterbalance orders decreases internal validity.

## Latin Square

Counterbalancing can be accomplished by simply randomly assigning, but there is one specific type of counterbalancing strategy used in experimental research called the **Latin square** that equalizes the number of positions under which each stimulus occurs. It ensures that each experimental message or stimulus occurs in the first position one time, in the last position one time, and in each in-between position one time. Also, each condition or stimulus follows the other exactly once. This is more efficient than simple random assignment.[110] Here is an illustration of how it works: A hypothetical experiment uses three different advertisements as stimuli. If the researcher randomly assigns the ads to order, there are six possible order combinations:

| A | B | C |
|---|---|---|
| A | C | B |
| B | C | A |
| C | B | A |
| C | A | B |
| B | A | C |

But using Latin squares produces three combinations:

| A | B | C |
|---|---|---|
| B | C | A |
| C | A | B |

Each advertisement is shown first one time, last one time, and in the middle one time. The two key features of a Latin square are that a row or column never contains the same letter twice and that every row and column contains the same letters. This is much more efficient than simple random assignment to order,[111] as it reduces the number of subjects needed to receive each order.[112] Latin squares are especially useful in large factorial designs where it would be quite costly to administer all possible order combinations.[113] This type of counterbalancing is achieved by randomly selecting stimuli to represent A, B, and C in the first row.[114] Next, the stimuli are simply rotated by moving the first-place stimulus to last place in each row and sliding the others over one place. This works for three or more stimuli; obviously with two stimuli, there are only two possible order combinations.

In reporting Latin squares, as in reporting random assignment, it is common to just see it mentioned in passing. For example, in this study of public service announcements (PSAs) in a health study, the authors said, "The order of the presentation of PSAs was counterbalanced according to a diagram-balanced Latin square."[115]

And in another study of decision making in TV newsrooms, the author described the rotation of the three story scenarios this way: "The order of which story participants received was counterbalanced using a Latin squares design."[116]

In studies that use multiple factors, Latin squares help avoid confounding of the factors. For example, in a study of the use of humor in advertising,[117] the authors had subjects listen to radio broadcasts that featured different advertisements. The factors used to make up each ad consisted of the type of product (e.g., cereal, cheese, batteries), brand name, and jokes, which they called one-liners. Here is how they describe their counterbalancing strategy:

Rotations for the three versions of radio broadcasts were designed such that a particular one-liner was not presented with a particular brand name or product type more than once in the study. . . . Within each combination, product types, brand names, and one-liners were rotated in order or presentation for each of the three audiotapes. To arrange three commentaries in three rotations, a Latin square counterbalancing technique (Keppel, 1991) was used.[118]

The Latin squares design got its name from an ancient puzzle on the different ways Latin letters could be arranged in a square.[119] It was introduced as a rotation experiment,[120] popularized by R. A. Fisher,[121] and has been the preferred method in psychology ever since.[122]

# RANDOM ASSIGNMENT RESISTANCE

Most researchers are quickly persuaded of the abilities of randomization to solve a multitude of problems, but that is frequently not the case for nonresearchers whose participation may be needed in a study. Disciplines that perform program evaluations or conduct studies in real-world or field environments may encounter resistance to random assignment. For example, school administrators allowed some students to bypass the random assignment process in one study.[123] Education researchers, for example, find that school personnel may object to offering some students a treatment opportunity and denying it to others.[124] Business researchers have found that executives may refuse to allow their employees to be randomly assigned, instead insisting on hand-picking those assigned to each group themselves.[125] In a health study, "a substantial number" of subjects refused to participate in the randomization because they did not want to be involved if they were not assured of receiving the potentially beneficial treatment.[126] Ethical concerns also raise opposition to randomization; for example, in an experiment on treatment for crime victims, some subjects who exhibited self-harming tendencies were moved from the control group to the treatment group, disrupting the randomization.[127] This can lead to researchers abandoning a true experiment in favor of a quasi experiment, discussed in chapter 4. This topic is discussed in more detail in More About box 7.3.

As elegant a procedure as random assignment is in all its forms, it is not perfect. But as Campbell and Stanley say, "It is nonetheless the only way of doing so, and the essential way."[180]

With a firm understanding of how subjects (and other things) should be assigned, the next chapter will deal with ways to sample subjects and how to determine the optimum number of them.

# MORE ABOUT . . . BOX 7.3
## Resistance to Random Assignment

When it comes to random assignment, compliance is critical.[128] As with pregnancy, there is no such thing as being "a little bit random"[129]— it is an all-or-nothing proposition. That distinction is often lost on nonresearchers; for example, in one study, when told that random assignment had been compromised, staff implementing it acted surprised and responded that they believed the assignments were "in fact, more-or-less random."[130] One employee directly involved with the process believed the instructions were merely "recommendations."[131]

Another example of random assignment gone wrong includes a murder by a subject who dropped out of a program, which led the prosecutor to refuse to deny treatment to anyone in need.[132]

Not all threats to random assignment are this dramatic. Any actions that compromise randomization can undermine the internal validity of an experiment by leading to nonrandom differences between subjects in treatment and control conditions. In the following table, the first column lists some common objections to random assignment from practitioners in the field tasked with assigning subjects to conditions for researchers. The column on the right contains advice for overcoming these objections. Researchers who have reported their results with these techniques have seen compliance with randomization go from as low as 19% to 94%.[133]

The advice here is drawn from education, counseling, criminal justice, and business fields but applies to attempts to assess the effectiveness of an intervention in a field setting in any discipline.

The best approach is for researchers to insist on conducting random assignment themselves and to carry out the procedure at the researcher's site, not the study site.[134] This should always be done in conjunction with communication with the site staff, allowing them to voice concerns, have questions answered, and participate in the design process.[135] Monitoring the assignment process is also essential. Subjects have been known to try to sneak into groups to which they are not assigned.[136] It is also important to observe the extent to which the intervention is actually being implemented; for example, if teachers are supposed to use technology, check to see how much they are doing so.[137]

| OBJECTION | RESPONSE |
|---|---|
| FAIRNESS<br><br>Giving a perceived benefit, even if unproven, to some and not all is intrinsically unfair.[138]<br><br>School personnel, in particular, are not inclined to offer interventions to some and deny others the same opportunity. [139] | Explain that when resources are limited and there are more people who need services than slots available, random assignment is one of the fairest ways to distribute services.[140]<br><br>Point out that random assignment protects the organization from accusations of favoritism.[141]<br><br>Explain the random assignment process as a lottery, which gives everyone an equal chance, which is fair.[142]<br><br>Alter the control group so they receive a lower dose of the treatment instead of no treatment.[143]<br><br>Agree to give those in the control group priority to participate in the treatment group during another run of the experiment.[144] |

*(Continued)*

(Continued)

| OBJECTION | RESPONSE |
|---|---|
| **NEED**<br><br>Fears that the most in need of the treatment would not be chosen by random assignment.[145] | Offer to categorize some of the most in need as "wildcards" who can bypass the random assignment process and are put in the treatment group; then exclude these subjects from the analysis.[146]<br><br>Divert the most needy into an alternative intervention that is not part of the study.[147]<br><br>Explain that the treatment has not yet been shown to work—that is what the study is for. If it does not provide benefit, then the needy in the control group will not have lost anything.[148]<br><br>Explain that if the treatment is shown to work in this randomized experiment, everyone can be offered it later.[149] |
| **EVALUATION FEARS**<br><br>If the experiment shows the program has no impact, it could be eliminated.[150] | Be sensitive to this issue and collaborate on the outcome variables. Add in qualitative data that can provide insights beyond the quantitative. Also include measures that may show more sensitivity to the program.[151] |
| **CONFLICTS WITH PRACTICE**<br><br>Randomly assigning people to get special training or be enrolled in certain classes conflicts with normal procedures.[152]<br><br>It may be difficult to assign certain interventions to only parts of existing units. For example, in schools where classes are taught by teams of teachers, assigning an intervention to only one set of teachers can lead to group planning issues.[153]<br><br>In one study, special education students needed to be in the same class, resulting in special education students being overenrolled in one condition.[154]<br><br>Staff is uncomfortable with an outsider telling them what to do.[155]<br><br>It might send unintended signals to high-performing employees if they were not chosen for the treatment.[156]<br><br>Staff may object to the extra work of implementing random assignment, experience scheduling conflicts, or key people may leave due to illness or turnover.[157] | Get to know staff, the environment, and their needs.[158]<br><br>Suggest procedures that afford a minimum of disruption.[159]<br><br>Allow practitioners to exempt up to 10% of subjects from random assignment for practical reasons. Track them and exclude from the analysis.[160] |

| OBJECTION | RESPONSE |
|---|---|
| **ACCIDENTAL**<br><br>Subjects may be accidentally assigned to the wrong condition due to misunderstanding, lack of time to make assignments properly, or staff turnover.[161]<br><br>In one study of schools, staff did not understand the lists of students already included random assignment to group, and they devised their own method to randomly assign from the lists.[162] | Improve communication.[163]<br><br>Assign a randomization liaison from the research team to the organization.[164]<br><br>Schedule multiple meetings and information sessions to explain the research design.[165]<br><br>Include everyone. For example, in one study, security guards were in charge of checking subjects into the program, so they needed to know why it was important that subjects go to the group they were assigned.[166]<br><br>Include staff in initial planning sessions for random assignment.[167]<br><br>Look for staff and organizations that have prior experience with random assignment and research studies. In one study, a staff member involved with random assignment said it took a year and a half before she fully understood the assignment process.[168]<br><br>Use color-coded forms to make it easier to quickly see to which condition a subject should be assigned. A study of domestic violence treatment trained police officers in random assignment using color-coded report forms.[169] |
| **SUBJECTS OBJECT**<br><br>Subjects request being put in different groups, refuse to participate in the randomization, withdraw in the middle of treatment, or complain to administrators, who reassign them.[170]<br><br>Subjects drop out for a variety of reasons including health, lack of childcare, and transportation issues.[171] | Make the control group more attractive by giving subjects some sort of "treatment as usual" such as normal classroom instruction or other interesting activities that will not confound the outcome.[172] One set of researchers considered an open-ended discussion group as an enhancement to the basic treatment.[173]<br><br>Establish a procedure so that those requesting to be moved must meet with the researchers, who explain the reasons behind the assignment.[174]<br><br>Offer the intervention to the subject at a later time.[175]<br><br>Put control group subjects who wish to receive the intervention on a waiting list for future programs.[176]<br><br>In one study, a principal insisted that siblings of those chosen for the treatment group also had to be included. Exclude these subjects from statistical analysis.[177]<br><br>Have staff refer subjects' requests to researchers, who are in a better position to turn them down and explain why[178]<br><br>Track subjects who leave and learn why.[179] |

# STUDY SPOTLIGHT 7.4
Taking advantage of random assignment in a natural setting

**From: Abrams, David S., and Albert H. Yoon. 2007. "The Luck of the Draw: Using Random Case Assignment to Investigate Attorney Ability."** *University of Chicago Law Review* 74 (4) (Fall): 1145–1177.

This study took advantage of naturally occurring random assignment when the researchers discovered that a county in Nevada was assigning incoming felony cases randomly to attorneys in the pool, which allowed for a natural experiment free from selection bias.

Clark County, which includes Las Vegas, began assigning attorneys to cases after a defendant's death sentence was overturned because he was assigned to an inexperienced public defender. Under the previous nonrandom assignment method, the better attorneys might be assigned the more difficult cases, thus confounding attorney ability with case difficulty. This opportunity allowed the researchers to examine the performance of attorneys that cannot be explained by case characteristics. Conventional wisdom says that lawyers who attend better law schools may get clients lower sentences, for example. The study discovered that Hispanic attorneys and those with more experience achieve better outcomes for clients than others, but gender and law school attended made no difference.

For the purposes of this book, the study is important because it illustrates in depth the value of random assignment.

The researchers began by checking to see that random assignment was indeed being implemented and not thwarted. This helped rule out alternative explanations for trial outcomes, such as case difficulty. Cases were assigned to attorneys without the judges, prosecutor, or team chief knowing any characteristics of the defendant or even the alleged offense, helping to ensure against any subconscious efforts to assign cases purposively. The researchers used nonparametric tests (chi-square) to see if cases were indeed being assigned randomly using the defendants' age, gender, and race. They explain that these three variables are highly correlated with other defendant characteristics on unobserved variables. They say, "Crucially, we assume that this provides evidence that unobservables are also randomly assigned (due to correlation with observables)."[181]

| TESTING FOR RANDOM ASSIGNMENT | | |
|---|---|---|
| **Case characteristic** | **$p$-value** | **Observations** |
| Defendant sex | 0.851 | 10,129 |
| Defendant age | 0.253 | 9,803 |
| Defendant race | 0.098 | 7,145 |

Note: Each row reports results from a separate simulation to test for the equality of public defender fixed effects. Defendant sex is a dummy variable for whether the defendant is male. Defendant race is 0 for black defendants and 1 for white defendants.

Nonsignificant results showed the cases were indeed randomly assigned (see figure 7.6). This then allowed the researchers to test their hypotheses concerning the differences among attorneys' abilities and other variables that predict better trial outcomes for defendants.

These researchers were creative in spotting an opportunity for a natural experiment. As with most journal articles, this one does not mention the researchers gaining approval from an Institutional Review Board (IRB) before collecting data. The data used may have been exempt from informed consent because it was a matter of public record, or the researchers may have given informed consent after the fact.

New researchers sometimes assume that because data are already collected, this constitutes "secondary data" and one does not need approval from an IRB. True secondary data occurs when subjects have received informed consent—for example, in existing data sets such as the American National Election Studies or Pew polls. The organizations collecting these data sets and making them available to researchers have obtained permission from a human subjects committee of an IRB and have provided subjects with informed consent. This is not the case with all existing data. For example, students who fill out evaluations about satisfaction with their classes have not been given the information contained in informed consent documents. In any research that involves information collected from human subjects, researchers should contact their IRB to determine if they need to obtain IRB approval and subjects' informed consent, even if data have already been collected. Chapter 11 will discuss informed consent and IRB approval in more detail. Researchers should be attuned to opportunities for naturally occurring randomization but should also be careful to secure permission from an IRB and follow protocols for obtaining informed consent from the people whose data will be used.

## Common Mistakes

- Not randomly assigning subjects to groups, or not doing random assignment appropriately
- Failing to randomly assign other elements of a study, such as the experimenters, to sessions
- Not counterbalancing stimuli

## Test Your Knowledge

1. When a participant has an equal chance of being in the treatment or control group in an experiment, it is called _____.

    a. Random sampling

    b. Random assignment

c. Random error

d. Selection bias

2. The main reason for using random assignment in an experiment is to ensure which of the following?

a. A sample representative of the population

b. That neither subject nor experimenter knows which group someone is in

c. That groups are as equivalent as possible on known and unknown variables

d. That the dependent variable does not differ across conditions

3. Which of the following is NOT a way to randomly assign subjects to groups?

a. Drawing names out of a hat

b. Flipping a coin

c. Using a random number generator

d. Rotating subjects so that groups come out even (e.g., 1, 2, 1, 2 . . .)

4. Groups need to be equivalent on all variables that can be measured.

a. True

b. False

5. Which is the preferred way to ensure that systematic variation does not confound a study?

a. Pretesting

b. Blocking or matching

c. Simple random assignment

d. Balancing groups by moving subjects around after random assignment

6. What besides subjects should be randomly assigned?

a. Nothing, only the subjects

b. Experimenters

c. All of the study's procedures

d. All but A

7. Latin square is a technique for _____.

a. Creating equivalent groups

b. Controlling for extraneous individual variables

c. Minimizing order effects

d. Randomly assigning subjects to groups

8. Complete the following to make a Latin square:

| A | B | C | D |
|---|---|---|---|
|   |   |   |   |
|   |   |   |   |
|   |   |   |   |

9. If men and women are paired and then assigned to the treatment or control group as a pair, this is called _____.

    a. Blocking or matching

    b. Random assignment

    c. Stratified random assignment

    d. Latin square

10. One drawback to random assignment is that experimenters must anticipate and be able to measure confounding variables before conducting the study, so it is no help for confounding variables that are not known.

    a. True

    b. False

Answers

1. b

2. c

3. d

4. b

5. c

6. d

7. c

8.

| A | B | C | D |
|---|---|---|---|
| B | C | D | A |
| C | D | A | B |
| D | A | B | C |

9. a

10. b

## Application Exercises

1. Using the experimental study you began developing in chapter 1 and continued by creating a design table and control group for in chapter 5, decide how you will randomly assign subjects to groups. Write one page on which strategy you will use and why—random number generator, drawing out of a hat, etc. Do a "test run" of this. Assume forty subjects in each of the groups in your study. Use your choice of randomizer to assign subjects. Analyze the results; were they balanced or unbalanced? Repeat the

process with a different type of randomizer to see how it turns out (i.e., if you used an online randomizer first, repeat by drawing out of a hat).

2. Write one page about all the elements of your study that could be randomly assigned. Besides the subjects, what other procedures might be randomly assigned? Why? Assume you will use at least three stimuli in your study (e.g., three different treatments, interventions, teaching techniques, ads, PSAs, stories, messages, etc.). Design a plan for counterbalancing them.

3. Write one page about the possible confounding variables that random assignment will need to help equalize across groups. Read literature about your outcome variable to see what others have found to be highly correlated with your dependent variable. Use your imagination and common sense to identify as many as you can.

## Suggested Readings

Chapter 5 in: R. Barker Bausell. 1994. *Conducting Meaningful Experiments: 40 Steps to Becoming a Scientist.* Thousand Oaks, CA: Sage.

Chapter 8, "Randomized Experiments: Rationale, Designs, and Conditions Conducive to Doing Them," pp. 246–278, in: Shadish, William R., Thomas D. Cook, and Donald T. Campbell. 2002. *Experimental and Quasi-Experimental Designs for Generalized Causal Inference.* Belmont, CA: Wadsworth Cengage Learning.

Read these two articles, one critical of random assignment and one more supportive, for a comparative perspective:

- Krause, Merton S., and Kenneth I. Howard. 2003. "What Random Assignment Does and Does Not Do." *Journal of Clinical Psychology* 59 (7): 751–766.

- Strube, M. J. 1991. "Small Sample Failure of Random Assignment: A Further Examination." *Journal of Consulting & Clinical Psychology* 59 (2): 346–350.

## Notes

1. W. A. McCall, *How to Experiment in Education* (New York: MacMillan, 1923), 41.
2. R. Barker Bausell, *Conducting Meaningful Experiments: 40 Steps to Becoming a Scientist* (Thousand Oaks, CA: Sage, 1994).
3. Richard A. Berk, "Randomized Experiments as the Bronze Standard," *Journal of Experimental Criminology* 1 (2005): 416–433.
4. Graeme D. Ruxton and Nick Colegrave, *Experimental Design for the Life Sciences,* 3rd ed. (Oxford, UK: Oxford University Press, 2011).
5. Bausell, *Conducting Meaningful Experiments.*
6. D. T. Campbell and J. C. Stanley, *Experimental and Quasi-Experimental Designs for Research* (Chicago: Rand McNally, 1963).
7. Charles Sanders Peirce and Joseph Jastrow, "On Small Differences of Sensation," *Memoirs of the National Academy of Sciences* 3, no. 75–83 (1885): 8.
8. William R. Shadish, Thomas D. Cook, and Donald T. Campbell, *Experimental and Quasi-Experimental Designs for Generalized Causal Inference* (Belmont, CA: Wadsworth Cengage Learning, 2002).

9. J. M. Gueron, "The Politics of Random Assignment: Implementing Studies and Impacting Policy," in *Evidence Matters: Randomized Trials in Education Research*, ed. F. Mosteller and R. Boruch (Washington, DC: Brookings Institution Press, 2002), 26.

10. Diana C. Mutz and Robin Pemantle, "Standards for Experimental Research: Encouraging a Better Understanding of Experimental Methods," *Journal of Experimental Political Science* 2, no. 2 (2016): 192–215.

11. Martin T. Orne, "Demand Characteristics and the Concept of Quasi Controls," in *Artifacts in Behavioral Research: Robert Rosenthal and Ralph L. Rosnow's Classic Books*, ed. Robert Rosenthal and Ralph L. Rosnow (Oxford: Oxford University Press, 2009), 110–137.

12. Cathaleene Macias et al., "Preference in Random Assignment: Implications for the Interpretation of Randomized Trials," *Administration & Policy in Mental Health & Mental Health Services Research* 36, no. 5 (2009): 331–342.

13. T. D. Cook and D. T. Campbell, *Quasi-Experimentation: Design and Analysis Issues for Field Settings* (Chicago: Rand-McNally, 1979).

14. Colin Ong-Dean, Carolyn Huie Hofstetter, and Betsy R. Strick, "Challenges and Dilemmas in Implementing Random Assignment in Educational Research," *American Journal of Evaluation* 32, no. 1 (2011): 40.

15. Macias et al., "Preference in Random Assignment," 331–342.

16. Ibid.

17. D. F. Halpern, *Thought and Knowledge: An Introduction to Critical Thinking*, 4th ed. (Mahwah, NJ: Erlbaum, 2003); M. Patricia King et al., "Impact of Participant and Physician Intervention Preferences on Randomized Trials: A Systematic Review," *Journal of the American Medical Association* 293, no. 9 (2005): 1089–1099.

18. Macias et al., "Preference in Random Assignment," 331–342.

19. Ibid.

20. Ibid.

21. Sameer B. Srivastava, "Network Intervention: Assessing the Effects of Formal Mentoring on Workplace Networks," *Social Forces* 94, no. 1 (2015): 427–452.

22. Shadish, Cook, and Campbell, *Experimental and Quasi-Experimental Designs*.

23. Cengiz Erisen, Elif Erisen, and Binnur Ozkececi-Taner, "Research Methods in Political Psychology," *Turkish Studies* 13, no. 1 (2013): 17.

24. Diana Mutz, *Population-Based Survey Experiments* (Princeton, NJ: Princeton University Press, 2011); Steven L. Nock and Thomas M. Guterbock, "Survey Experiments," in *Handbook of Survey Research*, ed. P. V. Marsden and J. D. Wright (Bingley, UK: Emerald Group Publishing Limited, 2010), 837–864.

25. Erin C. Cassese et al., "Socially Mediated Internet Surveys: Recruiting Participants for Online Experiments," *PS: Political Science & Politics* 46, no. 4 (2013): 1–10; James N. Druckman, "Priming the Vote: Campaign Effects in a US Senate Election," *Political Psychology* 25, no. 4 (2004): 577–594; Julio J. Elias, Nicola Lacetera, and Mario Macis, "Markets and Morals: An Experimental Survey Study," *PLoS ONE* 10, no. 6 (2015): 1–13.

26. Erisen, Erisen, and Ozkececi-Taner, "Research Methods in Political Psychology," 17.

27. Scott Clifford and Jennifer Jerit, "Is There a Cost to Convenience? An Experimental Comparison of Data Quality in Laboratory and Online Studies," *Journal of Experimental Political Science* 1, no. 2 (2014): 120–131.

28. Rebecca B. Morton and Kenneth C. Williams, *Experimental Political Science and the Study of Causality: From Nature to the Lab* (New York: Cambridge University Press, 2010).

29. Jona Linde and Barbara Vis, "Do Politicians Take Risks Like the Rest of Us? An Experimental Test of Prospect Theory under MPs," *Political Psychology* 38, no. 1 (2017): 101–117.

30. Clifford and Jerit, "Is There a Cost to Convenience?" 120–131.

31. Cassese et al., "Socially Mediated Internet Surveys"; Kevin J. Mullinix et al., "The Generalizability of Survey Experiments," *Journal of Experimental Political Science* 2 (2015): 109–138.

32. Renita Coleman and Lee Wilkins, "The Moral Development of Journalists: A Comparison With Other Professions and a Model for Predicting High Quality Ethical Reasoning," *Journalism and Mass Communication Quarterly* 81, no. 3 (2004): 511–527.

33. Renita Coleman and Lee Wilkins, "Searching for the Ethical Journalist: An Exploratory Study of the Ethical Development of News Workers," *Journal of Mass Media*

*Ethics* 17, no. 3 (2002): 209–255; Renita Coleman and Lee Wilkins, "The Moral Development of Journalists"; R. Coleman and L. Wilkins, "The Moral Development of Public Relations Practitioners: A Comparison with Other Professions," *Journal of Public Relations Research* 21, no. 3 (2009): 318–340.

34. Renita Coleman, "The Moral Judgment of Minority Journalists: Evidence from Asian American, Black, and Hispanic Professional Journalists," *Mass Communication and Society* 14, no. 5 (2011): 578–599.

35. Erisen, Erisen, and Ozkececi-Taner, "Research Methods in Political Psychology," 17.

36. Kate E. West, "Who Is Making the Decisions? A Study of Television Journalists, Their Bosses, and Consultant-Based Market Research," *Journal of Broadcasting & Electronic Media* 55, no. 1 (2011): 27.

37. Jun Myers, "Stalking the 'Vividness Effect' in the Preventive Health Message: The Moderating Role of Argument Quality on the Effectiveness of Message Vividness," *Journal of Promotion Management* 20, no. 5 (2014): 634.

38. Mutz and Pemantle, "Standards for Experimental Research," 192–215.

39. Bausell, *Conducting Meaningful Experiments*.

40. Mark L Davison and Stephen Robbins, "The Reliability and Validity of Objective Indices of Moral Development," *Applied Psychological Measurement* 2, no. 3 (1978): 391–403; James R. Rest, *Development in Judging Moral Issues* (Minneapolis, MN: University of Minnesota Press, 1979).

41. Bausell, *Conducting Meaningful Experiments*.

42. Christopher H. Rhoads and Charles Dye, "Optimal Design for Two-Level Random Assignment and Regression Discontinuity Studies," *Journal of Experimental Education* 84, no. 3 (2016): 421–448.

43. Srivastava, "Network Intervention."

44. D. Fergusson et al., "Post-Randomisation Exclusions: The Intention to Treat Principle and Excluding Patients from Analysis," *BMJ* 325 (2002): 652–654.

45. Howard Levene, "Robust Tests for Equality of Variances," in *Contributions to Probability and Statistics: Essays in Honor of Harold Hotelling*, ed. Ingram Olkin et al. (Stanford, CA: Stanford University Press, 1960), 278–292.

46. Mutz and Pemantle, "Standards for Experimental Research," 192–215

47. M. J. Strube, "Small Sample Failure of Random Assignment: A Further Examination," *Journal of Consulting & Clinical Psychology* 59, no. 2 (1991): 346–350.

48. Shadish, Cook, and Campbell, *Experimental and Quasi-Experimental Designs*

49. John Graham et al., "Random Assignment of Schools to Groups in the Drug Resistance Strategies Rural Project: Some New Methodological Twists," *Prevention Science* 15, no. 4 (2014): 516–525.

50. Ibid.

51. L. M. Hsu, "Random Sampling, Randomization, and Equivalence of Contrasted Groups in Psychotherapy Outcome Research," *Journal of Consulting and Clinical Psychology* 57 (1989): 131–137.

52. Alan Gerber et al., "Reporting Guidelines for Experimental Research: A Report from the Experimental Research Section Standards Committee," ibid.1, no. 1 (2014): 81–98.

53. Myers, "Stalking the 'Vividness Effect,'" 636.

54. Shirley S. Ho and Douglas M. McLeod, "Social-Psychological Influences on Opinion Expression in Face-to-Face and Computer-Mediated Communication," *Communication Research* 35, no. 2 (April 2008): 190–207.

55. Ibid., 197.

56. Gary W. Ritter and Rebecca A. Maynard, "Using the Right Design to Get the 'Wrong' Answer? Results of a Random Assignment Evaluation of a Volunteer Tutoring Programme," *Journal of Children's Services* 3, no. 2 (2008): 4–16.

57. Merton S. Krause and Kenneth I. Howard, "What Random Assignment Does and Does Not Do," *Journal of Clinical Psychology* 59, no. 7 (2003): 751–766.

58. Ibid.

59. Bausell, *Conducting Meaningful Experiments*; Hsu, "Random Sampling"; Strube, "Small Sample Failure of Random Assignment," 346–350.

60. James R. Rest et al., *Postconventional Moral Thinking: A Neo-Kohlbergian Approach* (Mahwah, NJ: Erlbaum, 1999).

61. Krause and Howard, "What Random Assignment Does and Does Not Do."

62. Mutz and Pemantle, "Standards for Experimental Research."

63. Ibid.

64. Ibid.

65. Hsu, "Random Sampling."
66. Strube, "Small Sample Failure of Random Assignment."
67. Graham et al., "Random Assignment of Schools."
68. Hsu, "Random Sampling."
69. Strube, "Small Sample Failure of Random Assignment."
70. Bausell, *Conducting Meaningful Experiments.*
71. Ibid.
72. Donald P. Green and Daniel Winik, "Using Random Judge Assignments to Estimate the Effects of Incarceration and Probation on Recidivism among Drug Offenders," *Criminology* 48, no. 2 (2010): 357–387.
73. Mutz and Pemantle, "Standards for Experimental Research."
74. Shadish, Cook, and Campbell, *Experimental and Quasi-Experimental Designs.*
75. Ibid.
76. Strube, "Small Sample Failure of Random Assignment," 346–350.
77. Krause and Howard, "What Random Assignment Does and Does Not Do"; Strube, "Small Sample Failure of Random Assignment."
78. Graham et al., "Random Assignment of Schools."
79. Campbell and Stanley, *Experimental and Quasi-Experimental Designs for Research.*
80. Murray Webster and Jane Sell, *Laboratory Experiments in the Social Sciences* (Amsterdam: Elsevier, 2007).
81. Bausell, *Conducting Meaningful Experiments*; Campbell and Stanley, *Experimental and Quasi-Experimental Designs for Research.*
82. Srivastava, "Network Intervention."
83. Ibid., 438.
84. Graham et al., "Random Assignment of Schools."
85. David Alan Free, "Perpetuating Stereotypes in Television News: The Influence of Interracial Contact on Content" (unpublished dissertation, University of Texas, 2012).
86. E. W. Gondolf, "Lessons from a Successful and Failed Random Assignment Testing Batterer Program Innovation," *Journal of Experimental Criminology* 6 (2010): 355–376.
87. Mutz and Pemantle, "Standards for Experimental Research."
88. Campbell and Stanley, *Experimental and Quasi-Experimental Designs for Research.*
89. Ruxton and Colegrave, *Experimental Design for the Life Sciences.*
90. For example, see ibid.; Murray R. Selwyn, *Principles of Experimental Design for the Life Sciences* (Boca Raton, FL: CRC Press, 1996).
91. Campbell and Stanley, *Experimental and Quasi-Experimental Designs for Research*; Strube, "Small Sample Failure of Random Assignment."
92. Krause and Howard, "What Random Assignment Does and Does Not Do."
93. Campbell and Stanley, *Experimental and Quasi-Experimental Designs for Research,* 15.
94. Selwyn, *Principles of Experimental Design for the Life Sciences.*
95. Graham et al., "Random Assignment of Schools."
96. Ibid.
97. Ibid.
98. Ibid.
99. Bausell, *Conducting Meaningful Experiments.*
100. Graham et al., "Random Assignment of Schools," 521.
101. Ibid.
102. Shadish, Cook, and Campbell, *Experimental and Quasi-Experimental Designs,* 253.
103. Bausell, *Conducting Meaningful Experiments.*
104. Linde and Vis, "Do Politicians Take Risks Like the Rest of Us?"
105. Ibid., 107–108.
106. Ibid., 111.
107. Bausell, *Conducting Meaningful Experiments,* 78.
108. Shadish, Cook, and Campbell, *Experimental and Quasi-Experimental Designs.*
109. Bausell, *Conducting Meaningful Experiments.*
110. Roger Kirk, *Experimental Design: Procedures for the Behavioral Sciences,* 4th ed. (Los Angeles, CA: Sage, 2013).
111. Campbell and Stanley, *Experimental and Quasi-Experimental Designs for Research.*
112. Ruxton and Colegrave, *Experimental Design for the Life Sciences.*
113. Shadish, Cook, and Campbell, *Experimental and Quasi-Experimental Designs.*
114. Kirk, *Experimental Design.*
115. Zhang Jueman, Zhang Di, and T. Makana Chock, "Effects of HIV/AIDS Public Service Announcements on Attitude and Behavior: Interplay of Perceived Threat

and Self-Efficacy," *Social Behavior and Personality: An International Journal* 42, no. 5 (2014): 799–809.

116. West, "Who Is Making the Decisions?" 27.

117. Eron M. Berg and Louis G. Lippman, "Does Humor in Radio Advertising Affect Recognition of Novel Product Brand Names?" *Journal of General Psychology* 128, no. 2 (2001): 194.

118. Ibid., 199.

119. Kirk, *Experimental Design*, 671.

120. E. L. Thorndike, W. A. McCall, and J. C. Chapman, *Ventilation in Relation to Mental Work*, vol. 78, Teachers College Contribution to Education (New York: Teachers College, Columbia University, 1916).

121. Ronald A. Fisher, *Statistical Methods for Research Workers* (Edinburgh: Oliver and Boyd, 1925).

122. Campbell and Stanley, *Experimental and Quasi-Experimental Designs for Research*.

123. Ritter and Maynard, "Using the Right Design to Get the 'Wrong' Answer?"

124. Ibid.

125. Srivastava, "Network Intervention."

126. Yun Hyung Koog and Byung-Il Min, "Does Random Participant Assignment Cause Fewer Benefits in Research Participants? Systematic Review of Partially Randomized Acupuncture Trials," *Journal of Alternative and Complementary Medicine* 15, no. 10 (2009): 1107–1113.

127. Richard A. Berk, Gordon K. Smyth, and Lawrence W. Sherman, "When Random Assignment Fails: Some Lessons from the Minneapolis Spouse Abuse Experiment," *Journal of Quantitative Criminology* 4, no. 3 (1988): 209–223.

128. Ong-Dean, Huie Hofstetter, and Strick. "Challenges and Dilemmas."

129. Gueron, "The Politics of Random Assignment," 26.

130. Ong-Dean, Huie Hofstetter, and Strick, "Challenges and Dilemmas," 39.

131. Ibid., 45.

132. Gondolf, "Lessons from a Successful and Failed Random Assignment."

133. Ong-Dean, Huie Hofstetter, and Strick, "Challenges and Dilemmas."

134. Gary W. Ritter and Marc J. Holley, "Lessons for Conducting Random Assignment in Schools," *Journal of Children's Services* 3, no. 2 (2008): 28–39.

135. Ibid.

136. Ibid.

137. Ibid.

138. Ibid.

139. Ritter and Maynard, "Using the Right Design."

140. Ritter and Holley, "Lessons for Conducting Random Assignment in Schools."

141. Ibid.

142. Bausell, *Conducting Meaningful Experiments*; Ritter and Holley, "Lessons for Conducting Random Assignment in Schools."

143. Ibid.

144. Ibid.

145. Ong-Dean, Huie Hofstetter, and Strick, "Challenges and Dilemmas"; Ritter and Holley, "Lessons for Conducting Random Assignment in Schools."

146. Ong-Dean, Huie Hofstetter, and Strick, "Challenges and Dilemmas"; Ritter and Holley, "Lessons for Conducting Random Assignment in Schools."

147. Berk, "Randomized Experiments as the Bronze Standard"; Ong-Dean, Huie Hofstetter, and Strick, "Challenges and Dilemmas."

148. Bausell, *Conducting Meaningful Experiments*

149. Ibid.

150. Ritter and Holley, "Lessons for Conducting Random Assignment in Schools."

151. Ibid.

152. Ong-Dean, Huie Hofstetter, and Strick, "Challenges and Dilemmas."

153. Ritter and Holley, "Lessons for Conducting Random Assignment in Schools."

154. Ong-Dean, Huie Hofstetter, and Strick, "Challenges and Dilemmas."

155. Ibid.

156. Srivastava, "Network Intervention."

157. Gondolf, "Lessons from a Successful and Failed Random Assignment."

158. Ritter and Holley, "Lessons for Conducting Random Assignment in Schools."

159. Bausell, *Conducting Meaningful Experiments*.

160. Ong-Dean, Huie Hofstetter, and Strick, "Challenges and Dilemmas."

161. Ibid.

162. Ibid.

163. Ibid.

164. Ibid.

165. Ritter and Holley, "Lessons for Conducting Random Assignment in Schools."
166. Ibid.
167. Ong-Dean, Huie Hofstetter, and Strick, "Challenges and Dilemmas."
168. Ibid.; Ritter and Holley, "Lessons for Conducting Random Assignment in Schools."
169. Berk, Smyth, and Sherman, "When Random Assignment Fails."
170. Ong-Dean, Huie Hofstetter, and Strick, "Challenges and Dilemmas"; Koog and Min.
171. Berk, Smyth, and Sherman, "When Random Assignment Fails."
172. Bausell, *Conducting Meaningful Experiments*, 74.
173. Gondolf, "Lessons from a Successful and Failed Random Assignment."
174. Ong-Dean, Huie Hofstetter, and Strick, "Challenges and Dilemmas."
175. Ibid.
176. Ritter and Holley, "Lessons for Conducting Random Assignment in Schools."
177. Ibid.
178. Ibid.
179. Ibid.
180. Campbell and Stanley, *Experimental and Quasi-Experimental Designs for Research*, 15.
181. David S. Abrams and Albert H. Yoon, "The Luck of the Draw: Using Random Case Assignment to Investigate Attorney Ability," *University of Chicago Law Review* 74, no. 4 (2007): 1145–1177.

# SAMPLING AND EFFECT SIZES

*When some would have us eliminate college students as a source of information we could ask, tongue-in-cheek, "What is it that occurs when a person's hand touches their degree that suddenly makes him or her a valid subject in a . . . study where they would not have been a minute earlier?*[1]

**—Michael Basil**

*Our findings would be substantially more credible if students were not so often the first and only choice.*[2]

**—William Wells**

## LEARNING OBJECTIVES

- Think critically about the use of students and subjects from various sources.

- Create a plan for recruiting and incentivizing subjects for an experiment.

- Describe the relationships between power and sample size.

- Explain effect sizes.

- Prepare and report the results of a power analysis.

There is nothing more important to experiments than the topic of the last chapter—random assignment. It may seem as if this book has put the cart before the horse in that it discusses how subjects are assigned before it addresses subjects themselves. The reason for this is that understanding random assignment is key to recognizing why certain subjects are appropriate for experiments when they may not be for other methods. This chapter is concerned with the primary focus of what is being randomly assigned—that is, the subjects in the sample. Exploring the related issues of power, which helps determine how many subjects are needed and effect sizes, or how well the treatment worked, is another aim of this chapter.

This chapter builds upon the discussion of external validity from chapter 5 while drawing from the understanding of random assignment in chapter 7. To briefly recap, the type of subjects that are used in an experiment can affect how well the results generalize to others. One of the most serious criticisms of experiments is that they usually cannot be generalized beyond the specific people in the study.[3] As was pointed out in chapter 5, most experiments use **convenience samples**—that is, people who are easily available—rather than those who are randomly sampled from a population.[4] Rather than random *sampling*, the counterpart in experiments is random *assignment*, which helps assure that subjects in different groups are equivalent on key characteristics. Equivalence is far more important in experiments than is the ability to generalize. Experiments then rely on logical inference to extend causal findings beyond the subjects of the study.

Experiments' superiority on internal validity and the benefits of random assignment do not give researchers a "pass" to use any-old subjects that are easily available. While we do refer to them as "convenience samples," the researchers' convenience is not the only thing that matters when selecting subjects. Researchers should carefully think through their choice of subjects for every study and then explain the reasons in the methods section of resulting papers. This chapter will supply fodder for those thoughts and explanations, and give an overview of some of the common sources of samples in experimental research. Assuming readers have now become reasonably assured that random sampling is, in most cases, an "inadequate" way to collect subjects for an experiment,[5] and that the use of nonrepresentative convenience samples in experiments is justified,[6] this chapter turns to one of the most often used and most frequently criticized type of subjects—students.

## STUDENT SAMPLES

There is no more convenient subject for a researcher in academia than a college student. Studies have shown that between 75% and 90% of experimental subjects in marketing and communication journals are students.[7] The tax discipline runs around 52%.[8]

Some departments make it easy to use student subjects by providing **subject pools** or **participant pools** where students are required to sign up to take part in a certain number of research studies per semester for course credit. This is common in courses with a research focus, such as methods classes, and in fields like psychology and advertising where students learn about the methods and procedures in practice firsthand. For example, in advertising, many of the decisions that go into determining what type of ad is produced result from advertising or market research, so it is logical that students should learn about the process that influences these choices. Students in subject pools are available to faculty researchers and sometimes also to graduate students. Even in departments where there is no pool of easily available student subjects, researchers find ways to entice students to participate in research with extra credit, gift cards, pizza, and the like. Yet one of the most common criticisms from reviewers is that a study is limited by the use of students as subjects. Some even feel that using students is "prescientific" or only valid in exploratory research and pilot studies.[9] Reviewers have been known to reject studies primarily on the basis of the use of student subjects. Before reaching that point, it behooves experimentalists to think carefully about the use of students—or anyone, for that matter—as subjects, choose the best subjects for the study, and then provide a strong theoretical rationale for the subjects used in the study. Examples of how researchers have done this are in How To Do It box 8.1. What follows lays the groundwork for that thinking, decision making, and subsequent rationale.

Using students as samples can sometimes be problematic, not only for external validity in that they may not be generalizable but also for internal validity when their responses may be biased because they are students. Obviously, generalizability is not an issue where students are the population to be generalized to, such as education studies, but for others, problems with the use of students as subjects seems to fall into the following categories outlined by Sears.[17]

## Higher Than Average Cognitive Skills

Because college is a place designed to foster critical thinking, and also because taking tests and filling out questionnaires is a common activity, students may perform better on studies than people who have never been to college or who have been out for some time.[18] This may "change the nature of the mental processes that are performed," says Basil,[19] who gives an example of research that investigates decision making as one area that may be different for students. The flip side is that students' higher cognitive skills can actually lower random error because they can answer questions on studies and report their thoughts more accurately.[20] Researchers should be careful to assess whether cognitive functioning will bias a study; if there is no theory, evidence, or logical reason why it

**HOW TO DO IT 8.1**

Rationales for Subjects

Here are some examples of how researchers have described and justified their choice of samples.

College Students Examples

Here is the justification for use of college students from a political study that goes beyond the usual statements of how student samples are adequate and there is no reason to envision differences between students and nonstudents, and instead refers specifically to evidence on the topic of the study to support the claim:

"One criticism of this methodology (e.g., Graber, 2004) is that because, like many other media experiments (e.g., Druckman, 2001a; Miller & Krosnick, 2000; Nelson & Oxley, 1999), the present studies use college students as participants, the findings cannot be generalized to other populations. However, media effects such as agenda setting, priming, and framing have been replicated in experiments that use a variety of samples, from college students (e.g., Druckman, 2001a; Nelson & Oxley, 1999; Miller & Krosnick, 2000) to adult volunteers from cities in which the investigators live (e.g., Iyengar & Kinder, 1987) to the general population (e.g., Nelson & Kinder, 1996), and in studies that match content analyses of the media to surveys of the general population (e.g., Iyengar & Simon, 1993). Therefore, the criticism that using a college student sample will lead to qualitatively different conclusions than a general population sample is not supported by the evidence."[10]

Miller, J. M. 2007. "Examining the Mediators of Agenda Setting: A New Experimental Paradigm Reveals the Role of Emotions." *Political Psychology* 28 (6): 689–717.

Here is another one that goes well beyond the usual to give information specific to the study:

"Experiments generally require a well-defined participant population that can be tracked, a treatment that can be randomized and administered to the correct person, and the ability to measure the outcome of interest for both the treatment and control groups. Voter mobilization experiments fit these requirements by focusing on registered voters, of whom there is an official list that can be randomized and later updated with turnout. Unfortunately, an official list of unregistered persons does not exist. Even if such a list did exist, residential mobility is much higher among unregistered persons and the reliability of such a list would be suspect. Conducting the experiments on college campuses solves the problem with defining a participant population . . . .

College students are an interesting population to study with regard to voter registration for four reasons. First, college students are geographically mobile and are extremely likely to have moved in the recent past, necessitating re-registration (Squire, Wolfinger, and Glass 1987). This mobility can also remove students from social support networks (like parents) who can help students engage civically. Second, college students are young and less likely to have developed a habit of voting (Plutzer 2002; Bendor, Diermeier, and Ting 2003; Green, Green, and Shachar 2003; Fowler 2006). The flipside of habit formation is that gains in participation at a young age will translate into greater participation in the future. Third, college students fall into many of the demographic categories associated with low levels of electoral participation: young (Wolfinger and Rosenstone 1980), disinterested in politics (Verba, Schlozman, and Brady 1995), and news nonconsumers (Wattenberg 2007).

Finally, the federal government has mandated that colleges and universities make an effort to register students. A 1998 amendment to the Higher Education Act requires colleges and universities to distribute voter registration forms to students enrolled in all degree or certificate programs. Institutions that fail to comply with the provision could jeopardize their federal student aid funds. Thus, college students present an empirically, pragmatically, and normatively interesting population to study with regard to registration habits.

College students are an especially interesting population to study with regard to e-mail and online registration tactics because they are more reliant on and frequent users of e-mail and the Internet relative to other age cohorts (Tedesco 2006). E-mail has not been found to be effective at boosting voter turnout (Nickerson 2007a), but college students should be the population most responsive to e-mail and Internet appeals. If e-mail messages encouraging registration and driving traffic to Web-based registration tools will work for any population, it would be college students."[11]

Bennion, E. A., and D. W. Nickerson. 2011. "The Cost of Convenience: An Experiment Showing E-Mail Outreach Decreases Voter Registration." *Political Research Quarterly* 64 (4): 858–869.

Here is another one that uses college students, justifying them because of their experience in the profession:

"One-hundred-and-ninety-four journalism students at a large Midwestern university participated. Use of students is appropriate because this is designed to see if effects are present at all; it is not concerned with generalizability. The sample was limited to journalism students to approximate the thought processes of journalists.

Many students had significant professional experience before entering school. Once admitted, these students are required as part of their courses to work in the newsrooms of the newspaper, magazine, or network-affiliate television station which serve the entire community but are run by the school." [12]

Coleman, R. 2006. "The Effect of Visuals on Ethical Reasoning: What's a Photograph Worth to Journalists Making Moral Decisions?" *Journalism and Mass Communication Quarterly* 83 (4): 835–850.

AGE Journal Article: study.sagepub.com/coleman

## MTurk Example

In this political communication study on belief echoes, or how false information can continue to influence a person's inferences even when corrected, the author used MTurk for subjects. Here is the reporting and justification:

"The experiments were conducted between August 2011 and November 2012. Participants accessed the experiment through Amazon's Mechanical Turk platform (MTurk).[2] Mechanical Turk is an online platform where subjects are paid to perform tasks ranging from captioning photos to taking surveys. The study was restricted to only United States participants over the age of 18.[3] Participants were paid between $0.61 and $0.75 for their participation (payment varied based on the length of the survey) and the surveys took most people between eight and 12 minutes to complete. All subjects were screened to ensure that none participated in more than one study. The three experiments described in this article each contain a unique set of participants.[4] A table describing the demographic characteristic of each sample is in the supplemental Appendix.

Several studies suggest that MTurk is a reasonable alternative to other traditionally used convenience samples.[5] While similar to the general population in many respects, the MTurk sample skews younger and more liberal. There is no theoretical reason to expect the formation of belief echoes to vary by age, as the cognitive processes that generate them should be similar among all ages. While partisanship might plausibly shape belief echoes, the experiments take this into consideration by randomly presenting subjects with misinformation that either reinforces or contradicts their preexisting partisan preferences. Each experiment followed a similar format. I explain this format in detail in the description of Experiment 1, then describe any variations in the descriptions of Experiments 2 and 3."[13]

*(Continued)*

(Continued)

Thorson, Emily. (2016). "Belief Echoes: The Persistent Effects of Corrected Misinformation." *Political Communication* 33 (3): 460–480.

## Panel Subjects Examples

In this study on the impact of government funding on donations to arts organizations, the authors use subjects from a firm that provides participants for research and marketing studies. Here is how they described it:

"Participants in the experiment were members of the CivicPanel project, an opt-in email panel of approximately 12,000 active panelists at the time of this study. CivicPanel is a university-affiliated online research project created to provide a general population of volunteers to participate in surveys and online studies about public and civic affairs. Voluntary panelists have been continuously recruited from various online postings including Google advertising, Craislist.org, and the open directory Dmoz.org. . . . Given the substantive focus on the U.S. nonprofit sector, 133 responses from non-U.S. residents were dropped from the analysis. An additional 24 of those with partially completed responses were also removed, resulting in a final analytical sample n = 562.

Table 2 displays the number of participants in each of the four arms or treatment groups as well as their demographic characteristics and political attitudes. . . . In a typical full randomized setup, treatment, and control groups should have the same characteristics except for the treatment they are given (Remler & Van Ryzin, 2011). The lack of statistically significant differences across groups randomly assigned to each condition in Table 2 confirms the statistical equivalence of the experimental groups."[14]

Kim, M., and G. G. Van Ryzin. 2014. "Impact of Government Funding on Donations to Arts Organizations: A Survey Experiment." *Nonprofit and Voluntary Sector Quarterly* 43 (5): 910–925.

Here is another example of a study that uses a panel of participants:

"Participants were recruited from a census representative panel maintained by the Qualtrics research firm, which uses the stratified quota sampling method. In exchange for their participation, cash value rewards were credited to panelists' online accounts. A total of 2,301 adult citizens aged 18 and older were randomly selected from the panel and invited via e-mail to participate in an online study; 861 members agreed to participate, and 768 individuals successfully completed the study. This represents a cooperation rate of 33.4% (COOP1, AAPOR)."[15]

Lee, H., and N. Kwak. 2014. "The Affect Effect of Political Satire: Sarcastic Humor, Negative Emotions, and Political Participation." *Mass Communication and Society* 17 (3): 307–328.

## Professional Samples

Here is a study that used professionals as subjects:

"Participants were professional journalists at newspapers and television stations across the South and Southwest region of the United States. They were recruited by the researcher writing and telephoning managers for permission to come to their newsrooms to conduct a study. No managers refused to allow the researcher to come. Newsroom managers announced the study, its date, time, and location to employees in advance via email. The researcher then traveled to the newsrooms where participants completed the questionnaire, usually in a conference room, and the researcher provided either lunch on the premises or gift cards to local restaurants in exchange for participation. The entire study took approximately 30 minutes."[16]

Coleman, R. 2011. "Journalists' Moral Judgment About Children: Do As I Say, Not As I Do." *Journalism Practice* 5 (3): 257–271.

would not, then students are appropriate.[21] Unless the phenomenon or process is different for students than for others, the findings should be valid.[22]

## Compliance With Authority

Because following instructions and pleasing authority is key to doing well in college, students may be more likely to try to give researchers the outcome they are looking for.[23] This phenomenon was covered in chapter 2 under demand characteristics. Recall from that chapter how Stanley Milgram rejected the use of students for his studies on obedience to authority for this very reason. Students also may more easily detect a study's hypothesis because of their experience participating in research,[24] which leads to more biased responses.[25] Others have shown that subjects who are savvy about research can deliberately control their responses and undermine the results.[26] Researchers should always conceal the hypothesis and use measures that reduce hypothesis-guessing from all kinds of subjects.[27] More about these kinds of measures will be covered in chapter 9. Also, students' regular interactions with authority figures (professors) may make students respond differently than nonstudents. One researcher testing two variations of stress reduction treatment found that one treatment worked on a sample of students but had no effect on community members, and the other treatment worked on people from the community but had no effect on students.[28] Greater compliance also can argue in favor of students as subjects under some circumstances, which may result in more accurate answers and less error from nonresponses.[29]

## Weaker Sense of Self

Having a weaker sense of self may be true not just of college students but also of other eighteen- to twenty-one-year-olds outside of college, as young people are typically in the process of discovering who they are at this stage of the life cycle. For the purpose of research, however, this contributes to more volatile opinions and being more easily swayed by persuasive arguments.[30] This argues against the use of students in studies of attitude change, for example.[31] Again, researchers should consider whether this characteristic is related to the outcome variable and, if so, steer away from students as subjects.[32] Basil gives an example of studies of attitude change as being less appropriate for a sample of students; however, the process of opinion formation may not be different, and so students could be appropriate.[33]

## Myriad Other Differences

College students are systematically different from others on many fronts; for example, they are likely to use social media more and traditional media less,[34] and are less conservative and dogmatic.[35] As with all research, careful consideration of a sample's systematic differences must be taken into account. When a study makes no claim of inferring to a larger population, and the outcome variable is not influenced by their differences, then college students are usually appropriate.[36] Evidence for or against differences potentially biasing a study should be drawn from theory, existing evidence, and logic. Without such evidence, the researcher should proceed with students if there are good reasons to use them instead of others.[37] Studies with student samples have the ability to add to our knowledge, and that should privilege their use when no objections can be confirmed.

## Homogeneity

One argument *for* students as subjects that is not based upon it being easier or cheaper for the researcher is that students are homogeneous—that is, they are similar to each other on several characteristics. Homogeneity of subjects in experiments aids internal validity by helping control for confounds—differences in subjects' age, education, use of technology, or whatever else cannot account for differences in outcomes if they do not vary.[38] Possible contaminants are minimized and the variability of measures is decreased, which helps reject the null hypothesis and identify when a theory is false.[39] In the pursuit of equivalence in treatment and control groups, as we saw in chapter 7, having subjects who are similar on variables related to the outcome is key. Students are more homogeneous than nonstudents on some variables[40] but vary as much as the general public on others.[41]

Students are similar to each other in age, education, media use,[42] life experiences, political engagement,[43] and political knowledge,[44] for example. When it comes to political knowledge and engagement, they tend to be lower than the average adult, so researchers should avoid conducting studies of political issues with students.[45] Likewise, students have little experience with paying taxes,[46] or interest rates and mortgages, and should be avoided as subjects in studies of these issues.[47] This argument applies to any set of homogeneous subjects; for example, people who are politically engaged, knowledgeable, and active do not resemble the average person.[48] Therefore, subjects drawn from political organizations, such as the League of Women Voters, provide the benefits of homogeneity but should not be generalized to others. In some fields such as cross-cultural research, for example, students' similar education levels give good estimates of representative samples.[49]

## Basic Psychological Processes

The main argument for using students is when research is concerned with basic psychological processes that should be the same for everyone.[50] That is, when the process studied operates among all people, then results with students are generalizable.[51] If there is no reason to believe the cognitive processes of students are different from nonstudents, then the use of student samples is appropriate.[52] Others go further to say that if the research aims to draw theoretical conclusions, such as for fundamental research and theory testing, then the sample does not matter.[53] Yet others have argued that even this is suspect because of demonstrated inabilities to generalize from students at one college to another,[54] or even from students in one major to another, and in different years of their schooling.[55]

Other research has identified the task subjects perform in the study as key to determining whether students are appropriate subjects. Analytical tasks with simple decisions are more appropriate for students than those with complex decisions and moral or ethical dilemmas.[56]

## Guarding Against Bias With Students

There are some steps that experimentalists can take to reduce problems associated with the use of students as subjects. Studying students when they are the population of interest is, of course, appropriate[57]—for example, in studies of teaching techniques or when they are the target market in advertising or consumer research.[58]

Researchers should also compare studies of students to nonstudents to see if there are differences.[59] A good place to start is with the literature; much can be found that demonstrates students are no different from others in many fields, such as accounting, nursing, and education, among others.[60] But there is also much that says students are not a good proxy for other populations, and some of it contradicts findings in the same fields.[61] This is another instance where the subject of chapter 3, knowing the literature, is crucial. Researchers should undertake at least a cursory review of the empirical evidence expressly for the purpose of discovering what it has to say about student samples.

Student samples also can be compared statistically to population data using percentages and a technique known as *average variability* or *variance of the mean*, which adds knowledge of expected variability.[62] (Formulas can be found in Cochrane 1977.)[63]

Using a combination of students and subjects from another population and then doing a statistical analysis to demonstrate if there are differences, which are reported in the text or a footnote, is another good approach.[64] When no differences are found, that helps assure readers that the student subjects are not inappropriate for this particular issue. If there are differences, then the study has shown that effects may be contingent on sample characteristics.[65] Furthermore, using different sources for samples within the same study is key to both internal and external validity.[66]

Researchers can also replicate their own studies (as well as those of others) with a nonstudent sample to see if it makes a difference.[67] As Lindsay and Ehrenberg say, "If a study is worth doing at all, it's worth doing twice."[68] Some have called for a minimum of two within-study replications with qualitatively different subjects as a requirement for publication in top-tier journals.[69] When conducting replications, do heed the advice in chapter 5 in order to extend the findings in some meaningful way.

Another way to ensure student subjects do not confound results can be to use statistical controls or covariates. These should be variables that are related to the outcome variable or are very different in students than in others, such as demographics of age and education.[70] The differences between students and others are not problematic as long as they can be predicted and controlled.[71] Report these in the paper and discuss findings honestly if they did confound the results.

Finally, some[72] recommend testing for prior knowledge of the theory and method used, as well as experience with research in general, in order to determine the likelihood of hypothesis guessing.

As pointed out in chapter 5, it is best to use subjects that are as similar as possible to those being studied; if the research is concerned with some phenomenon about teaching, and teachers can be reasonably expected to agree to be subjects, then that is better than using students. However, using education majors can be a reasonable proxy, as they will be teachers in the foreseeable future. As Basil said in the quote opening this chapter, a person is no less qualified to be in a study the minute before receiving a diploma than the minute after. For example, an argument can be made that undergraduates at elite journalism schools already had significant experience with student media before being admitted to serve as a proxy for journalists.[73] Others have used students in the master of public administration program who had previously been professionals in the field.[74] The real concern for experiments is whether the sample is appropriate to what is being studied, and less about how it was drawn.[75] Applying the yardstick for surveys and other methods is not an appropriate way to measure the quality of subjects in experimental designs.

Finally, the paper should always discuss why students, or any type of subject for that matter, are appropriate for the study.[76] Peterson says this should be justified by the theoretical relevance of the subjects to test the specific research questions.[77] In some fields, this is rare; for example, Marriott found that in ten tax discipline journals over twenty years, 80% did not provide justification for their sample or acknowledge any limitations associated with the use of students.[78] In marketing and consumer research, 63% ignored limitations of the sample, according to one study.[79]

It is also important to limit generalizations from studies that use student samples, or provide any policy changes or practice recommendations to professionals from such studies.

For example, extrapolating findings from students to the tax-paying public or making tax policy suggestions is not appropriate, although studies routinely do this.[80] Instead, conclusions should not focus on "people," "individuals," or the professionals the study is aimed at, but on "participants in this study," "these subjects," or "the professionals in this study."

This is also a good place in the paper to reiterate the purpose of experiments—to establish causality, not generalize to a population—as explained in chapter 5. Much space in this chapter is devoted to the use of students as subjects, for it is one of the most prominent issues in experimental studies. The next section discusses other types of samples for experiments and also the objections that have been raised to them.

Using a sample that is not comprised of students does not automatically solve all a researcher's problems. Many of the issues described earlier also apply to other types of samples. In general, convenience samples are biased because subjects volunteer. They do this for a reason, perhaps because they care deeply about the subject being studied or because they are motivated by the incentive, whether it is money or something else.[81] While there is no perfect sample, even one randomly drawn from a population, there are other good sources of subjects for experimental studies. Next is a discussion of some of the most popular sources.

# AMAZON'S MECHANICAL TURK

One of the newest sources of subjects for experiments is Amazon's **Mechanical Turk**, an online crowdsourcing platform where people are paid to perform various tasks that computers cannot.[82] Amazon developed MTurk, as it is known, in 2005 for its own use[83] but opened it up to others who needed the services that only human beings could provide, such as writing book summaries, comments, or captions, identifying items in photographs, transcribing audio and even grocery receipts,[84] among other things.[85] Amazon calls these **Human Intelligence Tasks**, or **HITs**.[86] One of the most unusual tasks is having workers look for missing persons in satellite images.[87] No one has yet been found this way. The name Mechanical Turk comes from a chess-playing machine popular at eighteenth-century carnivals designed to look like a Turkish sorcerer. In reality, a small man was hidden inside who played (and usually beat) the opponents—thus, the name of the platform designed to hide human workers.[88] In 2010, social scientists discovered it as a means for recruiting people to participate in surveys and experiments.[89] Advantages include that it is easy, affordable, and potentially representative of the population.

## Is MTurk Representative?

The early criticism of MTurk subjects was that they were younger, better educated, and had more females than the population.[90] But that has been changing, with demographics growing more representative of the U.S. population.[91] Now, many studies show that MTurk samples are comparable to U.S. workers, standard Internet samples, and other subject pools,[92] and are more diverse than students,[93] especially when it comes to young Asians and young Hispanic females.[94] But not all studies show this; in one study, students were actually more representative of the population than MTurk workers.[95] Other studies compare representativeness of MTurk workers to international populations.[96]

As MTurk has grown in popularity, so have the challenges to its external validity.[97] Exploring differences between MTurk and other sample sources has become almost a cottage industry. For a review of some of this literature, see More About box 8.2, Research on MTurk's Representativeness.

As with using students as subjects, researchers should think critically about using MTurk workers for samples, considering whether they are different from other subject pools and the population of interest.[110] Also, relying on one type of sample, whether it is students, MTurk workers, or subjects from any other source, brings drawbacks of its own.[111] Using a variety of sources within the same study is one important way that greater external validity can be achieved in experiments.[112]

## Advantages and Drawbacks

MTurk has gained widespread popularity in the social sciences because of its benefits, but it has some disadvantages as well. In addition to a large general population, low cost is probably one of the biggest reasons researchers use it. Workers are paid by the task. Some researchers have paid between sixty-one cents and seventy-five cents for eight to twelve minutes of work.[113] Workers with high approval ratings from other **requesters**, the term MTurk uses for those who post HITs, command higher pay. For example, workers with 95% approval ratings were paid $3 in one study.[114] The average hourly wage works out to between $1 and $1.38.[115] Amazon also tacks on a percentage for its own fee. Even at the higher rates, MTurk pay can be considerably less than what is required for students and adults. The savings achieved by using MTurk samples can be used to run more subjects or add more conditions.

Recruiting subjects and collecting data are also fast and easy in MTurk. Once the HIT is posted, hundreds of thousands of workers are automatically notified. Contrast this with going from class to class to pitch a study, or spending several days in a library or coffee shop soliciting subjects. Data collection is equally swift. Researchers report gathering enough subjects in the span of a few hours to less than a day,[116] with one

# MORE ABOUT . . . BOX 8.2
## Research on MTurk's Representativeness

Much research revolves around the question of how representative of the population MTurk workers are. This has important implications for the generalizability of studies that use them as subjects, especially for survey research but also to experimental work. Here is a brief overview of some of the research on this topic, both pro and con. As more work is always being done, readers should check for more and newer literature.

Bartneck and colleagues found that subjects recruited through MTurk were different from those recruited on campus or online, but declared that the difference was of "no practical consequence."[98]

Huff et al. compared MTurk with the Cooperative Congressional Election Survey and found strong similarities, with a maximum difference of less than seven percentage points on variables including age, gender, race, and political, occupational and geographic information. They say, "There are strong reasons for researchers to consider using MTurk to make inferences about a number of broader populations of interest," and encourage researchers not to automatically dismiss a study because it used MTurk subjects.[99]

However, Levay et al. replicated questions from the American National Election Studies (ANES) series in 2012 with MTurk workers and found significant differences. These were reduced by the use of covariates for nine variables—age, gender, race and ethnicity, income, education, marital status, religion, ideology, and partisanship. The authors conclude that "MTurk respondents do not appear to differ fundamentally from population-based respondents in unmeasurable ways"[100] and recommend including the nine variables as covariates. For experimentalists, they say that "representativeness of MTurk does not threaten experimental inferences in most cases"[101] but caution against unmeasurable variables that might also differ.

Similar conclusions were reached with an earlier ANES from 2008–2009 by Berinsky et al., who found that MTurk subjects were less representative than ANES subjects or those from Internet panels but more representative of the U.S. population than in-person convenience samples.[102]

When it comes to individual differences in demographics and political variables, MTurk subjects can be different from the U.S. population.[103] Yet researchers still claim that conclusions can be drawn from MTurk samples that are better in many cases than samples of students, as long as one understands the differences.[104]

Comparisons are not limited to demographic similarities though; research also examines the type of task in the experiment and outcome variables for differences between MTurk and other subjects. For example, Paolacci et al. and Birnbaum found only slight differences in MTurk subjects and others in decision-making experiments.[105] Buhrmester et al. found no meaningful differences between MTurk and other subjects on various psychometric tests.[106] Bartneck et al. found no differences in the outcome of studies that used subjects from MTurk, online services, or students. They say that MTurk is more "suitable for studies on the general population rather than specific subgroups."[107] Crump et al. found mixed results with a host of tasks including subliminal priming and learning tasks.[108] And Krupnikov found that MTurk subjects produced results significantly different from students and a nationally representative sample of adults when they were asked to read articles.[109]

While all these conflicting results may seem confusing, the key is to know what individual variables, outcomes, and tasks MTurk workers are different from the population on, and then act accordingly.

study receiving between 5.6 and 40.5 responses in an hour.[117] Furthermore, researchers do not need to be present or reserve a lab. And there is always a steady supply of MTurk workers, unlike the ebb and flow of students across the semester and breaks between them.[118]

These same benefits come with drawbacks, however. The low pay causes workers to try to complete a task as fast as possible, which can result in them not paying attention, pressing the same response button repeatedly, or just randomly checking off answers. Subjects taking experiments online, whether on MTurk or any other platform, have significantly more distractions than subjects in the lab.[119] To help control for that, an **attention check** question or two can be incorporated. For example, at a couple of points in the study, a factual question about what subjects just read can be asked, or an instruction can be inserted to provide a certain answer to the next question, no matter what their actual response would be. For example, "To the following question, please respond by selecting '4' regardless of what your answer would be." Make it clear in the instructions, consent form, and at the beginning of the study that the study includes questions designed to ensure they are paying attention and that failure to answer these correctly will result in not being paid. Workers are keenly interested in getting paid, not only for the money but because not getting paid results in bad ratings that can reduce the number of higher-paying HITs they are eligible to do in the future. Questions about details of the stimulus also can be asked at the end.[120] In order to help reduce response error, it is also recommended that researchers visually check for patterns such as repeatedly pressing the same button, or use pairwise agreement for the same question worded differently and other mechanisms to detect subjects rushing through a questionnaire.[121] Studies have shown that subjects in MTurk and traditional surveys are no different in terms of attentiveness.[122] Workers can be identified by their Amazon ID to ensure they do not complete the same study more than once.

Paying more seems to correlate with more completed tasks,[123] but quality of data is not related to rate of pay.[124] Turkers say they participate in research for entertainment as well as pay.[125]

Other disadvantages include a researcher's inability to control the environment of MTurk subjects the way they could in a laboratory.[126] In addition, gathering demographics and measuring response times require additional software such as the Qualtrics survey platform or AdobeFlash because the Amazon platform does not support this.[127] MTurk can be used to both recruit subjects and also host the questionnaire directly, or the questionnaire can be hosted using a survey package like Qualtrics, SurveyMonkey, and others.[128]

These drawbacks may easily be outweighed for researchers with few students, such as those at small colleges, without subject pools, or in nonacademic settings.[129]

# OTHER SUBJECT SOURCES

Other more traditional sources for obtaining subjects can be more expensive but usually do not come with the concerns of the student and MTurk samples described earlier. These include **opt-in participant panels** from commercial survey and market research including Qualtrics, Survey Sampling International, and Knowledge Networks, now known as GfK KnowledgePanel. Others include SurveySavvy, Harris Poll Online, YouGov's PollingPoint Panel, Polimetrix, and Survey Spot. Some researchers have used Craigslist. There are many more, but these seem to appear regularly in published academic papers. These firms have a pool of people who have agreed to take studies for compensation and choose which research projects they will participate in. Some also offer the ability to target a sample that is representative of a population or has certain characteristics—for example, registered voters.[130] Costs depend on the number of questions, type of subjects, and other details. Researchers report paying as low as $3 to $5 per subject and as high as $15 per person.[131]

When a survey experiment is conducted using subjects from a defined population, such as that provided by opt-in data platforms, some disciplines and journals ask for a response rate to be reported. In fact, the American Political Science Association's (APSA) experimental research section's standards committee guidelines specify that response rates be provided for every experiment that uses survey data collection methods,[132] and even for college student samples.[133] There is debate about whether this is appropriate or necessary, with some researchers saying that it is meaningless if the study does not make any claims to generalizability.[134] Currently, not many social sciences disciplines, with the exception of political science, require response rates for survey experiments; however, researchers should follow the standards and guidelines in their field and journal they are submitting to.

A more traditional approach is to recruit subjects through advertisements in newspapers,[i] flyers posted around town, and mailing lists. These methods have been applied to new media, with social media and online forums now sources for subjects. For example, one study used a LEGO forum on the Internet for a study about judging emotional expressions that manipulated the faces on LEGO toys.[135] The authors noted the potential bias in that the subjects were homogeneous in their interest in and experience with LEGOs. Another group of researchers developed a method for recruiting from social media that allows for targeting subjects around specific themes, such as the politically engaged—a particular weakness of student samples.[136] It appeals to online opinion leaders, such as

---

[i]Qualtrics provides respondents for research and also has survey software that can be used to administer a study regardless of whether subjects are drawn from the firm's pool. Researchers can use the software without using subjects from the pool.

bloggers and discussion forum moderators, to recruit subjects. This type of recruiting is especially good for studying a targeted sample. For political scientists, for example, being able to find politically sophisticated subjects, who make up a small percentage of the overall population, can give more accurate estimates of effects while improving external validity. Another example is a study that uses subjects from chat rooms for hate groups to study the types of messages that trigger aggression.[137] The authors write, "This insight would not be possible through the use of nationally representative probability samples, conventional student samples, or other online opt-in methods such as MTurk.[138] (See Study Spotlight 8.3 for more about a study of social media sites as sources of subjects.) Researchers can also enlist the help of organizations for specific subgroups—for example, public relations professionals who join the Public Relations Society of America.

Other researchers have found subjects in the staff of their schools,[139] lists of jury pools, which are drawn by randomly sampling citizens and are more heterogeneous, and election rolls.[140] (See Study Spotlight 8.3 for more about a study of jury pools as sources of subjects.) Some researchers are able to include experimental questions on a large-scale survey for free—for example, the Time-Sharing Experiments for the Social Sciences—while others, such as the Cooperative Congressional Election Study, can be costly.[141]

Another advantage with this recruitment strategy is that subjects are homogeneous, reflecting shared interests, issue attitudes, beliefs, and values. They are also the types of people who are likely to self-select to be exposed to the types of messages being studied, overcoming the problem of using natural settings that artificially expose people to messages that they would not otherwise see.

## RECRUITING

Subjects also can be recruited in public places such as parks and outdoor cafes. One researcher sat at tables outside coffee shops and other businesses, with the owners' permission, and recruited passersby with gift cards to the establishment.[148] Another found that fire departments were receptive to researchers' visits, as the firefighters had a lot of free time when waiting for calls. Subjects can also be recruited through social organizations such as Lions Clubs and church groups who invite speakers to their meetings. After having members take the study with paper and pencil for fifteen to twenty minutes, researchers can provide a fascinating talk about their research. This approach also has been used in newsrooms with ethics research; managing editors are usually receptive to having a professor give their journalists an ethics miniworkshop. Other strategies can be to set up tables at conferences to recruit working professionals—for example, at a conference for Internet domain name investors.[149] No doubt the creative display—an open briefcase full of money—helped attract subjects. When subjects need to represent a particular population—for example, working professionals—this

# STUDY SPOTLIGHT 8.3
Jury Pools and Social Media as Subject Sources

**Murray, G. R., C. R. Rugeley, D-G. Mitchell, and J. J. Mondak. 2013. "Convenient Yet Not a Convenience Sample: Jury Pools as Experimental Subject Pools."** *Social Science Research* **42 (2013): 246–253.**

Instead of relying on college students, these authors found another convenient, diverse, and inexpensive source of experimental subjects—people who have been summoned for jury duty. This paper discusses practical concerns such as gaining access and administering the experiment, and evidence including response rates, sample quality, and representativeness.

Other researchers have used prospective jurors, including Niven,[142] Sigelman et al.,[143] Terkildsen,[144] and Lewis et al.[145]

Some concerns with the use of jurors as study subjects include gaining the cooperation of court officials and judges. These authors, who have been conducting experiments with jury pools since 2009, report no problems and say that the good relationship the county has with the university helps. Not all have found this to be the case; for example, a nationwide study that used jury pools had only a 15% cooperation rate.[146]

Other issues include concerns by court administrators about increased workload and disruption of court proceedings by judges. Judges also are concerned that jury members are treated fairly and the study does not bias them. Other concerns aligned with Institutional Review Board (IRB) requirements, such as that subjects be free to not answer questions or stop the study at any time.

Judges are concerned about the content of the study, wishing to avoid anything to do with legal issues; political topics were OK. Judges review the study and approve it, and these authors have only had one question removed in all their experience.

Procedurally, the researchers use paper-and-pencil formats but say that handheld electronic devices might also be possible. They suggest limiting studies to ten to fifteen minutes because of potential jurors' limited free time. They administer the study when jurors first arrive and are waiting for the selection process to begin. They place clipboards with pencils attached, the cover letter, and instructions and questionnaire on seats before jurors arrive. They spent $350 on clipboards and incentives. One researcher should be present to monitor the study and answer questions. They have not found it necessary to offer incentives and estimate the cost at fifty-seven cents per subject—comparable to the cost on MTurk—which includes photocopying and supplies but not transportation to the courthouse.

In these researchers' county, jury pools are called twice a week with approximately seventy-five to 200 people in the pool. They estimate an average of 400 completed studies per month in a county of 100,000. Their response rate was 79% among potential jurors who showed up; adjusting for all those summoned, the response rate was between 39% and 68%.

Because jury pools are drawn from voter registration and driver's license lists, among other sources, jury pools are diverse and representative of the community. These authors compared jurors to a sample of students and a telephone survey using the same study. You can read their results in a table. They conclude, "Overall, we contend that jury pool data equal or exceed the alternatives under consideration on cost effectiveness, response rates, diversity of respondents, and representativeness."[147]

*(Continued)*

(Continued)

**Cassese, E. C., L. Huddy, T. K. Hartman, L. Mason, and C. R. Weber. 2013. "Socially Mediated Internet Surveys: Recruiting Participants for Online Experiments."** *PS: Political Science & Politics* **49 (4): 1–10.**

This study reports on a method the authors have used in six studies to recruit experimental subjects using social media, which they call the Socially Mediated Internet Survey (SMIS) method. It works by asking bloggers, discussion forum moderators, and Facebook and Google+ page administrators—all of whom are "central nodes" in the social network—to help recruit readers and visitors to their sites as study subjects.

Among the advantages of this method is that special subpopulations, such as political sophisticates and activists for a specific social issue, can be recruited. Political scientists, the discipline of these researchers, are often interested in highly engaged, knowledgeable, and politically active citizens, but they are not widely found in the general population. Using traditional recruitment methods would result in many subjects that do not fit the requirements of political sophisticates. With this method, they can be specifically targeted. For example, politically involved people interested in immigration issues can be recruited via the Stand With Arizona (and Against Illegal Immigration) Facebook page, which had 600,000 followers in early 2013. Researchers of various disciplines could use this; for example, a study of health messages about vaccines could recruit subjects via Facebook pages Vactruth.com and Anti-Anti-Vaccine-Campaign.

Researchers use the SMIS method by first identifying social networks that appeal to the subpopulation of interest, and then by appealing to bloggers and page administrators to endorse their study and solicit participation from their readers, contacts, and followers. They suggest Technorati (www.technorati.com) and lists of blogrolls (e.g., BlogHer.com for a directory of women bloggers) to identify blogs and forums. Because the request to participate in a study comes from a known opinion leader rather than an unknown researcher, the personal connection helps increase the likelihood of participation.

The authors give advice for gaining trust and cooperation by contacting the social mediator to obtain permission and answer questions about the project, noting that IRB approval is required for this contact. They give a link to an online supplemental appendix that contains the materials they used. In the six studies reported in this paper, about one of every eight bloggers the researchers contacted agreed to promote the study. They say they secured an average of 1,569 subjects per study, considerably more than they would have been able to recruit via student subject pools. Each social mediator recruited an average of 104 subjects. And unlike MTurk, these subjects were volunteers, and no incentive or payment was required.

The researchers compare their SMIS samples to samples from MTurk, students, and 2008 ANES subjects, and conclude that, while they are not representative, they are more diverse than students demographically and geographically.

approach works well. However, researchers should realize that in the cases of social clubs and organizations, the sample will be limited to self-selected groups who have time or are interested in the topic and share particular characteristics that may not be representative of the population—for example, retirees or women not employed outside the home. For this reason, sampling from a variety of sources to avoid systematic bias can be a good strategy.

## INCENTIVES

While some researchers have found they do not need to offer incentives,[150] many find that even a small token is important to convey to subjects that their time and effort in the research is valued.[151] Books, pencils, folders,[152] and postage stamps[153] are also used in addition to financial incentives. Gift cards can be more cost effective than cash; for example, more people may decline to participate for $10 in cash than for a $5 gift card. It may work best to describe the incentive as "a gift card to (name of coffee chain)" and leave out the amount; rarely does anyone ask how much it is for. It is a good idea to call ahead to make sure the store has enough cards on hand or if purchasing cards in bulk must be done at corporate headquarters.

Another approach is to tell participants they will be entered into a lottery for a drawing of a larger prize, such as an iPad. Two researchers raffled off a book and got twenty-nine students to participate.[154] Researchers also can raffle off a limited number of $10 gift cards, meaning they can buy fewer cards than the number of subjects.[ii] Not all IRBs will allow lottery incentives, so check first.

In addition to explaining the rationale for the use of the subjects in the study, researchers should also report the incentives, if any, and other details that will help readers evaluate the study. In the field of political science, the APSA's experimental research section's standards committee has codified a list of guidelines that includes who was eligible to participate, the dates of recruitment, when the study was conducted, and the number of subjects assigned to each group, among other things. For a complete list of guidelines, see Gerber et al. 2014 and 2016. Other disciplines and also individual journals may publish their own reporting standards. The most widely used standards are found in the *Publication Manual of the American Psychological Association*.

No doubt there are many other good sources of subjects for experiments and ways to recruit and incentivize them, limited only by one's imagination. When reading studies, pay attention to who the subjects are, where they came from, and how they were recruited. Also note the number of subjects used, which is the topic of the next section.

## SAMPLE SIZE AND POWER

"How many subjects do I need for my experiment?" is one of the first questions students ask. The good news is that experiments usually can require far fewer subjects than methods such as surveys. But the answer to the question is not quick or simple.

The topics of sample size and power are intertwined. **Sample size**, or the number of subjects in a study, is referred to as $N$ or $n$ in experiments, with the capital $N$ representing all subjects in the study and lower-case $n$ representing the subjects in one of the conditions. Estimating the sample size while in the process of designing an experiment is important

---

[ii]Many researchers self-fund their studies. Check with your department, college, and university for sources of funding, as well as outside grantors.

to ensure that statistical conclusions are accurate and reliable. If the sample is too small, the statistical test may not be significant because of low power, not because the hypothesis is incorrect.[155] If the sample is too big, the researcher will have spent time and money for little extra benefit. Thus, it is important to have the number of subjects be just right.[iii]

This is where statistical **power** comes in. Power is the probability of supporting a hypothesis, or, technically, rejecting a false null hypothesis when the alternative hypothesis is true. That is, power is the probability of achieving statistical significance when an effect actually exists. Power also is the concept behind **Type 2 errors**, which occur when the null hypothesis is not rejected but should be; that is, the alternative hypothesis should be supported, but it is not. This is indicated when the *p* value is not lower than .05. When a significance level of .05 or less is reached, there is more reason to be confident that the results are "real" and not due to chance. When statistical significance is not achieved due to a Type 2 error, besides being extremely disappointing for researchers, this means that some treatment that may actually work is now reported as not having an effect. Important interventions may never be adopted in practice.

Researchers tend to focus on **Type 1 errors**, which are the opposite of Type 2—that is, when the null hypothesis is rejected, but it should not be.[156] But Type 2 errors are also common in published research.[157] Researchers need to focus on both reducing errors and increasing power, and on guarding against Type 1 and Type 2 errors.[158]

One of the easiest ways to increase power, thereby reducing Type 2 errors, is to increase the sample size.[159] Larger samples mean more power because they more accurately represent the population from which they were drawn.[160] For an example of how this works, assume the entire population consists of one million people. It is difficult to measure all one million people, so scientists draw a sample from the population instead and estimate the mean on some variable. If the sample consisted of ten people, it would be possible to draw people with especially low or high scores. Increasing the sample to 100 increases the probability of drawing people with more moderate scores. The sample mean based on 100 people is closer to the population mean than the one based on ten people.

Another important statistic in this calculation is the **standard error**, which estimates the average difference between the sample and the population statistic.[161] It is the standard

---

[iii]American Psychological Association, *Publication Manual of the American Psychological Association,* 6th ed. (Washington, DC: Author, 2009). The APSA guidelines also include reporting an intent-to-treat analysis, which is found more in the medical field than social science. It is beyond the scope of this book to explain this statistical analysis, but instead, readers are referred to statistics books and courses, and articles such as Sally Hollis and Fiona Campbell, "What Is Meant by Intention to Treat Analysis? Survey of Published Randomised Controlled Trials," *BMJ* 319 no. 7211 (September 1999): 670–674.

deviation of the sampling statistic. Standard errors tend to be smaller when samples are larger; thus, larger samples increase power. But because time and money are limited in most cases, it is usually not practical to increase the sample size infinitely. Consequently, researchers need to balance the need for larger samples with the resources available.

It is also important not to have *too many* subjects, which could result in detecting relationships among all variables.[162] If power is too strong due to an excessively large sample, then finding statistical significance is almost certain. While it may seem like a great idea to assure one's hypotheses are supported, the relationships may be so small that they are unimportant practically.[163] The findings would then be substantively unimportant, which is the topic of the next section on effect sizes. Readers, reviewers, and editors are becoming savvy at detecting when a study has supported its hypotheses mainly by packing it with too many subjects. In addition, it is more ethical to minimize potential harm by using the least number of subjects necessary.[164]

It is also important to know any specific issues in your discipline that might affect the size of a sample; for example, in advertising, a phenomenon known as **ad blindness** occurs where subjects subconsciously tune out ads.[165] Advertising researchers may need to sample as many as 30% more subjects just to account for purging those who are unable to provide meaningful answers to questions about an advertisement because they did not recall seeing it. In moral development research, about 8% of subjects fail questions designed to detect those trying to fake a higher score and are purged.[166]

## Effect Sizes

The term *power* also refers to a study's **effect size**,[167] which is a statistic that describes the strength of the relationship between the independent variable (IV) and the dependent variable (DV), or the amount of variance in the DV that is explained or accounted for by the IV. The effect size statistic serves as a complement to the statistical significance represented by the $p$ value. Effect size statistics refer to the *practical* significance of the relationship. In other words, the $p$ value tells whether the treatment worked; the effect size tells how well it worked. More About box 8.4 explains the different effect size statistics.

Effect sizes may or may not be related to the $p$ value. For example, a highly significant $p$ value may be accompanied by a low effect size statistic, indicating that there is a low probability of the treatment affecting the outcome by chance, but the size of the effect is practically meaningless. The best possible outcome is when the $p$ value is significant and the effect size is large; this means that the treatment effect is not only real but also important. The effect of the treatment is meaningful in a practical sense.

# MORE ABOUT . . . BOX 8.4
## Effect Size Statistics

Different statistics represent effect sizes for different statistical tests. The effect size estimates the amount of variance explained or accounted for by the independent variables in an experiment. The first column contains the statistical test and the second the effect size statistic with its symbol and an explanation. These vary from 0 to 1.

| ANOVA, MANOVA | Eta-squared, $\eta2$ |
|---|---|
| Tests differences between two or more groups. Multiple analysis of variance (MANOVA) tests multiple dependent variables. | Eta-squared measures the variance explained in the sample, not the population, so it overestimates the effect size. The bias gets smaller as the sample size increases. |
| | SPSS does not calculate this; it must be calculated by hand. http://www.theanalysisfactor.com/calculate-effect-size/ |
| | **Partial Eta-squared, $\eta^2_p$**<br>SPSS calculates partial eta-squared for all analysis of variances (ANOVAs), but calls it eta-squared. It is the same value as eta-squared with one IV designs, but different for repeated measures designs. With more than one IV, partial eta-squared is the variance explained for one IV controlling for the other IVs. In other words, it excludes or "partials out" the variance explained by the other IVs. It is preferred when more than one IV is tested, as it is more conservative. |
| | **Omega-squared, $\omega^2$**<br>Estimates the variance explained in the population. Limited to between-subjects designs with equal cell sizes. Less biased than eta-squared or partial eta-squared. |
| **Correlation and Regression** | **$r$-squared, $r^2$ or $R^2$** |
| Tests the association or relationship between two or more variables; tests variables that predict an outcome variable. | The correlation between two variables is $r$, then the squared value of $r$ is $r^2$. This represents the amount of variance in each that is accounted for or explained by the other. For example, if $r = 0.21$, $r^2 = 0.0441$. 4.4% of the variance of either variable is shared with the other variable. |
| | In multiple regression, it is expressed as $R^2$ and explains the variance accounted for by all the independent variables together. |

| ANOVA, MANOVA | Eta-squared, η2 |
|---|---|
| **Odds Ratio** | **OR** |
| | This effect size measure is commonly used in medicine for binary variables or a dichotomous outcome, such as survival or not. It is expressed as, for example, the odds of a treatment success are three times higher than in the control group. |
| **Chi-Square** | **Phi coefficient, Cramer's V or Phi, φ** |
| Test of difference between categorical variables. | **Cohen's *d*** |
| | Examines the strength of the relationship between two variables; V may be used with more than two levels of a variable. |

Effect sizes are important to report along with significance tests because this allows readers to see the effect of a treatment not confounded by sample size. Whereas statistical significance is heavily influenced by sample size, effect sizes are less so. For example, a sample of 500 may show high statistical significance but have small effect sizes. The reverse is also true; a sample of fifty may not show statistical significance, but the effect size may be large. Having both statistics reported in a study allows readers to decide for themselves the substantive importance of the treatment. Reporting of effect sizes is standard practice in psychology[168] and is considered good practice in other disciplines.[169] Many journals are now requiring it. Whereas in the past a study that failed to reach statistical significance was likely to be rejected,[170] nowadays, one that reaches significance is not guaranteed publication if it is accompanied by a very low effect size.

Reporting effect sizes merely requires the addition of the proper statistic in the results section at the end of the list of values showing the results of the significance tests. In the following examples, the effect sizes are underlined:

- "Using condition (action exemplar, inaction exemplar, and control) as the independent variable and negative affect as dependent variable, a one-way analysis of variance (ANOVA) reported a significant effect, $F(2, 192) = 9.24$, $p < .001$, $\underline{\eta2 = .09}$."[171]

- "The impact on candidate 'image' evaluation under three issue conditions resulted in a significant finding ($F = 6.92$, $df = 6, 450$, $p < .01$, $\underline{\eta2 = .16}$); the finding also was significant for candidate 'capability' ($F = 11.80$, $df = 6, 450$, $p < .01$, $\underline{\eta2 = .25}$)."[172]

These examples used eta-squared because the test performed was ANOVA. Next is an example that uses $r^2$ for a correlation test:

> "H3 was supported: there was a significant positive correlation between the participants' liking of stories on the experimental website and civic engagement ($r = .811$, $p < .001$, $\underline{r^2 = .66}$)."[173]

Cohen[174] categorized the relative effect sizes according to this convention, also called "T-shirt effect sizes,"[175] and used in most social science disciplines:

| Cohen's Conventions for Effect Sizes | |
|---|---|
| Small | < 0.20 |
| Medium | 0.20–0.50 |
| Large | > 0.50 |

While Cohen provides a general rule of thumb, the magnitude of an effect size depends on the context; .25 may be practically significant for some disciplines and .50 considered large.[176] As you read studies in your field, notice what the reported effect sizes are in order to get a sense of your discipline and the specific variables' effect sizes. In the planning stages of any experiment, it is important to determine a minimum effect size that would indicate a treatment or manipulation is useful or important.[177]

Sample size, effect size, power, and significance level are all connected; if you know any three of these, the fourth can be determined. How to do that with a power analysis is the topic of the next section.

## Power Analyses

Determining sample size is the most common use of power.[178] Power estimations and analyses should always be done before data are collected, known as **a priori** power analysis. There are also rule-of-thumb methods for determining how many subjects a study should have, but free online power analysis calculators have all but replaced these. (See table 8.1 for Rules of Thumb for Sample Sizes.) All analyses of power are dependent upon the statistical test to be performed. For example, experiments that use regression analysis or structural equation modeling require more subjects than those that use $t$ tests or ANOVA. So far in this text, we have concentrated on studies that test differences between groups, which are appropriately tested with statistics such as the $t$ test when two groups are compared, ANOVA for three or more groups, and MANOVA, which is a form of ANOVA used when there are multiple DVs. A separate statistics course is required to conduct these tests knowledgeably, and this book is not intended to replace that. But readers should be aware that the statistical test performed affects the power and thus the size of the sample needed.

| TABLE 8.1 ● RULES OF THUMB FOR SAMPLE SIZES WITH VARIOUS STATISTICAL TESTS | |
|---|---|
| *t* tests, ANOVA, MANOVA | n = 30 per cell (Cohen, 1988) |
| Correlation, regression | n > 50 + 8 per IV to N > 104 + 8 per IV (Green 1991)[179] |
| | The number of predictor variables + 50 (Harris 1985)[180] |
| | 30 subjects per variable (Cohen and Cohen 1975)[181] |
| Chi Square | No expected frequencies below 5 (Howell 1997)[182] |
| Factor Analysis | 300 subjects (Tabachnick and Fidell 1996)[183], |
| | 50 per factor (Pedhazur and Schmelkin 1991[184]; Comrey and Lee 1992[185]) |

Notes: These sample sizes are for medium to large effects sizes.

Cohen[186] suggests a minimum power of 80%.

Comparisons of fewer groups/cells requires more participants to maintain power.[187]

Once upon a time, a power analysis had to be conducted by hand. More commonly today, researchers calculate power analyses using statistical software such as Stata and R, or online tools, one of the most popular of which is G*Power. Created by a group of German researchers, the software is free, available at http://www.gpower.hhu.de/, and is accompanied by tutorials.[188]

Before conducting a power analysis, researchers should examine previous studies that are similar to the one they are conducting and collect basic data including means, standard deviations, and effect sizes from them. Prior studies that researchers have conducted themselves also are useful for this purpose. For example, for an experiment that looked at whether journalists used different levels of moral judgment when story subjects were children than adults,[189] data from previous work on photographs and moral judgment were used to figure power and determine the sample size.[190]

In order to determine the sample size, *N*, at least three of the following four pieces of data are required:

- Alpha level, α—The convention in the social sciences is to use .05 or lower. A test will have more power with an alpha level of .05 than .01.

- Power—At least 80%, or .8 or higher, is recommended.[191]

- Effect size, *d*—Cohen's conventions, listed earlier, offer a rule of thumb. Read existing studies to determine what is typical for a study of a specific topic.

- Means and standard deviations—Obviously, means and standard deviations are not available on a study that has not yet been conducted, so these can come from previous research similar to the study to be conducted,[192] prior studies the researcher has done on the topic, or pilot studies. Meta-analyses are another good place for finding means from many different studies.

In the example of a moral development study, two groups were used—a treatment (stories about children) and control (stories about adults)—so *t* tests were specified in G*Power. A directional hypothesis was not predicted, so two-tailed tests were used. (If a direction had been predicted—for example, that journalists would use higher levels of moral judgment for stories with children than adults—a one-tailed test would have been used.) The a priori mode was specified because the power analysis was conducted before the study was performed to discover how many subjects to use. The means and standard deviations from the previous study of photographs were inserted; these were 5.27 (1.18) for the treatment group (photographs) and 4.25 (1.50) for the control group (no photographs). For power, .8 was specified; researchers can vary this between .8 and .95 to see how it affects the sample size. The Alpha error probability should be .05, which is standard in the social sciences. When these data are entered, the G*Power command will calculate the results. In this case, G*Power indicated a total of 94 subjects, with 37 in each of the two groups. Because the means and standard deviations were used, it calculated an effect size of .75, which is considered large by Cohen's conventions. If you do not know or cannot estimate the means and standard deviations, then input the desired effect size instead. Vary it to see how it changes the sample size requirements. Increasing the effect size can increase the sample size dramatically; specify smaller effect sizes if those are common for the research topic.

To review, it takes three of the pieces of information to calculate the fourth—alpha level (.05) and power (.8 minimum) are already determined; examine the literature to determine either effect size or the means/standard deviations. Experiment with the G*Power analysis to see how many subjects it takes to get a larger effect size. Performing a power analysis can help you decide if you need to switch to a cheaper form of subjects, such as MTurk, or if you can afford a sample from the general adult population.

This illustration of a G*Power analysis is fairly basic; there is actually much more to it. For example, G*Power allows the use of F tests using one-way ANOVA, main effects and a one-way interaction, and ANOVA between-subjects or within-subjects, among others. This requires a more advanced understanding of statistics, and more in-depth G*Power tutorials are available from many sources. Some are listed some in the "Suggested Readings" section.

Reporting a power analysis can range from a sentence to all the details in an appendix. Some examples include:

- "An a priori power analysis was completed based on the effect size of $d = 0.65$ for self-referential encoding compared to semantic encoding as reported in Symons and Johnson's large-scale meta-analysis (1997). The power analysis indicated that with power at 95% and an alpha of .05, a sample size of 33 would be sufficient to detect an effect of self-referential encoding."[193]

- "Data were analyzed from a final sample of 20 participants (mean age = 19.70, 15 females) who completed the study procedures. This sample size was chosen based on a priori power analyses (see supplemental materials)."[194]

- "An a priori power analysis, conducted in G*Power 3, indicated that a total sample size of approximately 60 participants would yield acceptable power (i.e., $1\text{-}\beta > 0.80$) for testing moderate effect sizes."[195]

## Observed Power

Finally, there is something called **observed power**, **post hoc power**, or **a posteriori power**, among other terms, that a few journals request researchers include when a statistical test was not significant.[196] This refers to a power test done after the study has been conducted, with the aim of understanding if the reason the null was not rejected could be attributed to the study being underpowered.[197] This is a controversial and complicated topic, the details of which will not be discussed here. To simplify, statistical tests that are not significant *always* have low power.[198] There is, in fact, a one-to-one correspondence between power and the $p$ value.[199] Many studies inappropriately report low power as a possible explanation for failure to support a hypothesis.[200] This is especially true when reporting the observed power values provided by SPSS or G*Power.[201] Instead, post hoc power should be based on population effect sizes of independent interest,[202] or results should be described using $p$ values, effect sizes, and confidence intervals.[203] As this is beyond the scope of this book, readers are instead referred to statistics books and courses.

The next chapter is concerned with the stimuli that subjects will receive in an experimental study and the instrumentation or observations that will be used to measure their responses.

# Common Mistakes

- Using student samples without considering how they might be different from the population of interest

- Not providing a rationale for the use of subjects of any type

- Generalizing beyond the subjects in the study

- Not conducting a power analysis prior to executing the study to determine the number of subjects needed

- Not reporting effect sizes, power, alpha, and number of subjects for each group

# Test Your Knowledge

1. Most experiments use which kind of samples?
    a. Random samples
    b. Representative samples
    c. Probability samples
    d. Convenience samples

2. Which of the following is NOT of concern when students are used as experimental subjects?
    a. Higher than average cognitive skills
    b. Homogeneity
    c. Compliance with authority
    d. Weaker sense of self

3. Which of the following is a disadvantage of using Amazon's Mechanical Turk for subjects?
    a. It is expensive
    b. Data collection is slow
    c. Subjects not paying attention to questions
    d. Subjects are not diverse

4. A Type 2 error is _____.
    a. The null hypothesis is *not* rejected when it should be
    b. The null hypothesis is rejected when it should be
    c. The null hypothesis is rejected when it should *not* be
    d. None of these

5. Power is related to _____.

   a. Sample size

   b. Effect size

   c. Significance level

   d. All of these

6. Which of the following is a problem related to a large sample?

   a. It raises the cost and time required to conduct the study

   b. Detecting relationships among all variables

   c. Finding significant relationships that are practically unimportant

   d. All of these

7. Effect size is _____.

   a. The amount of variance in the DV that is explained or accounted for by the IV

   b. The same as the significance level

   c. Heavily influenced by sample size

   d. Something that should not be reported in the study

8. In the social sciences, an effect size of .35 is considered to be:

   a. Very Small

   b. Small

   c. Medium

   d. Large

   e. Very Large

9. Estimating sample size with a power analysis before a study is conducted is called:

   a. A posteriori power

   b. A priori power

   c. Post hoc power

   d. Observed power

   e. Abuse of power

10. Power is not dependent upon the statistical test to be performed

    a. True

    b. False

**Answers**

| | | | |
|---|---|---|---|
| 1. d | 4. a | 7. a | 9. b |
| 2. b | 5. d | 8. c | 10. b |
| 3. c | 6. d | | |

## Application Exercises

1. Do a power analysis using data from studies similar to the one you are working on. Use G*Power or some similar power calculator. A free download of G*Power, the manual, and a tutorial can be found at http://www.gpower.hhu.de/.

2. Write up the sampling portion for the methods section of the experiment you are creating. Follow the examples in this chapter and other studies that are similar to yours. Address the following: Who are you going to use and how do they relate to the target population, how many do you need, how will you recruit them, what incentives will you use, and any other topics pertinent to your study. Incorporate your power analysis. Justify the use of your sample. One to two pages.

## Suggested Readings

**On student subjects:**

Basil, Michael D. 1996. "The Use of Student Samples in Communication Research." *Journal of Broadcasting and Electronic Media* 40 (3) (Summer): 431–440.

**On effect size:**

Levine, T. R., and C. R. Hullett. 2002. "Eta Squared, Partial Eta Squared and the Misreporting of Effect Size in Communication Research." *Human Communication Research* 28: 612–625.

**On G*Power:**

Mayr, S., E. Erdfelder, A. Buchner, and F. Faul. 2007. "A Short Tutorial of Gpower." *Tutorials in Quantitative Methods for Psychology* 3 (2): 51–59.

**On Post Hoc Power:**

O'Keefe, Daniel J. 2007. "Post Hoc Power, Observed Power, A Priori Power, Retrospective Power, Prospective Power, Achieved Power: Sorting Out Appropriate Uses of Statistical Power Analyses." *Communication Methods and Measures* 1 (4): 291–299.

# Notes

1. Michael D. Basil, "The Use of Student Samples in Communication Research," *Journal of Broadcasting and Electronic Media* 40, no. 3 (1996): 439.

2. William D. Wells, "Discovery-Oriented Consumer Research," *Journal of Consumer Research* 19 (1993): 492.

3. Elizabeth Tipton, "How Generalizable Is Your Experiment? An Index for Comparing Experimental Samples and Populations," *Journal of Educational and Behavioral Statistics* 39, no. 6 (2014): 478–501.

4. Basil, "The Use of Student Samples"; John A. Courtright, "Rationally Thinking About Nonprobability," *Journal of Broadcasting & Electronic Media* 40, no. 3 (1996): 414–421; Annie Lang, "The Logic of Using Inferential Statistics with Experimental Data From Nonprobability Samples: Inspired by Cooper, Dupagne, Potter, and Sparks," *Journal of Broadcasting & Electronic Media* 40, no. 3 (Summer 1996): 422–430; William R. Shadish, Thomas D. Cook, and Donald T. Campbell, *Experimental and Quasi-Experimental Designs for Generalized Causal Inference* (Belmont, CA: Wadsworth Cengage Learning, 2002).

5. Shadish, Cook, and Campbell, *Experimental and Quasi-Experimental Designs*, 373.

6. Basil, "The Use of Student Samples."

7. Robert A. Peterson, "On the Use of College Students in Social Science Research: Insights from a Second-Order Meta-Analysis," *Journal of Consumer Research* 28 (2001): 450–461; I. Simonson et al., "Consumer Research: In Search of Identity," in *Annual Review of Psychology*, ed. S. T. Fiske, D. L. Schacter, and C. Zahn-Waxler (Palo Alto, CA: Annual Reviews, 2001): 249–275.

8. Lisa Marriott, "Using Student Subjects in Experimental Research: A Challenge to the Practice of Using Students as a Proxy for Taxpayers," *International Journal of Social Research Methodology* 17, no. 5 (2014): 503–525.

9. W. J. Potter, R. Cooper, and M. Dupagne, "The Three Paradigms of Mass Media Research in Mainstream Communication Journals," *Communication Theory* 3 (1993): 317–335.

10. Joanne M. Miller, "Examining the Mediators of Agenda Setting: A New Experimental Paradigm Reveals the Role of Emotions," *Political Psychology* 28, no. 6 (2007): 696.

11. Elizabeth A. Bennion and David W. Nickerson, "The Cost of Convenience: An Experiment Showing E-Mail Outreach Decreases Voter Registration," *Political Research Quarterly* 64, no. 4 (2011): 861.

12. Renita Coleman, "The Effect of Visuals on Ethical Reasoning: What's a Photograph Worth to Journalists Making Moral Decisions?" *Journalism and Mass Communication Quarterly* 83 no. 4 (Winter 2006): 840.

13. Emily Thorson, "Belief Echoes: The Persistent Effects of Corrected Misinformation," *Political Communication* 33, no. 3 (2016): 466–467.

14. M. Kim and G. G. Van Ryzin. "Impact of Government Funding on Donations to Arts Organizations: A Survey Experiment." *Nonprofit and Voluntary Sector Quarterly* 43, no. 5 (2014): 916.

15. Hoon Lee and Nojin Kwak, "The Affect Effect of Political Satire: Sarcastic Humor, Negative Emotions, and Political Participation," *Mass Communication and Society* 17, no. 3 (2014): 315.

16. Renita Coleman, "Journalists' Moral Judgment About Children: Do as I Say, Not as I Do?" *Journalism Practice* 5, no. 3 (Summer 2011): 257–271.

17. D. O. Sears, "College Sophomores in the Laboratory: Influences of a Narrow Database on Social Psychology's View of Human Nature," *Journal of Personality and Social Psychology* 51 (1986): 515–530.

18. Ibid.

19. Basil, "The Use of Student Samples," 434.

20. Ibid.

21. Ibid.

22. Ibid.

23. Ibid.; Sears, "College Sophomores in the Laboratory."

24. B. H. Newberry, "Truth Telling in Subjects with Information About Experiments: Who Is Being Deceived?" *Journal of Personality and Social Psychology* 25 (1973): 369–374.

25. R. Hertwig and A. Ortmann, "Deception in Experiments: Revisiting the Arguments in Its Defense," *Ethics & Behavior* 18 (2008): 59–92.

26. C. D. Kam, "Implicit Attitudes, Explicit Choices: When Subliminal Priming Predicts Candidate Preference," *Political Behavior* 29 (2007): 343–367.

27. Basil, "The Use of Student Samples."

28. Deborah Nazarian and Joshua M. Smyth, "Context Moderates the Effects of an Expressive Writing Intervention: A Randomized Two-Study Replication and Extension," *Journal of Social & Clinical Psychology* 29, no. 8 (2010): 903–929.

29. Basil, "The Use of Student Samples."

30. Ibid.; Sears, "College Sophomores in the Laboratory."

31. Basil, "The Use of Student Samples."

32. Ibid.

33. Ibid.

34. Renita Coleman and H. Denis Wu, *Image and Emotion in Voter Decisions: The Affect Agenda* (New York: Lexington Books, 2015), chapter 9.

35. W. A. Cunningham, T. Anderson, and J. Murphy, "Are Students Real People?" *The Journal of Business* 47 (1974): 399–409.

36. Basil, "The Use of Student Samples."

37. Ibid.

38. Yair Levy, Timothy J. Ellis, and Eli Cohen, "A Guide for Novice Researchers on Experimental and Quasi-Experimental Studies in Information Systems Research," *Interdisciplinary Journal of Information, Knowledge and Management* 6 (2011): 151–161.

39. J. W. Lucas, "Theory-Testing, Generalization, and the Problem of External Validity," *Sociological Theory* 21 (2003): 236–253; J. G. Lynch Jr., "On the External Validity of Experiments in Consumer Research," *Journal of Consumer Research* 9 (1982): 225–239; John G. Lynch Jr., "The Role of External Validity in Theoretical Research," *Journal of Consumer Research* 10 (1983): 109–111.

40. Peterson, "On the Use of College Students."

41. Paul H. P. Hanel and Katia C. Vione, "Do Student Samples Provide an Accurate Estimate of the General Public?" *PLoS ONE* 11, no. 12 (2016): 1–10.

42. Coleman and Wu, *Image and Emotion in Voter Decisions.*

43. C. D. Kam, J. R. Wilking, and E. J. Zechmeister, "Beyond the 'Narrow Data Base': Another Convenience Sample for Experimental Research," *Political Behavior* 29 (2007): 415–440; P. J. Henry, "College Sphomores in the Laboratory Redux: Influences of a Narrow Databse on Social Psychology's View of the Nature of Prejudice," *Psychological Inquiry* 19, no. 2 (2008): 49–71.

44. M. H. Birnbaum, ed., *Psychological Experiments on the Internet* (San Diego, CA: Academic Press, 2000); M. H. Birnbaum, "Human Research and Data Collection Via the Internet," *Annual Review of Psychology* 55, no. 1 (2004): 803–832; Henry, "College Sphomores in the Laboratory Redux"; U. D. Reips, "The Web Experiment Method: Advantages, Disadvantages and Solutions," in *Psychological Experiments on the Internet,* ed. M. H. Birnbaum (San Diego, CA: Academic Press, 2000); M. P. Wattenberg, *Is Voting for Young People?* (Upper Saddle River, NJ: Pearson, 2011).

45. Erin C. Cassese et al., "Socially Mediated Internet Surveys: Recruiting Participants for Online Experiments," *PS: Political Science & Politics* 46, no. 4 (2013): 1–10.

46. Marriott, "Using Student Subjects in Experimental Research."

47. Cassese et al., "Socially Mediated Internet Surveys."

48. Ibid.

49. E. Diener, M. Diener, and C. Diener, "Factors Predicting the Subjective Well-Being of Nations," *Journal of Personality and Social Psychology* 69 (1995): 851–864; R. Fischer and S. Schwartz, "Whence Differences in Value Priorities? Individual, Cultural, or Artifactual Sources," *Journal of Cross-Cultural Psychology* 42 (2011): 1127–1144.

50. F. R. Kardes, "In Defense of Experimental Consumer Psychology," *Journal of Consumer Psychology* 5 (1996): 279–296; Lucas, "Theory-Testing, Generalization."

51. Basil, "The Use of Student Samples"; Lang, "The Logic of Using Inferential Statistics."

52. J. Alm and M. McKee, "Extending the Lessons of Laboratory Experiments on Tax Compliance to Managerial and Decision Economics," *Managerial and Decision Economics* 19 (1998): 259–275.

53. D. Bello et al., "From the Editors: Student Samples in International Business Research," *Journal of International Business Studies* 40 (2009): 361–364; D. G. Mook, "In Defense of External Invalidity," *American Psychologist* 38 (1983): 379–387; R. E. Pernice et al., "On Use of Student Samples for Scale Construction," *Psychological Reports* 102 (2008): 459–464.

54. Peterson, "On the Use of College Students"; Robert A. Peterson and Dwight R. Merunka, "Convenience Samples of College Students and Research Reproducibility," *Journal of Business Research* 67, no. 5 (2014): 1035–1041.

55. A. Bardi et al., "Value Stability and Change During Self-Chosen Life Transitions: Self-Selection Versus Socialization Effects," *Journal of Personality and Social Psychology* 106 (2014): 131–147.

56. M. Host, B. Regnell, and C. Wohlin, "Using Students as Subjects—A Comparative Study of Students and Professionals in Lead-Time Impact Assessment," *Empirical Software Engineering* 5 (2000): 201–214; G. Liyanarachchi, "Feasibility of Using Student Subjects in Accounting Experiments: A Review," *Pacific Accounting Review* 19, no. 1 (2007): 47–67; Marriott, "Using Student Subjects in Experimental Research."

57. Marriott, "Using Student Subjects in Experimental Research."

58. C. M. Megehee, "Advertising Time Expansion, Compression, and Cognitive Processing Influences on Consumer Acceptance of Message and Brand," *Journal of Business Research* 62, no. 4 (2009): 420–431.

59. Basil, "The Use of Student Samples."

60. For example, see: S. Hazari, C. Brown, and R. Rutledge, "Investigating Marketing Students' Perceptions of Active Learning and Social Collaboration in Blogs," *Journal of Education for Business* 88 (2013): 101–108; Host, Regnell, and Wohlin, "Using Students as Subjects"; Jin Huang et al., "Individual Development Accounts and Homeownership Among Low-Income Adults with Disabilities: Evidence from a Randomized Experiment," *Journal of Applied Social Science* 10, no. 1 (2016): 55–66; Yanna Krupnikov and Adam Seth Levine, "Cross-Sample Comparisons and External Validity," *Journal of Experimental Political Science* 1, no. 1 (2014): 59–80; Liyanarachchi, "Feasibility of Using Student Subjects"; G. Liyanarachchi and M. Milne, "Comparing the Investment Decisions of Accounting Practitioners and Students: An Empirical Study on the Adequacy of Student Surrogates," *Accounting Forum* 29 (2005): 121–135; D. W. Schanzenbach, "What Have Researchers Learned from Project Star?" in *Brookings Papers on Education Policy* (2007): 205–228; Valmi D. Sousa, Jaclene A. Zauszniewski, and Carol M. Musil, "How to Determine Whether a Convenience Sample Represents the Population 1," *Applied Nursing Research* 17, no. 2 (2004): 130–133; T. Waller, C. Lampman, and G. Lupfer-Johnson, "Assessing Bias against Overweight Individuals Among Nursing and Psychology Students: An Implicit Association Test," *Journal of Clinical Nursing* 21 (2012): 3504–3512; James N. Druckman and C. D. Kam, "Students as Experimental Participants: A Defense of the "Narrow Data Base," in *Cambridge Handbook of Experimental Political Science*, ed. James N. Druckman, et al. (New York: CUP, 2011), 41–57.

61. A. Abdel-Khalik, "On the Efficiency of Subject Surrogation in Accounting Research," *The Accounting Review* 49 (1974): 743–750; D. Bean and J. D'Aquila, "Accounting Students as Surrogates for Accounting Professionals When Studying Ethical Dilemmas: A Cautionary Note," *Teaching Business Ethics* 7 (2003): 187–204; R. Copeland, A. Francia, and R. Strawser, "Students as Subjects in Behavioral Business Research," *The Accounting Review* 48 (1973) 365–372; M. T. Gordon, A. Slade, and N. Schmitt, "The 'Science of the Sophomore' Revisited: From Conjecture to Empiricism," *Academy of Management Review* 11 (1986): 191–207.

62. Sousa, Zauszniewski, and Musil, "How to Determine Whether a Convenience Sample Represents the Population 1."

63. W. G. Cochran, *Sampling Techniques,* 3rd ed. (New York: Wiley, 1977).

64. Renita Coleman, Esther Thorson, and Lee Wilkins, "Testing the Impact of Public Health Framing and Rich Sourcing in Health News Stories," *Journal of Health Communication* 16, no. 9 (2011): 941–954; Rebecca S. McEntee, Renita Coleman, and Carolyn Yaschur, "Comparing the Effects of Vivid Writing and Photographs on Moral Judgment in Public Relations," *Journalism and Mass Communication Quarterly* 94 no. 4 (2017): 1011–1030; Aimee Meader et al., "Ethics in the Digital Age: A Comparison of the Effects of Moving Images and Photographs on Moral Judgment," *Journal of Media Ethics* 30, no. 4 (2015): 234–251.

65. Nazarian and Smyth, "Context Moderates the Effects."

66. Krupnikov and Levine, "Cross-Sample Comparisons."

67. Peterson, "On the Use of College Students"; Peterson and Merunka, "Convenience Samples of College Students."

68. R. M. Lindsay and A. S. C. Ehrenberg, "The Design of Replicated Studies," *American Statistician* 47 (1993): 236.

69. Peterson and Merunka, "Convenience Samples of College Students."

70. Basil, "The Use of Student Samples."

71. Hanel and Vione, "Do Student Samples Provide an Accurate Estimate of the General Public?"

72. Christine E. Meltzer, Thorsten Naab, and Gregor Daschmann, "All Student Samples Differ: On Participant Selection in Communication Science," *Communication Methods and Measures* 6 (2012): 251–262.

73. Coleman, "The Effect of Visuals."

74. Claire A. Dunlop and Claudio M. Radaelli, "Teaching Regulatory Humility: Experimenting with Student Practitioners," *Politics* 36, no. 1 (2016): 79–94.

75. Basil, "The Use of Student Samples."

76. T. D. Cook and D. T. Campbell, *Quasi-Experimentation: Design and Analysis Issues for Field Settings* (Chicago: Rand-McNally, 1979).

77. Peterson, "On the Use of College Students."

78. Marriott, "Using Student Subjects in Experimental Research."

79. Peterson, "On the Use of College Students"; Peterson and Merunka, "Convenience Samples of College Students."

80. Marriott, "Using Student Subjects in Experimental Research."

81. Sousa, Zauszniewski, and Musil, "How to Determine Whether a Convenience Sample Represents the Population 1."

82. Winter Mason and Siddharth Suri, "Conducting Behavioral Research on Amazon's Mechanical Turk," *Behavioral Research* 44 (2012): 1–23.

83. Srinivas Rao and Amanda Michel, "ProPublica's Guide to Mechanical Turk," *ProPublica* (Oct. 15, 2010).

84. Bassam Tariq, "Turking for a Living," *New Yorker* (March 20, 2015).

85. Mason and Suri, "Conducting Behavioral Research."

86. Christoph Bartneck et al., "Comparing the Similarity of Responses Received From Studies in Amazon's Mechanical Turk to Studies Conducted Online and With Direct Recruitment," *PLoS ONE* 10, no. 4 (2015): 1–23.

87. http://en.wikipedia.org/wiki/The_Turk. Accessed June 24, 2017.

88. http://en.wikipedia.org/wiki/The_Turk. Accessed June 24, 2017.

89. http://en.wikipedia.org/wiki/The_Turk; Bartneck et al., "Comparing the Similarity of Responses."

90. J. Ross et al., "Who Are the Crowdworkers? Shifting Demographics in Mechanical Turk" (paper presented at the ACM, 2010).

91. Adam J. Berinsky, Gregory A. Huber, and Gabriel S. Lenz, "Evaluating Online Labor Markets for Experimental Research: Amazon.Com's Mechanical Turk," *Political Analysis* 20, no. 3 (2012): 351–368; Gabriele Paolacci, Jesse Chandler, and Panagiotis Ipeirotis, "Running Experiments on Amazon Mechanical Turk," *Judgment and Decision Making* 5, no. 5 (2010); Ross et al., "Who Are the Crowdworkers?"

92. Berinsky, Huber, and Lenz, "Evaluating Online Labor Markets."

93. Michael Buhrmester, Tracy Kwang, and Sam Gosling, "Amazon's Mechanical Turk: A New Source of Inexpensive, yet High-Quality, Data?" *Perspectives on Psychological Science* 6, no. 1 (2011): 3–5; R. Kosara and C. Ziemkiewicz, "Do Mechanical Turks Dream of Square Pie Charts?" *Proceedings BEyond Time and Errors: Novel EvaLuation Methods for Information Visualization (BELIV)* 10 (2010): 373–382.

94. Connor Huff and Dustin Tingley, "'Who Are These People?' Evaluating the Demographic Characteristics and Political Preferences of MTurk Survey Respondents," *Research and Politics* July-September (2015): 1–12.

95. Krupnikov and Levine, "Cross-Sample Comparisons."

96. Thomas Bernauer, Robert Gampfer, and Aya Kachi, "European Unilateralism and Involuntary Burden-Sharing in Global Climate Politics: A Public Opinion Perspective from the Other Side," *European Union Politics* 15, no. 1 (2014): 132–151; Robert Gampfer, Thomas Bernauer, and Aya Kachi, "Obtaining Public Support for North-South Climate Funding: Evidence from Conjoint Experiments in Donor Countries," *Global Environmental Change* 29 (2014): 118–126.

97. Huff and Tingley, "'Who Are These People?'"

98. Bartneck et al., "Comparing the Similarity of Responses," 1/23.

99. Huff and Tingley, "'Who Are These People?'" 8.

100. Kevin E. Levay, Jeremy Freeze, and James N. Druckman, "The Demographic and Political Composition of Mechanical Turk Samples," *SAGE Open* January-March (2016): 1–17

101. Ibid., 10.

102. Berinsky, Huber, and Lenz, "Evaluating Online Labor Markets."

103. Ibid.; Buhrmester, Kwang, and Gosling, "Amazon's Mechanical Turk"; Huff and Tingley, "'Who Are These People?'"; Panagiotis G. Ipeirotis, "Demographics of Mechanical Turk," *CeDER Working Paper No. 10-10* New York University, no. Retrieved from http://www.ipeirotis.com/wp-content/uploads/2012/02/CeDER-10-01.pdf (2010); Krupnikov and Levine, "Cross-Sample Comparisons"; Kevin J. Mullinix et al., "The Generalizability of Survey Experiments," 2 (2015): 109–138.

104. Berinsky, Huber, and Lenz, "Evaluating Online Labor Markets"; Krupnikov and Levine, "Cross-Sample Comparisons"; Mullinix et al., "The Generalizability of Survey Experiments."

105. Birnbaum, *Psychological Experiments on the Internet*; Paolacci, Chandler, and Ipeirotis, "Running Experiments on Amazon Mechanical Turk."

106. Buhrmester, Kwang, and Gosling, "Amazon's Mechanical Turk."

107. Bartneck et al., "Comparing the Similarity of Responses," 5/23.

108. Matthew J. C. Crump, John V. McDonnell, and Todd M. Gureckis, "Evaluating Amazon's Mechanical Turk as a Tool for Experimental Behavioral Research," *PloS One* 8, no. 3 (2013): 1–18.

109. Krupnikov and Levine, "Cross-Sample Comparisons."

110. Ibid.; Levay, Freeze, and Druckman, "The Demographic and Political Composition."

111. Krupnikov and Levine, "Cross-Sample Comparisons."

112. Ibid.

113. Emily Thorson, "Belief Echoes: The Persistent Effects of Corrected Misinformation," *Political Communication* 33, no. 3 (2016). 460–480.

114. Huff and Tingley, "'Who Are These People?'"

115. Ellen Cushing, "Amazon Mechanical Turk: The Digital Sweatshop," *Utne Reader* January-February, http://www.utne.com/science-and-technology/amazon-mechanical-turk-zm0z13jfzlin (2013); John Horton and Lydia Chilton, "The Labor Economics of Paid Crowdsourcing," in Proceedings of the 11th ACM Conference on Electronic Commerce (2010).

116. Bartneck et al., "Comparing the Similarity of Responses."

117. Buhrmester, Kwang, and Gosling, "Amazon's Mechanical Turk."

118. Travis Simcox and Julie Fiez, "Collecting Response Times Using Amazon Mechanical Turk and Adobe Flash," *Behavioral Research* 46 (2014): 95–111.

119. Scott Clifford and Jennifer Jerit, "Is There a Cost to Convenience? An Experimental Comparison of Data Quality in Laboratory and Online Studies," *Journal of Experimental Political Science* 1, no. 2 (2014): 120–131.

120. Berinsky, Huber, and Lenz, "Evaluating Online Labor Markets."

121. Bartneck et al., "Comparing the Similarity of Responses"; Berinsky, Huber, and Lenz, "Evaluating Online Labor Markets"; A. J. Berinsky, M. F. Margolia, and M. W. Sances, "Separating the Shirkers from the Workers? Making Sure Respondents Pay Attention on Self-Administered Surveys," *American Journal of Political Science* 58, no. 3 (2014): 739–753; Huff and Tingley, "'Who Are These People?'"

122. D. Rand, "The Promise of Mechanical Turk: How Online Labor Markets Can Help Theorists Run Behavioral Experiments," *Journal of Theoretical Biology* 299 (2012): 172–179.

123. J. Heer and M. Bostock, "Crowdsourcing Graphical Perception: Using Mechanical Turk to Assess Visualization Design" (paper presented at the Proceedings of the SIGCHI Conference on Human Factors in Computing Systems, New York, 2010).

124. Buhrmester, Kwang, and Gosling, "Amazon's Mechanical Turk"; Mason and Suri, "Conducting Behavioral Research."

125. Paolacci, Chandler, and Ipeirotis, "Running Experiments on Amazon Mechanical Turk."

126. Buhrmester, Kwang, and Gosling, "Amazon's Mechanical Turk"; Heer and Bostock, "Crowdsourcing Graphical Perception"; D. Kelly, D. Harper, and B. Landau, "Questionnaire Mode Effects in Interactive Information Retrieval Experiments," *Information Processing and Management* 44 (2008): 122–141.

127. Bartneck et al., "Comparing the Similarity of Responses"; Simcox and Fiez, "Collecting Response Times."

128. Paolacci, Chandler, and Ipeirotis, "Running Experiments on Amazon Mechanical Turk."

129. M. Smith and B. Leigh, "Virtual Subjects: Using the Internet as an Alternative Source of Subjects and Research Environment," *Behavior Research Methods* 29 (1997): 496–505.

130. Marriott, "Using Student Subjects in Experimental Research."

131. Gregg R. Murray et al., "Convenient Yet Not a Convenience Sample: Jury Pools as Experimental Subject Pools," *Social Science Research* 42, no. 1 (2013): 246–253.

132. Alan Gerber et al., "Reporting Guidelines for Experimental Research: A Report from the Experimental Research Section Standards Committee," *Journal of Experimental Political Science* 1, no. 1 (2014): 81–98.

133. Alan S. Gerber et al., "Reporting Balance Tables, Response Rates and Manipulation Checks in Experimental Research: A Reply from the Committee That Prepared the Reporting Guidelines," *Journal of Experimental Political Science* 2, no. 2 (2016): 216–229.

134. Diana C. Mutz and Robin Pemantle, "Standards for Experimental Research: Encouraging a Better Understanding of Experimental Methods," *Journal of Experimental Political Science* 2, no. 2 (2016): 192–215.

135. Bartneck et al., "Comparing the Similarity of Responses."

136. Cassese et al., "Socially Mediated Internet Surveys."

137. Ibid.

138. Ibid., 777.

139. Kam, "Implicit Attitudes, Explicit Choices."

140. Murray et al., "Convenient Yet Not a Convenience Sample."

141. For an example of a study that incorporated experimental conditions in the British Election Study 2012, see Rosie Campbell and Philip Cowley, "What Voters Want: Reactions to Candidate Characteristics in a Survey Experiment," *Political Studies* 62, no. 4 (2013): 745–765; Murray et al., "Convenient Yet Not a Convenience Sample."

142. David Niven, "The Other Side of Optimism: High Expectations and the Rejection of Status Quo Politics," *Political Behavior* 22, no. 1 (2000): 71–88.

143. Lee Sigelman, Carol K. Sigelman, and Barbara J. Walkosz, "The Public and the Paradox of Leadership: An Experimental Analysis," *American Political Science* 36 (1992): 366–385.

144. Nayda Terkildsen, "When White Voters Evaluate Black Candidates: The Processing Implications of Candidate Skin Color, Prejudice, and Self-Monitoring," *American Journal of Political Science* 37 (1993): 1032–1053.

145. Christopher J. Lewis, Dona-Gene Mitchell, and Cynthia R. Rugeley, "Courting Public Opinion: Utilizing Jury Pools in Experimental Research," in *Political Methodology Conference* (Tallahassee, FL 2005).

146. Ibid.

147. Murray et al., "Convenient Yet Not a Convenience Sample," 252.

148. McEntee, Coleman, and Yaschur, "Comparing the Effects of Vivid Writing."

149. Mitchell Hoffman and John Morgan, "Who's Naughty? Who's Nice? Experiments on Whether Pro-Social Workers Are Selected out of Cutthroat Business Environments," *Journal of Economic Behavior & Organization* 109 (2015): 173–187.

150. Kim and Ryzin, "Impact of Government Funding"; Murray et al., "Convenient Yet Not a Convenience Sample."

151. Gary W. Ritter and Marc J. Holley, "Lessons for Conducting Random Assignment in Schools," *Journal of Children's Services* 3, no. 2 (2008): 28–39.

152. Ibid.

153. Willem Wetzels et al., "Impact of Prepaid Incentives in Face-to-Face Surveys: A Large-Scale Experiment with Postage Stamps," *International Journal of Public Opinion Research* 20, no. 4 (2008): 507–516.

154. Dunlop and Radaelli, "Teaching Regulatory Humility."

155. S. Mayr et al., "A Short Tutorial of Gpower," *Tutorials in Quantitative Methods for Psychology* 3, no. 2 (2007): 51–59.

156. Ibid.

157. Ibid.

158. Ibid.

159. For example, see J. Cohen, "Things I Have Learned (So Far)," *American Psychologist* 45 (1990): 1304–1312; Jacob Cohen, "The Earth Is Round (P < .05)," *American Psychologist* 49, no. 12 (1994): 997–1003.

160. L. J. Cronbach et al., *The Dependability of Behavioral Measurements: Theory of Generalizability for Scores and Profiles* (New York: Wiley, 1972); G. A. Marcoulides, "Maximizing Power in Generalizability Studies under Budget Constraints," *Journal of Educational Statistics* 18, no. 2 (1993): 197–206.

161. Wilson Van Voorhis and Morgan, "Understanding Power and Rules of Thumb."

162. Barbara G. Tabachnick and Linda S. Fidell, *Using Multivariate Statistics* (New York: HarperCollins, 1996);

Esther Thorson, Robert H. Wicks, and Glenn Leshner, "Experimental Methodology in Journalism and Mass Communication Research," *Journalism and Mass Communication Quarterly* 89, no. 1 (2012): 112–124.

163. J. Descôteaux, "Statistical Power: An Historical Introduction," *Tutorials in Quantitative Methods for Psychology* 3, no. 2 (2007): 28–34; Thorson, Wicks, and Leshner, "Experimental Methodology in Journalism."

164. Rebecca B. Morton and Joshua A. Tucker, "Experiments, Journals, and Ethics," *Journal of Experimental Political Science* 1, no. 2 (2015): 99–103.

165. Chia-Hu Chang et al., "Virtual Spotlighted Advertising for Tennis Videos," *Journal of Visual Communication & Image Representation* 21, no. 7 (2010): 595–612; Justin W. Owens, Evan M. Palmer, and Barbara S. Chaparro, "The Pervasiveness of Text Advertising Blindness," *Journal of Usability Studies* 9, no. 2 (2014): 51–69.

166. James R. Rest, *Development in Judging Moral Issues* (Minneapolis, MN: University of Minnesota Press, 1979).

167. Thorson, Wicks, and Leshner, "Experimental Methodology in Journalism."

168. Leland Wilkinson and Task Force on Statistical Inference, American Psychological Association Science Directorate, "Statistical Methods in Psychology Journals: Guidelines and Explanations," *American Psychologist* 54, no. 8 (1999): 594–604.

169. Thorson, Wicks, and Leshner, "Experimental Methodology in Journalism."

170. D. R. Atkinson, M. J. Furlong, and B. E. Wampold, "Statistical Significance, Reviewer Evaluations, and the Scientific Process: Is There a (Statistically) Significant Relationship?" *Journal of Counseling Psychology* 29 (1982): 189–194.

171. Graham N. Dixon, "Negative Affect as a Mechanism of Exemplification Effects," *Communication Research* 43, no. 6 (2015): 768.

172. H. Denis Wu and Renita Coleman, "The Affective Effect on Political Judgment: Comparing the Influences of Candidate Attributes and Issue Congruence," *Journalism and Mass Communication Quarterly* 91, no. 3 (2014), 530–543.

173. Renita Coleman et al., "Public Life and the Internet: If You Build a Better Website, Will Citizens Become Engaged?" *New Media & Society* 10, no. 2 (2008): 179–201.

174. J. Cohen, *Statistical Power Analysis for the Behavioral Sciences,* 2nd ed. (Hillsdale, NJ: Erlbaum, 1988).

175. Russell V. Lenth, "Java Applets for Power and Sample Size," Division of Mathematical Sciences, the College of Liberal Arts of the University of Iowa, https://homepage.divms.uiowa.edu/~rlenth/Power/.

176. Erik Westlund and Elizabeth A. Stuart, "The Nonuse, Misuse, and Proper Use of Pilot Studies in Experimental Evaluation Research," *American Journal of Evaluation* 38, no. 2 (2017): 246–261.

177. Descôteaux, "Statistical Power."

178. Wilkinson and Task Force on Statistical Inference, American Psychological Association Science Directorate, "Statistical Methods in Psychology Journals."

179. S. B. Green, "How Many Subjects Does It Take to Do a Regression Analysis?" *Multivariate Behavioral Research* 26 (1991): 499–510.

180. R. J. Harris, *A Primer of Multivariate Statistics,* 2nd ed. (New York: Academic Press, 1985).

181. J. Cohen, and P. Cohen, *Applied Multiple Regression/ Correlation Analysis for the Behavioral Sciences* (Hillsdale, NJ: Erlbaum, 1975).

182. D. C. Howell, *Statistical Methods for Psychology*, 4th ed. (Belmont, CA: Wadsworth, 1997).

183. Tabachnick and Fidell, *Using Multivariate Statistics.*

184. E. J. Pedhazur and L. P. Schmelkin, *Measurement, Design, and Analysis: An Integrated Approach* (Hillsdale, NJ: Erlbaum, 1991).

185. A. L. Comrey and H. B. Lee, *A First Course in Factor Analysis,* 2nd ed. (Hillsdale, NJ: Erlbaum, 1992).

186. Cohen, *Statistical Power Analysis for the Behavioral Sciences,* 2nd ed.

187. A. Aron and E. N. Aron, *Statistics for Psychology,* 2nd ed. (Upper Saddle River, NJ: Prentice Hall, 1999).

188. Also see: F. Faul et al., "G*Power 3: A Flexible Statistical Power Analysis Program for the Social, Behavioral, and Biomedical Sciences," *Behavior Research Methods* 39, no. 2 (2007): 175–191; Mayr et al., "A Short Tutorial of Gpower."

189. Coleman, "Journalists' Moral Judgment About Children."

190. Coleman, "The Effect of Visuals."

191. Cohen, *Statistical Power Analysis for the Behavioral Sciences,* 2nd ed.

192. Descôteaux, "Statistical Power."

193. Sarah V. Bentley, Katharine H. Greenaway, and S. Alexander Haslam, "An Online Paradigm for

Exploring the Self-Reference Effect," *PLoS ONE* 12, no. 5 (2017): 1–21.

194. Erica A. Hornstein and Naomi I. Eisenberger, "Unpacking the Buffering Effect of Social Support Figures: Social Support Attenuates Fear Acquisition," *PLoS ONE* 12, no. 5 (2017): 1–9.

195. Satoris S. Culbertson, William S. Weyhrauch, and Christopher J. Waples, "Behavioral Cues as "Indicators of Deception in Structured Employment Interviews," *International Journal of Selection & Assessment* 24, no. 2 (2016): 119–131.

196. John M. Hoenig and Dennis M. Heisey, "The Abuse of Power," *The American Statistician* 55, no. 1 (2001): 19–24; Daniel J. O'Keefe, "Post Hoc Power, Observed Power, A Priori Power, Retrospective Power, Prospective Power, Achieved Power: Sorting Out Appropriate Uses of Statistical Power Analyses," *Communication Methods and Measures* 1, no. 4 (2007): 291–299; J. Descôteaux, "Editor's Note: The Uncorrupted Statistical Power," *Tutorials in Quantitative Methods for Psychology* 3, no. 2 (2007): 26–27.

197. Hoenig and Heisey, "The Abuse of Power."

198. Ibid.; O'Keefe, "Post Hoc Power, Observed Power."

199. Hoenig and Heisey, "The Abuse of Power"; O'Keefe, "Post Hoc Power, Observed Power."

200. Hoenig and Heisey, "The Abuse of Power."

201. O'Keefe, "Post Hoc Power, Observed Power."

202. Ibid.

203. Cohen, *Statistical Power Analysis for the Behavioral Sciences,* 2nd ed.; Hoenig and Heisey, "The Abuse of Power"; O'Keefe, "Post Hoc Power, Observed Power."

# STIMULI AND MANIPULATION CHECKS

*Look for a large object rather than a small one.*[1]

**—R. Barker Bausell**

The heart of any experiment is the stimulus. This is also the fun part. Experimentalists seldom define the term **stimulus**, instead relying on the dictionary definition of it as something that causes a response or reaction.[2] For example, Freud called a stimulus a motivating force, mirroring the dictionary definition.[3] The most common usage of the term is likely in the context of the economy—discussion of a "stimulus package" is

# STUDY SPOTLIGHT 9.1
## Creating Realistic Stimuli

SAGE Journal Article:
study.sagepub.com/
coleman

From: Chen, Gina Masullo. 2013. "Losing Face on Social Media." Communication Research 42 (6): 819–838. doi:10.1177/0093650213510937.

In this study, the author goes to great lengths to create realistic stimuli and conduct manipulation checks in order to create a fictitious but believable social networking site for college students. She first began with a focus group of seven college students and used a procedure that asked them to think out loud (see chapter 10 for more on this) while brainstorming ideas for the topic of the site (e.g., "Leggings Aren't Pants," "How Do They Expect Me to Learn at 8 a.m. When I'm Still Drunk"), questions on it (e.g., "Top 5 songs on my iPod are . . ." "On the weekend, you're most likely to find me . . ."), and the types of messages they might receive when trying to join such a site.

She used a customizable online platform called Ning to create the fictitious social networking site called "The College Network." Subjects were told they were beta testing a new social media site for college students.

For this, she adapted a procedure advocated by Graesser (1981) to create stimuli for experiments. Information about this book can be found in the "Suggested Readings" section at the end of this chapter.

## FIGURE 9.1 ● THE COLLEGE NETWORK

Gina Masullo Chen

pervasive when the economy is sluggish. When politicians and economists talk about a stimulus, they mean something that will increase employment and encourage spending. They are interested in doing something that will cause the economy to react positively. The term is similar for social science experiments—a stimulus is the vehicle that an experimenter uses to deliver the manipulation hypothesized to cause some effect. And as the advice from Bausell in the opening quote says, a "large object"—in this case, a big or strong stimulus—is better suited to create a response than is a small one.

Stimuli (the plural form of stimulus) for an experiment can be in whatever form best delivers the manipulation, treatment, or intervention to the subjects. For Ivan Pavlov, the stimulus was a ringing bell. Stanley Milgram built an "electric shock generator" as a stimulus, which was nothing more than a box with switches and labels. Philip Zimbardo created an entire mock prison as his stimulus. In many different disciplines in the social sciences, researchers commonly use messages as a principal source of stimuli[4]—for example, campaign websites in political studies, advertisements for marketing research, clips of movies to induce mood in a psychology study. Stimuli are often conceived of in terms of their physical features,[5] such as the functionality or organization of a website, which makes up the concept of interest.[6] Another form of stimulus is as instructions—for example, telling subjects to list what worries them about an issue such as immigration.[7] Stimuli can range from the very simple, such as text on a piece of paper or computer screen, to the complex, such as an entire fictitious TV news show or website. Many are somewhere in between—posters, web pages, press releases, tweets, social media posts, and the like. One political study sent subjects text messages as the stimuli.[8] For some disciplines that assess the effectiveness of programs or interventions, the stimuli are those programs or interventions, such as a computer-assisted learning curriculum or a training seminar given to police to teach them how to better handle people with mental illness, for example. In these cases, the stimuli already exist, and researchers may only need to create something else for the control group to receive.

Creating high-quality stimuli is key to a successful experiment, so this chapter is devoted to advice and suggestions to achieve this.

## EXAMPLES OF STIMULI

Probably the best way to illustrate a stimulus in a social science experiment is with examples:

- In a political science study aimed at determining which politicians make it into the news and why, the stimuli were fictional press releases about parliamentarians.[9]

- In a marketing experiment designed to see what messages were most effective at getting people to cook on fuel-efficient stoves instead of using fires in Uganda, the experimenters created posters touting the new stoves.[10]

- In a study of a public relations crisis, the voice pitch of a spokesperson was manipulated with radio broadcasts of a fictitious press conference.[11]

- In an education study, students were taught on a computer instead of by a teacher; the computer-assisted curriculum was the stimulus.[12]

In all these examples, the stimuli are designed to represent the categories of theoretical interest to the study. They are the vehicle through which the experimenters manipulate the levels of the factors hypothesized to cause some effect or outcome. Specifically:

- In the political science study, the press releases were written to represent characteristics hypothesized to make politicians newsworthy, such as which party they belonged to and the issue they specialized in.[13] These represent the levels of the factors that were manipulated, or changed, in the stimulus press releases.

- In the marketing experiment for stoves, the posters were the stimuli that delivered the manipulated messages representing the levels of the factor—for example, one on health benefits and one on saving time and money.[14]

- In the PR crisis study, the radio broadcasts of a press conference were the stimuli created by having a student pretending to be an organization's spokesperson record a statement, which was then manipulated to create one high-pitched version and one low-pitched version; the pitch represented the levels of the factor being studied.[15]

- In the education experiment, the computer-assisted lessons were the stimuli that manipulated the concepts in a theory of language learning that was being tested by changing how visual and auditory information was presented, and with different question-and-answer strategies, for example.[16]

In journalism, stories are often created to look like they have appeared in a newspaper or on a website. For example, a study of the effects of speed versus accuracy on readers' perceptions of news organizations' credibility created stimuli that consisted of stories in blog-roll format that showed inaccurate information being corrected as the story updated.[17]

In this study of the effects of speed and accuracy on readers' perceptions of credibility of news organizations, the researcher created stimuli designed to look like a news organization's blog roll. These were presented to subjects on a computer screen the way they would see them if they were real. She imitated actual news organization's blog rolls to create the stimuli. Figures 9.2a and 9.2b show an example of a story in the fast condition, with inaccuracies, and in the slow condition, with no inaccuracies. In the fast condition, the manipulation is achieved with the term "CORRECTION."

## FIGURE 9.2A ● FAST CONDITION

**Lee, Angela Min-Chia. 2014. How Fast Is Too Fast? Examining the Impact of Speed-Driven Journalism on News Production and Audience Reception (unpublished dissertation, The University of Texas at Austin).**

Dozens Dead in San Antonio Flooding, Landslides

Live Text As It Happened

By NICHOLAS KULISH

**10:02 a.m.**: Torrential rains began on Sunday night and continued into Monday morning, causing power failures and cutting off roadways near The Far Northwest.

**9:40 a.m.**: Mayor Martinez de Vera said burials for the dead and treatment for the injured are being organized.

**9:28 a.m.**: "Many houses in the suburbs were destroyed by the rain," Greenberg said. "Many of the victims are children, and the houses collapsed on them."

**9:23 a.m.**: Police spokesman, Jon Hermes, said that hundreds more had been displaced because of damage to their homes. Willy Greenberg, spokesman for Mayor Art Martinez de Vera, said the damage is extensive.

**9:17 a.m.**: *CORRECTION*—At least 60, not 100, people were killed.

**9:12 a.m.**: At least 100 people were killed and dozens injured in San Antonio, after heavy rains caused flooding and landslides in Bexar County, officials said.

## FIGURE 9.2B ● SLOW CONDITION

Dozens Dead in San Antonio Flooding, Landslides

By NICHOLAS KULISH

At least 60 people were killed and dozens injured in San Antonio after heavy rains caused flooding and landslides in Bexar County, officials said.

Police spokesman Jon Hermes said hundreds more had been displaced because of damage to their homes. Willy Greenberg, spokesman for Mayor Art Martinez de Vera, said the damage is extensive.

"Many houses in the suburbs were destroyed by the rain," Greenberg said. "Many of the victims are children, and the houses collapsed on them."

Martinez de Vera said burials for the dead and treatment for the injured are being organized. Torrential rains began on Sunday night and continued into Monday morning, causing power failures and cutting off roadways near The Far Northwest.

Quite a lot of work is involved in creating realistic-looking posters, radio broadcasts, ads, and websites; however, not all stimuli need to be this complex. In a business study on corporate social responsibility, the researchers manipulated how socially responsible a business was by describing it as either nonprofit or for-profit in text scenarios that participants read; the scenarios were the stimuli.[18] Text on paper or on computer screens is among the simplest to create, and many experiments use these as stimuli. For example, in a political science study where subjects were given information about fictional candidates' positions on issues and then asked to cast a vote, the information was presented as text on a computer screen rather than being billed as coming from a candidate's website or a news source, eliminating the need to mock up a website or newspaper editorial.[19] In another experiment, subjects were given an essay to read that primed their feelings of disgust or concerns about harm, and then asked to make a moral judgment about gay adoption.[20] The essay was not presented as coming from an editorial in a magazine or newspaper, so there was no need to make it look like one. However, if an experiment calls for some message that is typically delivered via a medium such as TV commercials or Twitter, then having subjects read text that describes a TV commercial or tweet is far less realistic than creating a fictional TV commercial.

This is one of the reasons why there is so much criticism about the lack of external validity in experiments (see chapter 5 on validity). (For an online tool that creates fake social media such as Twitter, Facebook, and more, see More About box 9.2.)

Sometimes, the stimulus itself is not complicated to create but the accompanying parts of the experiment are. For example, if the manipulation is embedded in written instructions, as it was in an economics experiment where subjects performed a task and were told that a contribution would either go to an organization or not, there is no need to create stimuli such as posters or ads. The written instructions are the stimuli. However, the researchers did need to create the task that subjects would perform—decoding letters into numbers. Thus, they used software to create tables consisting of one column of letters and an adjacent column with the corresponding numbers, which was displayed to subjects on a computer screen.[24]

Stimuli do not always have to be fictitious or created by researchers; some studies use the real thing. For example, in a study designed to see if reality TV shows could encourage altruistic behavior, researchers used actual segments from reality shows.[25] The TV shows were the stimuli, selected to represent either game-style reality shows (*Survivor, Amazing Race*) or meaningful and inspiring reality shows (*Undercover Boss* and *Supernanny*). In another study, three stimuli testing the effects of Internet messages on political efficacy were an online quiz created by Minnesota Public Radio, a story from the TV

# MORE ABOUT . . . BOX 9.2
## Creating Realistic Social Media Stimuli

More and more information is delivered to people via social media such as Facebook and Twitter—especially to millennials, who represent the college students so often used as subjects in academic experiments. Online tools are available to help researchers create believable social media. For example, Twister, Tweeterino, and Simitator all offer tools to create fictitious Tweets, with Simitator also able to create fictitious Facebook posts and chats, SnapChat messages, and iPhone texts. PrankMeNot is another source for creating tweets, Facebook posts, and message chats. The Simitator website touts the ability to "prank your friends," but educators have also found it useful as a teaching tool in schools that block Internet access for students,[21] for instance, or to create handouts that students can relate to.[22]

One researcher who used Simitator to create believable Tweets for experiments[23] started by randomly sampling actual published tweets from the *New York Times*, *Wall Street Journal*, and *Washington Post*. He then used the tool to recreate the tweets but made them look like they came from fictitious journalists. He also simulated the way journalists cover multiple stories throughout the day for a realistic Twitter-following experience.

For a more ambitious project, creating a fully working social media site is possible with Ning, although it is not interactive. It allows the creator to add news stories, pictures, headlines, and to manipulate the number of likes and followers. Another site that allows for custom editing of web pages is CloneZone. No doubt there are others. These are free, but some others charge.

Another way to adapt real web pages for experiments is by using the "inspect element" tool in a web browser. Simply open up a web page and right click, then scroll down to the bottom of the box and select "Inspect Element." A source code pane will open up at the bottom. Click and drag to highlight the text you wish to change in the top pane, then right click and select "Inspect Element" again. The text will be highlighted in the bottom pane. Simply type over the old words and the new words will automatically appear on the website. Close the bottom pane by clicking the X on the right side, then take a screenshot and use this as a (noninteractive) web page in an experiment. You can use Command+Shift+4 on a Mac, then use the crosshair pointer to edit out the top and bottom of the browser. On a PC, use Alt+PrtScn or Snipping Tool. The changes are not permanent; the page returns to normal once you refresh it. There are tutorials online with more detail.

Find these tools at:

Ning: https://www.ning.com/

CloneZone: clonezone.link

Prank Me Not: www.prankmenot.com

Twister: http://www.classtools.net/twister/

*(Continued)*

(Continued)

Tweeterino: https://tweeterino.com/

Simitator: www.Simitator.com

At top is the original tweet from the New York Times. The text was used to create realistic tweets using fictitious journalists as stimuli for an experiment.

**From: Boulter, Trent. 2017. "Following the Familiar: Effect of Exposure and Gender on Credibility of Journalists on Twitter." (Dissertation, The University of Texas at Austin),https:// repositories.lib.utexas.edu/bitstream/handle/2152/62635/BOULTER-DISSERTATION-2017. pdf?sequence=1&isAllowed=y).**

## FIGURE 9.3 ● TWEETS CREATED FOR STUDY

**The New York Times** @nytimes · 12m

Sumner Redstone, 92, has resigned as chairman of CBS as questions swirl about his mental competence nyti.ms/1StNpTa

View summary

**Richard Smith**
@richard_smith

Follow

Sumner Redstone, 92, has resigned as chairman of CBS as questions swirl about his mental competence bit.ly/1StNpTa

Reply  1  Favorite  More

3 Feb 16 · 12 minutes ago

**Linda Miller**
@linda_miller

Follow

Sumner Redstone, 92, has resigned as chairman of CBS as questions swirl about his mental competence bit.ly/1StNpTa

Reply  1  Favorite  More

3 Feb 16 · 12 minutes ago

show *20/20*, and the MyBarackObama.com video.[26] Actual news photographs that have run in various magazines and newspapers can also be used as the stimuli that convey the treatment. In the educational study described earlier, a software company created the stimulus—the computer-assisted curriculum. Frequently, studies in education, social work, and other fields that test interventions or assess programs already or about to be put into practice in the field use preexisting stimuli.

# ADVICE ON CREATING STIMULI

## Keep It Real

When stimuli are fictitious, researchers should endeavor to make them as realistic as possible. One way to achieve this is to start with actual news articles, ads, posters, study guides, websites, or whatever, and then rewrite or edit them to reflect the manipulation. For example, in a study of how health stories were framed, the researchers used real stories and then rewrote them to replace all instances of one kind of frame with another that was being studied.[27] Researchers can also use actual stimuli, such as study guides, movies, or TV broadcasts, and edit in different wording or video to reflect the conditions of the study. Actual candidates' websites can be altered to remove party identification, change the issue positions, and replace names and photos with fictitious ones. (For an example of advertisements created this way, see figure 9.4.)

Here are some examples of advertisements used as stimuli in an experiment. The researchers collected actual advertisements in order to make the stimuli as realistic as possible and then altered them to meet the requirements of the treatment and control conditions.

Another way to achieve more realistic stimuli is to have professionals (or former professionals, often graduate students) write the press releases, create websites, alter study guides, etc. Researchers may think they can create a realistic-looking newspaper clip, for example, but the finished product will have the headlines centered and in all capital letters, which real newspapers tend not to do. There are a lot of subtle things that go into creating a professional-looking product that nonprofessionals are not always aware of. Two researchers acknowledge this in a study where they created news articles, writing, "We undertook considerable effort to adjust the news articles to the common lay-out and journalistic style of day-to-day Dutch news coverage."[28] On some subconscious level, subjects are likely to recognize an amateur effort and not respond in the

FIGURE 9.4 ● ADVERTISEMENTS

Source: Kim, Sunny Jung, and Jeffrey T. Hancock. 2016. "How Advertorials Deactivate Advertising Schema." *Communication Research*, 10.1177/0093650216644017.

same way as if they believed the stimuli were real. This does not always require a large outlay of funds, as often students with professional knowledge can be recruited to help with these tasks.

## Control as Much as Possible

Use the literature and common sense to recognize what needs to be controlled when creating stimuli. Fictitious events, people, and places are frequently used in experiments to avoid contamination by subjects' prior knowledge about real people, places, or events. Thus, in the voice pitch study,[29] the researchers used a fake organization and a fictitious health crisis. To prevent subjects from suspecting they were fake, they set the event in a different area of the country, reasoning that subjects might think it was real and they just had not heard about it because it was not in their geographic area. This represents a form of control known as **experimental control**, when the stimuli themselves are designed to be free of confounds. Another example of this is in a study of politicians in the news that was careful to select political issues that were not clearly linked to one particular party. Steering clear of issues that are favorites of either the Republicans or Democrats avoids having subjects rate the fictional candidate based on party rather than the thing being manipulated.[30] This is an experimental control because something in the stimulus is being controlled.

In other situations, using fictitious stimuli might compromise the findings. One group of researchers reasoned that might be the case in a study of what makes politicians newsworthy, and so used real members of the Dutch parliament.[31] To control for the subjects' previous knowledge about the real politicians, the study asked subjects how often they thought each parliamentarian succeeded in making it into the news and then used that as a covariate in the analysis, removing the effects of prior knowledge from the results. This is a form of control known as **statistical control**; when it is not possible or desirable to control something in the stimuli, researchers measure it and use it as a covariate in the statistical analysis. When there are things that cannot be controlled in a manipulation—how much people already know about something, for example—then it should be measured and controlled for statistically. Be sure to collect the information on this *before* giving subjects the treatment if there is any chance that they could have learned it from the manipulation. The variables used as covariates should all be something related to the outcome variable; if the dependent variable is assessment of credibility, and gender of the source is not related to credibility, then there is probably no need to measure and control for it. Gender and race are variables that are frequently thought to interact with manipulated variables and confound the results; however, this depends on what is being studied. Consult the literature.

In summary, there are two ways to control for confounds: with experimental control, which is in the manipulation or stimuli, and with statistical control, by measuring and including it in the analysis as a covariate. For example, if race is important in how a person rates the interaction between a police officer and citizen in a video, then having half of the officers in the video be White and half Black is an experimental control. If the race of the subject is important, then measuring and including the subjects' race in the analysis is a statistical control.[i] One should always prefer experimental controls to statistical controls if possible.

## Vary Only the Things Being Studied

Everything except the thing being manipulated should be kept the same in all the control and treatment versions. In a study of voice pitch,[32] that meant keeping the speed with which the statement was read and the emphasis on certain words, pauses, accent, pronunciation, and wording the same for all the different recordings. Another study used eight press releases that were all written to be the same length, had the same kind of a quote, and were all negatively framed.[33] This will often be described as something "being held constant"; for example, in the political study the negative framing was described this way: "We held

---

[i] I thank an anonymous reviewer for providing this clear and concise example.

the news value of conflict constant . . . with all MPs criticizing the government."[34] When things vary that are not meant to, the study is said to be confounded. This was explained in chapter 1 and can be as innocent as designing an advertisement in horizontal format for the treatment group and as a vertical for the control group, or putting one picture at the top for the treatment group and at the bottom for the control group. In these cases, there is no way to know if the horizontal or vertical format or picture placement is what actually caused any effects. It would be better to keep all ads horizontal and all pictures at the top.

Confounds can be created not just when designing stimuli but also when the experiment is conducted. For example, using two different researchers to run the study, or giving some subjects the treatment in the morning and others in the afternoon, also can be a form of confounding. Frequently, researchers are careful to hold constant the elements of the stimuli but forget about the procedural components. Any unavoidable differences can be compensated for by random assignment (see chapter 7)—for example, by randomly assigning the two researchers to run subjects in both treatment and control groups. But it is much better to avoid confounds entirely. Bausell recommends "a microscopic examination of every element in the study's design"[35] in order to uncover any possible differences, whether in the stimuli or the procedure. This involves scrutinizing every conceivable aspect of an experiment and possibly even performing a dry run or dress rehearsal, called a *pilot study*, which is a subject of chapter 11.

As with most everything else about experiments, common sense and the literature should be used as a guide in determining what is likely to be related to the outcome variable and thus should be controlled.

## MAXIMIZE COMPARISONS

When creating stimuli for experiments, it is important to make the manipulation or treatment strong enough to detect a true effect. This means maximizing the comparisons between the treatment and control groups, what Bausell calls looking for large objects rather than small ones.[36] This is so important, it has even been called the first rule of experimentation.[37] Weak manipulations are a common problem that can have important consequences.[38] For example, if a study is interested in determining the effects of a newspaper's reputation on readers' assessments of credibility, the researcher would be wise to use news organizations at opposite ends of the reputation spectrum, such as the *New York Times* and the *National Enquirer*. If no effects are found with this size of a chasm in reputation, then it is highly unlikely that more subtle differences will produce effects. However, if effects *are* found between the highest- and lowest-reputation newspapers, the researcher can then go on to explore differences among newspapers with less of a reputation gap. The studies of photographs' effects on moral judgment[39] used photographs that had won prestigious national awards, which have been shown to represent the highest level of the concept of novelty. If the study did not find effects with the strongest manipulation possible—the award-winning novel photographs—then it would be unlikely to find effects with lesser manipulations, such as photographs of the everyday variety. Award-winning photographs are not what people usually see in their daily newspapers. Because effects were found with the award-winning photographs, it would be logical to then go on to test photographs that are more commonly used in local daily newspapers, eventually testing the least novel type of photograph, such as head shots.

Stanley Milgram employed this approach in his studies of obedience to authority.[40] In the first study, he had the experimenter in the white lab coat that was ordering subjects to continue giving shocks stand in the same room, right next to the subjects. When he found effects at this close proximity, he began moving the experimenter farther and farther away from the subjects. Eventually, the experimenter was out of the room entirely. As the authority figure got farther away from the subject, obedience declined and the subjects refused to administer shock treatments.[41]

Making the manipulation that the treatment and control groups receive as different as possible is important for increasing the likelihood that an experiment will find a positive result, should one actually exist.[42] For example, if the study calls for manipulating the framing in a story, then make half or more of the story contain the frame being studied. This is much more than a real story would contain, but if no effects are found when so much of the story is framed a certain way, it is unlikely there would be effects when even less of the story is framed that way. Many researchers underestimate the strength of a manipulation needed to produce results,[43] so something that seems like overkill may in fact not even register with subjects.

## Employ Message Variance

Up to this point, this chapter has mainly been concerned with how to create variance in the stimuli based on the treatment or manipulation—that is, the levels of the independent variables of theoretical interest to the study. That is referred to as **treatment variance**.[44] But there is also another kind of variance that needs to be considered when creating stimuli—that is, message variance. **Message variance** refers to the number of messages or stimuli used to represent each treatment level.[45] For example, in studies of how the race of people affects attitudes and judgments, photographs are often used as the stimuli to manipulate the levels of the independent variable race. Rather than using one photograph of a Black person and one photograph of a White person, using three photographs of people of each race is a better strategy. This results in a

**multiple-message design** because it used more than one "message"—in this case a photograph—per treatment level. If only one photograph is used to represent each race, it would be a **single-message design**. When there is more than one message or stimulus to represent each level of a treatment or factor, it may also be referred to as a **repetition factor.**[46] It is important to use more than one stimulus to represent a factor, because rarely are researchers interested in a specific stimulus or message, such as one particular person, TV show, or commercial, but they are actually interested in the category, or level of the factor, that person, show, or commercial represents. For example, in the reality TV study,[47] the researchers were interested in two kinds of shows—game-style and inspiring shows. They used two shows at each level in a multiple-message design: two episodes of *Survivor* and *Amazing Race* to represent game-style, and two episodes of *Supernanny* and *Undercover Boss* to represent inspiring shows. This is important because stimuli or messages will vary in their effects, no matter how carefully researchers attempt to make them similar.[48] Multiple versions of the stimuli help ensure that effects are not due to the individual attributes of a single stimulus.

Single-message designs also are much weaker in allowing researchers to generalize beyond one specific message or stimulus—in this example, one TV show.[49] Dependable generalization requires multiple stimuli.[50] Had the reality TV researchers only used one show to represent each factor level, they only would have been able to say any effects were due to a specific episode of *Survivor* or *Undercover Boss,* not the more general categories these two shows represented. That is, they would not be able to say that a certain type of show caused effects, only that exactly the one show used had an effect. It is rarely useful to know that one particular episode of *Survivor* caused some outcome, and in any event, there may well be unknown features of that one episode that could have caused the outcome, thus confounding the results. For example, one episode may have angered or offended subjects, had a smoother transition to the commercial, or been more compatible in tone with the commercial.[51]

It is never possible to account for all confounds with a single stimulus. By using multiple stimuli to represent each level of a factor, the chances of anything other than the independent variable of interest being responsible for the outcome are reduced. As an illustration of why it is important to use more than one stimulus or message, a study of how health stories were framed used messages representing four different health issues and obtained similar effects for three of the four.[52] However, one issue—smoking—did not produce the same results. There was something about the idiosyncrasies of that particular issue or story that made people react differently to it than the others. Had the study used only this one story, it would never have been known that the frames actually worked in other contexts.

## How Many Stimuli to Create?

Obviously, creating multiple stimuli is more work for the researcher. But exactly how many messages or stimuli does an experiment need? The answer is "it depends." Some studies, such as those employing latency responses where the measure is how long a subject takes to react, are unreliable unless a large number of different stimuli are used.[53] Thorson and colleagues recommend using as many as you can "reasonably expect a participant to attend to without fatigue or boredom setting in."[54] In a study of TV public service announcements (PSAs), the researchers used six stimuli for each factor level.[55] A good idea is to start with four or more stimuli if they do not take subjects long to process, such as a short story or photograph. For stimuli that take longer to process, start with three. The advice to "start with" a certain number is because sometimes the different stimuli do not always adequately represent the concept or level of the independent variable one is attempting to create. That is the subject of the next section of this chapter. Of course, it is never possible to make multiple stimuli exactly the same on every possible category, so message variance is treated as random error when testing the differences between levels of treatments.[56]

Even though creating more stimuli is more work, it pays off in the long run, as experiments that use single-message designs will eventually need to be conducted again and again with different stimuli and then meta-analyzed in order to be generalized.[57]

## Fixed vs. Random Factors

When multiple stimuli are used to represent a single level of a factor, the standard way to treat the various responses is by averaging each individual subject's responses into all the stimuli that represent each level.[58] So, for example, if a subject sees three photographs of Black people and three photographs of White people and is asked to make an ethical decision, then the subjects' ethics scores on three Black photographs are averaged, resulting in one score for that level of the race factor, and the same done for the three White photographs. These are then analyzed with traditional statistical techniques such as analysis of variance (ANOVA).[59] This is appropriate when the levels of the factors are considered **fixed factors** rather than **random factors**. Fixed factors are those whose levels are limited,[60] or researchers choose the levels,[61] whereas random factors are those that represent a sample of a larger population rather than every conceivable level within that population.[62] The most common use of a random factor is with subjects of an experiment who are samples from a larger population and do not exhaust the universe of potential subjects.[63]

Sometimes, the stimuli also should be treated as random factors. Using the example of a study whose stimuli are photographs of Black people and White people, the individuals in the photographs are obviously not the only Black and White people in the world but are sampled from a larger universe. If researchers have sampled these particular photographs and use them to generalize to a larger population of all people of those two races, those photographs would be considered random factors. In such a study, both the subjects who participate in the study and the stimulus photographs are random factors, and special statistical techniques for mixed-effects models should be used.[64] This allows for generalizing to the population of stimuli as well as to the population of subjects.[65]

Using random effects models also helps avoid making a Type 1 error, which was described in chapter 8 as a "false positive," or when one finds an effect that is not really real.[66] These special statistical techniques are not commonly used in some social science fields, or even in clinical and social psychology.[67] Random effects models are recommended when there is an infinite number of levels or many more than are being tested and the levels of the factor are sampled. This allows for generalizing beyond the particular levels in the experiment.[68]

In contrast, a fixed factor has a limited number of levels—a drug that exists only in certain dosages, such as 10 mg, 20 mg, and 40 mg, for instance. A drug with an infinite number of levels would be a random factor. If only two interventions exist—for example, there are only two training programs for social workers dealing with violence-prone clients—that is a fixed factor. An education study comparing three different tests when no other tests exist is another example of a fixed factor. Another common use of fixed factors is with panel data that compare the same people, companies, states, schools, or other entities **longitudinally**, or across some longer period of time. A fixed factor also can be the levels of a factor that are chosen by the researcher. For example, it is common to treat stimuli such as the photographs of Black and White people as fixed factors when the researcher is only interested in generalizing to the specific stimuli used in the experiment, not beyond. This can lead to the necessity to replicate findings with different stimuli so as to aid generalizability.

The discussion surrounding the appropriate use of fixed vs. random effects models is complicated and beyond the scope of this book. Interested readers will find several articles for further information in the "Suggested Readings" section.

## MANIPULATION CHECKS

Once the stimuli are created, it is often advisable to conduct a manipulation check to determine if subjects perceive the stimuli the way researchers intend.[69] Failure to ensure that a stimulus is what is intended in concrete terms can doom an experiment to failure, specifically of the Type 2 variety, which is not supporting a hypothesis when it should. Scientific knowledge is not advanced and doubt may be cast upon theories that are actually correct when this happens. In addition, researchers are less likely to publish studies that result in null findings.[70] It has been suggested that manipulation checks be added to the checklist of requirements for experiments in numerous social sciences,[71] with some such as social psychology requiring them before a paper is accepted for publication.[72] However, this is a contested point, with some saying that manipulation checks are rarely, if ever, necessary.[73]

## Manipulation Check, Pretest, or Pilot Study?

A manipulation check is a way of determining that the stimuli have actually manipulated the independent variable the way the researcher intends.[74] The terms *pilot study* and *pretest* are frequently used interchangeably with *manipulation check*. Often when researchers conduct the manipulation before the actual study, they will refer to it as a pretest. This book delineates the three as distinct procedures. In this text, a pretest, as in "pretest–posttest design," is part of the actual study, given before the treatment or manipulation, and is either equivalent to or the same as the posttest so before-and-after comparisons can be made. A pretest is different from a manipulation check because their purposes are different, with a manipulation check designed to determine if the researcher's manipulation of latent constructs have been done effectively, no matter when it is carried out. Chapter 11 discusses pilot studies in detail, but briefly, a pilot study is a larger undertaking than a manipulation check, intended to be a "test run" of the entire experiment.

Manipulation checks are conducted to help ensure that stimuli are what the researcher intends them to be so as to aid the best possible chance of having an effect on the theoretically relevant outcome variables.[75] For example, in a study to determine if vivid writing had an effect on moral judgment,[76] the manipulation check was designed to see if the three stories the researchers had written were "vivid," which was defined theoretically as concrete, descriptive writing that helped people paint a mental picture. The manipulation check determined if ordinary people found the vivid stories to be more concrete, descriptive, and mental-picture-painting than the control stories written in traditional news style. This was achieved by asking subjects who were not involved in the actual experiment to answer questions specifically about the vividness of the stories rather than to take the entire study. Some of the questions to that effect were: "This story was very descriptive," "This story was very colorful," "This story was very vivid," "This story had a lot of details," and others designed to measure the features that the literature said defined the theoretical construct of vividness. In this manipulation check, one of the four stories was not significantly different from the nonvivid stories, so it was rewritten and checked again before being used with subjects for the actual experiment. In this case, the manipulation check uncovered a problem so that the researchers could fix it before it was too late. A manipulation check is not a measure of what the stimulus does in terms of effects on the dependent variable; rather, it is a measure of what the stimulus is.[ii]

## Direct vs. Indirect Manipulations

In the study on vivid writing, the construct of vividness could only be manipulated indirectly—for example, with descriptions of people and scenes. A manipulation check is needed for this kind of latent independent variable in order to know if the researchers have successfully created vivid stories.[77] This is not the case for all manipulated variables; for example, in a study where the manipulation is the number of sources in a story, a manipulation check is not necessary if one group of stories contains five sources and the other contains one source. In this case, the operationalization is the same as the construct—there is no need to conduct a manipulation check to see if some stories have five sources and some have one; it is indisputable that they do. "So long as the operationalization of the treatment and the independent variable are one and the same, there was no need for a manipulation check."[78] Similarly, gender may not need to be subjected to a manipulation check if names and physical features are not ambiguous. For example, in one study, researchers used the names "John" and "Sarah" in short profiles of hypothetical political candidates.[79] Nor would political party affiliation need a manipulation check as long as it was clearly labeled. Concrete attributes of the stimuli or intrinsic structural properties do not always need a manipulation check. For example, it is not necessary to ask subjects how long two stories are if one is 500 words and one is 100 words. No matter what subjects say, they clearly are different lengths.[80]

## Mediators and Psychological States

Manipulation checks should be conducted not on the indisputable structural features of the stimuli but on the psychological states that these features arouse. For example, in the vividness study, in addition to ensuring that the stories were colorful, descriptive, and contained details—all content features—the manipulation check also ensured that the stories were constructed to have the desired psychological effect on subjects—that is, that they helped them paint a mental picture, a theoretical construct called "imaging."[81] The manipulation check also included questions about this, including, "I formed a mental image from this story," "It was easy to imagine what this scene looked like," and "I could easily visualize this."

---

[ii]There is some dispute over what researchers call manipulation checks actually being measures of mediating psychological states. Manipulation checks measure structural or content attributes of the stimuli rather than attitudes or perceptions that subjects have of the content; these are attributes of the participant rather than attributes of the stimulus. A detailed discussion of this is beyond the scope of this book, but interested readers can learn more in O'Keefe, "Message Properties, Mediating States, and Manipulation Checks."

These represent the subjects' perception of the stories as vivid or not, which is theorized to induce the psychological state of imaging, or painting a mental picture. The psychological state represents the causal explanation referred to in chapter 1. In many cases, researchers use psychological states in manipulation checks but then fail to analyze them in the actual study as potential mediators of the dependent variable.[82] When this is the case, researchers miss an opportunity to provide an explanation for an effect. Including potential mediators in studies enables researchers to explain why a certain effect occurred (see More About box 9.3, Mediators and Moderators). For example, in one study, researchers examined the effect of the number of terms or phrases used in a web search on users' perceptions of control or mastery, a concept called *dominance*.[83] Dominance was the dependent variable (DV) and Search Term was the independent variable (IV) represented by two levels, high and low, operationalized by three, and one search term or phrase. The search terms or phrases are physical attributes of the stimuli. The psychological state, or mediator, that the number of search terms were expected to activate in subjects was perceived relevance; three search terms were intended to be perceived by subjects as resulting in highly relevant results, and one search term was expected to return a search result that subjects perceived as low in relevance. The researchers conducted a manipulation check to ensure that three search terms led to subjects' perceiving results to be highly relevant and one search term leading to results perceived to be of low relevance. This study also took the additional step of measuring perceived relevance in the actual study so that it could be analyzed as a mediator; that is, it was hypothesized that perceived relevance was the causal mechanism that would mediate the relationship between the number of search terms and dominance.[iii] In this case, three hypotheses are proposed: one proposing the direct effect of the IV (number of search terms) on the DV; one proposing the direct effect of the mediator (perceived relevance) on the DV; and one proposing the effect of the IV, indirectly through the mediator, on the DV.

One argument for conducting a manipulation check is that without it, the scientific community loses valuable information. When no manipulation check is done in a study that fails to support a hypothesis, researchers cannot know if the theory needs revision or if it was the treatment that was unsuccessful. The hypothesis may even be abandoned.[93] As Mutz and Pemantle say, "Ignoring manipulation checks thus impedes the growth of scientific knowledge."[94]

---

[iii]It is beyond the scope of this book to discuss the analysis of mediators beyond saying they can be tested using regression as described by Baron and Kenny (1986), or with bootstrap distribution tests as described by Efron and Tibshirani (1993) via a free macro for certain statistical software called PROCESS (Hayes, 2013). It is available at http://www.processmacro.org/index.html. R. M. Baron and D. A. Kenny, "The Moderator-Mediator Variable Distinction in Social Psychological Research: Conceptual, Strategic, and Statistical Considerations," *Journal of Personality and Social Psychology* 51, no. 6 (December 1986): 1173–1182; Andrew F. Hayes, *Introduction to Mediation, Moderation, and Conditional Process Analysis, Second Edition: A Regression-Based Approach* (New York: Guilford Press, 2013).

# MORE ABOUT ... BOX 9.3
## Mediators and Moderators

Chapter 1 discussed the importance of including a causal mechanism in an experiment, which is something to explain *why* the effect an experiment found actually occurred. The example given there was of an experiment to determine if photographs improved moral judgment. In that study, photographs did improve moral judgment, and that was the effect. The causal mechanisms examined were involvement and elaboration, or being absorbed or interested in the stories and thinking deeply about the people in them. These causal mechanisms were found to be mediators—that is, they were the psychological states that served as the pathways by which the independent variable influenced the dependent variable.[84] There is often confusion about when something is a mediator and when it is a moderator. This supplement is designed to help sort that out.

## Mediators

Mediators are psychological states or conditions that explain how and why the observed effect happened.[85] They represent the mechanisms by which some effect occurs.[86] In James Lind's experiment on scurvy described in chapter 2, he found that citrus like limes and lemons cured scurvy. He did not study the mediators or mechanisms in that study, but later it was found that vitamin C was the mediating variable between limes and scurvy. In the earlier example, central route processing or thinking deeply about the photographs was the cognitive process or psychological condition that led to better moral judgment. Fear could be the psychological state that leads to intentions to quit smoking after seeing PSAs. In addition to representing psychological states, mediators come after the treatment or manipulation is given. Continuing the previous examples, fear came after watching the PSA, while elaboration was induced by seeing the photograph. Finally, the mediator must be correlated with the independent variable. Thus, the PSAs themselves had scary messages, which correlate with subjects' feelings of fear, and the photographs had elements of novelty and unusualness, which has been correlated with greater cognitive elaboration. Treatments probably have many mediators or causal mechanisms, but the only ones that researchers can know about are the ones they test.

## Moderators

Unlike mediators, moderators explain when and under what conditions effects might be larger or smaller, or when and for whom certain effects will be found.[87] A moderator is a third variable that, when combined with the independent variable, has an effect on the strength of the relationship to the dependent variable. Examples of moderators include older age decreasing the likelihood of finding a job; attending a preschool moderating the effect of a mother's age on a child's cognitive development;[88] and personality traits such as hypermasculinity increasing aggression after viewing violent

TV shows.[89] In all of these examples, the moderators are observable traits that are preexisting, or come before the treatment, rather than being induced by the treatment. For example, age and a hyper-masculine personality are traits or characteristics of the job applicant and TV viewer, not something induced by a treatment such as a job training program or watching violent TV. Also, moderators are uncorrelated with the independent variable or manipulation. For example, whether a child attends preschool is not correlated with the mother's age.

The following chart summarizes the differences between mediators and moderators.

| Mediator | Moderator |
| --- | --- |
| Explains why and how an effect occurred; the causal mechanism | Answers for whom and when the effect occurs; affects the strength of the relationship between the IV and DV |
| Is a psychological state | Is an observable trait |
| Comes after the IV | Comes before the IV |
| Is correlated with the IV | Is uncorrelated with the IV |

In addition, there is a graphic display that helps visualize the relationship between mediators and moderators in an experiment. This graphic is frequently found in journal articles to represent the processes of an experiment. Mediation is identified with the abbreviation Me, moderation with the abbreviation Mo. The following example uses photographs as the IV and moral judgment as the DV. In the mediator graphic, elaboration, or thinking deeply, is the mediator, while education level is the moderator. The arrows represent the process and also the different hypotheses, printed underneath.

## Mediation graphic

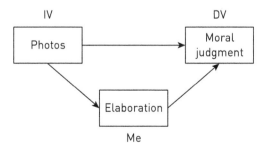

(Continued)

(Continued)

H1: Seeing photographs will significantly increase the level of moral judgment compared to not seeing photographs.

H2: Seeing photographs will lead to greater elaboration.

H3: Elaboration will lead to significantly higher levels of moral judgment.

H4: Seeing photographs will lead to higher levels of moral judgment, mediated by elaboration.

## Moderation graphic

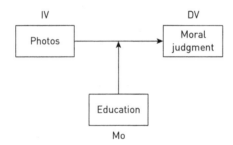

H1: Photographs will significantly increase levels of moral judgment.

H2: Education moderates the effect of photographs on moral judgment, with higher education leading to higher levels of moral judgment.

Here is an example from a published study of the graphic display for a mediator and the hypotheses.[90] This experiment tested the effect of interactive features of a website on subjects' assessments of the credibility of the news on the website. The IV was interactivity, with the treatment group instructed to use the interactive features, operationalized as voting in an online poll, e-mailing the news organization, and viewing a slide show. The noninteractive group subjects were asked to read three articles. The mediator was the psychological state of perceived interactivity— that is, the causal mechanism was how interactive subjects perceived the website to be. You can see the elements that define a mediator here: Perceived interactivity comes after the treatment is given; that is, being presented with online polls, e-mail, and a slide show should lead subjects to perceive the website as interactive. It is correlated with the IV, in that interactive features are related to perceptions of interactivity. Perceived interactivity is also a psychological state—that is, it is a perception. And it explains why the IV has an effect on the DV; giving people websites with polls, e-mail, and slide shows leads them to perceive it as interactive, which increases their assessment of the site as credible.

From: Tao, C., and E. P. Bucy. 2007. "Conceptualizing Media Stimuli in Experimental Research: Psychological Versus Attributed-Based Definitions." *Human Communication Research* 33: 397–426.

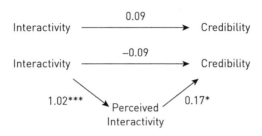

H1: Credibility ratings of online news sites will be higher for interactive conditions than noninteractive conditions.

H2: Perceived interactivity will be positively associated with assessments of media credibility.

H3: Perceived interactivity will mediate the relationship between interactive tasks and evaluations of media credibility.[91]

It is beyond the scope of this textbook to explain how to analyze mediators and moderators. The classic way uses a series of regressions as explained in step-by-step detail by Baron and Kenny, and the Sobel Test; newer procedures use bootstrapping and can be accomplished using a free macro called PROCESS.[92] It is available at http://www.processmacro.org/index.html.

## Manipulation Checks in Survey Experiments

The trend of using survey experiments also argues for the need for manipulation checks.[95] With a survey experiment where subjects are taking the experiment at remote locations where the researcher cannot observe, it is impossible to know if subjects were actually exposed to the stimuli. Embedding a manipulation check into the actual experiment can help researchers identify subjects who paid attention to the stimuli versus those who randomly checked off answers.[96] Screener questions are not a substitute for manipulation checks in survey experiments because screeners are designed to test if subjects were merely exposed to the manipulation, not whether it was effective.[97]

One last reason to conduct a manipulation check is to determine if the stimuli are similar on things that are not intended to vary and could confound the results. For example, in designing multiple advertisements, experiments might use different models who should be similar in appearance and attractiveness; stories should be similarly interesting or likeable; political ads should be similarly toned, whether negative or positive. Manipulation checks can confirm these similarities so that confounds are not the cause of results.

Many experiments do not report manipulation checks,[98] leading readers to believe that none were conducted. Some articles say that a manipulation check was conducted and that it worked but provide no supporting evidence. It is becoming more common to see details about manipulation checks provided in appendices or in online supplements. Manipulation checks may not need to be conducted when the manipulations or stimuli have been used previously, in which case that is mentioned.

## Practical Issues

Three practical concerns about manipulation checks are when to conduct them, how many subjects to use, and how to measure things.

There are two options for when to conduct a manipulation check: before the actual study and separate from it, or embedded within the actual study with its assessment placed at the end. Actually, there are three options, as manipulation checks can be done both ahead of the study and also within it. This can be the preferred option, which will be explained next.

Conducting a manipulation check before running the actual study is a helpful way to design successful stimuli. It allows researchers to spot problems and tweak the stimuli before testing it on actual subjects. Two researchers did this in their political study, using students for the manipulation check to validate the stimuli but not administering it to the real politicians in the actual study so as not to make it too lengthy.[99] For this type of a manipulation check during stimulus development, fewer subjects are needed than for the actual study, but still enough to find significant differences between the treatment and control group stimuli. The study on vivid writing used twenty-six subjects for the manipulation check conducted prior to the actual study, for example.[100] But this is probably the least that should be used, as fewer than twenty subjects can make it hard to conduct significance tests.

Another common way that social science researchers report manipulation checks is embedded within the study itself. The advantage of this is that they are assured the actual subjects of the experiment perceived the stimuli manipulations as they were intended. This should be done with the manipulation check assessment asked at the end of the study, after the dependent variable measures are given, so as not to alert subjects to the manipulations or purpose of the study.[101] This also has the benefit of measuring the psychological state expected to cause the outcome in the actual study, affording researchers the ability to test mediators.

The third way to conduct manipulation checks combines the two approaches: a separate group of subjects who are not involved in the study and then another manipulation check within the study itself so that actual experimental subjects also receive it. The benefits to this are threefold: this allows researchers time to revise the stimuli if necessary, ensures that actual experimental subjects perceive the stimuli as intended, and incorporates a mediator into the study. The only cost to doing this is that it lengthens the study by the amount of time subjects spend on the manipulation check questions.[102] One way around this is to reduce the number of manipulation check questions for the actual study based on an internal consistency analysis such as Cronbach's alpha or factor analysis, and then eliminate the weaker items from the actual study. The vivid writing study described earlier used nine items assessing vividness in the first manipulation check and reduced the number of questions to the three most predictive items for the actual study. Many researchers' experiences with stimuli that fail manipulation checks and need to be revised, and even prestudy manipulation checks, go on behind the scenes and do not get reported in journal articles because of word-length limits. Readers should not despair; research can be messy, and what appears in print is not necessarily the whole story.

When measuring for a manipulation check, one does not ask all the same questions as in the study itself; the goal of the manipulation check is to determine if the operationalization reflects theoretical constructs, so assessments should focus on that, not on measuring outcome DVs. As always, common sense and the literature should guide the writing of manipulation check questions. If other researchers have already conducted manipulation checks on the construct in a study, that is a natural place to begin before attempting to create one's own assessment. But when none can be found, it is perfectly acceptable to create one using the literature as a basis.

If a manipulation check embedded within the actual study fails—that is, if subjects do not perceive it the way it was intended—that stimulus should be dropped from the analysis if it cannot be revised and rerun.

# REPORTING THE STIMULI
# AND MANIPULATION CHECKS

## Stimuli Write-Up

When writing the paper for an experiment, a portion of the methods section, usually labeled *stimuli*, *stimulus materials*, or *procedures*, is where information about the stimuli and any issues associated with them are presented. This should appear early in the methods section and describe the stimuli in enough detail for readers to visualize them. It also addresses any issues that might be of concern, such as the fictitious nature of people, organizations, etc.

For experiments where the details of the stimuli are not too extensive, they should be reported in the body of the paper, including the exact wording of all the messages and description of any visual images. In the marketing experiment on cookstoves, the posters' wording was short, so it was all contained in the text, one of which is reproduced here:

> Smoke from the cook fire is poison. It makes you feel light-headed or dizzy, makes you cough, and can cause sore eyes or a sore throat from the smoke. Smoke from cook-stoves causes serious diseases, including pneumonia and bronchitis. These diseases from cook-stove smoke caused as many child deaths in Uganda as malaria.[103]

The text also describes the picture on the poster as a baby smoking a cigarette.

For studies with many stimuli or stimuli that are more complicated to describe, it is appropriate to give the full description of one stimulus as an example and refer readers to an appendix or a website for the others.[104] It is also a good idea to make it easy for readers to see what the manipulations were by highlighting or italicizing the items that vary while using regular type for the parts that are constant. For example, in the study of parliamentarians who made it into the news, one of the twenty-four press releases was described this way:

> "The B61-nuclear bombs do not need to be modernized, but rather destroyed," *responds Green Member* of Parliament *Wouter Devriendt* to the recent news about *the modernization of the nuclear weapons stored in Kleine Brogel*. "Nuclear weapons are dangerous and useless. Moreover, the modernization, the storage, the maintenance and the surveillance of the nuclear bombs are extremely expensive. The government needs to undertake action to commence and finish a complete nuclear disarmament." Devriendt wants to gain clarity about the measures concerning nuclear weapons in Belgium *by asking a written question* to the authorized cabinet member.[105]

Finally, for very complex stimuli and when there are many of them, the text should describe the stimuli briefly and then refer readers to an appendix or supplemental website where they can read and view the entire body of stimuli. In the study of corporate social responsibility (CSR), for example, the stimuli section gave only a general description of the scenarios and the dimensions that they represented, such as whether the corporation was harmful to the environment or not, a good business partner, and how it treated employees.[106] Because there were six lengthy text scenarios, presenting it in the appendix was more efficient than in the text. The description in the body of the paper was detailed enough that most readers were not left with many questions. Here is the text:

> For this task, six different scenarios were created and distributed to the participants. In each scenario, the participants were provided with information on a fictive organization operating university canteens. In accordance with Bardsley (2000), the participants were not informed that the survey subject was fictional as this does not constitute a deception of participants, and the scenarios could potentially be true. In scenarios 1, 3, and 5, the organization was described as a "for-profit organization" and in scenarios 2, 4, and 6 as a "nonprofit organization." The scenarios also differed in terms of the organization's CSR performance. In the first two scenarios, no information was given about CSR performance. Scenarios 3 and 4 contained information about the organization's positive CSR performance and scenarios 5 and 6 provided information about negative CSR performance. The CSR performance was manipulated by providing information on organizational behavior along three fundamental dimensions of CSR: The environment (environmentally friendly vs. environmentally harmful waste disposal), society (respectful vs. disrespectful treatment of employees), and economy (pleasant vs. unpleasant business partner). . . . The original texts describing each scenario can be found in the Appendix.[107]

Elements to be included in the written description of the stimuli include, in no particular order,

- the number of stimuli created and the number in each condition;
- if the stimuli were real or fictitious:
  - if fictitious, describe how subjects were persuaded they were real, and
  - if real, describe how subjects' prior knowledge was not a confounding factor;
- if deception was involved, how subjects were debriefed;
- how the concepts of theoretical interest were operationalized;

- the physical attributes of the stimuli that are posited to cause the changes in the dependent variable (i.e., pictures, format, length, word count, etc.);

- discussion of any potential confounds, whether of the stimuli or procedure, linked to the independent variables and how they were controlled (e.g., statistically or in the manipulation);

- how differences were maximized; and

- explanation of all decisions in theoretical terms—for example, if gender has been found to be related to a particular outcome or not, and how the operationalization reflects theoretical constructs.

For more examples of writing the stimuli portion of the methods section, see How To Do It box 9.4.

One piece of advice for writing up the stimuli section is to do it immediately after creating the stimuli. It may be hard to remember everything that was done or the reasoning behind the decisions that were made after the study is completed. The same advice goes for writing up the manipulation check results; rerunning manipulation check data because the original output could not be found is unnecessarily time consuming. Develop a habit of writing each portion of the methods as soon as it is finished, even if it is just in note format.

## Manipulation Check Write-Up

Some journals put the manipulation check in the methods section, immediately after the stimuli are described, while others save it for the results section, especially if the manipulation check was conducted on the subjects of the actual study. Some studies do a combination of both, reporting the measures used in the manipulation check in the methods section and then the test of those measures reported in the results section[108] (see How To Do It box 9.5, Writing Up Manipulation Check Results). If the journal has no preference, then it should be included where it makes the most logical sense and will not leave readers with lingering questions. Another option for very long manipulation checks, or when checks were done before and during the actual experiment, is to include the results in an appendix or refer readers to a supplemental website.

Here are some examples of how researchers have described their stimuli. The description should be detailed enough for readers to visualize what the stimuli looked like and to be able to recreate them for their own study.

## Example 1

*In this study, the description of the stimuli is combined with the details of the study design, covered in chapter 6. Notice also how this addresses the use of fictitious stimuli and debriefing of subjects regarding deception, and also how it discusses confounds and how they were addressed:*

## "Methodology

## Design and stimuli

Study 1 used a single-factor design in order to examine the impact of lowered and raised voice pitch on the perceptions of an organizational spokesperson. Each participant first received a small text online informing them of the crisis events that were taking place in a fictitious company, followed by the voice recording of an organizational spokesperson. The use of a fictitious organization allows us to avoid potential confounding effects of pre-existing knowledge and prior reputation (Laufer & Jung, 2010). However, to avoid suspicion among participants due to the fact that they had not heard of the organization or the events, the crisis was situated in a different region of the country. At the end of the experiment, the respondents were notified that the crisis was fictitious.

The introductory text explained that a company, which cultivates salad, was at that moment confronted with a food contamination crisis. Consumers who had eaten the salad were reporting to hospitals with stomach problems. In addition, it appeared that the salad got contaminated because the company had used a pesticide which was forbidden by the local government. The crisis thus posed a threat to the public, which increased the demand for an adequate organizational response.

Voice pitch was manipulated by means of a brief sound fragment from a fictitious press conference given by the organization in crisis. An organizational spokesperson confirmed the information that had been offered in the introductory text, informed potential victims, elaborated briefly on the corrective action that was taken, and took responsibility and apologized for the crisis. We audio-recorded a male student in radio journalism while reading this statement about the crisis events. Prior research found no impact of gender on the relation between voice pitch and attributions of competence and dominance (DeGroot & Motowidlo, 1999; Jones, Feinberg, DeBruine, Little, & Vukovic, 2010; McHenry et al., 2012). Similar to previous studies, we manipulated the voice pitch in the recordings by means of computer software (i.e., Audacity) (Imhof, 2010; Jones et al., 2010; O'Connor et al.,

*(Continued)*

(Continued)

2011; Puts et al., 2006, 2007). The software allowed us to manipulate one specific aspect of the voice, namely pitch, while keeping all others (e.g., speed, emphasis, pausing, accent, and pronunciation) constant. This method also allowed us to control for content (Imhof, 2010).

Two versions of the original voice recordings were made, one with raised voice pitch and one with lowered voice pitch (cf. Jones et al., 2010; Puts et al., 2006; Tigue et al., 2012). The baseline level was raised and lowered by one-and-a-half semitone (cf. Puts et al., 2006, 2007)."

**From: Claeys, An-Sofie, and Verolien Cauberghe. 2014. "Keeping Control: The Importance of Nonverbal Expressions of Power by Organizational Spokespersons in Time of Crisis."** Journal of Communication **64: 1162–1163.**

## Example 2

*The next two examples are particularly concerned with making the stimuli as realistic as possible. In the first write-up of stimuli, notice how the researchers report adapting actual messages for the study:*

## "Stimulus materials

An array of advertorials and advertisements were collected from media sources to generate the stimulus materials for Study 2. Each advertorial contained both a text-based information section focusing on healthy eating or sleeping and an advertising section presenting visuals with advertising captions. The delivered information on healthy eating and sleeping was similar to the information used in Study 1. Using visual editing programs, we separated and placed informational content before advertising content for info-first advertorial stimuli, and placed advertising sections ahead of informational sections for ad-first advertorial stimuli. Except for this experimental manipulation in structure, the messages and conveyed information were identical. Advertising-only sections were used as regular advertisements (see Appendix A for sample stimulus materials)."

**From: Kim, Sunny Jung, and Jeffrey T. Hancock. 2016. "How Advertorials Deactivate Advertising Schema: MTurk-Based Experiments to Examine Persuasion Tactics and Outcomes in Health Advertisements."** Communication Research **44 (7): 1019–1045. 10.1177/0093650216644017.**

## Example 3

*In this example, the researchers used an expert to help them create realistic stimuli. Notice also the informal "manipulation check" in this study from 2003; today, "squaring nicely" is unlikely to pass the test for adequate reporting of manipulation check results:*

"First, we ran copies of our ads by a local political consultant to see if they were realistic. He indicated that the spots were plausible representations of the kind of ads one might hear run during an election, which gives us greater confidence in the generalizability of our results. Second, we asked students from one of the author's university to rate how negative and how positive were each of the simulated ads. We wanted to make sure that our ads captured accurately the variables of interest. The undergraduates' ratings of the ads squared nicely with our judgments of them. In other words, students viewed our 'attack' ads as attacks and viewed our 'positive' ads as positive. This verification increased our confidence in the manipulation."

**From: Geer, John G., and James H. Geer. 2003. "Remembering Attack Ads: An Experimental Investigation of Radio."** Political Behavior **25 (1): 69–95.**

## HOW TO DO IT 9.5

## Writing Up Manipulation Check Results

Manipulation checks are reported in different sections of a study, depending on the journal's preference and where it makes the most sense. Here are some examples.

## Example 1

*In this study, the manipulation check results were reported in the methods section after the stimulus material, and said:*

"On a seven-point scale (1 = strongly disagree to 7 = strongly agree), participants were asked to what extent the article dealt with the (1) positive or the (2) negative consequences of the issue. The manipulation check showed successful manipulation with slightly elevated standard deviations. When asked for positive consequences, participants in the opportunity condition ($M = 5.94$, $SD = 1.63$) perceived their article to be more positive than participants in the risk condition ($M = 2.35$, $SD = 1.93$; $t(612) = 2.75$, $p < .001$). When asked for negative consequences, participants in the risk condition ($M = 5.87$, $SD = 0.146$) perceived the article to be more negative than participants in the opportunity condition ($M = 3.24$, $SD = 2.09$; $t(611) = 4.53$, $p < .001$)."

**From: Lecheler, Sophie, and Claes H. de Vreese. 2013. "What a Difference a Day Makes? The Effects of Repetitive and Competitive News Framing Over Time."** *Communication Research* **40 (2): 157.**

## Example 2

*In this study, the manipulation check was reported in the results section:*

"Using condition (action exemplar, inaction exemplar, and control) as the independent variable and negative affect as dependent variable, a one-way analysis of variance (ANOVA) reported a significant effect, $F(2, 192) = 9.24$, $p < .001$, $\eta2 = .09$. A Bonferroni post hoc test reported that those in the action exemplar condition, $M = 3.56$, $SD = 1.2$, reported higher negative affect scores than those in the control condition, $M = 2.85$, $SD = 1.33$, $p < .01$, and inaction exemplar condition, $M = 2.62$, $SD = 1.2$, $p < .001$. Therefore, the manipulation for the action risk exemplar worked.

However, those in the inaction exemplar condition produced negative affect scores no different than the control condition, $p = .95$, indicating that the manipulation for the inaction exemplar condition did not achieve the desired result."

**From: Dixon, Graham N. 2015. "Negative Affect as a Mechanism of Exemplification Effects."** *Communication Research* **43 (6): 768**

## Example 3

*In another study, the manipulation check results were included in a supplementary online site; the text gave this summary of the results:*

"The priming manipulations were pretested for their effect on various associations and discrete emotions. Results confirmed that the manipulations are effective. Thus, t-tests indicate that the harm prime generated significantly more injury and harm associations compared to the other primes, that

*(Continued)*

(Continued)

the damage prime generated associations with convenience, and the disgust and sadness primes each generated the relevant emotion significantly more than the other three primes. Further, primes were overall comparable in the level of perceived negativity (the only pair of essays that significantly differed on a t-test were disgust and damage; see the online supporting materials for full pretest results)."

**From: Ben-Nun Bloom, Pazit. 2014. "Disgust, Harm and Morality in Politics."** *Political Psychology* **35 (4): 501.**

## Example 4

*Finally, in this study, part of the manipulation check was reported in the methods section and part in the results:*

### In Methods

"Measures were rated on 7-point Likert scales except where noted as otherwise.
   Manipulation check.
   At both pretest and posttest perceived threat was assessed using items adapted from prior studies (Rimal et al., 2009; Tyler & Cook, 1984; Witte, 1994). To measure perceived susceptibility, participants were asked how likely it was that they themselves or others around them might be exposed to HIV/AIDS. Participants were also asked how serious and threatening HIV/AIDS was and how important or urgent HIV/AIDS prevention was to individuals and to society. Responses were averaged into indices of perceived severity ($\alpha = .86$ at pretest, $\alpha = .95$ at posttest)."

### And in Results

"From pretest to posttest, participants with main partners perceived higher susceptibility at the personal level, $M = .50$, $SD = 1.34$, $t(157) = 4.68$, $p < .001$; and at the societal level, $M = .37$, $SD = 1.23$, $t(157) = 3.88$, $p < .001$. From pretest to posttest, participants with nonmain partners perceived higher susceptibility at the personal level, $M = .47$, $SD = 1.38$, $t(111) = 3.62$, $p < .001$; and at the societal level, $M = .43$, $SD = 1.30$, $t(111) = 3.49$, $p < .001$. Perceived severity did not increase from pretest to posttest. Hypothesis 1 was, therefore, partially supported. The manipulated difference in perceived threat was reflected by perceived susceptibility."

**From: Zhang, Jueman (Mandy), Di Zhang, and T. Makana Chock. 2014. "Effects of HIV/AIDS Public Service Announcements on Attitude and Behavior: Interplay of Perceived Threat and Self-Efficacy."** *Social Behavior and Personality* **42 (5): 802–803.**

Regardless of where it appears, elements that should be included in the manipulation check description include:

- if manipulation checks were conducted prior to the actual study, within the study itself, or both;

- a statement of whether the manipulation was successful or not;

- *N*s, statistical tests, and values that indicate significant differences and the direction of the differences;
- the measures used and response sets; and
- if items were created by others (cite them) or the researchers.

With stimuli created and deemed successful via a manipulation check, the design of the experiment is nearing completion. The next chapter deals with construction of the instrument used to measure the dependent variables, covariates, mediators, and moderators. Of course, the steps in experiment design can be reversed, with instrument design coming before stimuli construction, or be done at the same time.

## Common Mistakes

- Not using stimuli that look realistic
- Using one stimulus rather than many
- Not doing a manipulation check when necessary, or not reporting it
- Underestimating the strength of a manipulation needed to produce results
- Not including psychological states as mediators in the actual study

## Test Your Knowledge

1. In a study, journalists read press releases that highlighted different features of politicians, such as their political party and favorite issues, and were asked how likely they would be to write a story about them. What was the category of theoretical interest manipulated in the stimuli?

   a. The likelihood that journalists would write stories

   b. Different features of politicians that make them newsworthy

   c. The length of the press releases

   d. The size of the news organization the journalist worked for

2. Stimuli represent categories of theoretical interest because they _____.

   a. Serve as the vehicle through which the experimenters manipulate the factors hypothesized to cause some effect or outcome

   b. Are complex and take a lot of work to create

c. Control for confounding variables

d. Measure and statistically control for confounds

3. In an experiment that uses real politicians in the stimulus materials, it is important to control for subjects' prior knowledge about the politicians.

a. True

b. False

4. A statistical control is _____.

a. Something that cannot be controlled in the stimuli

b. Something that is measured and controlled for

c. Both A and B

d. A statistical technique like ANOVA or chi-square

5. Statistical controls should be measured _____.

a. Before the stimuli are given

b. After the stimuli are given

c. During the administration of the stimuli

d. Two weeks after the study

6. Fictitious people, places, and events are often used in experiments to avoid contamination by subjects' prior knowledge. These are called _____.

a. Statistical controls

b. Experimental controls

c. Control groups

d. Treatments

7. Selecting political issues that are not clearly linked with a particular party represents a form of _____.

a. Statistical control

b. Experimental control

c. Control group

d. Treatment

8. Covariates should _____.

a. Always include demographics

b. Be included in the manipulation check

c. Be randomly assigned

d. Be related to the outcome or dependent variable

9. Fixed factors are _____.

a. Those whose levels are unlimited

b. Those whose levels are chosen by the researchers

c. Those that represent a sample of the population

d. Both A and B.

10. Random factors are _____.

a. Those whose levels are unlimited

b. Those whose levels are chosen by the researchers

c. Those that represent a sample of the population

d. Those that are randomly assigned

Answers

| | | | |
|---|---|---|---|
| 1. b | 4. c | 7. b | 9. d |
| 2. a | 5. a | 8. d | 10. c |
| 3. a | 6. b | | |

## Application Exercises

1. For the experiment you are designing in this course, describe how you will create your stimuli. Address the following:

- **How will you make it realistic?** For example, will you start with an actual website or stimuli and adapt it? Do you have professional experience designing ads? Will you employ someone who does? Will you use software or online tools? Or will you use existing stimuli such as a TV show or curriculum plan?

- **How do your stimuli represent the categories of theoretical interest?** For example, do comments at the end of an online story represent the theoretical category of reader engagement?

- **How will your stimuli maximize comparisons?** Are you employing the strongest manipulation or the largest difference possible?

- **How will you employ message variance?** That is, how many stimuli will you create? Why?

Once you have planned all the details of your stimuli, begin creating them.

2. Design a manipulation check for the stimuli you have created. What questions will you use to determine if the manipulation is perceived as you intend? How many subjects will you recruit and from where? How long will it take? Once you have created your stimuli and manipulation check, get some subjects to take it and see if your stimuli worked. Obtain IRB approval first if required by your institution. Write up this portion of the paper.

3. Read methods sections from four studies in your area of interest and label the items that are reported. What in this chapter is included? What isn't? What special issues are reported? Identify where in the article manipulation checks are reported—in methods, results, a footnote, appendix, or online?

## Suggested Readings

**Creating stimuli for research:**

Graesser, A. C. 1981. *Prose Comprehension Beyond the Word*. New York, NY: Springer-Verlag.

Reeves, B., and S. Geiger. 1994. "Designing Experiments That Assess Psychological Responses." In *Measuring Psychological Responses to Media*, edited by A. Lang, 165–180. Hillsdale, NJ: LEA.

Slater, M. D. 1991. "Use of Message Stimuli in Mass Communication Experiments: A Methodological Assessment and Discussion." *Journalism Quarterly* 68 (3): 412–421.

**Manipulation checks:**

O'Keefe, D. J. 2003. "Message Properties, Mediating States, and Manipulation Checks: Claims, Evidence, and Data Analysis in Experimental Persuasive Message Effects Research." *Communication Theory* 13 (3): 251–274.

Tao, C., and E. P. Bucy. 2007. "Conceptualizing Media Stimuli in Experimental Research: Psychological Versus Attributed-Based Definitions." *Human Communication Research* 33: 397–426.

**Fixed vs. random factors:**

Chang, Yu-Hsuan A., and David M. Lane. 2016. "Generalizing Across Stimuli as Well as Subjects: A Non-Mathematical Tutorial on Mixed-Effects Models." *Quantitative Methods for Psychology* 12 (3): 201–219.

Clark, H. 1973. "The Language as Fixed-Effect Fallacy: A Critique of Language Statistics in Psychological Research." *Journal of Verbal Learning and Verbal Behavior* 12: 335–359. 10.1016/S0022-5371(73)80014-3.

Raaijmakers, J. G. W. 2003. "A Further Look at the 'Language-As-Fixed-Effect Fallacy.'" *Canadian Journal of Behavioral Science* 57: 141–151. 10.1037/h0087421

Raaijmakers, J. G. W., J. M. C. Schrijnemakers, and F. Gremen. 1999. "How to Deal With 'The Language-As-Fixed-Effect Fallacy': Common Misconceptions and Alternative Solutions." *Journal of Memory and Language* 41: 416–426. 10.1006/jmla.1999.2650.

# Notes

1. R. Barker Bausell, *Conducting Meaningful Experiments: 40 Steps to Becoming a Scientist* (Thousand Oaks, CA: Sage, 1994), 95.

2. James J. Gibson, "The Concept of the Stimulus in Psychology," *American Psychologist* 15, no. 11 (1960): 694–703.

3. Ibid.

4. Michael D. Slater, "Messages as Experimental Stimuli: Design, Analysis, and Inference." Paper presented at the Annual Meeting of the Association for Education in Journalism and Mass Communication (72nd, Washington, DC, August 10–13, 1989).

5. Esther Thorson, Robert H. Wicks, and Glenn Leshner, "Experimental Methodology in Journalism and Mass Communication Research," *Journalism and Mass Communication Quarterly* 89, no. 1 (2012): 112–124.

6. S. Shyam Sundar, "Theorizing Interactivity's Effects," *Information Society* 20 (2004).

7. Shana Kushner Gadarian and Bethany Albertson, "Anxiety, Immigration, and the Search for Information," *Political Psychology* 35, no. 2 (2014): 133–164.

8. Elizabeth A. Bennion and David W. Nickerson, "The Cost of Convenience: An Experiment Showing E-Mail Outreach Decreases Voter Registration," *Political Research Quarterly* 64, no. 4 (2011): 858–869.

9. Debby Vos, "How Ordinary MPs Can Make It Into the News: A Factorial Survey Experiment with Political Journalists to Explain the Newsworthiness of MPs," *Mass Communication and Society* 19, no. 6 (2016): 738–757.

10. Theresa Beltramo et al., "The Effect of Marketing Messages and Payment Over Time on Willingness to Pay for Fuel-Efficient Cookstoves," *Journal of Economic Behavior and Organization* 118 (2015): 333–345.

11. An-Sofie Claeys and Verolien Cauberghe, "Keeping Control: The Importance of Nonverbal Expressions of Power by Organizational Spokespersons in Time of Crisis," *Journal of Communication* 64 (2014): 1160–1180.

12. Horacio Alvarez-Marinelli et al., "Computer Assisted English Language Learning in Costa Rican Elementary Schools: An Experimental Study," *Computer Assisted Language Learning* 29, no. 1 (2016): 103–126.

13. Vos, "How Ordinary MPs Can Make It Into the News."

14. Beltramo et al., "The Effect of Marketing Messages."

15. Claeys and Cauberghe, "Keeping Control."

16. Alvarez-Marinelli et al., "Computer Assisted English Language Learning."

17. Angela Min-Chia Lee, "How Fast Is Too Fast? Examining the Impact of Speed-Driven Journalism on News Production and Audience Reception" (unpublished dissertation, University of Texas, 2014); Angela M. Lee, "The Faster the Better? Examining the Effect of Live-Blogging on Audience Reception," *Journal of Applied Journalism and Media Studies* 8, no. 1 (in press).

18. Nick Lin-Hi, Jacob Horisch, and Igor Blumberg, "Does CSR Matter for Nonprofit Organizations? Testing the Link between CSR Performance and Trustworthiness in the Nonprofit Versus For-Profit Domain," *Voluntas* 26 (2015): 1944–1974.

19. André Blais, Cengiz Erisen, and Ludovic Rheault, "Strategic Voting and Coordination Problems in Proportional Systems: An Experimental Study," *Political Research Quarterly* 67, no. 2 (2014): 386–397.

20. Pazit Ben-Nun Bloom, "Disgust, Harm and Morality in Politics," *Political Psychology* 35, no. 4 (2014): 495–513.

21. Nicole LaFave, "Fake Tweets & More—Simitator," http://edtechpicks.org/2016/05/fake-tweets-more-simitator/.

22. Canterbury College, "Simitator," https://www.canterburycollege.ac.uk/teaching-learning-hub/technology/simitator/.

23. Trent R. Boulter, "Following the Familiar: Effect of Exposure and Gender on Credibility of Journalists on Twitter," (dissertation, The University of Texas at Austin), https://repositories.lib.utexas.edu/bitstream/handle/2152/62635/BOULTER-DISSERTATION-2017.pdf?sequence=1&isAllowed=y).

24. Agne Kajackaite, "If I Close My Eyes, Nobody Will Get Hurt: The Effect of Ignorance on Performance in a Real-Effort Experiment," *Journal of Economic Behavior and Organization* 116 (2015): 518–524.

25. Mina Tsay-Vogel, "Me Versus Them: Third-Person Effects Among Facebook Users," *New Media & Society* 18, no. 9 (2016): 1956–1972.

26. John C. Tedesco, "Political Information Efficacy and Internet Effects in the 2008 U.S. Presidential Election," *American Behavioral Scientist* 55, no. 6 (2011): 696–713.

27. Renita Coleman, Esther Thorson, and Lee Wilkins, "Testing the Impact of Public Health Framing and Rich Sourcing in Health News Stories," *Journal of Health Communication* 16, no. 9 (2011): 941–954.

28. Sophie Lecheler and Claes H. de Vreese, "What a Difference a Day Makes? The Effects of Repetitive and Competitive News Framing over Time," *Communication Research* 40, no. 2 (2013): 147–175.

29. Claeys and Cauberghe, "Keeping Control."

30. For an example, see H. Denis Wu and Renita Coleman, "The Affective Effect on Political Judgment: Comparing the Influences of Candidate Attributes and Issue Congruence," *Journalism and Mass Communication Quarterly* 91, no. 3 (2014): 530–543.

31. Vos, "How Ordinary MPs Can Make It Into the News."

32. Claeys and Cauberghe, "Keeping Control."

33. Vos, "How Ordinary MPs Can Make It Into the News."

34. Ibid., 752.

35. Bausell, *Conducting Meaningful Experiments*, 76.

36. Ibid., 95.

37. C. Sansone, C. C. Morf, and A. T. Panter, *The Sage Handbook of Methods in Social Psychology* (Thousand Oaks, CA: Sage Publications, 2008).

38. Diana C. Mutz and Robin Pemantle, "Standards for Experimental Research: Encouraging a Better Understanding of Experimental Methods," *Journal of Experimental Political Science* 2, no. 2 (2016): 192–215.

39. Renita Coleman, "The Effect of Visuals on Ethical Reasoning: What's a Photograph Worth to Journalists Making Moral Decisions?" *Journalism and Mass Communication Quarterly* 83, no. 4 (2006): 835–850.

40. Stanley Milgram, *Obedience to Authority: An Experimental View* (New York: Harper & Row, 1974).

41. Ibid.

42. Bausell, *Conducting Meaningful Experiments*; Sansone, Morf, and Panter, *The Sage Handbook of Methods in Social Psychology*.

43. Mutz and Pemantle, "Standards for Experimental Research."

44. Thorson, Wicks, and Leshner, "Experimental Methodology in Journalism."

45. Ibid.

46. Ibid.

47. Tsay-Vogel, "Me Versus Them."

48. Daniel J. O'Keefe, "Trends and Prospects in Persuasion Theory and Research," in *Persuasion: Theory & Research*, ed. Daniel J. O'Keefe (Thousand Oaks, CA: Sage, 2002).

49. Ibid.

50. Ibid.

51. S. Jackson and S. Jacobs, "Generalizing About Messages: Suggestions for Design and Analysis of Experiments, Plus Responses by James J. Bradac and Dean E. Hewes," *Human Communication Research,* 9, no. 2 (1983): 169–181.

52. Coleman, Thorson, and Wilkins, "Testing the Impact of Public Health Framing."

53. Charles M. Judd, Jacob Westfall, and David A. Kenny, "Treating Stimuli as a Random Factor in Social Psychology: A New and Comprehensive Solution to a Pervasive but Largely Ignored Problem," *Journal of Personality and Social Psychology* 103, no. 1 (2012): 54–69.

54. Thorson, Wicks, and Leshner, "Experimental Methodology in Journalism," 119–120.

55. Glenn Leshner, Paul D. Bolls, and Erika Thomas, "Scare 'Em or Disgust 'Em: The Effects of Graphic Health Promotion Messages," *Health Communication* 24 (2009): 447–458.

56. Thorson, Wicks, and Leshner, "Experimental Methodology in Journalism."

57. D. J. O'Keefe, "Message Properties, Mediating States, and Manipulation Checks: Claims, Evidence, and Data Analysis in Experimental Persuasive Message Effects Research," *Communication Theory* 13, no. 3 (2003): 251–274.

58. Judd, Westfall, and Kenny, "Treating Stimuli as a Random Factor."

59. Ibid.

60. Ibid.

61. Yu-Hsuan A. Chang and David M. Lane, "Generalizing Across Stimuli as Well as Subjects: A Non-Mathematical Tutorial on Mixed-Effects Models," *Quantitative Methods for Psychology* 12, no. 3 (2016): 201–219.

62. Judd, Westfall, and Kenny, "Treating Stimuli as a Random Factor."

63. Ibid.

64. Chang and Lane, "Generalizing Across Stimuli"; Judd, Westfall, and Kenny, "Treating Stimuli as a Random Factor."

65. Chang and Lane, "Generalizing Across Stimuli."

66. Ibid.

67. Ibid.

68. Ibid.

69. Thorson, Wicks, and Leshner, "Experimental Methodology in Journalism."

70. Annie Franco, Neil Malhotra, and Gabor Simonovits, "Publication Bias in the Social Sciences: Unlocking the File Drawer," *Science* 345, no. 6203 (2014): 1502–1505.

71. M. Foschi, "Hypotheses, Operationalizations, and Manipulation Checks," in *Laboratory Experiments in the Social Sciences*, ed. Murray Webster and Jane Sell (New York: Elsevier, 2007); Mutz and Pemantle, "Standards for Experimental Research"; Thorson, Wicks, and Leshner, "Experimental Methodology in Journalism."

72. Sansone, Morf, and Panter, *The Sage Handbook of Methods in Social Psychology*.

73. D. J. O'Keefe, "Message Properties, Mediating States and Manipulation Checks."

74. Sansone, Morf, and Panter, *The Sage Handbook of Methods in Social Psychology*.

75. Mutz and Pemantle, "Standards for Experimental Research."

76. Rebecca S. McEntee, Renita Coleman, and Carolyn Yaschur, "Comparing the Effects of Vivid Writing and Photographs on Moral Judgment in Public Relations," *Journalism and Mass Communication Quarterly* 94, no. 4 (2017): 1011–1130.

77. P. C. Cozby, *Methods of Behavioral Research*, 10th ed. (New York: McGraw-Hill, 2009); B. C. Perdue and J. O. Summers, "Checking the Success of Manipulations in Marketing Experiments," *Journal of Marketing Research* 23, no. 4 (1986): 317–326.

78. Mutz and Pemantle, "Standards for Experimental Research," 194.

79. Rosie Campbell and Philip Cowley, "What Voters Want: Reactions to Candidate Characteristics in a Survey Experiment," *Political Studies* 62, no. 4 (2013): 745–765.

80. O'Keefe, "Message Properties, Mediating States, and Manipulation Checks."

81. McEntee, Coleman, and Yaschur, "Comparing the Effects of Vivid Writing."

82. O'Keefe, "Message Properties, Mediating States, and Manipulation Checks."

83. C. Tao and E. P. Bucy, "Conceptualizing Media Stimuli in Experimental Research: Psychological Versus Attributed-Based Definitions," *Human Communication Research* 33 (2007): 397–426.

84. C. Tao and E. P. Bucy, "Conceptualizing Media Stimuli."

85. Ibid.

86. Amery D. Wu and Bruno D. Zumbo, "Understanding and Using Mediators and Moderators," *Social Indicators Research: An International Interdisciplinary Journal for Quality of Life Measurement* 3 (2008).

87. Ibid.

88. James Hall and Pamela Sammons, "Mediation, Moderation & Interaction," in *Handbook of Quantitative Methods for Educational Research*, ed. Timothy Teo (Rotterdam, Netherlands: Sense, 2013).

89. Erica Scharrer, "Hypermasculinity, Aggression, and Television Violence: An Experiment," *Media Psychology* 7, no. 4 (2005): 353–376.

90. Tao and Bucy, "Conceptualizing Media Stimuli."

91. Ibid., 413–414.

92. R. M. Baron and D. A. Kenny, "The Moderator-Mediator Variable Distinction in Social Psychological Research: Conceptual, Strategic, and Statistical Considerations," *Journal of Personality and Social Psychology* 51, no. 6 (1986): 1173–1182; M. D. Sobel, "Asymptotic Confidence Intervals for Indirect Effects in Structural Equation Models," in *Sociological Methodology*, ed. S. Leinhardt (San Francisco: Jossey-Bass, 1982), 212–290; Andrew F. Hayes, *Introduction to Mediation, Moderation, and Conditional Process Analysis, Second Edition: A Regression-Based Approach* (New York: Guilford Press, 2013).

93. Mutz and Pemantle, "Standards for Experimental Research"; B. Efron and R. J. Tibshirani, *An Introduction to the Bootstrap* (New York: Chapman & Hall, 1993).

94. Mutz and Pemantle, "Standards for Experimental Research," 197.

95. Ibid.

96. Ibid.

97. Ibid.

98. Ibid.

99. Jona Linde and Barbara Vis, "Do Politicians Take Risks Like the Rest of Us? An Experimental Test of Prospect Theory Under MPs," *Political Psychology* 38, no. 1 (2017): 101–117.

100. McEntee, Coleman, and Yaschur, "Comparing the Effects of Vivid Writing."

101. Mutz and Pemantle, "Standards for Experimental Research."

102. Ibid.

103. Beltramo et al., "The Effect of Marketing Messages," 336.

104. For an example, see Vos, "How Ordinary MPs Can Make It Into the News."

105. Ibid., 747.

106. Lin-Hi, Horisch, and Blumberg, "Does CSR Matter for Nonprofit Organizations?"

107. Ibid., 1955.

108. Jueman (Mandy) Zhang, Di Zhang, and T. Makana Chock, "Effects of HIV/AIDS Public Service Announcements on Attitude and Behavior: Interplay of Perceived Threat and Self-Efficacy," *Social Behavior and Personality* 42, no. 5 (2014).

# INSTRUMENTS AND MEASURES

*I have been struck again and again by how important measurement is to improving the human condition.*

**—Bill Gates**

## LEARNING OBJECTIVES

- Summarize the advantages and disadvantages of questionnaires as the instrument of an experiment.

- Discuss when single-item indicators are appropriate and when indexes are superior.

- Identify some unobtrusive instruments and be able to link them to what psychological or physiological processes they measure.

- Describe how observations are used in experiments and how reliability is ensured.

- Explain the levels of measurement required for independent variables (IVs) and dependent variables (DVs) in an experiment.

- Devise an instrument for an experiment that includes appropriate levels of measurement and response choices, and verify the validity of its constructs.

Creating stimuli is only half the job in preparing the materials of an experiment for launch. The other half involves creating the **instrument** that will be used to measure the responses provoked by the stimuli. The instrument differs from the stimulus in that it is the actual device used to measure a response, whereas the stimulus is the vehicle used to deliver the manipulation or treatment. Put another way, the instrument is the measurement device, tool, or procedure researchers use to collect data produced in response to the stimuli. Measurement is not only important to improving the human condition, as the opening quote says, but also to improving the chances for success in an experiment.

Instruments can be thought of in three main categories: (1) as self-reports, completed by the experimental subject, such as a questionnaire; (2) as technological equipment like B. F. Skinner's kymograph, a device that used a stopwatch to record movement; and (3) as observations recorded by a researcher—for example, behavior of children in classrooms. This chapter will discuss the pros and cons of these types of instruments, then follow with a discussion of measurement issues.

# INSTRUMENTS

## Questionnaires

In many social science experiments today, the instrument is frequently a questionnaire, similar to a survey, designed to measure people's self-reported responses to some manipulation or treatment. The questionnaire is the set of questions used to gather and record subjects' responses. Questionnaires can be administered in a variety of ways—on computers, with paper and pencil, in face-to-face interviews, or on the phone.[1] Ronald Fisher's experiment of the lady tasting tea used a face-to-face interview as the instrument; the lady simply told the experimenter whether the tea or milk came first.

Writing questions is a complicated art form, with many decisions about wording, content, and placement, among other issues. There are many good texts and articles about this topic, so I do not belabor it here. Rather, I recommend sources in the "Suggested Readings" list and hit the highlights of problems I commonly see with experimental questionnaires in More About box 10.1 in this chapter.

Importantly, the questionnaire of an experiment needs to capture the abstract concepts of the dependent variables, covariates, and intervening variables (mediators and moderators) in a concrete way. The actual questions asked of subjects are the applied translations of the theoretical concepts outlined in the literature review, known as the *operationalizations*. For example, one way the concept of attention has been measured is by how much

# MORE ABOUT . . . BOX 10.1
## Writing Questionnaires

- Do not ask about more than one thing per question. Watch for "and," as in: "Rate your attitude toward Blacks *and* Hispanics on the following scale." People may have different attitudes for each. Having them give one answer only invites error.

- Check to see that questions make sense to ordinary people. For example, "How involved were you in this dilemma?" is meant to operationalize involvement as being absorbed by something, but could be interpreted as being *personally* involved with the issue.

- Keep questions short and direct. Make them clearly written. Avoid using researcher language like "operationalize."

- Examine each question to see if it is needed and what level of detail is required. Every question just adds time to the study, which may cause subjects to lose interest or get tired, which introduces error. If income is not going to be used in the analysis, for example, then there is no need to ask about it.

- Avoid biased and leading questions. Take out adjectives and adverbs.

- Whenever possible, use questions that have been used in other studies. The methods section, an appendix, supplemental website, or cited studies should give exact wording and response choices. Cite these.

- Double check to be sure that all variables in the hypotheses are operationalized in the methods section and that a conceptual definition for each is in the literature review. If there are any "orphans," ask if that question is really needed.

subjects remember.[2] The concept of anxiety can be measured or operationalized with questions such as "How anxious did you feel?" To measure trustworthiness of a fictitious business, one study asked subjects how much they agreed with four statements: "I find it easy to trust (the business)," "I can trust (the business) completely," "(The business) is a trustworthy organization," and "I trust the management of (the business)."[3] Exact wording of questions used in studies can be found in the methods section, footnotes, appendix, or a supplemental website. Some studies cite another study that used the same questions previously, and researchers will need to read the cited studies to track down the exact wording.

Questions also can be less directly worded than using "anxious" to measure anxiety and "trust" to measure trustworthiness, as in the previous illustrations. For example, to measure social marketing effectiveness, one experiment used questions asking subjects about their intentions to change, behavioral intentions, and willingness to communicate.[4] These three measures had all been used by others, which the researchers cited. The researchers also included a new measure of their own creation, asking subjects about their intentions to express an attitude by clicking a "like" button.

As illustrated by this marketing study, using questions—also called **items**—that have been developed and tested by other researchers should be the first choice to ensure reliability and validity. Taking existing questions and modifying them for some specific use also is frequently done. When previous studies lack a good measure, or researchers think there is another or better way to measure a concept, developing original questions, as with the "like" button example, is appropriate. These new items should be adequately tested to ensure they measure what they are supposed to.[5] More about that in the "Measurement Issues" section later in this chapter.

### Single Items vs. Indexes

Using only one question—called a **single-item indicator**—should be reserved for concrete concepts such as age, education level, other demographics, and simple concepts such as overall ratings—for example, overall effectiveness of teachers as rated by students,[6] and overall job satisfaction.[7] It pays to know which variables are valid as single items, because fewer questions can shorten a study. However, studies with inappropriate single-item measures are more likely to be rejected by journal editors and reviewers because of issues with measurement validity and reliability.[8] Abstract and multidimensional concepts such as credibility, persuasion, and anxiety should be made up of multiple questions, which are used to form an **index**, as was done in the social marketing study with the four questions. An abstract concept that is measured with only one question tends to be weaker and less stable than one with multiple questions, and stronger measures are more likely to show significance if it exists. This is illustrated by a study that measured religiosity with two questions, "Would you describe yourself as extremely religious (7) to extremely nonreligious (1)?" and "Where would you place your religious beliefs?" with response choices from extremely fundamentalist (7) to extremely liberal (1).[9] When the two-question index was used in the analysis, it showed significant differences at the level of $p < .001$. After a reviewer suggested the fundamental-to-liberal question could have biased the analysis, it was removed and the analysis done with only the single-item asking about religious beliefs. That analysis produced the same conclusion as the previous one but was significant at $p < .05$ rather than $p < .001$, presumably because the single-item indicator was weaker than the original two-question index.[10] This illustrates one reason why single-item indicators are discouraged for all but the most obvious, concrete, and single-dimensional of variables.

Instead, complex theoretical concepts should be measured with an index of multiple questions. A good example is the concept of self-efficacy, which describes a person's belief in his or her ability to execute a task successfully.[11] People draw from four sources to gauge their abilities, including their own past performance, watching others, praise and criticism, and their emotional state. Thus, questions measuring self-efficacy should capture each of these four sources. Many self-efficacy indexes, which are also sometimes called *scales*, have been tailored for specific domains from education[12] to health care[13] and beyond. There are even specific indexes for pornography avoidance[14] and information retrieval on the web in China,[15] as well as general indexes for children, parents, teachers, and much more.[16] (For a guide on constructing self-efficacy indexes, see Bandura, 2006.[17]) As an example, an education self-efficacy index in one study[18] consisted of nine items previously developed by other researchers,[19] including: "I expect to do very well in this class," "I am sure that I can do an excellent job on the problems and tasks assigned for class," and "I know that I will be able to learn the material for my class."[20]

Slight wording changes to developed indexes can make a difference. For example, asking what one "can do" is different from asking what one is "able to do"[21] and what one "will do" in self-efficacy studies.[22] It is important to read articles on index development for such guidance. Another example can be found in the reasoned action model,[23] where injunctive norms are perceptions of what other people should or ought to do, and descriptive norms are perceptions of what people are actually doing; the questions are worded to ask how much someone *approves of* a certain behavior for injunctive norms, and how much someone *does* a certain behavior for descriptive norms.[24] This is not meant to discourage researchers from adapting questions or writing their own, only to point out the steps that should be taken to ensure that newly created questions adhere to the theory guiding the concepts. In fact, many concepts are better studied with measures developed especially for particular contexts,[25] and creating new questions is encouraged.

## Pros and Cons

The use of questionnaires as the instrument to measure outcomes from experimental manipulations has its strengths and weaknesses. Questionnaires mainly rely on self-reports—that is, subjects answer the questions themselves, reporting on their own attitudes, opinions, and behaviors. Self-reports are fast, cheap, and easy. Subjects can do them privately, and the anonymous nature is thought to encourage honest answers. Survey experiments conducted online may reduce demand effects, as subjects are not being influenced by the presence of an experimenter.[27] Questionnaires are a much-used instrument in social science experiments, measuring all manner of things such as memory, attitudes, emotions, personality traits, behaviors, and behavioral intentions. Yet self-reports are inherently weak and can lead to inaccurate results.[28]

# QUESTIONNAIRE EXAMPLE

Figure 10.1 contains an example of a questionnaire used in a study of the framing of health stories.[26] The double underlined areas were not shown to subjects but are here for the researcher's purpose. The labels represent the theoretical constructs the questions are meant to operationalize. For example, Factual Knowledge is measured with multiple-choice questions, and the number each subject got correct is the score. Attribution of Responsibility is the theoretical construct represented by the next set of questions. To ensure that the questions measured the construct accurately, a Cronbach's alpha measure of reliability for the purpose of internal consistency was computed; that is reported as Alpha = .805. The "R" in double underline indicates a question that needs to be reverse coded. In other words, some questions are worded negatively and some positively; reverse coding allows for responses of 7 to indicate positive responses and 1 to indicate negative.

| FIGURE 10.1 ⬣ QUESTIONNAIRE |
| --- |

*Please respond to the following items about the immigrant health story.*

FACTUAL KNOWLEDGE; correct answer is in italics

What is the fastest growing segment of the U.S. population?

[a]   Asian immigrants          *[b]   Latino immigrants*          [c]   European immigrants

What percentage of foreign-born adults lacks a primary health care provider?

*[a]   1 in 4*          [b]   1 in 3          [c]   1 in 5

What percent of immigrant workers in Santa Clara County are uninsured?

[a]   37%          *[b]   54%*          [c]   65%

Latinos are how much more likely to die from prostate cancer than Caucasians?

[a]   four times as likely          *[b]   twice as likely*          [c]   three times as likely

*Please indicate how much you agree with the following statements:*

ATTRIBUTION OF RESPONSIBILITY ALPHA = .805

|  | Strongly Disagree |  |  |  |  |  | Strongly Agree |
| --- | --- | --- | --- | --- | --- | --- | --- |
| The government should spend more money on health care prevention and treatment for immigrants | 1 | 2 | 3 | 4 | 5 | 6 | 7 |
| Immigrant health care is a societal problem | 1 | 2 | 3 | 4 | 5 | 6 | 7 |
| R Immigrant health care is an individual problem | 1 | 2 | 3 | 4 | 5 | 6 | 7 |

| | Strongly Disagree | | | | | | Strongly Agree |
|---|---|---|---|---|---|---|---|
| R̲ Immigrants have only themselves to blame for lack of health care | 1 | 2 | 3 | 4 | 5 | 6 | 7 |
| R̲ If people work hard they can almost always find a way to obtain health care | 1 | 2 | 3 | 4 | 5 | 6 | 7 |
| Employers are to blame for providing unsafe working conditions for immigrants | 1 | 2 | 3 | 4 | 5 | 6 | 7 |
| Health care providers are partly to blame for not learning about the culture of immigrants they serve | 1 | 2 | 3 | 4 | 5 | 6 | 7 |
| Communities can help immigrants by offering free English language lessons focused on health issues | 1 | 2 | 3 | 4 | 5 | 6 | 7 |
| Employers are to blame for not providing insurance for immigrant workers | 1 | 2 | 3 | 4 | 5 | 6 | 7 |
| Lack of access to health insurance makes it harder for immigrants to manage their health | 1 | 2 | 3 | 4 | 5 | 6 | 7 |
| R Poor access to health care is something t̲hat people voluntarily put themselves at risk for | 1 | 2 | 3 | 4 | 5 | 6 | 7 |
| People who have a hard time getting health care are innocent victims | 1 | 2 | 3 | 4 | 5 | 6 | 7 |

There are many reasons for inaccuracies in self-reports. People may be managing their own self-image or responding with socially desirable answers.[29] For example, few people will admit to holding racial prejudices. Self-reports have attempted to overcome this by asking people not what *they* think but what they think others think (e.g., "However, *we are not asking for your opinions on these matters. In this study, we are interested in how the opinion items are perceived.*").[30] However, self-reports are notorious for being unable to overcome the social desirability bias or impression management; thus, other instruments should be considered. Additionally, people may be reluctant to answer questions honestly about illegal behavior or sensitive questions with moral overtones.[31]

Another reason why questionnaires that rely on self-reports may produce incorrect answers is that some things may be beyond a person's ability to introspectively assess.[32]

For example, some feelings are inaccessible to people, as are some of their own personality traits.[33] In these cases, people are not intentionally answering incorrectly but are simply not even aware of their true feelings or traits. When this is the case, other instruments can produce different results. An example is research that shows conservatives are happier than liberals when measured with self-reports, but that liberals show happier behavior when unobtrusive measures are used, such as observing smiling and use of positive emotional language.[34]

In addition, people can be mistaken, misremember, exaggerate, or minimize their answers to self-reports. Another explanation may be misunderstanding of a question; with survey experiments given online, subjects cannot ask a researcher for clarification of questions they may not understand. Similarly, people may interpret the meaning of questions differently than researchers intended. I once measured involvement by asking several standard questions, including, "How involved were you with this story?" with the question intended to measure how much it engaged or interested them. The graduate students used in a pilot test of the questionnaire responded the way that was intended; the undergraduates that were the subjects of the actual study wrote notes or said during debriefing, "I'm not involved with (drugs/prostitution/homelessness/elder abuse) at all!" That question was eliminated from the index. Along the same lines, some people interpret response scales differently, with some consistently giving the most extreme ratings (1s and 7s, for example) and others sticking to the middle (3s and 4s, for example).[35]

Validity studies are often conducted to compare self-reports to other instruments. For example, questions asking about criminal offenses committed can be compared against conviction rates in criminology research. Education research is frequently concerned with the accuracy of students' self-reports; for example, a study that compared high school transcripts of courses in music with self-reports of music participation found students' self-reported participation with music ensembles to be quite accurate, but students typically overreported the amount of time they spent practicing.[36] Teachers' reports of practice time was not much more accurate.[37]

On a final note, one tip for success in experiments is that **open-ended response** options in questionnaires can prove quite enlightening and helpful. These are simply questions that have no set answers or scales for subjects to choose from but allow them to answer in their own words—for example, questions such as "Tell me about . . ." or "Why did you choose this answer?" Comments from subjects as examples to illustrate statistical findings can make results "come alive." And they can be useful for backing up claims. For example, a reviewer once asked if the subjects in a study had met the criteria of carefully

scrutinizing all sides of an issue rather than merely trying to bolster their own preconceived position in a decision-making experiment; being able to pull examples from the
open-ended responses to demonstrate that they had was extremely valuable.[38] There is a
rich literature in the analysis of qualitative data, but these open-ended responses also can
be categorized, counted, and measured to turn qualitative data into quantitative. They
do need to be categorized by a human, however (see the "Observations" section in this
chapter), so are not as easy to use as closed-ended questions.

For more tips on creating successful instruments and measurements in experiments, see
More About box 10.2.

Some disciplines are more inclined to use self-reports than others; economics, for example, prefers observations of behavior[39] or performance-based measures.[40] Those types of
instruments and other alternatives to self-reports are covered next.

## Unobtrusive and Nonreactive Measures

In addition to the many weaknesses of self-reports described earlier, they are also subject
to reactivity and demand characteristics, a concept introduced in chapter 2 where it was
explained that bias is introduced when a subject changes his or her responses as a reaction to being studied. To overcome these biases, instruments have been devised that are
nonreactive.[46] Nonreactive instruments are those that ensure the subject is not aware of
what is being tested so that the act of being measured does not influence the responses.
Another term often used to mean the same thing is *unobtrusive*. Unobtrusive and nonreactive measures exist on a continuum;[47] in the most unobtrusive studies, subjects are
unaware they are in a study, and even the researchers do not know the hypotheses. More
commonly, subjects know they are participating in a study but do not know the aims
of the research so are unable to influence their responses for or against the hypothesis.
The psychological instruments described in the next section are nonreactive in the sense
that subjects are unable to distort their responses, but they definitely know they are
participating in a study.

## Technological Instruments

Another way to measure the outcomes or responses to experimental treatments is with
instruments of the technological tool, mechanical, or equipment variety. Some researchers also refer to these as *devices, hardware,* and *software*.[48] B. F. Skinner invented his own,
such as the "cumulative recorder" that used a pen and roll of paper to automatically
record when a rat pressed a lever or a pigeon pecked a key.[49] While computer-administered

# MORE ABOUT. . . BOX 10.2
## Successful Measurements

- Always give the measurement immediately after a subject receives a treatment stimulus. For example, subjects read one story and immediately answer questions or list all thoughts about it before reading the next story, then answering questions or listing thoughts about it. Do not give all questions or all thought listings after all stories have been read.

- Employ multiple measures of the dependent variable—for example, a feeling thermometer, six trait evaluations, and two agree–disagree statements.[41] This offers comparisons of the measures and reduces the chance for any particular instrument to drive results. One measure may be better than the other.

- Another approach to foiling the social desirability bias is to introduce irrelevant questions or tasks so that subjects will not be able to easily guess what the study is about. Other terms for this include intervening items, buffer items, and distractor tasks. For an example, see Emily Thorson's study on belief echoes.[42]

- Remember to reverse code items that are worded the opposite way of the majority of questions. For example, 1 should become 7, 2 becomes 6, etc.

- Data from experimental subjects does not have to be collected all at once. Many experiments, especially those using technological instruments, are conducted over a period of time. Space and equipment constraints are among the most prevalent reasons. For example, a researcher showing subjects a TV show in a laboratory setting would not likely have a large-enough room; many of the psychological and physiological instruments are expensive, and only one or a few are available, so subjects are run one at a time. Other reasons for running the experiment over time include the need to include additional treatments after learning the results from one experiment.[43] However, researchers should be cognizant of threats to validity (see chapter 5) such as events that may bias the results (e.g., history).

- Include covariates judiciously. The purpose of a covariate is to reduce variance caused by nuisance variables that are related to the dependent variable. These need to be planned in advance and measured before the treatment is given if the treatment might affect the covariate. When done correctly, covariates can increase the power of an experiment. When too many variables that are not predictors of the DV are included, they can actually reduce the power. Covariates should not be used because they correlated with the independent variables, but with dependent variables.[44]

- Demographics need only be included as covariates if they are strong predictors of the dependent variable.[45] Only the demographics that are necessary to describe the sample or are to be used in the analysis need to be included in the questionnaire. For example, questions about income can be particularly sensitive for subjects; unless income is necessary for the analysis, it may be better to not ask about it.

questionnaires also require technology, they are different from the high-tech instruments in the following section, such as functional magnetic resonance imaging (fMRI) machines that detect changes in blood flow to the brain, allowing researchers to see what parts of the brain are being activated; eye-tracking devices that record eye movement; heart rate monitors that measure attention, arousal, emotion, and effort;[50] and galvanometric skin response receptors that measure changes in the skin, like sweating, as a proxy for emotion, arousal, and attention.[51] Many of these instruments today do consist of technology and software; for example, latency response, or how fast subjects respond to a question that measures cognitive processing, is done with computer software that measures response rates in milliseconds, and web tracking software that records the links a person clicks on and how long they spend on a certain site. Here these are classified separately from questionnaires that are recorded with software because subjects are not self-reporting their responses.

These and other instruments not included here, for the list is too long, represent **implicit tests**—that is, ones where the subject is not necessarily consciously aware of his or her responses. Many of these record psychological or physical responses such as heart rate. Some of these are used in social sciences more frequently than others, and some tend to be used in specific disciplines within the social sciences. Next are highlights of some of the more popular of these instruments in the social sciences. Space prohibits a full discussion of the strengths and weaknesses of each; this is instead an introduction, and interested readers should seek more comprehensive texts on the problems and how to address them.

## Functional Magnetic Resonance Imaging

One of the newest instruments to catch on in social science is functional magnetic resonance imaging, or **fMRI**, a noninvasive brain scanner that produces cross-sectional images of the brain that captures brain activity as opposed to static brain structure. It is used to identify areas of the brain associated with certain mental processes such as trusting, or when experiencing emotions such as fear.[52] There is a growing interest in fMRI and similar neuroimaging tools across the social sciences,[53] becoming especially popular in marketing and consumer research, with many books on the

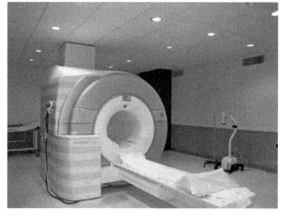

Dimoka (2012)

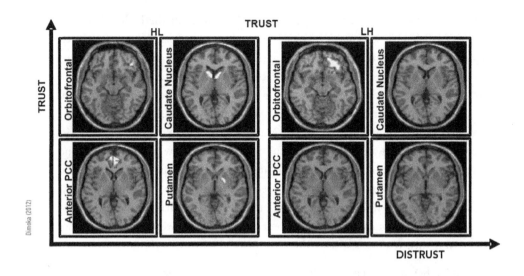

topic.[54] Marketing studies that use fMRI have included research on cognitive processing when people see their favorite brand label,[55] or choose between brands of beer and coffee,[56] to understand willingness to pay,[57] to see the effect of expert statements,[58] and to forecast sales changes based on point-of-sale ads.[59] In political science, fMRI has been used to predict changes in attitudes toward candidates[60] and to examine the relationship between emotion and voting,[61] among other things. In health communication, fMRI has been used to examine memory for health messages[62] and to test the effectiveness of public service announcements (PSAs) about risky alcohol use.[63] In economics, it has been used to examine reputation and trust in exchanges.[64] This is not an exhaustive list of all fMRI studies in social science; nearly every discipline has at least some, including one that used fMRI to see the differences in cognitive processing between artistic and popular music.[65]

Using fMRI as an instrument is not as simple as using an instrument like a questionnaire. It takes a considerable amount of training,[66] time, and effort to conduct such a study.[67] It may even require a trained lab technician and possibly even a radiologist to look for brain abnormalities if required by an Institutional Review Board.[68] The equipment is expensive and large, consisting of a full-body tube where subjects lay down flat inside.[69] Subjects can view stimuli through goggles or on a screen, and respond verbally or on a keyboard.[70] Their heads must stay perfectly still, and they cannot have any metal piercings, implants, or medical issues.[71] The scanner is noisy, and experimental tasks need to be limited to forty-five to sixty seconds.[72] Because of the high cost and time it takes to run subjects one at a time, sample sizes are small, usually between ten and twenty subjects per study.[73] Currently, fMRI in the social sciences is used mainly to complement other instruments, allowing for triangulation with self-reports or interviews, for example, or to measure concepts subject to the biases discussed earlier.[74]

## Heart Rate

Another instrument that measures physiological responses to stimuli is a heart rate monitor. Compared to fMRI, it is relatively cheap and easy to use, although not without the need for special safety training as it involves electricity.[75] Heart rate, measured via electrocardiogram, abbreviated as ECG or EKG, is used to assess attention, arousal, cognitive effort, and emotion.[76] It affords a real-time record of a person's emotional and cognitive changes while they are performing some task,[77] such as watching a political ad or listening to music. EKG measures the time between heartbeats using electrical impulses via electrodes attached to a subject's skin and requires special hardware and software.[78] It has been used in social science, including education to understand test anxiety,[79] in music to examine the differences in listening to live versus recorded music,[80] in marketing to test different breakfast drinks,[81] with public service advertising,[82] and for health messages,[83] while subjects watched jerky motion in TV and film[84] as well as commercials with celebrities,[85] while subjects read the news,[86] looked at political ads,[87] saw political leaders making inappropriate faces,[88] and with children using information technology, among other things.[89]

## Skin Conductance

Changes in the skin also can provide measures of emotion, arousal, and attention.[90] Known by a variety of terms, including galvanic skin response (GSR) and electrodermal response (EDR), these instruments measure fluctuations in the skin including sweating, voltage, and resistance.[91] **Skin conductance** instruments are especially useful for commercial advertising, sales and marketing, and consumer research to overcome issues with self-reports.[92] In addition to these fields, skin conductance has been used in political science[93] to study the effect of anxiety on political beliefs, for example,[94] and with media violence,[95] television dramas,[96] health messages,[97] marketing,[98] teachers' stress,[99] and gaming.[100] Skin conductance instruments involve attaching electrodes to subjects' fingers or palms.[101] As with most of these high-tech instruments, subjects must be run individually, and computer or software malfunctions can further erode a small sample.[102]

## Other Physiological Instruments

In addition to those already mentioned, there are instruments that measure virtually every psychological and physiological reaction a human can make. These include acoustic startle reflexes activated by loud noises,[103] saliva tests that measure stress, and voice frequency analysis and voice pitch instruments used to measure dominance,[104] among others. One health communication study used a CPR mannequin

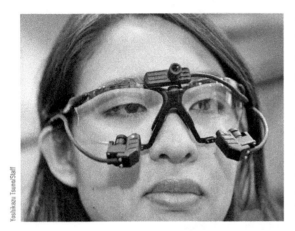

Yoshikazu Tsuno/Staff

that recorded measurements of the quality of the compressions given, including rate, depth, complete release, and the length of time the subjects' hands were off the mannequin.[105]

## Eye Tracking

Unlike the more difficult and costly instruments such as fMRI, eye-tracking devices are relatively cheap and easy to use. Eye tracking is used to unobtrusively capture a subject's visual attention patterns and direction.[106] Eye-tracking instruments measure eye fixation or position (where the eye rests), fixation frequency (how often), duration (how long),[107] and movement.[108] It is used to provide information on what a person looks at, in what order, and for how long.[109] It has been used to explain cognitive load effects[110] and to measure arousal using pupil dilation.[111]

Eye-tracking equipment used in social science experiments include devices made by companies such as SensoMotoric Instruments,[112] Tobii Technology,[113] iView Systems,[114] Applied Science Laboratories,[115] and EyeTribe,[116] among others. The cost can be as low as $200 for a unit.[117] The tracking devices are embedded in a headset[118] or glasses[119] that subjects wear, at the bottom of a mobile device or computer screen,[120] or mounted above the device.[121] Infrared cameras can be used to identify the location of the corneal reflection.[122]

Finger touches on the screen, such as zooming and swiping, also can be measured with these devices.[123] In addition to data about the eye movement and fixations, a heat map of the most looked-at areas of the stimuli can be generated,[124] among other graphics.[125]

Drawbacks of the eye-tracking instruments are some of the same as with fMRI—sample sizes are small, around twenty,[126] because the time required to run each subject is intensive.[127] For example, calibrating the device for each subject takes about ten minutes per person. Incorrectly calibrating the devices can result in a loss of subjects.[128]

Eye-tracking instruments have been used to study all manner of subjects in the social sciences, including the process of decision making;[129] news photographs;[130] the nonverbal behavior of political candidates;[131] impulse buying;[132] consumer behavior when shopping on mobile devices;[133] advertising;[134] television;[135] economics;[136] education,[137] including how long teachers looked at students in a study where teachers wore glasses with eye-tracking devices;[138] and all things online.[139]

Eye tracking has been used in conjunction with other instruments, such as electroencephalogram, for triangulation purposes,[140] and also to validate other instruments—for example, to identify problems with questionnaires.[141] One study used eye tracking with face-to-face interviews as a measure of visual attention to study how asking different forms of questions affects answers.[142]

## Eyes on Screen

A type of measure similar to eye tracking but specific to television is "eyes on screen."[143] This instrument is used to measure attention, capturing how much a subject looks at the TV screen, for how long, when, and how often the looking occurs, also known as "orienting." It requires a video camera behind a one-way mirror to record subjects as they watch TV. It is used to study TV programs and commercials, and often as a complement to or substitute for self-reports.[144] Unlike eye tracking devices which automatically collect data about where a subject looks, eyes on screen requires a human to review the video in order to determine when, how often, and how long the subjects' eyes are on the TV screen.[145] More about that under the "Observations" section.

## Web Tracking

Another instrument similar to eye tracking is web tracking, which records a subject's every click and the time spent on various parts of websites. Web tracking or monitoring software has been used in various social science disciplines, including with online news use,[146] website design,[147] and political information.[148] Web monitoring software allows researchers—with subjects' informed consent—to see their actual online behavior, including when, how, and where they enter websites, their navigation paths,[149] and the queries they use in searches.[150] Advantages of this type of instrument are that users are unaware they are being observed, it is not subject to lapses in memory, and it records real-world behavior in real time.[151] Data can be collected in the lab or in subjects' own natural environments. Some researchers design their own software,[152] while others use commercially available software[153] such as Camtasia,[154] and still others analyze the log files[155] or web browser histories.[156]

### Latency Response

One time-tested implicit measure that has been adopted from psychology is the latency response or reaction time instrument. This measures how quickly people respond to a question or stimulus to implicitly gauge memory, implicit attitudes, attitude accessibility, and cognitive processing.[157] It is measured in milliseconds as the length of time it takes a subject to remember something,[158] connect a stimulus to a preconceived attitude, or process new information.[159]

Latency response is well known for its use measuring attitudes about sensitive subjects, such as racial prejudice,[160] with tests such as the Implicit Associations Test (IAT).[161] These tests are designed to capture people's thoughts, attitudes, and feelings that they may be reluctant to admit, such as stereotypes.[162] They are called "implicit" because subjects are not aware of what is being measured the way they are with overt questions. The IAT, for example, shows subjects words paired with faces and asks if the word is positive or negative. Subjects who dislike certain faces, such as those of minorities, will respond significantly faster to negative words paired with them than to positive words.[163] The facial stimuli are essentially subliminal, being shown to subjects for only milliseconds, a time so short that people are not even conscious of seeing them.[164] But subconsciously, the faces of people they dislike are working to slow down their response times when the tone of the word is incongruent; that is, it takes longer to overcome a negative reaction to a disliked face and decide that the word is positive. An implicit association test is available online at Harvard's Project Implicit, https://implicit.harvard.edu/implicit/takeatest.html. Latency response also has been adapted for use in social science studies of sensitive subjects.

Another use for latency response in social science is to measure memory. For example, subjects might be shown something such as a TV show and later be shown a portion of it and asked to respond as quickly as possible to whether they saw it before or not.[165] Latency has been used as a

measure of memory in advertising effectiveness[166] and is commonly found in communication studies.[167] It is also useful for education research[168]—for example, learning from multimedia.[169]

A related way of using latency is to measure attitude accessibility, or how automatically something is retrieved from memory, with stronger and more accessible attitudes retrieved faster than weaker attitudes.[170] For example, studies of political attitudes and behavior have used latency this way.[171]

Latency is also commonly used as a measure of information or cognitive processing, with longer times indicating deliberative or central route cognitive processing and shorter times

indicating peripheral or heuristic processing.[172] For example, it took subjects longer to solve ethical dilemmas with photographs than without, which resulted in better moral judgment due to more careful cognitive processing.[173] Researchers also saw this phenomenon in a business study of faking on personnel tests by job applicants; creating fake answers took more mental processing and thus more time for subjects to think up than did answering honestly.[174] Similarly, in an information technology study where subjects evaluated web pages,[175] more attractive pages were linked to shorter response latencies. It took people less time to decide a page was attractive than to decide that it was not. This study also compared results from this implicit measure (latency) to explicit questions about web page attractiveness and found correspondence.

Also in this vein, latency has been used to assess persuasion knowledge, or how aware people are that they are being shown persuasive messages.[176] The theory explains that cognitive capacity is required to be aware of persuasion knowledge, and when capacity is low, people are less likely to be aware of it.[177] For example, when watching television that requires a lot of cognitive capacity, an indirect measure such as reaction time is more appropriate for measuring persuasion knowledge than is a direct measure such as asking explicit questions.

Latency responses can be measured as simply as with a researcher operating a stopwatch, or can require special equipment and software. For example, Meyer used in-person interviews where the researchers started a timer as soon as they had finished asking a question and then stopped the timer when the subject began answering.[178] Latency can also be measured over the telephone and in the laboratory with equipment consisting of a computer and software that delivers the stimulus, collects the response, and has a precision timer built in.[179] In laboratory settings or with survey experiments, computer software such as Inquisit,[180] SuperLab, or MediaLab[181] measures latency responses, reducing measurement error.[182] Within-subjects designs are preferable to control for individual differences, as some people simply read and respond faster than others. With between-subjects designs, scores should be standardized. Because of the potential for errors such as equipment malfunctions or subjects failing to respond, data should be cleaned.[183] Also, computer keyboards can be less accurate than special response devices.

## Secondary Reaction Tasks

**Secondary reaction task** (SRT) instruments are similar to latency response in that time between a stimulus and response is measured; however, with secondary reaction tasks, there is the addition of a "distractor" task. SRT measures attention rather than memory. In this type of study, subjects perform some task while also processing a message, effectively doing two things at one time.[184] For example, subjects may be asked to watch TV and press a button whenever they see a light flash. SRT measures cognitive processing and the limits of a person's resources to "provide clues about how much capacity is being used by the message."[185] The idea is that the increasing demands or difficulty of the first task (watching TV, reading a story, etc.) will slow down subjects' reactions to the second task (pressing a button when a tone sounds or light flashes). SRT can answer questions about attention, arousal, and involvement.[186] SRT measures the length of time in milliseconds between the time of the tone or light and when the subject presses the button. Typically, people make more mistakes on the second task or take longer to respond if the first task is more difficult or requires more effort. SRT can be important for understanding when and why people do not learn from information.

Because the measures are in milliseconds, the timing of cues must be precise and requires special equipment such as Inquisit,[187] SuperLab, or MediaLab.[188] Practice runs must be conducted to verify that the equipment works, and each subject must be familiarized with it. Multiple measures, and thus stimuli, are important to control for individual differences in baseline reaction times. For example twelve[189] to twenty[190] stimuli are typical. This also ensures against atypical messages, as discussed in the section on message variance in the last chapter. Subjects can be run a few at a time—for example, six to eight in a sitting.[191] Participants can respond on a regular computer keyboard, or with a special response pad, which may be more accurate than a keyboard. Subjects can be lost for technical reasons such as equipment failure, and for other reasons such as subjects failing to ever press the button.[192]

### Continuous Response Instruments

Self-reports of attitudes, emotions, and other sensory responses reported via questionnaire have the drawback of being measured at one moment in time. But people typically experience things continuously, with their cognitive states changing. For example, when watching a TV show, emotions can range from fear to happiness to sadness and back. Questionnaires only capture the subjects' emotions at the time they answered the question. To overcome this, researchers use **continuous response instruments** that allow subjects to report their feelings or valence of thoughts and attitudes moment by moment.[193] Continuous response devices typically consist of a handheld box with a dial corresponding to 7-point scales.[194] As the subject views the stimuli, such as a TV show, film, or advertisement, he or she can turn the dial to correspond to his or her evaluations, attitudes, emotions, or other DV. The dial hardware is connected to the TV or screen with the stimuli so that data are overlaid, showing the researcher exactly what the subject is responding to. Social science researchers use this to study PSAs,[195] facial expressions of political candidates[196] and their performance in debates,[197] and teacher effectiveness,[198] among other things.

Of particular concern with all technological instruments is calibration and decay.[199] On all such instruments, buttons may become easier to push with use, creating threats to internal validity.[200] If using more than one instrument—for example, two heart rate monitors—a check should be run on the same subject at the same time to make sure that the two devices record the same value. Researchers should check the function and settings of instruments before each subject to ensure accuracy of data collected. Research assistants should be trained in the proper use of the equipment.

## Thought Listing and Think Aloud

Finally, one last implicit measure that requires a simple instrument—a recording device—is the think-aloud protocol. It is discussed here with its twin measure, thought listing, which does not require any special instrument but is so similar that it is natural to discuss them together. These techniques measure how people think and solve problems and the changes in their thought processes with either a recording device (think aloud) or low-tech paper and pencil, or computer software such as those used for online survey experiments (thought listing).[201] Thought listing avoids the use of explicit questions by exposing subjects to some stimuli or having them do a task and then asking them to write down all the thoughts they had during that time. The think-aloud version accomplishes the same goal but involves having subjects say out loud everything that goes through their heads while they are being exposed to the stimuli or doing the task. Subjects are recorded and a researcher is there to prompt them to keep talking, saying everything that comes to mind. These techniques are used to investigate the mental processes that people go through for everything from using a website[202] or searching the Internet[203] to evaluating a game design[204] and making ethical decisions[205] to how people understand attempts to persuade them[206] or how they make sense of conflicting political information.[207]

These protocols avoid the problems associated with asking subjects to introspect and analyze their thought processes but do not get at the automatic processing that people are not consciously aware of.[208] The procedures can be used to measure the amount and type of

You just read about a journalist's investigation of domestic violence in middle-class families. Please write down all the thoughts and feelings you had while reading this, including thoughts and feelings that are not necessarily relevant to the issue. Put one thought in each box below and mark whether you felt this thought was positive, negative, or neutral.

☐ Positive
☐ Neutral
☒ Negative

> PUBLISHING A STORY W/ UNWANTED SOURCES DOESN'T GIVE IT
> THE CREDIBILITY IT NEEDS

☒ Positive
☐ Neutral
☐ Negative

> BY DOING MORE REPORTING, THE REPORTER MIGHT FIND COMFORT
> TO BE ON RECORD

☐ Positive
☒ Neutral
☐ Negative

> THE REPORTER SHOULD CONTINUE TO WORK ON STORY AND
> EMPATHIZE W/ VICTIMS

☒ Positive
☐ Neutral
☐ Negative

> A STORY ABOUT DOMESTIC VIOLENCE WITH FEWER ON'T SOURCES
> ON RECORD IS BETTER THAN A HUNDRED SOURCES W/O A
> DOCUMENTED SOURCE.

☐ Positive
☐ Neutral
☐ Negative

☐ Positive
☐ Neutral
☐ Negative

☐ Positive
☐ Neutral
☐ Negative

☐ Positive
☐ Neutral
☐ Negative

☐ Positive
☐ Neutral
☐ Negative

☐ Positive
☐ Neutral
☐ Negative

☐ Positive
☐ Neutral
☐ Negative

cognitive processing, whether someone thinks about the stimulus deeply and with effort or superficially, as well as the content and valence of their thoughts.

Thought listings are relatively easy to obtain, simply requiring subjects to write down all their thoughts. Researchers must count and code all the thoughts according to category or type of thought, which is covered next in the "Observations" section. One way to simplify that task is to ask subjects to write each discrete thought in a separate box. Asking them to also check a box that indicates whether the thought was positive, negative, or neutral can take some of the guesswork out of interpreting the data. Of course, this is also subject to bias, including subjects failing to record some thoughts to make the study go faster.

Think-alouds require more time and resources to collect but overcome the issue of subjects not actually writing down every thought they had in thought listings. Using think-alouds, subjects can only be run one at a time, one per experimenter. Subjects must first be trained, as saying everything that comes to mind is not normal. Training can be done with simple math problems or word scrambles.[209] Once subjects are comfortable saying all their thoughts out loud, the stimuli are presented and the experiment begins. A researcher is positioned near the subject but out of sight to remind the subject to keep talking whenever he or she stops. It is important that the researcher not talk directly to the subjects, answer questions, or probe how or why they made some decision; researchers should only prompt them to "keep talking," or "keep saying out loud everything that comes into your head."[210] The subjects' responses should be recorded and transcribed so that, as with thought listing, they can be analyzed using content analysis methods.

## Observations

Another common "instrument" in social science experiments are human observations—for example, when researchers watch students play and interact with others and record what they see.[211] Philip Zimbardo's prison experiment used researchers' observations of the subjects' behavior as they interacted as prisoners and guards. Stanley Milgram combined observations of his shock experiment subjects' comments and nonverbal behavior with the numerical data of how severe a shock the subjects were willing to give.

Observing is frequently thought of in the qualitative realm—for example, with participant observation or ethnography—but can be employed in experiments as well. Education is a field that commonly uses this technique, as it can be more reliable than asking children explicit questions they may not be able to answer. For example, in an experiment designed to assess the effectiveness of a physical education program on children's moral development, teachers observed children in physical education classes, during intramural sports, and at recess.[212] Teachers rated the students on ten prosocial behaviors, including arguing, complaining, teasing, sharing, breaking rules, and not taking turns.

Observations can be used as an instrument in other domains as well. For example, one famous study is Albert Bandura's Bobo doll experiment on violence and media content.[213] In this study, Bandura showed children TV shows with characters punching and throwing balls while shouting things like "pow" to a life-size blow-up clown that pops back up after being punched. After children saw the TV clip, they were put in a room with a similar doll. Researchers observed through a two-way mirror and wrote down if the children imitated any of the behaviors they saw in the TV clip. In this study, none of the observers knew which children were in which treatment condition—that is, this was a double-blind study.[214] In other disciplines, observations can be used in experiments on disruptive classroom behavior, time students spend on a task, nurses' hand-washing behaviors,[215] and facial expressions,[216] among others. Experimental economics is another field that prefers observing behavior—for example, whether subjects choose a competitive or piece-rate payment for paid tasks.[217]

## Interobserver Reliability

Whenever human observers are used to rate, score, judge, or code something, including data measured with instruments such as eyes on screen, thought listing, and think-alouds, reliability should be assessed to ensure that the humans doing the rating are measuring things the same way. For example, if one observer judges a child's statement as "teasing," then others should also count it as teasing, not as "arguing." This was first discussed in chapter 5 on validity and reliability. Typically, these interobserver reliability checks should involve two or more observers judging the same facial expression, behavior, thought, or other behavior independently, and then a calculation of agreement performed. For example, in one health communication study, observers recorded the time it took for subjects to start CPR; the observations of time were calculated for agreement by the different observers.[218] Training sessions using data not included in the actual experiment may be necessary in order to achieve acceptable levels, usually around .80.[219] (For more about interobserver reliability, see More About box 10.3.) As with technological instruments, human instruments can change over time as well—for example, by getting better at coding things accurately—and need to be checked periodically through the process.[220] There are many good guides to conducting interobserver reliability, which uses the same approach as intercoder reliability in the content analysis method. There are several recommendations in the "Suggested Readings" section.

Related to training judges or coders is the issue of training research assistants who may be administering the experiment. Subjects must believe the experimental stimuli and even the situation are real, that the study is important, and find it at least somewhat interesting for good results to be obtained. Research assistants who administer the study or act as confederates—that is, they are pretending to be real subjects à la Milgram's shock study learner—must be trained to play the role, doing more acting than reading a script.[222]

# MORE ABOUT . . . BOX 10.3
## Interobserver Reliability

There are different statistical tools used to analyze interobserver reliability based on whether the measure is nominal, ordinal, interval, or ratio. For example, smiles can be coded as dichotomous (smiling or not smiling) or on a scale, for example 1 = frowning, 7 = smiling, 5 = neutral mouth expression, and the points in between as intermediate levels. When the measure is nominal, Scott's Pi or Cohen's Kappa are appropriate statistical tests of agreement. These calculations take into account the probability of two judges agreeing by chance rather than because they actually are interpreting things the same way. It is considered superior to Holsti's formula, which is a straight percentage of agreement that does not factor in chance. For experiments with ratio or interval level data, such as 1- to 5-point scales, Krippendorf's Alpha and Fleiss' Kappa can be used. These also allow for more than two judges.

Typical is 80% (.80) or higher agreement, although 70% (.70) is sometimes acceptable.[221]

Free online calculators for interobserver reliability exist, such as

- ReCal2, GraphPad QuickCalcs, and VassarStats for two coders (http://dfreelon.org/utils/recalfront/recal2/ and https://www.graphpad.com/quickcalcs/kappa1.cfm; http://vassarstats.net/kappa.html);

- ReCal3 for three coders (http://dfreelon.org/utils/recalfront/recal3/); and

- ReCal OIR, which calculates Krippendorf's Alpha for any number of coders (http://dfreelon.org/utils/recalfront/recal-oir/).

Others are also available. Simply search online for interobserver, interrater, or intercoder reliability calculators. In addition, there are software packages that can be purchased, including Excel, Simstat, and SPSS, which calculates Cohen's Kappa. For an overview, see http://matthewlombard.com/reliability/.

| Test Name | Number of Observers | Corrects for chance? | Level of data |
|---|---|---|---|
| Holsti's formula | 2 | No; calculates a straight percentage | Nominal |
| Scott's Pi | 2 | Yes | Nominal |
| Cohen's Kappa | 2 | Yes | Nominal |
| Fleiss' Kappa | 2 or more | Yes | Nominal |
| Krippendorf's Alpha | 2 or more | Yes | All levels |

### Other Unobtrusive Instruments

There are many other unobtrusive instruments colloquially termed *oddball measures*.[223] For example, going to auto repair shops to see what channels radios are tuned to is an unobtrusive way to assess people's favorite radio stations. One of the more ingenious non-reactive instruments to measure attitudes is the "lost letter" technique.[224] In one classic study, stamped letters addressed to different religious groups and organizations such as Christian churches, mosques, and synagogues were scattered about a neighborhood. The address was actually a researcher's post office box, and the number of letters good Samaritans returned to a particular religious group was the measure of prejudice by people in the neighborhood. Most of these creative measures have fallen out of favor, but new approaches are taking their place. For examples such as list experiments and real effort tasks, see Study Spotlight box 10.4 for details.

### Unobtrusive Questions

While this section has concentrated on nonreactive instruments other than questionnaires, it is also possible to construct questions that are unobtrusive, in the sense that subjects are unable (or less likely) to alter their responses to be socially desirable or give answers they think support the hypotheses (or refute them). The Defining Issues Test used to measure moral judgment uses such a questionnaire.[239] While subjects are aware that the study is about making ethical decisions, they are told there are no "right" answers and that the researcher is interested in what issues were most important in making the decision. The ethical dilemmas presented to subjects are written so that either course of action could be defended as ethical. Yet researchers are still able to gauge how high or low a person's moral judgment is because the twelve statements that subjects rate on a scale of importance are written to represent the six stages of moral judgment.[240] Choosing higher-staged statements results in a higher score than choosing lower-stage statements. Unless subjects are familiar with Kohlberg's theory, they are unlikely to be able to choose high-stage statements unless they have developed to that level. In fact, the instrument also includes a way for researchers to detect if subjects are trying to fake a higher score.[241] When subjects are unable to purposely alter their responses to questions, they are considered unobtrusive.

## MEASUREMENT ISSUES

Measurement is another topic that is covered in greater depth in many books, textbooks, and articles, so this text does not attempt to address everything. Rather, topics of particular importance to experiments are touched on here.

## STUDY SPOTLIGHT 10.4
### Unobtrusive Instruments—List, Choice, and Real Effort Task Experiments

Experimentalists do not necessarily have to avoid using questionnaires in order for an instrument to be unobtrusive. Several methods have been developed that still use questionnaires but avoid asking questions directly, increasing truthful answers and avoiding nonresponses.[225] Among them are three popular with political scientists but adaptable to any social science field. In fact, the two choice-experiment studies described here come from marketing and food policy. This spotlight focuses on three types of unobtrusive instruments—the list experiment, choice experiment, and the real effort task—but there are others, such as the endorsement experiment. It should also be noted that these instruments can be used for surveys as well as experiments.

### List Experiment

Kramon[226] demonstrated how a list experiment can be more externally valid in that it is more reflective of reality when the topic was the sensitive issue of vote buying. The strength of the list experiment is that it avoids the social desirability bias that can encourage participants to give socially acceptable answers rather than truthful ones. It does this by giving subjects a list of activities that are both sensitive and not sensitive, such as taking a bribe in exchange for their vote, or having seen political signs in their neighborhoods. Subjects are specifically told *not* to identify which particular items are true for them but to simply indicate *how many* items are true for them. This assumes subjects are more truthful when asked to give a number rather than answer questions directly. The control group receives only nonsensitive items, while the treatment group receives the same items as the control group but with the addition of sensitive items. The difference between group means gives the estimate of the existence of sensitive attitudes or behaviors.[227] Kramon's results showed significantly more reports of vote buying in the experiment than on surveys, which aligned with actual instances of vote buying.

Read the study at:

**Kramon, Eric. 2016. "Where Is Vote Buying Effective? Evidence From a List Experiment in Kenya."** *Electoral Studies* 44: 397–408. 10.1016/j.electstud.2016.09.006

### Choice Experiment

In choice experiments, subjects make decisions based on trade-offs and preferences—for example, between job offers with trade-offs between salary and benefits,[228] or other types of consumer decisions including willingness to pay for certain attributes. Subjects make choices based on the characteristics of the different products or services offered, and researchers then use those to infer values the subjects hold—for example, if a higher salary is more important than a pension.

Subjects are asked to choose between alternatives rather than to rank or rate them.[229] This avoids the social desirability bias by not asking subjects what they prefer directly, but by observing the attributes of the things they choose over those they do not. For example, in a study of recycling, respondents may

*(Continued)*

(Continued)

self-report that they will recycle even if the packaging requires cleaning, but in a choice experiment they may actually only choose packages that do not need cleaning. That is what happened in a choice experiment that had subjects choose between two types of sandwich containers.[230] The trade-offs included how much cleaning the packages needed before recycling, how many parts it had to be separated into (paper or plastic, or both), and how long it would take to recycle. Subjects were more likely to recycle when a package had to be separated than when it had to be cleaned or took more time to recycle.

Another choice experiment on food policy found that subjects valued labels certifying the safety of beef over the country the beef came from, tenderness, or the ability to trace where food-borne diseases came from.[231] Subjects were asked to choose between two types of rib-eye steaks that came with labels indicating different prices per pound, food safety inspections, country of origin, if tenderness was guaranteed, and if it was traceable to the farm of origin.

Experts recommend choice experiments limit the number of attributes in a choice to six so as not to overwhelm subjects and make it harder for them to decide.[232] The food safety study used five attributes, for example.[233] It is also recommended that researchers use between twenty-five and ninety choice sets or scenarios in order to estimate main effects and two-way interactions.[234] The recycling study used twenty different choice scenarios, with each subject evaluating five.[235] A no-choice option is also recommended for these types of experiments because that is a realistic element that is commonly available in settings such as consumer decisions.[236]

Read these two studies at:

Klaiman, K., D. L. Ortega, and C. Garnache. 2017. "Perceived Barriers to Food Packaging Recycling: Evidence From a Choice Experiment of US Consumers." *Food Control 73*, 291–299.

Loureiro, M. L., and W. J. Umberger. 2007. "A Choice Experiment Model for Beef: What U.S. Consumer Responses Tell Us About Relative Preferences for Food Safety, Country-of-Origin Labeling and Traceability." *Food Policy 34* (4): 496–514.

## Real Effort Task

Another instrument that helps overcome demand effects of a laboratory setting where subjects might behave differently because researchers are watching is a real effort task experiment. In one study, researchers sought to learn the optimal frequency of reminders to increase charitable giving but wanted to avoid having subjects in a lab experiment give more to charity than they actually would if they were not being observed.[237] The study, conducted across three months, paid subjects for performing a task where they counted the 1s in a 5 x 5 matrix and received payment for correct answers in an online account. The researchers sent subjects reminders to check their online balances and told them they had the opportunity to donate to a charity via their online account. The online web portal linked to the charity's website so subjects could find out more about it. The treatment conditions were three reminder intervals: none, weekly, or monthly. The monthly reminders worked the best, and money donated was actually given to the charity.

Read this study at:

Sonntag, A., and D. J. Zizzo. 2015. "On Reminder Effects, Drop-Outs and Dominance: Evidence From an Online Experiment on Charitable Giving." *PLoS ONE* 10 (8): 1–17.

---

### A Validation Study

Another study is of special interest for this spotlight because it tested three unobtrusive methods against direct questions to determine the strengths and weaknesses of each.[238] It found that all three unobtrusive instruments—list experiments, choice experiments, and the randomized response method—were better than direct questions on sensitive issues for reducing nonresponse and providing results closer to actual behavior—in this study, votes. It found the randomized response technique performed the best but was harder for subjects to do unless they were given a practice question. All three unobtrusive instruments were significantly better than direct questions at avoiding the social desirability bias and nonresponse. Drawbacks of list experiments included ceiling and floor effects. This study also provides details on how to construct these three types of instruments.

Read this study at:

**Rosenfeld, B., K. Imai, and J. N. Shapiro. 2016. "An Empirical Validation Study of Popular Survey Methodologies for Sensitive Questions."** *American Journal of Political Science* 60 (3): 783–802

---

## Levels of Measure

No matter how data are collected, variables must be measured appropriately for an experiment. In the case of experiments where a test of differences such as a *t* test or analysis of variance are to be used to analyze data, the dependent variable must be measured continuously—that is, at the interval or ratio level—and the independent variables must be categorical. As the independent variable is typically the treatment and control groups, this is less of an issue than how the dependent variable is measured. Intervening variables can be measured either continuously or categorically; I typically recommend continuous measures for these as well. One reason is because continuous measures can be collapsed into categories and used as independent variables; for example, in one study, involvement was used as both an intervening variable as a continuous measure and then collapsed into high, medium, and low categories and used as an independent variable to test an interaction effect.[242] While continuous variables can be turned into categorical ones, categorical variables cannot become continuous.

## Response Choices

In questionnaires, the choice of responses an experimenter gives to subjects are known as **response scales.** These choices of answers to questions range on a continuum of direction and intensity that allows researchers to assign scores to subjects. For example, a **Likert scale**[243] offers a fixed-choice response format that measures levels of agreement, frequency, importance, or likelihood—for example, Strongly

Agree (7) to Strongly Disagree (1), with the in-between points of Agree (6), Somewhat Agree (5), Neither Agree Nor Disagree (4), Somewhat Disagree, (3), and Agree (2). On a 5-point scale, the "somewhat" choices are eliminated. The wording changes to reflect the most appropriate answer to the question. For example, to "How much did you experience the following emotions," the response choices would range from Never to A Lot. As with question wording, following the lead of previous research is recommended; often, questions that have been used repeatedly and demonstrate reliability and validity will have a set response scale accompanying them. Scales are preferable to binary response options such as yes/no, true/false, or other categorical responses such as three choices of yes/no/maybe for questions about attitudes, opinions, beliefs, emotions, and other variable items. In politics especially, research has shown that scales are better at capturing people's uncertainty about their beliefs and attitudes than are dichotomous measures.[244] Categorical questions, such as one's political party, can be answered with categories, but typically, political identification is also measured with the strength of party affiliation (Would you call yourself a strong Republican/Democrat or not so strong?) and which party one feels closer to (Democrat, Republican, Neither).

At the other end of the spectrum, feeling thermometers range from 0 to 100; for example, a typical feeling thermometer from political science says, "Please rate both the candidates you read about on the thermometer below. The thermometer runs from 0 to 100 degrees. Rating above 50 means that you feel favorable and warm toward the person. Rating below 50 means that you feel unfavorable and cool toward the person."[245]

An odd number of response choices allows for a neutral point. There is debate of whether this is good or bad, and it also depends on what is being measured. For example, real attitudes may be missed with a neutral option.[246] Some questions do not need a neutral or would allow subjects with real opinions to opt out of the question. For example, "How interested are you in politics and public affairs" logically has no neutral; the four choices of very, somewhat, slightly, and not at all interested covers all bases.

Measuring things the same way as much as possible is also recommended so that they can be indexed more easily. More about indexing follows.

## Ceiling and Floor Effects

Having enough response choices is important to avoid **ceiling effects**, which occur when a variable has not been measured highly enough and so scores bunch up at the top because subjects cannot respond any higher—for example, using income responses that top out at $100,000. Today, there are many more people with incomes of $100,000 or more than there used to be, so this is no longer high enough. This results in not enough variation in the data, which means some effects on the dependent variable may not be detected. If the means of the groups are not significantly different, it could be because of ceiling effects. This can be tested by examining the distribution for normality in the curve. A similar phenomenon is called **floor effects**, when the response choices do not go low enough. Ceiling and floor effects can occur with Likert-scale responses as well as categories; for example, one study used 5-point scales and found ceiling effects.[247] Seven-point scales may have been a better choice.

## Construct Validity

As was covered in chapter 5, validity is designed to test how much an instrument measures what it claims to measure. That chapter was devoted to the theoretical concept of validity; this section is about how to test it.

One of the benefits of using questions that have been used before is that they have likely undergone testing to ensure they measure what they claim to, which is called **construct validity**, first introduced in chapter 5. Other kinds of validity include face, convergent, and discriminant validity, and readers are referred to other texts in the "Suggested Readings" section for more about those. Construct validity ensures that the variable represents the theoretical ideas or concepts behind it—for example, "personality," "happiness," or "depression." A test must measure what it claims to, not something similar. Construct validity is measured by expert assessment of the degree to which the instrument measures the construct, or by comparison to other instruments that measure the same or similar constructs.

Construct validity can be assessed with statistical methods that show whether there is a common factor underlying the individual items that make up the composite index or combination of several questions. To form an index, questions measured with the same response set are usually summed and averaged, or divided by the total number of questions. Before constructing the index, however, it is necessary to determine that all the questions "hang together" or are related to each other and represent the same concept. A simple way of looking at it is if the multiple questions designed to measure one concept are correlated with each other. Correlation coefficients are rarely used to determine this, however; instead, special statistics that are used to determine validity include factor analysis, among others. Cronbach's alpha is a measure of the correlation of two tests of the same construct and is used as an internal consistency estimate of reliability. These statistical tools have the advantage of helping improve the strength of an index by identifying items that should not be included.

## HOW TO DO IT 10.5

### Writing Up the Instrument and Measurement Sections

After the description of the stimuli (chapter 9), the methods section contains details about the instrument and measurements, and the procedures used to carry them out. All measurements for dependent variables, covariates, mediators, and moderators should give exact wording for questionnaires. Demographics are not usually given in this much detail; some articles will specify the demographics by name (e.g., age, education, gender), while others will just say "the usual demographics." If there are very many variables to operationalize, examples can be given in the text with the complete questionnaire in an appendix.[248] The response choices also should be provided—the first time in detail, and then other measures can give a briefer version. For example, that the response scale is a 5-point Likert scale ranging from strongly disagree (1) to strongly agree (5) should be explained the first time it is described, but can be more concisely explained as "the same 5-point scales" or with the endpoints in parentheses (e.g., 1 = never, 5 = all the time) on future references.

Cronbach's alpha or factor analyses for indexes and explanations of how they were formed must also be reported. Some journals use symbols, while others spell out statistical tests (e.g., Cronbach's alpha vs. the symbol $\alpha$). Some journals include this in the methods section, and others put it in results; follow the style of the journal to which the paper is being submitted. The reporting of instruments and measures should be comprehensive enough that other researchers could replicate a study without having to contact the authors. Here are some examples of how authors have written about their instruments and measures. Only some of the more common social science instruments are included here; for others, see any of the studies cited in this chapter.

### Example 1: Questionnaire

*This experiment used a questionnaire, with the instrument items and indices' statistics in the text. Notice also how the response choices are given.*

"Assessment of the current climate of opinion. We measured the participants' perceptions of the current climate of opinion using two items ("At the moment, the majority of Cologne's citizens are against the extension" [CC 1, current climate of opinion 1] and "Right now Cologne's citizens do not want an extension of the express line" [CC 2, current climate of opinion 2]). Participants could answer on a five-point Likert-type scale ranging from 1 (I don't agree at all) to 5 (I totally agree). Both items made up a scale measuring participants' perception of disagreement within the population (Spearman-Brown coefficient = .70, M = 3.75, SD = 1.21)."[249]

**From: Zerback, T., T. Koch, and B. Kramer. 2015. "Thinking of Others: Effects of Implicit and Explicit Media Cues on Climate of Opinion Perceptions."** *Journalism and Mass Communication Quarterly* **92 (2): 421–443.**

### Example 2: Questionnaire

*This experiment also used a questionnaire, with a feeling thermometer and two other measures, with the exact wording in an appendix. It gives the reliability statistics of the index in parentheses.*

"The candidate evaluation index consisted of nine variables: a feeling thermometer, six trait evaluations, and two agree-disagree statements about McKenna's suitability for office.[6] Evaluations of McKenna formed a highly reliable index ($\alpha$. = 924)."[250]

SAGE Journal Article
study.sagepub.com
coleman

From: Thorson, Emily. 2016. "Belief Echoes: The Persistent Effects of Corrected Misinformation." *Political Communication* 33 (3): 460–480.

## Example 3: Construct Validity

*This experiment reported more details from factor analysis and Cronbach's alpha within the text.*

"To ensure construct, convergent, and discriminant validity (Perdue and Summers 1986), we conducted a confirmatory factor analysis. The items of each factor loaded only on that factor. We estimated Cronbach's (1951) alpha values to measure the reliability of any group of indicators that formed one factor. The values of all but one construct were greater than 0.70 (Nunnally 1978), in support of internal consistency; we also accepted the perceived self-efficacy construct, whose Cronbach's alpha was 0.61, which was greater than 0.60 (Robinson et al. 1991). Finally, to assess discriminant validity, we compared the average variance extracted with the squared correlations for all other constructs; the average variance extracted was always higher, indicating discriminant validity (Fornell and Larcker 1981; see Table 4 in Appendix). Thus the factor analyses revealed satisfactory results for all variables (Bagozzi et al. 1991; Cronbach et al. 1963; Nunnally 1978). We provide the constructs and results in Table 3 in the Appendix."[251]

From: Thaler, Julia, and Bernd Helmig. 2013. "Promoting Good Behavior: Does Social and Temporal Framing Make a Difference?" *Voluntas: International Journal of Voluntary and Nonprofit Organizations* 24 (4): 1006–1036.

## Example 4: Eye Tracking

*For technological instruments, the description of the instrument and procedure can be longer than for questionnaires. Here is an example of an eye-tracking study.*

"The study was conducted in individual sessions. Participants were verbally informed that the study was about visual perception. Further instructions were given on a computer screen. The instruction stated that the participants would see several pictures, and that their task would be to rate the pictures. The instructions also explained the process of the experiment to the participants: that (a) they would see a cross in the middle of the screen, (b) the cross disappears when they look at it, (c) the picture is presented for a few seconds, and (d) they would be asked for their rating.

"The presentation screen was a 22-inch monitor with a resolution of 1680 x 1050 pixels and a refresh rate of 60 Hz. Participants were seated approximately 60 cm away from the monitor. Lighting was kept constant and the participants wore headphones to control for background noises. The grey background during the task was equal to the mean luminosity of the pictures (RGB: 127,127,127).

"The experiment consisted of 40 trials. Each trial started with a fixation cross in the location where the pictures were later presented. After participants had fixated on the cross for 1,500 ms, a blank screen was presented for 500 ms. Then, one of the 40 pictures from the four categories (neutral and positive non-shopping situations, hedonic and utilitarian shopping situations) was presented on the screen for 4,000 ms. The order of the pictures was fully randomized. During the picture presentation, we assessed pupil diameter using an SMI RED 500 remote eye-tracker (Sensomotoric Instruments GmbH, Teltow, Germany) with a sampling rate of 250 Hz. After the

*(Continued)*

(Continued)

presentation of each picture, the participants rated how much they liked the picture (1= not at all, 7 = very much) and how positively they perceived the scene presented in the picture (i.e., valence; 1= negative, 7= positive).

"After the 40 trials, the participants answered a questionnaire that contained questions on demographics and the buying impulsiveness scale (BIS $\alpha$ =.83) from Rook and Fisher [1]. The BIS consists of nine items, such as 'I often buy things spontaneously.' Participants indicated on a five-point rating scale how much they agreed with each statement (1= strongly disagree, 5 = strongly agree). The authors of the BIS propose that buying impulsiveness represents a continuum; thus, the BIS does not have a cut-off point, but uses the scale score as a continuous measure of buying impulsiveness (possible range: 9–45, observed range: 9–36, M=18.3, SD=6.1)."[i]

**From: Serfas, B. G., O. B. Büttner, and A. Florack. 2014. "Eyes Wide Shopped: Shopping Situations Trigger Arousal in Impulsive Buyers." *PLoS ONE* 9 (12): 1–9.**

## Example 5: Latency Response

*When psychological or physiological instruments are used, there are not typically questions that must be operationalized. In this example of a study that uses latency response, the procedure and how the instrument records the measures are described instead.*

"Dependent Measure: Response Latencies. The recorded response time for participants in the lexical decision task was a measure of implicit stereotype activation. Participants received the target stimulus, which was either a word (e.g., *smart*) or a non-word (e.g., *tinpy*). All non-words had lengths matching words. Participants had to decide as quickly and accurately as possible whether the target stimulus was a word or non-word by using the appropriate response keys on the computer keyboard. The first round in this task was a practice session where participants received feedback on their performances. Here, 24 target stimuli (words or non-words) appeared in quick succession in random order. An exclamation point preceded each target stimulus for 300 milliseconds. Twelve of these stimuli were neutral words (e.g., *after, complete, more*) unrelated to stereotypes. The remaining stimuli were non-words of equal length.

"Once the practice round ended, 72 target stimuli appeared in a random order. Of these, 16 stimuli were stereotypical words (e.g., *lazy, spiritual, poor*) based on pre-tests. The remaining 48 stimuli equally presented neutral words (e.g., *lady, delicious, pour*) and non-words (e.g., *linr, foigpnafe, pkid*) of length equal to the stereotypical words. Of the stereotypical words, some related to benevolent stereotypes (e.g., *traditional, polite*) and some related to hostile stereotypes (e.g., *lazy, uneducated*). An output file for each participant recorded the speed of response to each stimulus in milliseconds."[252]

**From: Ramasubramanian, Srividya. 2007. "Media-Based Strategies to Reduce Racial Stereotypes Activated by News Stories." *Journalism and Mass Communication Quarterly* 84 (2): 249–264.**

---

[i]There are other types of scales, including Semantic Differential, Thurstone, and Guttman scales.

## Example 6: Think Aloud and Thought Listing

*As with the other unobtrusive measures, a think-aloud or thought-listing instrument describes the instructions subjects are given and procedures they follow. For example:*

"Participants were then given four search tasks to complete using search engines, while following a think aloud protocol. Although they were not instructed about what search engine to use, they all selected Google's general search engine, which is popular in Iran. They were briefed about the think aloud technique (i.e. to think aloud about their decisions, actions, emotions and thoughts). The search tasks are presented below. These tasks were purposefully designed to result in some hits in search engine results that were filtered by the government so when participants clicked on some of the links they could not access the pages and were redirected to the peyvandha.ir, which indicated that the page had been blocked by the government.

"Search tasks

"Suppose for one of your course assignments or due to your personal interests you need information on the items listed below. Please open a browser and use search engines to find relevant information on the topics. Think aloud about your actions, decision, emotions and thoughts while doing the tasks:

1. You need information on the biography, beliefs and a sample of works by Mr. Shojaeddin Shafa;

2. You need some information on the thoughts and opinions of Mr. Mehdi Jami, journalist, blogger and contemporary researcher and a sample of his works;

3. You need to find the lyrics of a song named "Stay with me" from Akcent band; and

4. Find a brief history or account of socialism in Iran."[253]

**From: Jamali, H. R., and P. Shahbaztabar. 2017. "The Effects of Internet Filtering on Users' Information-Seeking Behaviour and Emotions."** *Aslib Journal of Information Management* **69 (4): 408–425.**

Regardless of whether one is creating new questions to form an index or using one from previous research, experiments are expected to validate all indexes used in the study and report it in either the methods or results sections (see How To Do It box 10.5). A pilot study—one topic in the next chapter—is a good way to test out a new construct and its index before using it in an actual experiment. The next chapter also addresses getting approval from an IRB, which is a necessary step before collecting data from any subjects. Another important topic that connects with this chapter, especially the section on unobtrusive instruments, is obtaining subjects' informed consent, protecting them from harm, and other ethical considerations concerning experiments.

## Common Mistakes

- Using self-reports when unobtrusive instruments are better suited

- Using technological instruments without proper theoretical understanding or methodological training

- Using single questions to represent complex theoretical constructs; multiple items combined in an index should be used instead.

- Using new questions created by the researcher when validated items and indexes already exist

## Test Your Knowledge

1. In most cases, indexes of several questions _____.
   a. Are no better than single-item indicators
   b. Are superior for measuring multilevel constructs
   c. Help shorten a study
   d. Have more issues with reliability and validity

2. Single-item indicators are _____.
   a. Devices that subjects use to indicate their response
   b. Questions that are worded directly
   c. Multiple questions combined to measure a single item
   d. Inferior for measuring multilevel constructs

3. Advantages of questionnaires are that they _____.
   a. Are fast, cheap, and easy
   b. Can be private
   c. Reduce demand effects
   d. All of these

4. Disadvantages of questionnaires are _____.
   a. Self-reports can be inaccurate
   b. They can be subject to the social desirability bias
   c. They are not good for things people may not be able to introspect about
   d. All of these

5.  Functional magnetic resonance imaging, or fMRI, is a noninvasive brain scanner that is used to _____.

    a.  Measure how fast subjects can answer questions

    b.  Detect when a subject is lying

    c.  Identify areas of the brain associated with certain mental processes such as trusting or emotions

    d.  Measure how long a subject spends on a web page

6.  When researchers watch students play and interact with others and record what they see, which instrument are they using?

    a.  Latency response

    b.  Questionnaire

    c.  Observation

    d.  Eyes on screen

7.  In a study where teachers rate students on behaviors, including arguing, complaining, teasing, sharing, breaking rules, and not taking turns, what ensures they are rating them the same way?

    a.  Manipulation checks

    b.  Interobserver reliability

    c.  Cronbach's alpha

    d.  Factor analysis

8.  In an experiment, the independent variable is measured at which level?

    a.  Categorical

    b.  Interval

    c.  Ratio

    d.  Continuous

9.  At which level must the DV be measured in a typical experiment?

    a.  Categorical

    b.  Continuous

    c.  Nominal

    d.  Ordinal

10. At which level must covariates be measured?

    a.  Nominal

    b.  Ordinal

c. Interval

d. Any of these

**Answers**

| | | | | | | | |
|---|---|---|---|---|---|---|---|
| 1. b | | 4. d | | 7. b | | 9. b |
| 2. d | | 5. c | | 8. a | | 10. d |
| 3. d | | 6. c | | | | |

# Application Exercises

1. Read any two experimental journal articles of your choice and then analyze and critique their methods sections. Identify the items from this chapter including the instruments used and procedures. For example, what are the response choices? Which constructs use indexes and which use single-item indicators? Where in the article is exact question wording reported—in the methods text, a footnote, appendix, or online? How does the study address reactivity or demand characteristics and other biases, such as social desirability, misunderstanding, and inability to introspect, associated with the instrument used? Is there enough information for you to replicate it? Is one article's methods section better written than the other? If so, why? The purpose of this assignment is to think critically about methods sections so you can do your own.

2. For the study you are working on in this book, devise an instrument and measures appropriate to test your hypotheses or research questions. Write three pages describing the instrument, including appropriate levels of measurement and response choices. Discuss how you will verify the validity of the constructs. If your main instrument is a questionnaire, write briefly about an unobtrusive instrument that could also be used in your study.

# Suggested Readings

## Question Writing

Tourangeau, R. 2004. "Experimental Design Considerations for Testing and Evaluating Questionnaires." In *Methods for Testing and Evaluating Survey Questionnaires,* edited by S. Presser, J. M. Rothgeb, M. P. Couper, J. T. M. E. Lessler, J. Martin, and E. Singer, 209–224. Hoboken, NJ: Wiley.

## Single-Item Indicators

Petrescu, Maria. 2013. "Marketing Research Using Single-Item Indicators in Structural Equation Models." *Journal of Marketing Analytics* 1 (2): 99–117.

## fMRI

This paper gives guidelines on why and how to conduct fMRI studies.

Dimoka, Angelika. 2012. "How to Conduct a Functional Magnetic Resonance (fMRI) Study in Social Science Research." *MIS Quarterly* 36 (3): 811–840.

## Eye Tracking

Jankowski, Jaroslaw, Jaroslaw Watrobski, Katarzyna Witkowska, and Pawel Ziemba. 2016. "Eye Tracking Based Experimental Evaluation of the Parameters of Online Content Affecting the Web User Behavior." In *Selected Issues in Experimental Economics,* edited by K. Nermend and M. Latuszynska, 311–332. Cham, Switzerland: Springer.

## Technological Instruments

In addition to chapters on each instrument, there is a chapter on how to set up a lab for these measures.

Lang, Annie, ed. 1994. *Measuring Psychological Responses to Media*. Hillsdale, NJ: Erlbaum.

## Interobserver Reliability

For a tutorial, see:

Hallgren, K. A. 2012. "Computing Inter-Rater Reliability for Observational Data: An Overview and Tutorial." *Tutorials in Quantitative Methods for Psychology* 8 (1): 23–34.

## More on Validity

Messick, S. 1995. "Validity of Psychological Assessment: Validation of Inferences From Persons' Responses and Performances as Scientific Inquiry Into Score Meaning." *American Psychologist* 50: 741–749.

## Notes

1. Christoph Bartneck et al., "Comparing the Similarity of Responses Received from Studies in Amazon's Mechanical Turk to Studies Conducted Online and with Direct Recruitment," *PLoS ONE* 10, no. 4 (2015): 1–23.
2. Shana Kushner Gadarian and Bethany Albertson, "Anxiety, Immigration, and the Search for Information," *Political Psychology* 35, no. 2 (2014): 133–164.
3. Nick Lin-Hi, Jacob Horisch, and Igor Blumberg, "Does CSR Matter for Nonprofit Organizations? Testing the Link between CSR Performance and Trustworthiness in the Nonprofit

Versus For-Profit Domain," *Voluntas* 26 (2015): 1944–1974.

4. Julia Thaler and Bernd Helmig, "Promoting Good Behavior: Does Social and Temporal Framing Make a Difference?" *Voluntas: International Journal of Voluntary and Nonprofit Organizations* 24, no. 4 (2013): 1006–1036.

5. D. A. Dillman and C. D. Redline, "Testing Paper Self-Administered Questionnaires: Cognitive Interview and Field Test Comparisons," in *Methods for Testing and Evaluating Survey Questionnaires*, ed. S. Presser et al. (Hoboken, NJ: Wiley, 2004), 299–317; R. Tourangeau, "Experimental Design Considerations for Testing and Evaluating Questionnaires," in *Methods for Testing and Evaluating Survey Questionnaires*, ed. S. Presser et al. (Hoboken, NJ: Wiley, 2004), 209–224.

6. J. P. Wanous and M. J. Hudy, "Single-Item Reliability: A Replication and Extension," *Organizational Research Methods* 4, no. 4 (2001): 361–375.

7. J. P. Wanous and A. E. Reichers, "Estimating the Reliability of a Single-Item Measure," *Psychological Reports* 78, no. 2 (1996): 631–634.

8. C. Fuchs and A. Diamantopoulos, "Using Single-Item Measures for Construct Measurement in Management Research: Conceptual Issues and Application Guidelines," *Die Betriebswirtschaft* 69, no. 2 (2009): 195–210; Wanous and Hudy, "Single-Item Reliability."

9. Renita Coleman and Lee Wilkins, "The Moral Development of Journalists: A Comparison with Other Professions and a Model for Predicting High Quality Ethical Reasoning," *Journalism and Mass Communication Quarterly* 81, no. 3 (Autumn 2004): 511–527.

10. Ibid.

11. A. Bandura, *Self-Efficacy: The Exercise of Control* (New York: W. H. Freeman and Company, 1997); Albert Bandura, "Toward a Psychology of Human Agency," *Perspectives on Psychological Science* 1, no. 2 (2006): 164–180.

12. M. Kayhan Kurtuldu and Damla Bulut, "Development of a Self-Efficacy Scale Toward Piano Lessons," *Educational Sciences: Theory & Practice* 17, no. 3 (2017): 835–857.

13. Keiko Nanishi et al., "Determining a Cut-Off Point for Scores of the Breastfeeding Self-Efficacy Scale–Short Form: Secondary Data Analysis of an Intervention Study in Japan," *PLoS ONE* 10, no. 6 (2015): 1–12; R. C. Knibb, C. Barnes, and C. Stalker, "Parental Confidence in Managing Food Allergy: Development and Validation of the Food Allergy Self-Efficacy Scale for Parents (FASE-P)," *Clinical & Experimental Allergy* 45, no. 11 (2015): 1681–1689; Yanping Zhao et al., "Translation and Validation of a Condom Self-Efficacy Scale (CSES) Chinese Version," *AIDS Education & Prevention* 28, no. 6 (2016): 499–510; Franklin N. Glozah et al., "Assessing Alcohol Abstinence Self-Efficacy in Undergraduate Students: Psychometric Evaluation of the Alcohol Abstinence Self-Efficacy Scale," *Health & Quality of Life Outcomes* 13 (2015): 1–6.

14. Shane W. Kraus et al., "The Development and Initial Evaluation of the Pornography-Use Avoidance Self-Efficacy Scale," *Journal of Behavioral Addictions* 6, no. 3 (2017): 354–363.

15. Carole Rodon and Aline Chevalier, "Toward More Comprehensive Chinese Internet Users' Studies: Translation and Validation of the Chinese-Mandarin Version of the 8-Item Information Retrieval on the Web Self-Efficacy Scale (CH-IROWSE)," *International Journal of Human-Computer Interaction* 33, no. 10 (2017): 846–855.

16. A. Bandura, "Guide for Constructing Self-Efficacy Scales," in *Self-Efficacy Beliefs of Adolescents*, ed. Tim Urdan and Frank Pajares (Charlotte, NC: Information Age, 2006).

17. Ibid.

18. Syeda Shahida Batool, Sumaira Khursheed, and Hira Jahangir, "Academic Procrastination as a Product of Low Self-Esteem: A Mediational Role of Academic Self-Efficacy," *Pakistan Journal of Psychological Research* 32, no. 1 (Summer 2017): 195–211.

19. P. R. Pintrich and E. V. De Groot, "Motivation and Self-Regulated Learning Components of Classroom Academic Performance," *Journal of Educational Psychology* 82 (1990).

20. Batool, Khursheed, and Jahangir, "Academic Procrastination as a Product of Low Self-Esteem," 200.

21. Albert Bandura, "Much Ado Over a Faulty Conception of Perceived Self-Efficacy Grounded in Faulty Experimentation," *Journal of Social & Clinical Psychology* 26, no. 6 (2007): 641–658.

22. Bandura, "Guide for Constructing Self-Efficacy Scales," 308.

23. Martin Fishbein and Icek Ajzen, *Predicting and Changing Behavior* (New York, NY: Taylor & Francis, 2010).

24. Angela M. Lee, Renita Coleman, and Logan Molyneux, "From Thinking to Doing: Effects of Different Social Norms on Ethical Behavior in Journalism," *Journal of Media Ethics* 31, no. 2 (2016): 72–85.

25. Chang-Dae Ham, Michelle R. Nelson, and Susmita Das, "How to Measure Persuasion Knowledge," *International Journal of Advertising* 34, no. 1 (2015): 17–53.

26. Renita Coleman, Esther Thorson, and Lee Wilkins, "Testing the Impact of Public Health Framing and Rich Sourcing in Health News Stories," *Journal of Health Communication* 16, no. 9 (2011): 941–954.

27. Murray Webster and Jane Sell, *Laboratory Experiments in the Social Sciences* (Amsterdam: Elsevier, 2007).

28. Timothy Wilson, "Knowing When to Ask: Introspection and the Adaptive Unconscious," *Journal of Consciousness Studies* 10, no. 9/10 (2003): 131.

29. Rob Hoskin, "The Dangers of Self-Report," Science Brainwaves. http://www.sciencebrainwaves.com/the-dangers-of-self-report/

30. John B. McConahay, Betty B. Hardee, and Valerie Batts, "Has Racism Declined in America? It Depends on Who Is Asking and What Is Asked," *The Journal of Conflict Resolution* 25, no. 4 (1981): 563–579.

31. Cengiz Erisen, Elif Erisen, and Binnur Ozkececi-Taner, "Research Methods in Political Psychology," *Turkish Studies* 13, no. 1 (2013): 13–33.

32. A. I. Jack and A. Roepstorff, eds., *Trusting the Subject: The Use of Introspective Evidence in Cognitive Science*, 2 vols. (Exeter, UK: Imprint Academic, 2003); R. E. Nisbett and T. D. Wilson, "Telling More Than We Can Know: Verbal Reports on Mental Processes," *Psychological Review* 84 (1977): 231–259.

33. Wilson, "Knowing When to Ask."

34. Sean P. Wojcik et al., "Conservatives Report, But Liberals Display, Greater Happiness," *Science* 347, no. 6227 (2015): 1243–1246.

35. Hoskin, "The Dangers of Self-Report."

36. C. K. Madsen, "A 30-Year Follow-up Study of Actual Applied Music Practice Versus Estimated Practice," *Journal of Research in Music Education* 52 (2004): 77–88.

37. C. C. Wang and D. W. Sogin, "Self-Reported Versus Observed Classroom Activities in Elementary General Music," *Journal of Research in Music Education* 45 (1997): 444–456.

38. Renita Coleman, "The Effect of Visuals on Ethical Reasoning: What's a Photograph Worth to Journalists Making Moral Decisions?" *Journalism and Mass Communication Quarterly* 83, no. 4 (2006): 835–850.

39. Werner Bönte, Sandro Lombardo, and Diemo Urbig, "Economics Meets Psychology: Experimental and Self-Reported Measures of Individual Competitiveness," *Personality and Individual Differences* 116 (2017): 179–185.

40. Ralph Hertwig and Andreas Ortmann, "Experimental Practices in Economics: A Methodological Challenge for Psychologists?" *Behavioral and Brain Sciences* 24, no. 3 (2001): 383.

41. Emily Thorson, "Belief Echoes: The Persistent Effects of Corrected Misinformation," *Political Communication* 33, no. 3 (2016): 460–480.

42. Ibid.

43. Rebecca B. Morton and Kenneth C. Williams, *Experimental Political Science and the Study of Causality: From Nature to the Lab* (New York: Cambridge University Press, 2010).

44. Diana C. Mutz and Robin Pemantle, "Standards for Experimental Research: Encouraging a Better Understanding of Experimental Methods," *Journal of Experimental Political Science* 2, no. 2 (2016): 192–215.

45. Ibid.

46. Eugene J. Webb et al., *Unobtrusive Measures: Nonreactive Research in the Social Sciences* (Chicago: Rand McNally, 1966); Eugene J. Webb et al., *Unobtrusive Measures: Revised Edition* (Thousand Oaks, CA: Sage, 2000).

47. Immo Fritsche and Volker Linneweber, "Nonreactive (Unobtrusive) Methods," in *Handbook of Psychological Measurement—A Multimethod Perspection*, ed. M. Eid and E. Diener (Washington, DC: American Psychological Association, 2004).

48. Annie Lang, ed., *Measuring Psychological Responses to Media* (Hillsdale, NJ: Erlbaum, 1994).

49. B. F. Skinner, "Superstition in the Pigeon," *Journal of Experimental Psychology* 38 (1948): 168–172.

50. Annie Lang, "What Can the Heart Tell Us About Thinking?" in *Measuring Psychological Responses to Media*, ed. Annie Lang (Hillsdale, NJ: Erlbaum, 1994).

51. Lang, *Measuring Psychological Responses to Media*.

52. Angelika Dimoka, "How to Conduct a Functional Magnetic Resonance (fMRI) Study in Social Science Research," *MIS Quarterly* 36, no. 3 (2012): 811–840.

53. Ibid.

54. Simone Kühn, Enrique Strelow, and Jürgen Gallinat, "Multiple 'Buy Buttons' in the Brain: Forecasting Chocolate Sales at Point-of-Sale Based on Functional Brain Activation Using fMRI," *NeuroImage* 136 (2016): 122–128.

55. S. Kuhn and J. Gallinat, "The Neural Correlates of Subjective Pleasantness," *NeuroImage* 61 (2012): 289–294.

56. M. Deppe et al., "Nonlinear Responses within the Medial Prefrontal Cortex Reveal When Specific Implicit Information Influences Economic Decision Making," *Journal of NeuroImaging* 15 (2005): 171–182.

57. H. Plassmann, J. P. O'Doherty, and A. Rangel, "Appetitive and Aversive Goal Values Are Encoded in the Medial Orbitofrontal Cortex at the Time of Decision Making," *Journal of Neuroscience* 30 (2010): 10799–10808; Joshua B. Plavnick and Summer J. Ferreri, "Single-Case Experimental Designs in Educational Research: A Methodology for Causal Analyses in Teaching and Learning," *Education Psychology Review* 25 (2013): 549–569; H. Plassmann, J. O'Doherty, and A. Rangel, "Orbitofrontal Cortex Encodes Willingness to Pay in Everyday Economic Transactions," *Journal of Neuroscience* 27 (2007): 9984–9988.

58. V. Klucharev, A. Smidts, and G. Fernandez, "Brain Mechanisms of Persuasion: How 'Expert Power' Modulates Memory and Attitudes," *Social Cognitive and Affective Neuroscience* 3 (2008): 353–366.

59. Kühn, Strelow, and Gallinat, "Multiple 'Buy Buttons' in the Brain."

60. J. Kato et al., "Neural Correlates of Attitude Change Following Positive and Negative Advertisements," *Frontier in Behavioral Neuroscience* 3, no. 6 (2009).

61. N. O. Rule et al., "Voting Behavior Is Reflected in Amygdala Response Across Cultures," *Social Cognitive and Affective Neuroscience* 5 (2010): 349–355; M. I. Spezio et al., "A Neural Basis for the Effect of Candidate Appearance on Election Outcomes," *Social Cognitive and Affective Neuroscience* 3 (2008): 344–352.

62. D. Seelig et al., "Low Message Sensation Health Promotion Videos Are Better Remembered and Activate Areas of the Brain Associated with Memory Encoding," *PLoS One* 9, no. e113256 (2014).

63. Martin A. Imhof et al., "How Real-Life Health Messages Engage Our Brains: Shared Processing of Effective Anti-Alcohol Videos," *Social Cognitive and Affective Neuroscience* 12, no. 7 (2017): 1188–1196.

64. B. King-Casas et al., "Getting to Know You: Reputation and Trust in a Two-Person Economic Exchange," *Science* 308, no. 5718 (2005): 78–83.

65. Ping Huang et al., "The Difference Between Aesthetic Appreciation of Artistic and Popular Music: Evidence From an fMRI Study," *PLoS ONE* 11, no. 11 (2016): 1–14.

66. Dimoka, "How to Conduct a Functional Magnetic Resonance (fMRI) Study in Social Science Research."

67. J. C. Culham, "Functional Neuroimaging: Experimental Design and Analysis," in *Handbook of Functional Neuroimaging of Cognition*, ed. R. Cabeza and A. Kingstone (Cambridge, MA: MIT Press, 2006), 53–82; A. W. Song, S. A. Huettel, and G. McCarthy, "Functional Neuroimaging: Basic Principles of Functional MRI," in *Handbook of Functional Neuroimaging of Cognition*, ed. R. Cabeza and A. Kingstone (Cambridge, MA: MIT Press, 2006), 21–52.

68. Dimoka, "How to Conduct a Functional Magnetic Resonance (fMRI) Study in Social Science Research"

69. Ibid.

70. Ibid.

71. Ibid.

72. Ibid.

73. Ibid.

74. Ibid.

75. Lang, "What Can the Heart Tell Us About Thinking?"

76. Ibid.

77. Ibid.

78. Ibid.

79. A. Kadir ÖZer, Cemile Ekin Eremsoy, and Emel Kromer, "Physiological Measurement of the Process of Perspective Shift in the Mental Imagery of Test

Anxiety," *Electronic Journal of Social Sciences* 15, no. 58 (Summer 2016): 903–916.

80. Haruka Shoda, Mayumi Adachi, and Tomohiro Umeda, "How Live Performance Moves the Human Heart," *PLoS ONE* 11, no. 4 (2016): 1–11.

81. René A. de Wijk et al., "ANS Responses and Facial Expressions Differentiate Between the Taste of Commercial Breakfast Drinks," *PLoS ONE* 9, no. 4 (2014): 1–9.

82. Zachary Hohman et al., "A Biopsychological Model of Anti-Drug PSA Processing: Developing Effective Persuasive Messages," *Prevention Science* 18, no. 8 (2017): 1006–1016.

83. Jie Xu, "Message Sensation and Cognition Values: Factors of Competition or Integration?" *Health Communication* 30, no. 6 (2015): 589–597.

84. Himalaya Patel et al., "Receptive to Bad Reception: Jerky Motion Can Make Persuasive Messages More Effective," *Computers in Human Behavior* 32 (2014): 32–39.

85. Mareile Opwis et al., "Weird or Wired Celebrities: Effects of Celebrity Endorsers in Energy-Commercials on Psychophysiological Response Patterns," *NeuroPsychoEconomics Conference Proceedings* (2012): 54.

86. Kevin Wise, Paul D. Bolls, and Samantha R. Schaefer, "Choosing and Reading Online News: How Available Choice Affects Cognitive Processing," *Journal of Broadcasting & Electronic Media* 52, no. 1 (2008): 69–85.

87. Zheng Wang, Alyssa C. Morey, and Jatin Srivastava, "Motivated Selective Attention During Political Ad Processing: The Dynamic Interplay Between Emotional Ad Content and Candidate Evaluation," *Communication Research* 41, no. 1 (2014): 119–156.

88. Erik Bucy and Samuel D. Bradley, "Presidential Expressions and Viewer Emotion: Counterempathic Responses to Televised Leader Displays," *Social Science Information* 43, no. 1 (2004): 59–94.

89. Sandra Ononogbu et al., "Association Between Information and Communication Technology Usage and the Quality of Sleep Among School-Aged Children During a School Week," *Sleep Disorders* (2014): 1–6.

90. Robert Hopkins and James E. Fletcher, "Electrodermal Measurement: Particularly Effective for Forecasting Message Influence on Sales Appeal," in *Measuring Psychological Responses to Media*, ed. Annie Lang (Hillsdale, NJ: Erlbaum, 1994), 113–132; Marieke G. N. Bos et al., "Psychophysiological Response Patterns to Affective Film Stimuli," *PLoS ONE* 8, no. 4 (2013): 1–8; Jonathan Renshon, Jooa Julia Lee, and Dustin Tingley, "Physiological Arousal and Political Beliefs," *Political Psychology* 36, no. 5 (2015): 569–585; Xu, "Message Sensation and Cognition Values."

91. Hopkins and Fletcher, "Electrodermal Measurement."

92. Ibid.

93. Michael Bang Petersen, Ann Giessing, and Jesper Nielsen, "Physiological Responses and Partisan Bias: Beyond Self-Reported Measures of Party Identification," *PLoS ONE* 10, no. 5 (2015): 1–10.

94. Renshon, Lee, and Tingley, "Physiological Arousal and Political Beliefs."

95. Barbara Krahé et al., "Desensitization to Media Violence: Links With Habitual Media Violence Exposure, Aggressive Cognitions, and Aggressive Behavior," *Journal of Personality and Social Psychology* 100, no. 4 (2011): 630–646.

96. Andreas Gregersen et al., "Following the Viewers: Investigating Television Drama Engagement Through Skin Conductance Measurements," *Poetics* 64 (2017): 1–13.

97. Gabrielle Turner-Mcgrievy, Sri Kalyanaraman, and Marci K. Campbell, "Delivering Health Information Via Podcast or Web: Media Effects on Psychosocial and Physiological Responses," *Health Communication* 28, no. 2 (2013): 101–109; Chen-Bo Zhong and Julian House, "Hawthorne Revisited: Organizational Implications of the Physical Work Environment," *Research in Organizational Behavior* 32 (2012): 3–22.

98. Martin Reimann et al., "How We Relate to Brands: Psychological and Neurophysiological Insights Into Consumer–Brand Relationships," *Journal of Consumer Psychology (Elsevier Science)* 22, no. 1 (2012): 128–142; Peter Walla, Gerhard Brenner, and Monika Koller, "Objective Measures of Emotion Related to Brand Attitude: A New Way to Quantify Emotion-Related Aspects Relevant to Marketing," *PLoS ONE* 6, no. 11 (2011): 1–7.

99. Mohammed Al-Fudail and Harvey Mellar, "Investigating Teacher Stress When Using Technology," *Computers & Education* 51, no. 3 (2008): 1103–1110.

100. Guillaume Chanel, J. Matias Kivikangas, and Niklas Ravaja, "Physiological Compliance for Social Gaming Analysis: Cooperative Versus Competitive Play," *Interacting with Computers* 24, no. 4 (2012): 306–316.

101. Bos et al., "Psychophysiological Response Patterns"; Renshon, Lee, and Tingley, "Physiological Arousal and Political Beliefs."

102. Ibid.

103. Bos et al., "Psychophysiological Response Patterns."

104. Webster and Sell, *Laboratory Experiments in the Social Sciences.*

105. Hendrika Meischke et al., "Delivering 9-1-1 CPR Instructions to Limited English Proficient Callers: A Simulation Experiment," *Journal of Immigrant and Minority Health* 17, no. 4 (2015): 1049–1054.

106. Manuel Alonso Dos Santos et al., "The Influence of Image Valence on the Attention Paid to Charity Advertising," *Journal of Nonprofit & Public Sector Marketing* 29, no. 3 (2017): 346–363; Janet Hernández-Méndez and Francisco Muñoz-Leiva, "What Type of Online Advertising Is Most Effective for E-Tourism 2.0? An Eye Tracking Study Based on the Characteristics of Tourists," *Computers in Human Behavior* 50 (2015): 618–625; C. S. Longman, A. Lavric, and S. Monsell, "More Attention to Attention? An Eye-Tracking Investigation of Selection of Perceptual Attributes During a Task Switch," *Journal of Experimental Psychology: Learning, Memory, and Cognition* 39, no. 4 (2013): 1142–1151.

107. Zijian Harrison Gong and Erik P. Bucy, "When Style Obscures Substance: Visual Attention to Display Appropriateness in the 2012 Presidential Debates," *Communication Monographs* (2016): 1–24; Hernández-Méndez and Muñoz-Leiva, "What Type of Online Advertising."

108. Yi-Chun Lin, Tzu-Chien Liu, and John Sweller, "Improving the Frame Design of Computer Simulations for Learning: Determining the Primacy of the Isolated Elements or the Transient Information Effects," *Computers & Education* 88 (2015): 280–291.

109. Ibid.

110. Ibid.

111. Benjamin G. Serfas, Oliver B. Büttner, and Arnd Florack, "Eyes Wide Shopped: Shopping Situations Trigger Arousal in Impulsive Buyers," *PLoS ONE* 9, no. 12 (2014): 1–9.

112. Yunying Dong et al., "Eye-Movement Evidence of the Time-Course of Attentional Bias for Threatening Pictures in Test-Anxious Students," *Cognition & Emotion* 31, no. 4 (2017): 781–790; Serfas, Büttner, and Florack, "Eyes Wide Shopped."

113. Guillaume Hervet et al., "Is Banner Blindness Genuine? Eye Tracking Internet Text Advertising," *Applied Cognitive Psychology* 25, no. 5 (2011): 708–716; Yoon Min Hwang and Kun Chang Lee, "Using Eye Tracking to Explore Consumers' Visual Behavior According to Their Shopping Motivation in Mobile Environments," *CyberPsychology, Behavior and Social Networking* 20, no. 7 (2017): 442–447; Nicole S. Dahmen, "Photographic Framing in the Stem Cell Debate: Integrating Eye-Tracking Data for a New Dimension of Media Effects Research," *American Behavioral Scientist* 56, no. 2 (2012): 189–203; Nora A. McIntyre, Robert M. Klassen, and M. Tim Mainhard, "Are You Looking to Teach? Cultural, Temporal and Dynamic Insights into Expert Teacher Gaze," *Learning and Instruction* 49 (2017): 41–53; Cornelia Eva Neuert and Timo Lenzner, "Incorporating Eye Tracking Into Cognitive Interviewing to Pretest Survey Questions," *International Journal of Social Research Methodology* 19, no. 5 (2016): 501–519.

114. Marc Resnick and William Albert, "The Impact of Advertising Location and User Task on the Emergence of Banner Ad Blindness: An Eye-Tracking Study," *International Journal of Human–Computer Interaction* 30, no. 3 (2014): 206–219.

115. Gong and Bucy, "When Style Obscures Substance."

116. Alonso Dos Santos et al., "The Influence of Image Valence."

117. Ibid.

118. Olena Kaminska and Tom Foulsham, "Real-World Eye-Tracking in Face-to-Face and Web Modes," *Journal of Survey Statistics and Methodology* 2, no. 3 (2014): 343–359.

119. McIntyre, Klassen, and Mainhard, "Are You Looking to Teach?"

120. Hervet et al., "Is Banner Blindness Genuine?"

121. Hwang and Lee, "Using Eye Tracking to Explore"; Bartosz W. Wojdynski and Hyejin Bang, "Distraction Effects of Contextual Advertising on Online News Processing: An Eye-Tracking Study," *Behaviour & Information Technology* 35, no. 8 (2016): 654–664.

122. Jaroslaw Jankowski et al., "Eye Tracking Based Experimental Evaluation of the Parameters of Online Content Affecting the Web User Behaviour," in *Selected Issues in Experimental Economics*, ed. K. Nermend and M. Latuszynska (Cham, Switzerland: Springer, 2016), 311–332.

123. Hwang and Lee, "Using Eye Tracking to Explore."

124. Alonso Dos Santos et al., "The Influence of Image Valence"; Gong and Bucy, "When Style Obscures Substance"; Wojdynski and Bang, "Distraction Effects of Contextual Advertising."

125. Jankowski et al., "Eye Tracking Based Experimental Evaluation."

126. Dong et al., "Eye-Movement Evidence."

127. McIntyre, Klassen, and Mainhard, "Are You Looking to Teach?"

128. Hernández-Méndez and Muñoz-Leiva, "What Type of Online Advertising"; Hwang and Lee, "Using Eye Tracking to Explore."

129. Anastasia G. Peshkovskaya et al., "The Socialization Effect on Decision Making in the Prisoner's Dilemma Game: An Eye-Tracking Study," *PLoS ONE* 12, no. 4 (2017): 1–15.

130. Dahmen, "Photographic Framing in the Stem Cell Debate."

131. Gong and Bucy, "When Style Obscures Substance."

132. Serfas, Büttner, and Florack, "Eyes Wide Shopped."

133. Hwang and Lee, "Using Eye Tracking to Explore."

134. Alonso Dos Santos et al., "The Influence of Image Valence"; Hervet et al., "Is Banner Blindness Genuine?"; Resnick and Albert, "The Impact of Advertising Location"; Wojdynski and Bang, "Distraction Effects of Contextual Advertising."

135. Sabrina Heike Kessler and Lars Guenther, "Eyes on the Frame," *Internet Research* 27, no. 2 (2017): 303–320.

136. Jankowski et al., "Eye Tracking Based Experimental Evaluation."

137. Lin, Liu, and Sweller, "Improving the Frame Design."

138. McIntyre, Klassen, and Mainhard, "Are You Looking to Teach?"

139. Hernández-Méndez and Muñoz-Leiva, "What Type of Online Advertising."

140. Alonso Dos Santos et al., "The Influence of Image Valence."

141. Neuert and Lenzner, "Incorporating Eye Tracking Into Cognitive Interviewing"; Hervet et al., "Is Banner Blindness Genuine?"

142. Kaminska and Foulsham, "Real-World Eye-Tracking."

143. Esther Thorson, "Using Eyes on Screen as a Measure of Attention to Television," in *Measuring Psychological Responses to Media*, ed. Annie Lang (Hillsdale, NJ: Erlbaum, 1994), 65–84.

144. Ibid.

145. Ibid.

146. D. Tewksbury, "What Do Americans Really Want to Know? Tracking the Behavior of News Readers on the Internet," *Journal of Communication* 53, no. 4 (2003): 694–710; Martijn Kleppe and Marco Otte, "Analysing and Understanding News Consumption Patterns by Tracking Online User Behaviour with a Multimodal Research Design," *Digital Scholarship in the Humanities* 32 (2017): 158–170.

147. Renita Coleman et al., "Public Life and the Internet: If You Build a Better Website, Will Citizens Become Engaged?" *New Media & Society* 10, no. 2 (2008): 179–201.

148. E. Menchen-Trevino and C. Karr, "Researching Real-World Web Use with Roxy: Collecting Observational Web Data with Informed Consent," *Journal of Information Technology & Politics* 9, no. 3 (2012): 254–268; S. A. Munson, S. Y. Lee, and P. Resnick, "Encouraging Reading of Diverse Political Viewpoints with a Browser Widget," in *Proceedings of the Seventh International AAAI Conference on Weblogs and Social Media* (Cambridge, MA: AAI Press, 2013), 419–428, http://www.aaai.org/ocs/index.php/ICWSM/ICWSM13/paper/view/6119, accessed Sept. 25, 2015.

149. Kleppe and Otte, "Analysing and Understanding News Consumption Patterns."

150. P. Batista and M. Silva, "Mining Web Access Logs of an On-Line Newspaper," *Proceedings of the 2nd International Conference on Adaptive Hypermedia and Adaptive Web Based Systems*, http://xldb.di.fc.ul.pt/xldb/publications/rpec02.pdf. (2002).

151. Kleppe and Otte, "Analysing and Understanding News Consumption Patterns."

152. Ibid.; Menchen-Trevino and Karr, "Researching Real-World Web Use."

153. O. Findahl, *The Swedes and the Internet 2009* (Gavle: World Internet Institute, 2009).

154. Coleman et al., "Public Life and the Internet."

155. Batista and Silva, "Mining Web Access Logs."

156. S. Ebersole, "Uses and Gratifications of the Web Among Students," *Journal of Computer-Mediated Communication* 6, no. 1 (2000).

157. Ham, Nelson, and Das, "How to Measure Persuasion Knowledge."

158. Glen T. Cameron and David A. Frieske, "The Time Needed to Answer: Measurement of Memory Response Latency," in *Measuring Psychological Responses to Media*, ed. A. Lang (Hillsdale, NJ: Erlbaum, 1994), 149–164.

159. Marco Meyer and Harald Schoen, "Response Latencies and Attitude-Behavior Consistency in a Direct Democratic Setting: Evidence From a Subnational Referendum in Germany," *Political Psychology* 35, no. 3 (2014): 431–440.

160. Dermot Barnes-Holmes et al., "The Implicit Relational Assessment Procedure: Exploring the Impact of Private Versus Public Contexts and the Response Latency Criterion on Pro-White and Anti-Black Stereotyping Among White Irish Individuals," *Psychological Record* 60, no. 1 (Winter 2010): 57–79.

161. A. G. Greenwald, D. E. McGhee, and J. L. K. Schwartz, "Measuring Individual Differences in Implicit Cognition: The Implicit Association Test," *Journal of Personality and Social Psychology* 74, no. 6 (1998): 1464–1480.

162. A. G. Greenwald et al., "Understanding and Using the Implicit Association Test: III. Meta-Analysis of Predictive Validity," *Journal of Personality and Social Psychology* 97 (2009): 17–41.

163. Erisen, Erisen, and Ozkececi-Taner, "Research Methods in Political Psychology."

164. Ibid.

165. Cameron and Frieske, "The Time Needed to Answer."

166. W. Jeffrey Burroughs and Richard A. Feinberg, "Using Response Latency to Assess Spokesperson Effectiveness," *Journal of Consumer Research* 14, no. 2 (1987): 295–299.

167. Cheryl Bracken, Gary Pettey, and Mu Wu, "Revisiting the Use of Secondary Task Reaction Time Measures in Telepresence Research: Exploring the Role of Immersion and Attention," *AI & Society* 29, no. 4 (2014): 533–538; Justin Robert Keene and Annie Lang, "Dynamic Motivated Processing of Emotional Trajectories in Public Service Announcements," *Communication Monographs* 83, no. 4 (2016): 468–485; Glenn Leshner et al., "When a Fear Appeal Isn't Just a Fear Appeal: The Effects of Graphic Anti-Tobacco Messages," *Journal of Broadcasting & Electronic Media* 54, no. 3 (2010): 485–507.

168. Thierry Olive et al., "Children's Cognitive Effort and Fluency in Writing: Effects of Genre and of Handwriting Automatisation," *Learning and Instruction* 19, no. 4 (2009): 299–308.

169. Cornelia Schoor, Maria Bannert, and Roland Brünken, "Role of Dual Task Design When Measuring Cognitive Load During Multimedia Learning," *Educational Technology Research and Development* 60, no. 5 (2012): 753–768.

170. Meyer and Schoen, "Response Latencies and Attitude-Behavior Consistency."

171. Ibid.

172. Ibid.

173. Coleman, "The Effect of Visuals on Ethical Reasoning."

174. Saul Fine and Merav Pirak, "Faking Fast and Slow: Within-Person Response Time Latencies for Measuring Faking in Personnel Testing," *Journal of Business and Psychology* 31, no. 1 (2016): 51–64.

175. Noam Tractinsky et al., "Evaluating the Consistency of Immediate Aesthetic Perceptions of Web Pages," *International Journal of Human-Computer Studies* 64, no. 11 (2006): 1071–1083.

176. Ham, Nelson, and Das, "How to Measure Persuasion Knowledge."

177. Ibid.

178. Meyer and Schoen, "Response Latencies and Attitude-Behavior Consistency."

179. Cameron and Frieske, "The Time Needed to Answer."

180. Fine and Pirak, "Faking Fast and Slow."

181. Glenn Leshner, Paul D. Bolls, and Erika Thomas, "Scare 'Em or Disgust 'Em: The Effects of Graphic Health Promotion Messages," *Health Communication* 24 (2009).

182. Cameron and Frieske, "The Time Needed to Answer."

183. Ibid.

184. M. D. Basil, "Secondary Reaction-Time Measures," in *Measuring Psychological Responses to Media*, ed. A. Lang (Hillsdale, NJ: Erlbaum, 1994), 85–98.

185. Ibid., 85.

186. Ibid.

187. Bracken, Pettey, and Wu, "Revisiting the Use of Secondary Task Reaction."

188. Leshner, Bolls, and Thomas, "Scare 'Em or Disgust 'Em."

189. Bracken, Pettey, and Wu, "Revisiting the Use of Secondary Task Reaction."

190. Keene and Lang, "Dynamic Motivated Processing of Emotional Trajectories."

191. Ibid.; Schoor, Bannert, and Brünken, "Role of Dual Task Design."

192. Bracken, Pettey, and Wu, "Revisiting the Use of Secondary Task Reaction."

193. Gong and Bucy, "When Style Obscures Substance"; Frank Biocca, Prabu David, and Mark West, "Continuous Response Measurement (CRM): A Computerized Tool for Research on the Cognitive Processing of Communication Messages," in *Measuring Psychological Responses to Media*, ed. A. Lang (Hillsdale, NJ: Erlbaum, 1994), 15–64.

194. Ibid.

195. Keene and Lang, "Dynamic Motivated Processing of Emotional Trajectories."

196. Gong and Bucy, "When Style Obscures Substance."

197. Jeremy Saks et al., "Dialed In: Continuous Response Measures in Televised Political Debates and Their Effect on Viewers," *Journal of Broadcasting & Electronic Media* 60, no. 2 (2016): 231–247.

198. Jason M. Silveira, "The Perception of Pacing in a Music Appreciation Class and Its Relationship to Teacher Effectiveness and Teacher Intensity," *Journal of Research in Music Education* 62, no. 3 (2014): 302–318.

199. D. T. Campbell and J. C. Stanley, *Experimental and Quasi-Experimental Designs for Research* (Chicago: Rand McNally, 1963).

200. William R. Shadish, Thomas D. Cook, and Donald T. Campbell, *Experimental and Quasi-Experimental Designs for Generalized Causal Inference* (Belmont, CA: Wadsworth Cengage Learning, 2002).

201. M. A. Shapiro, "Think-Aloud and Thought-List Procedures in Investigating Mental Processes," in *Measuring Psychological Responses to Media Messages*, ed. Annie Lang (Hillsdale, NJ: Lawrence Erlbaum Associates, 1994), 1–14.

202. Coleman et al., "Public Life and the Internet."

203. Hamid R. Jamali and Pria Shahbaztabar, "The Effects of Internet Filtering on Users' Information-Seeking Behaviour and Emotions," *Aslib Journal of Information Management* 69, no. 4 (2017): 408–425; Pengyi Zhang and Dagobert Soergel, "Process Patterns and Conceptual Changes in Knowledge Representations During Information Seeking and Sensemaking: A Qualitative User Study," *Journal of Information Science* 42, no. 1 (2016): 59–78.

204. Heather Desurvire and Magy Seif El-Nasr, "Methods for Game User Research: Studying Player Behavior to Enhance Game Design," *IEEE Computer Graphics and Applications* 33, no. 4 (2013): 82–87.

205. Coleman, "The Effect of Visuals on Ethical Reasoning"; Carter Gibson et al., "A Qualitative Analysis of Power Differentials in Ethical Situations in Academia," *Ethics & Behavior* 24, no. 4 (2014): 311–325.

206. Ham, Nelson, and Das, "How to Measure Persuasion Knowledge"; Robert C. Sinclair, Tanya K. Lovsin, and Sean E. Moore, "Mood State, Issue Involvement, and Argument Strength on Responses to Persuasive Appeals," *Psychological Reports* 101, no. 3 (2007): 739–753.

207. Jeffrey L. Bernstein, "What Think-Aloud Protocols Can Teach Us About How People Manage Political Information." Conference presentation at the American Political Science Association Teaching and Learning Conference, San Jose, California, February 2008.

208. Shapiro, "Think-Aloud and Thought-List Procedures."

209. For examples, see Coleman et al., "Public Life and the Internet."

210. Shapiro, "Think-Aloud and Thought-List Procedures."

211. Debra Malmberg, Marjorie Charlop, and Sara Gershfeld, "A Two Experiment Treatment Comparison Study: Teaching Social Skills to Children with Autism Spectrum Disorder," *Journal of Developmental and Physical Disabilities* 27, no. 3 (2015): 375–392.

212. Sandra L. Gibbons, Vicki Ebbeck, and Maureen R. Weiss, "Fair Play for Kids: Effects on the Moral Development of Children in Physical Education," *Research Quarterly for Exercise and Sport* 66, no. 3 (1995): 247–255.

213. Albert Bandura, "Influence of Models' Reinforcement Contingencies on the Acquisition of Imitative Responses," *Journal of Personality and Social Psychology* 1, no. 6 (1965): 589–595.

214. Ibid.

215. R. Barker Bausell, *Conducting Meaningful Experiments: 40 Steps to Becoming a Scientist* (Thousand Oaks, CA: Sage, 1994).

216. Wojcik et al., "Conservatives Report."

217. Bönte, Lombardo, and Urbig, "Economics Meets Psychology."

218. Meischke et al., "Delivering 9-1-1 CPR Instructions."

219. K. A. Hallgren, "Computing Inter-Rater Reliability for Observational Data: An Overview and Tutorial," *Tutorials in Quantitative Methods for Psychology* 8, no. 1 (2012): 23–34.

220. Shadish, Cook, and Campbell, *Experimental and Quasi-Experimental Designs for Generalized Causal Inference.*

221. Kimberly A. Neuendorf, *The Content Analysis Guidebook* (Thousand Oaks, CA: Sage, 2002), 145.

222. Webster and Sell, *Laboratory Experiments in the Social Sciences.*

223. Webb et al., *Unobtrusive Measures.*

224. Stanley Milgram, Leon Mann, and Susan Harter, "The Lost-Letter Technique: A Tool of Social Science Research," *Public Opinion Quarterly* 29, no. 3 (1965): 437–438.

225. Bryn Rosenfeld, Kosuke Imai, and Jacob N. Shapiro, "An Empirical Validation Study of Popular Survey Methodologies for Sensitive Questions," *American Journal of Political Science* 60, no. 3 (2016): 783–802.

226. Eric Kramon, "Where Is Vote Buying Effective? Evidence From a List Experiment in Kenya," *Electoral Studies* 44 (2016): 397–408.

227. Rosenfeld, Imai, and Shapiro, "An Empirical Validation Study."

228. Jing Chen and Pallavi Chitturi, "Choice Experiments for Estimating Main Effects and Interactions," *Journal of Statistical Planning and Inference* 142, no. 2 (2012): 390–396.

229. Kimberly Klaiman, David L. Ortega, and Cloé Garnache, "Perceived Barriers to Food Packaging Recycling: Evidence From a Choice Experiment of US Consumers," *Food Control* 73 (2017): 291–299.

230. Ibid.

231. M. L. Loureiro and W. J. Umberger, "A Choice Experiment Model for Beef: What U.S. Consumer Responses Tell Us About Relative Preferences for Food Safety, Country-of-Origin Labeling and Traceability," *Food Policy* 32, no. 4 (2007): 496–514.

232. Chen and Chitturi, "Choice Experiments for Estimating Main Effects and Interactions."

233. Loureiro and Umberger, "A Choice Experiment Model for Beef."

234. Chen and Chitturi, "Choice Experiments for Estimating Main Effects and Interactions."

235. Klaiman, Ortega, and Garnache, "Perceived Barriers to Food Packaging Recycling."

236. Loureiro and Umberger, "A Choice Experiment Model for Beef."

237. Axel Sonntag and Daniel John Zizzo, "On Reminder Effects, Drop-Outs and Dominance: Evidence From an Online Experiment on Charitable Giving," *PLoS ONE* 10, no. 8 (August 7, 2015): 1–17.

238. Rosenfeld, Imai, and Shapiro, "An Empirical Validation Study."

239. James R. Rest et al., *Postconventional Moral Thinking: A Neo-Kohlbergian Approach* (Mahwah, NJ: Erlbaum, 1999).

240. Lawrence Kohlberg, *The Philosophy of Moral Development: Moral Stages and the Idea of Justice* (Cambridge, MA: Harper & Row, 1981); Lawrence Kohlberg, *The Psychology of Moral Development: The Nature and Validity of Moral Stages* (San Francisco: Harper & Row, 1984).

241. James R. Rest, Lynne Edwards, and Stephen J. Thoma, "Designing and Validating a Measure of Moral Judgment: Stage Preference and Stage Consistency Approaches," *Journal of Educational Psychology* 89, no. 1 (March 1997): 5–28.

242. Coleman, "The Effect of Visuals on Ethical Reasoning."

243. R. M. Alvarez and C. H. Franklin, "Uncertainty and Political Perceptions," *Journal of Politics* 56, no. 3 (1994): 671–688.

244. Emily Thorson, "Belief Echoes."

245. Erisen, Erisen, and Ozkececi-Taner, "Research Methods in Political Psychology."

246. H. Cho and F. J. Boster, "Effects of Gain Versus Loss Frame Antidrug Ads on Adolescents," *Journal of Communication* 58, no. 3 (2008): 428–446.

247. Alan Gerber et al., "Reporting Guidelines for Experimental Research: A Report From the Experimental Research Section Standards Committee," *Journal of Experimental Political Science* 1, no. 1 (2014): 81–98.

248. Thomas Zerback, Thomas Koch, and Benjamin Kramer, "Thinking of Others: Effects of Implicit and Explicit Media Cues on Climate of Opinion Perceptions," *Journalism and Mass Communication Quarterly* 92, no. 2 (2015): 421–443.

249. Thorson, "Belief Echoes," 467.

250. Thaler and Helmig, "Promoting Good Behavior," 1018.

251. Srividya Ramasubramanian, "Media-Based Strategies to Reduce Racial Stereotypes Activated by News Stories," *Journalism and Mass Communication Quarterly* 84, no. 2 (Summer 2007): 249–264.

252. Jamali and Shahbaztabar, "The Effects of Internet Filtering," 412.

# THE INSTITUTIONAL REVIEW BOARD AND CONDUCTING ETHICAL EXPERIMENTS

*The experimental method is the most nearly ideal method for scientific explanation, but unfortunately it can only rarely be used in political science because of practical and ethical impediments.*[1]

**—A. Lijphart**

## LEARNING OBJECTIVES

- Describe the purpose of the Institutional Review Board and its principles when conducting an experiment.

- Explain how deception can be avoided and its effects minimized in experiments.

- Illustrate examples of harm and abuse of power in social science experiments and ways to minimize them.

- Identify ways social science experiments can protect subjects' privacy and confidentiality.

- Create an Institutional Review Board proposal.

- Develop a pilot study.

In spite of the opening quotation's declaration more than forty-five years ago, political scientists and others have indeed found ways to overcome the practical and ethical impediments of experimentation, making it virtually a growth industry in social science.[2] Despite this, even the language of experiments—"manipulation," "control," and "subjects"—implies the power and authority researchers have over participants, with accompanying concerns for treating them fairly and with respect. This chapter expands on the discussion of ethics in chapter 2 by exploring these ethical impediments and some corrective measures, the process of gaining approval from an Institutional Review Board, and the conducting of a pilot study.

## INSTITUTIONAL REVIEW BOARDS

Institutional review boards, or IRBs, are committees that review research proposals to ensure that researchers treat subjects ethically and do not cause them harm. Most universities in the developed world have them, and in the United States, IRB approval and oversight is also required for federally funded research conducted outside university settings. IRBs were developed in the 1970s in response to the experiments of the Nazi physicians, the Tuskegee syphilis experiment, and other controversial studies. In the Tuskegee syphilis experiment, subjects, who were Black men, went untreated for forty years even when a cure was known, and some were never even told they had the disease. Claims by medical personnel that they were only doing their jobs or following orders mirrored comments of the Nazis during the Holocaust. Because of these and other experiments, efforts were begun to approve, oversee, and regulate research in order to avoid such abuses. The ***Belmont Report***, produced by the committee charged with laying out the basic ethical principles of research with human subjects, is the foundation that IRBs use to develop guidelines researchers must adhere to. Its three basic principles are *respect for persons,* defined as not coercing or deceiving subjects and providing them with informed consent; *beneficence*, which involves not harming subjects, minimizing risks, and maximizing benefits; and *justice*, which includes selecting subjects and administering procedures in a fair manner.[3]

IRBs were originally developed in response to abuses in biomedical experiments, but social science research also has a history of ethical transgressions, including the experiments described in chapter 2 such as Stanley Milgram's shock experiments and Philip Zimbardo's Stanford prison study.[4] Milgram's study is a frequently cited example of one of the main criticisms of experiments: deception (see More About box 2.3, Deception, in chapter 2). Specifically, the researchers falsely told subjects the purpose of the study was to test whether punishment improved learning, not that it was about obedience to authority. Thus, subjects agreed to be in the study without really knowing what they were consenting to. In addition, subjects were encouraged to harm another person, which led to psychological distress for many, if not most, of them.

Harm in the form of psychological distress was the primary ethical issue with the Stanford prison experiment. These issues of harm and informed consent, among others particularly prominent within experimentation, will be discussed in this chapter in the context of the IRB. Because IRBs were developed primarily to regulate biomedical research, there is some frustration among social scientists who say that IRBs apply an inappropriate yardstick to their fields, resulting in demands for changes that compromise the study.[5] (For more about understanding and negotiating with the IRB, see Study Spotlight 11.1.)

At the outset, it is important to state that ethical research is not merely what the IRB allows. Although the IRB rules and principles governing research with human subjects are meant to cover important ethical concerns, principled experimentation is more than simply following these rules. Designing an ethical experiment should be one's goal from the first inkling of an idea through every step of the process. However, because IRBs are the principal means of enforcing ethical behavior, their standards will be the framework for this discussion. Applying for IRB approval is different at every institution, so this chapter will not attempt to walk through an application process, but instead discusses the steps common to all IRBs in More About box 11.2, IRBs. What follows are some of the common ethical concerns with experiments and suggestions of ways to minimize or remedy them.

## STUDY SPOTLIGHT 11.1

### Risks and Wrongs in Social Science Research

SAGE Journal Article: study.sagepub.com/ coleman

**From: Oakes, J. Michael. 2002. "Risks and Wrongs in Social Science Research: An Evaluator's Guide to the IRB."** *Evaluation Review* **26 (5): 443.**

Social scientists have expressed frustration with an IRB process originally devised for biomedical research. In this article, the author explains the rationale for IRBs, helps readers understand the rules, and gives advice to navigate the process.

Many social scientists believe that IRBs do not understand social science inquiry or its methodologies. The author offers two reasons for this: "Regulations were developed for biomedical research. Interpretations of regulations have become more strict."[6] He points out that social scientists were

*(Continued)*

(Continued)

not involved in developing IRB rules. The focus on risk also has grown to include nonphysical harm, despite the lack of evidence of this kind of risk. However, he says, "The absence of data on risks and wrongs in social scientific research does not prove that subjects go unscathed."[7] He cites many of the same risks of harm included in this chapter, including invasion of privacy and stigmatization, giving specific examples such as a victim of domestic abuse whose loss of confidentiality allows a batterer to find her, and a victim of posttraumatic stress disorder who experienced flashbacks in response to a question.

Among the reasons for the increasing strictness of IRBs are the threat of fines, legal action, and having all research suspended at an institution for one study's infraction. I personally experienced this when researchers at the medical school associated with my university realized that patients were being randomly assigned to receive warm or cold blood transfusions. They gathered the previously collected data, analyzed it, and published a study—all without gaining the informed consent of the patients whose data were used. The entire university was prohibited from receiving approval for any new studies for a period of time, which hampered even the journalism doctoral students who were trying to get their dissertations done.

In addition to IRB actions that frustrate social scientists, Oakes lays blame on social scientists, too. He says, "In short, many researchers still believe, perhaps subconsciously, that they have an inalienable right to research. That is, they have the right to research other humans without interference from an IRB."[8] He compares IRBs to journal editors who have a right to ask for changes from study authors. The solution he proposes is education on both sides: Social scientists must learn about the IRB and must educate the IRB about social science. He goes on to give a primer on IRB issues, for example, defining **equipoise**—true uncertainty that one treatment is better than another—minimal risk, and vulnerable subjects. IRBs developed the exempt category explained in More About box 11.2 for social science research. It exempts from oversight evaluation of educational practices, survey research that does not collect any identifying data, and observational studies. Experiments that involve deception are not exempt, nor are those testing interventions.

The ethical recruitment of subjects is also discussed, with "equitable selection" one of the top priorities of IRBs. Poor and minority populations were historically overrepresented in research, such as the Tuskegee studies. Then, it shifted to exclude women and minorities between the mid-1970s and mid-1990s. Equitable selection of subjects ensures that everyone enjoys the benefits of the knowledge research produces. Practical evidence-based advice is offered on the amount of incentives, with $1 to $5 in mail surveys representing a balance between gaining cooperation and avoiding coercion. Research on lotteries for bigger incentives has shown they may be coercive, as people do not understand probabilities. He discusses issues unique to research on groups, where, for example, intact classrooms are the unit being studied. Problems range from one subject who declines to participate to whether leaders, such as a manager at a job site, have the right to consent for all. He explains how a Certificate of Confidentiality can prevent sensitive data from being subpoenaed for identifying information.

As for educating IRBs, Oakes recommends empirical research on harm subjects have actually experienced from social science research. He laments that social science researchers have not adequately attempted to provide data regarding the risks of their research, noting that "Results from experimental designs would be most helpful."[9] He offers a long list of research topics, including the optimal amount of compensation. It ends with a table of helpful tips for improving relationships with the IRB. The footnotes are full of fascinating and helpful information.

# MORE ABOUT . . . BOX 11.2
## IRBs

While every research institution with an IRB will have different criteria, there are some commonalities proscribed by federal regulations.[10] Among them are the three types of review: exempt, expedited, and full board. The term *exempt* can be misinterpreted; it does not mean that research in this category is exempt from *approval* by the IRB. Rather, it means that these studies have been judged as presenting minimal risk to subjects and are exempt from ongoing *oversight*. Much social science research falls into this category. When a researcher applies for IRB approval, he or she will be expected to suggest which type of review the study should receive. The IRB will decide whether that is the most appropriate level of oversight or if something more is required. Experiments that do not put subjects at more risk than they could expect in their normal lives typically fall into the exempt category. There are some exceptions; for example, if subjects are under eighteen, prisoners, mentally ill, or pregnant women[i], they are deemed to be vulnerable populations, and the level of review steps up a notch to "expedited." Studies of school children typically are in this category and involve assent of the child as well as informed consent of the parent or guardian. The expedited category may also include studies that involve video or audio recording, while some institutions will deem these to be exempt as well. This classification of research may require the researcher to report on the status of the project and any adverse events yearly, whereas a report in the exempt category is due only when the study is closed out and requires less information. Research classified as expedited is not necessarily approved by the IRB faster than research deemed exempt. Full board review is exactly what it says—research that requires the entire membership of the IRB to review the proposal at their regularly scheduled meeting. Exempt and expedited projects receive scrutiny from only a few members.

IRB proposals typically require researchers to provide a narrative research proposal, possibly following a standardized template. Other documentation includes the stimuli, instruments and measures, informed consent documents, and recruitment scripts. Explanation of procedures, debriefing text, and rationale for deception, if applicable, is also required, as are explanations of where subjects will come from and if the researcher has the resources to carry out the study. Drawing subjects from Amazon's Mechanical Turk comes with its own set of requirements, as these subjects are actually "workers" and their identities are available via their MTurk ID, which is required for them to be paid. Look for guidance on the language necessary for MTurk subjects on your IRB's website or contact a representative. Researchers will be expected to spell out the benefits of the study, any potential risks and how they will be minimized, and how researchers will deal with adverse events. The time a subject will spend on the study should be given truthfully, as IRB representatives have lots of experience with this. Take the study yourself if you are not good at judging time. Applying for IRB approval typically requires that the experiment be completely designed, with all materials at least in beta stage. Some IRBs will allow manipulation checks of stimuli to be conducted without

---

[i]This is not meant to suggest that if it is possible a pregnant woman will be among the subjects, that researchers should declare "pregnant woman" on the IRB application; rather, if pregnant women are specifically being targeted as subjects, then researchers should check this box.

*(Continued)*

(Continued)

IRB approval, usually if the data from them will not be combined with that from the actual study, and others require approval before conducting manipulation checks. There can be quite a lot of down time while waiting for approval, and researchers sometimes get frustrated that their study is ready to go and they must hurry up and wait. However, it is imperative that researchers not begin collecting data until they have received IRB approval. The IRB representative may require changes to the study—some minor and some major—before approving. If a researcher makes any changes to a study after approval—for example, after conducting a pilot study and discovering measures that needed to be changed—then an amendment may need to be filed with the IRB. Most IRBs will promptly review the amendments and give the OK (or require changes), and some do not require the researcher to halt data collection until the amendment is approved. The defining feature of whether an amendment will be approved is if it does not raise the level of risk to subjects.

Editors of many journals are now asking for proof of IRB approval when papers are submitted.[11] This may present problems for researchers who do not have review boards—for example, at institutions outside the United States. If you are doing research in a setting where there is no IRB, I recommend at a minimum giving informed consent to participants using the federal guidelines. In addition, it will help to act in an ethical manner, not use deception, minimize risk, protect subjects' privacy, allow them to withdraw, and debrief them, along with the other recommendations in this chapter. Having the proposal reviewed by an independent ethics expert is another approach.[12] Journal editors who receive papers that did not receive IRB oversight will evaluate a study for these ethical guidelines.[13] Here is an example from a published paper of an ethics statement provided where no IRB was in place:

"According to the Austrian Universities Act 2002 (UG2002), which was in place at the time the study was carried out, only medical universities were required to appoint ethics committees for clinical tests, application of medical methods, and applied medical research. Consequently, no ethical approval for this specific study was required. Nevertheless, the present study was part of a project that was funded by a European Union Marie Curie FP7 Integration Grant, and the project received ethical approval. As there was no institutional review board in charge at the time the project proposal was submitted, it was approved by an independent expert (Institute for Ethics and Law in Medicine, University of Vienna). The present study was conducted in accordance with the Declaration of Helsinki (revised 1983) and local guidelines of the Faculty of Psychology, University of Vienna. Written informed consent was given by all participants, who could also withdraw at any time during the experiment without further consequences. At the end of the experiment, participants were debriefed in detail."[14]

From: Serfas, Benjamin G., Oliver B. Büttner, and Arnd Florack. 2014. "Eyes Wide Shopped: Shopping Situations Trigger Arousal in Impulsive Buyers." *PLoS ONE* 9 (12): 1–9.

# ETHICAL ISSUES IN EXPERIMENTS

## Deception

As discussed in chapter 2, perhaps the leading ethical concern with experiments is that subjects will be deceived. No other methodology is quite as susceptible to misleading subjects as experimentation, with its focus on "manipulation." One predominant way deception occurs is when subjects are misinformed or misled about the purpose of the experiment during the informed consent process. This is often rationalized as necessary to avoid demand effects or hypothesis guessing, leading subjects to change their responses to please (or displease) the researcher. However, researchers sometimes think that deception is necessary when it is not. The use of unobtrusive questions or instruments, which do not point to the purpose of the study with direct questions, or distractor questions that mask the purpose, can all help eliminate the need to deceive subjects (see chapter 10 for more on these). For example, in moral judgment studies, it is rather obvious that the scenarios subjects are asked to make decisions about are ethical issues; telling them they represent something else fools no one and compromises the researcher's credibility with subjects. Rather than asking direct questions, however, having subjects rank unobtrusive statements that are designed to reflect different levels of ethical stages allows researchers to truthfully say the study is about ethical decision making without giving away the hypotheses. Researchers can also honestly say there is no right or wrong answer and tell subjects they are interested in the things that were important in making their decision.[15] It is not necessary to tell subjects every detail about the scoring of their responses when giving them informed consent. IRBs routinely approve studies of this nature and do not even require that subjects be told about the scoring system after the study is over, although that can certainly be done if the researcher chooses. Designing and conducting unobtrusive experiments can be more difficult and time consuming than simply deceiving subjects about the purpose of the study; however, this is the approach that ethical researchers should pursue.

It is important to understand that subjects need to be unaware of the specific hypotheses of an experiment or the relationship between variables and expected results; instead, they need to be told more globally about the general topic of the study.[16] Having experimenters such as graduate assistants who run the subjects also be unaware of the goals and hypotheses—the double-blind experiment described in chapter 5—also helps guard against hypothesis guessing by subjects.

When telling subjects the true purpose of the experiment would invalidate results, subjects should instead be deceived as little as possible, and the deception should not lead to harm or distress. In addition, subjects must be debriefed and told the true purpose of the study immediately after their participation in the experiment. If they have been deceived, they must be told this, and the reasons why should be explained. Researchers need to honestly answer any questions subjects ask. In the process of debriefing, experimenters should be careful not to cause embarrassment over the fact that subjects have been fooled.[17] An IRB may not approve an experiment that requires deception, even with debriefing.

There are other ways that subjects can be deceived in an experiment other than during the informed consent process—for example, when confederates who are in on the experiment are used and subjects are led to believe they are other subjects. Milgram's shock experiments used a confederate as "the learner" who was supposedly receiving the shocks administered by the subject.[18] Leon Festinger and James Carlsmith used a confederate who pretended to be a subject who had just completed a boring experiment turning pegs; the confederate's job was to tell the real subject that the study was fascinating and important.[19] In a more contemporary example, a study of different types of lying used confederates trained to lie by misleading and by omitting information who were paired with uninformed subjects in order to study face-to-face deception in negotiations for buying and selling property.[20] Subjects were debriefed, and no adverse reactions are reported in the paper.

## Harm

Deception may be the main ethical concern with experiments, but IRBs are charged primarily with preventing harm to subjects. That is also the researcher's first and foremost responsibility. While social science experiments may rarely harm people physically the way medical studies can, there are still risks of causing damage. Some of the harm caused by experiments can include loss of confidentiality or invasion of privacy, embarrassment, stigma, or being stereotyped.[21] Nor should subjects be made to feel unduly frightened or offended, experience self-hatred or worthlessness, or be at risk of ridicule or backlash from family, friends, colleagues, or employers. Psychological distress is the most likely kind of harm in social science experimentation.[22] In IRB language, the risk of harm to participants should be no greater than the risks encountered in everyday life. For many social science studies, this is not much of an issue; for example, answering questions about one's political attitudes could reasonably be expected to be a risk encountered in normal conversations about politics. But responding to questions about HIV status, sexual behavior, drug use, or illegal acts will be especially scrutinized by the IRB. To avoid psychological harm, researchers should refrain from asking subjects to divulge private information that could be embarrassing, reveal traumatic events, or be coerced into acting in ways they do not anticipate, as in Milgram's shock studies. When asking sensitive questions that have a greater risk of harm, IRBs will insist that they be crucial to the study and that researchers minimize harm as much as possible. What constitutes "daily life" is variable, however. Some recommend that the potential for harm be compared against a daily life that is nonviolent and includes freedom of speech, which may not be the case for all subjects.[23] One benchmark is for researchers to evaluate the risk of harm using their own daily lives.[24]

One IRB-approved way to minimize harm in experiments is to allow subjects to skip questions that make them uncomfortable, or withdraw from the study entirely anytime they wish without repercussions. For example, subjects who stop participating if they become uncomfortable with the violence in a TV show would still receive their incentives. Ensuring subjects that their participation in and responses to a study will be kept confidential also reduces the risk of harm via loss of privacy. Warning subjects about any potential risk of harm in the informed consent document is required by the IRB, as well as is telling them they may skip questions or withdraw without losing any benefits. Different people respond differently to experimental manipulations, with some feeling no harmful effects while others can become quite upset after the same treatment. Experimenters who sense a subject responding poorly should intervene and stop the experiment for that person.[25] Finally, the ability to withdraw from a study also allows subjects to have their responses excluded from the analysis even after the study is over.[26]

One corrective measure that can be taken if harm does occur is to provide subjects with resources to deal with the unintended effects—for example, referring student subjects to the college's counseling center or locating similar centers and providing referrals to nonstudent subjects. While the potential for harm from many, if not most, social science experiments is highly unlikely, it can never be ruled out completely. Not all harm is knowable before an experiment is conducted.

## Abuse of Power

Researchers also should be wary of the imbalance of power in relationships with subjects. A classic example is Milgram's shock experiments, where the researcher represented an authority figure subjects felt compelled to obey.[27] For university-based experimentalists, personally recruiting one's own students for an experiment can lead to students participating when they might not really want to for fear of getting a lower grade. Ways around this include not using students currently enrolled in one's own class or whom one is supervising. Having an uninvolved third party do the recruiting, such as a graduate student who does not grade for the class, is another approach, as is using students enrolled in subject pools, although these are not without their own challenges, especially considering they are not entirely voluntary (see Hegtvedt 2014 for more[28]). Students participating in a study for extra credit should be assured their names will be withheld from the instructor until after all grading has been completed, and extra credit will be awarded only at the end of the course. Even better is to use gift cards or other incentives instead of extra credit for those whom one has power over. Additionally, students who wish to earn extra credit without participating in the study must be offered an alternative assignment that is not more demanding than the study would be. Limiting the amount of an incentive is also important to avoid crossing the line into coercion.[29] Participation in an experiment must always be voluntary for IRB approval, so allowing subjects to withdraw or opt out of certain aspects without loss of extra credit or other incentives is another way to circumvent abuse of power.

## Random Assignment

Another area of experimentation that raises ethical questions is the defining feature of random assignment. Recall from chapter 7 that randomly assigning subjects to treatment and control groups is the single most important thing a researcher can do in a true experiment. However, subjects tend not to appreciate the elegance of this solution to a variety of problems that can bias the results of an experiment. One objection to random assignment is that if researchers think some treatment might work better than another or better than no treatment, it is unethical to refuse to give the treatment to everyone, or at least to those who request it. Education researchers find this to be common with school personnel and parents.[30] Criminology, business, social work, and other fields also experience ethical dilemmas when there is evidence that some subjects may need the treatment more than others.[31] Stoker calls this criticism "misplaced,"[32] explaining that researchers do not know that the treatment actually works, which is why they are testing it. Few subjects, apparently, believe this to be the case. In one study, subjects felt that random assignment was unacceptable whether the context was medical or nonmedical.[33] They refused to believe that doctors did not hold a preference for one treatment over the other. When researchers are unsure if a specific treatment will work better than another or no treatment, that is a condition known as equipoise.[34] Subjects in the study believed the same about whether a lawyer could really be unsure of whether it was better to settle a case or go to court. Furthermore, there was little the researchers could do to convince subjects otherwise.[35] After all, few scientists develop treatments and interventions that they do not think will work better than existing efforts. In fact, recruitment of subjects for medical randomized clinical trials is declining because of subjects' objections to being randomly assigned to the treatment or control group.[36] Some of the ways to overcome subjects' objections to randomization are discussed in chapter 7, including agreeing to allow control group subjects to receive the treatment in another run of the experiment.

# PROTECTING SUBJECTS

While lay people may view random assignment as unethical, most experimentalists and IRBs do not (for a dissenting view, see Fives et al. 2015[37]). They are more concerned with ways to protect subjects from deception, harm, and abuse of power. What follows is a more in-depth discussion of some of the methods that IRBs require of researchers in order to protect subjects. Most of these have been previewed earlier in this chapter but are covered in more detail next.

## Informed Consent

Ensuring that experimental subjects received informed consent is the lynchpin of ethical research as defined by IRBs. The *Belmont Report* acknowledges that intrusive or potentially harmful research may be outweighed by the benefits it produces but says researchers have a duty to fully inform subjects and obtain their permission before the study begins.[38] Consent must be voluntary, and the information provided to subjects must include the purpose of the research, what procedures are involved and what the subject must do, how long it will take, all foreseeable risks and harms including psychological distress, and any benefits, including those to the individual subjects and society at large. Incentives do not count as a benefit; rather, the creation of new scientific knowledge, development of best practices for professions, or, for students, a hands-on research experience are more commonly described benefits.

Informed consent takes various forms. The traditional written consent form is a physical piece of paper, signed by both the researcher and subject, with a copy for each. This is generally used for in-person experiments such as those conducted in a laboratory. A second type of consent is becoming more prevalent with the increase in online experiments. This is known as *waiver of documentation*, which means that the physical document or paper consent form is waived, not consent of the subject.[ii] This type of informed consent contains all the same information as the written consent form but is operationalized as a cover letter at the beginning of an online study. Rather than signing their names, subjects click "I agree" after reading the consent information. IRBs may require researchers to say which kind of consent form a study will use and explain why. Actual waiver of consent itself is also possible; however, there is a higher bar for this. IRBs typically grant requests to waive informed consent when it is not possible to get consent from subjects *and* the risks are no greater than in everyday life—for example, if a researcher is observing what people are reading on a subway and would not be able to give written informed consent forms to everyone on the subway, and being watched on public mass transit is something that typically happens anyway and carries no greater risk of harm than if the researcher was not observing. Failing to give informed consent in such cases may damage the image of social science research, however.[39]

---

[ii]The waiver of consent is also used for some face-to-face studies under certain conditions as outlined in federal guidelines §46.117.

While the subway example is not an experiment, there are similar unobtrusive instruments used in experiments, as covered in chapter 10. Just because a researcher *can* obtain data from subjects without their knowledge does not mean that it is acceptable to withhold informed consent. Giving subjects written or online consent is always preferable to not providing them with any information about the study. For example, this might occur with web-tracking software installed in public lab computers that record a person's Internet behavior without the person even being aware of it. Subjects should still be informed about the details of the study and be allowed to choose whether to participate or not before researchers collect log files from their computers. This also applies to other highly unobtrusive instruments such as audio or video recording and observations, among others. The requirements for waiver of informed consent apply to naturalistic observations in public places and when there is no risk of harm that is greater than normal. There are also exceptions for studies of normal educational practices in educational settings, job or organization effectiveness research that does not put subjects' employment at risk and confidentiality is protected, archival research where there is no risk to subjects, and anonymous questionnaires. All of these must have a risk of harm no greater than that of normal life.[40]

As more experiments move out of the laboratory and onto the Internet, these ethical concerns have grown to include worries about effects on more individuals and even people who are not part of the study.[41]

## Privacy and Confidentiality

Another major issue for experimental research is privacy and confidentiality. This goes beyond concerns about answering sensitive questions. **Privacy** is about what data are collected, whereas **confidentiality** relates to how data are stored and reported.[42] Only when researchers do not know who participated and collect no names or other identifying information is the study **anonymous**.[43] When experimenters know subjects' names or collect identifying information that would allow them to track subjects—for example, for follow-ups—subjects should be told their information is confidential. Collecting only the identifying information that will be used in the analyses not only reassures subjects that their identity will not be revealed but it shortens the time of the study. Additionally, subjects are more likely to provide honest responses when they are assured their identities will remain unknown. Names are not used in reports of experiments; if open-ended responses are used to illustrate a point, they are referred to with pseudonyms or labels such as "Subject A."[44] In order to maintain subjects' privacy, researchers should either not be able to link subjects' identities with their responses or they should de-identify the data, removing any information that would allow tracing back to the person from his or her data.

Confidentiality can be maintained by various methods, such as storing the data on a password-protected computer that is kept in a locked office or file cabinet, not sharing data with others unless it is de-identified, using data in aggregate rather than individually, and shredding hard copies or files with identifying information. Avoid e-mailing data.[45] It is also important not to share with subjects their own individual results; for example, subjects may want to know "how they did" on a moral judgment questionnaire. In addition to avoiding embarrassment or disappointment, not sharing their results give subjects more confidence that no one else will ever know their individual scores. Exceptions to this include certain legal conditions and when subjects make threats of harm to themselves or others; then the researcher has a duty to intervene.[46] There are also special circumstances that apply to vulnerable populations, such as children, prisoners, the elderly, and the disabled. It is beyond the scope of this book to go into detail; however, most IRB training programs will deal with these in depth.

In the next section, the discussion of ethics in experimentation moves beyond concerns about subjects to issues related to researchers' own behavior. Obviously, these concerns are not confined to experiments but are serious enough that these cautions bear repeating.

# RESEARCHER ISSUES

It should go without saying that researchers should analyze and present data as ethically as possible, but enough instances of researcher misconduct and retracted articles arise that this is apparently not as obvious as it seems. Unethical acts range from inaccuracies to intentional misconduct, fraud, and data forgery. This is not always attributable to honest mistakes or character deficits of the individual researcher but can also include societal-level factors such as the "publish or perish" mentality of academic research, where pressure to publish studies can result in researchers performing some of the unethical acts described earlier and in the next section.[47] In the belief that forewarned is forearmed, the following are some of the ways that experimentalists can run afoul of ethical research.

## Data Ethics

The well-known saying that "liars figure and figures lie" illustrates the idea that there are numerous ways to manipulate data to make a study's results come out a certain way or seem more interesting or important. Terms for this include **data mining**, **P-hacking**, and **HARKing**, or hypothesizing after the results are known.[48] These are all terms for researchers exploring data,[49] such as crunching numbers until something interesting is found. This is the opposite of what the scientific method prescribes.[50] Other misuse of data includes failing to report unfavorable results[51] and failed replications.[52] Some antidotes to this, beyond researchers simply resisting the temptation, include reporting effect sizes instead of relying only on $p$ values (see chapter 8), and sharing ones' (de-identified) data for others to analyze in replications (see chapter 5). This assumes that a researcher has not fabricated data or fraudulently altered it. Any changes to data, such as transformations to achieve normality or mean substitution of missing data, should always be disclosed. If one researcher sees another engaging in unethical behavior, he or she has a duty to report it. There are even researchers who practice **unmasking**, or policing other authors' perceived violations.[53] As Fiske says, "Transparency is good advice for everyone."[54]

Other ways of manipulating results that do not involve altering data include overclaiming, or going beyond what the data actually show.[55] This can be common in discussion and conclusion sections of papers where authors overextrapolate—for example, drawing conclusions about why subjects behaved a certain way or presuming their reasons for some response when there is no data to support such claims. If a mediator was not included in the study, no explanations can be offered for causal mechanisms by which the effect occurred. Another tendency of overclaiming arises in results sections when the standard $p$ level of .05 mysteriously changes to .059 or .06, or a $p$ level of .11 is described as almost significant or approaching significance.

Oversampling, or using an extremely large sample size to take advantage of the law of large numbers, which makes it easier to find statistical significance, is another form of misusing data. Ethically, this also violates the mandate to minimize interventions and, thus, possible harm.[56] Reporting power analyses (see chapter 8) provides transparency about how many subjects were appropriate and keeps this tendency in check.

Occasionally, experiments make use of **secondary data**, or existing data that were previously collected by someone else. Examples include the popular American National Election Studies (ANES) or General Social Survey (GSS). If secondary data are not publicly available and stripped of all identifying information, then the researchers who collected it must administer informed consent to the subjects for it to be acceptable to use in research. However, not all existing data follow informed consent procedures, making it unacceptable for published scientific studies. One example is students' evaluations of courses and instructors; because the students were not informed that their responses would be used in a study and allowed to give or withhold permission, it is not ethical to use these data in this manner and will not be approved by an IRB. For some existing data, IRBs may allow gaining informed consent after the fact.

## Plagiarism and Self-Plagiarism

One of the most serious ethical issues that plagues research of any kind is **plagiarism**, or not giving proper credit to words and ideas that are not the researcher's own. The remedy is simple—attributing sources appropriately. Giving proper credit is as simple as a citation, yet examples abound of these kinds of violations. Occasionally, it is done intentionally. In some cases, it results from honest mistakes or sloppy note taking and writing practices. In others, plagiarism is due to misunderstanding what needs to be cited. For example, two professors working with a new graduate student discovered from a journal editor that the student coauthor had plagiarized nearly the entire literature review of the paper they just submitted; the student did not understand what needed to be cited. I have also had students tell me the original author's English was better than theirs so they did not rewrite. It is important that researchers scour their own writing and that of any coauthors for language that sounds unlike their own and ensure that any words or ideas acknowledge the original source.

When quoting another author, care should be taken to put the verbatim language inside quotation marks and to include the page number along with the typical source information. There is no limit on the number of words that can be used verbatim without attribution; for example, conventional wisdom may say fifty words or fewer are OK to use without attribution. This is not true. Even a single term or phrase that is taken word for word from another source without proper credit constitutes plagiarism. Plagiarism is best avoided by rewriting to paraphrase someone else's statements. Paraphrasing does not mean changing a word or two, however; proper paraphrasing means even the sentence structure is different. Plagiarism can be committed with any type of work—unpublished, nonacademic, online, in speeches, etc. It also is necessary to guard against plagiarism in all types of writing, whether for a journal, conference, or even an unpublished class paper.

While it does not matter if the plagiarism is intentional or accidental, it frequently results unintentionally—for example, as a result of note taking that inadvertently excludes the source. Researchers need to develop ways to avoid this; for example, by not copying and pasting from electronic documents but always paraphrasing, or by highlighting material that is verbatim in notes and including the source. This takes longer but can eliminate embarrassment and even ruined reputations.

A subset of plagiarism is the act of **self-plagiarism**, or taking verbatim from one's own writing. This is also known as *duplication* or *text recycling*. Even though you wrote it, this is considered academic misconduct because the journal in which it was published deserves to receive credit. Avoiding self-plagiarism can sometimes involve compositional gymnastics, especially with experiments where multiple studies rely on the same stimuli and instruments in pursuit of self-replication. Having rewritten the stimuli and instruments descriptions a time or two, it becomes a challenge to say things another way and still be concise and readable.

A related ethical concern that is rising to the top in the field of communication is the practice of **data slicing**, or writing more than one paper from a single data set with only minor variations.[57] Several top journals in communication now require researchers to disclose in cover letters if a data set has been used to produce more than the one article being submitted. This can be problematic for surveys particularly, but also for experiments if researchers have been economical in including different dependent variables (DVs), mediators, or moderators in one study with the goal of producing two or more papers. To avoid this ethical lapse, experimentalists should ensure there are more than "minor variations" in each article.

## Authorship Issues

Questions revolving around authorship—who gets it, in what order, and when—are vexing to all methods of inquiry, but every time I have taught a course in experimental design, this is the class topic that receives the most participation from students in the form of horror stories: the professor going up for tenure who wanted a solo publication and took a student's name off a paper; one author who volunteered to shepherd the paper through publication and in the process changed the order, with his name coming first; four coauthors who disagreed about who had done the most work; even a professor who thought her name should be on a student's paper, but it was not. Associations such as the American Psychological Association and others offer guidelines on authorship questions, and those should be consulted as they may differ from one discipline to the other. In addition, talking with colleagues to gauge ethical norms is helpful.

One of the primary ethical concerns with authorship involves the previously mentioned power relationships—in this case, between faculty and graduate students rather than student subjects. For example, should the faculty member or student receive first author? If a student is being paid as a research assistant, is authorship also necessary? If a student does not write anything but does much work in preparing stimuli and instruments and collects and analyzes data, does that qualify for authorship? What if a student writes a good portion of the paper that is later cut out? These same issues apply to junior and senior faculty. For these and other questions, I have two rules of thumb: (1) err on the side of the student or junior researcher and (2) set the ground rules in advance, and discuss any changes prior to making them. Think of this second one as a kind of informed consent among researchers.[58] Before starting any experiment, a frank and open discussion should be had with all those involved, whether students or faculty. Who will get authorship and who will not? What will the order be? What will the duties be? What will happen if someone does not deliver? In the event that anything changes, a new round of discussion and negotiation should ensue and everyone's buy-in achieved. Get these in writing, via e-mail if necessary, as a summary of understanding. Research projects can take a long time, and memories fade; hard feelings may be avoided if a written record is available.

Occasionally, students want to give a professor authorship on their thesis, dissertation, or a research paper on which the professor did little more than give advice. Students sometimes misunderstand that supervising a thesis or dissertation, or giving advice, fall under the faculty member's job description and do not usually warrant authorship. Sometimes, students wish to honor a professor, and at other times they feel that having the professor's name on the paper will make it more favorably disposed to publication. In these cases, I decline and suggest that students give me an acknowledgment rather than authorship. No one's name should be on a paper if they did not substantially contribute to it. That includes giving students authorship that they did not earn (a too-generous interpretation of rule of thumb number 1). In my experience, having the original idea for the paper does qualify as a substantial contribution, but merely giving advice without doing any writing does not. I advise against making or accepting such offers.

Theses and dissertations are supposed to be independent research and are part of the faculty member's job description and compensation. However, some faculty find themselves doing more work than they anticipated in helping a student prepare a thesis or dissertation for publication. In these cases, see rule of thumb number 2—it is time for a frank discussion of what the student and faculty member expect; if the faculty member is unwilling to continue putting in more work without authorship credit, it is time for the student to learn to fly solo.

Authorship order, especially first place, matters. Not only will the first author's name be cited more frequently in journals where later authors are reduced to "et al.," but first authors are typically responsible for shepherding the paper through the publication process, with all the attendant work in answering reviewers' questions and making revisions. In addition, during the tenure process, first authorship is generally viewed more favorably than other positions; tenure committees also frequently ask the promotion candidate to describe others' contributions and give a breakdown of effort in percentages. Contacting all coauthors to get a sense of their perspective before allocating contribution rates can serve one well, as committees have also been known to contact coauthors and ask them the same question. It is always best if one is not seen as regularly overcrediting themselves.

Finally, authorship order should be based on relative contributions—that is, those with more ability should contribute more than those with less ability, such as students. Contributions should be considered authorship-worthy when they rise to the level of a student's competence—for example, if data analysis duties were shared but the student was only able to conduct descriptive statistics while the faculty member provided the tests of difference.[59]

Other ethical issues regarding authorship arise when dealing with journals and conferences. Briefly, one should not take his or her name off a paper because conference division limits have been reached and then attempt to restore one's name to the paper if it gets accepted. This is an attempt to skirt the rules, which are established in order to give everyone a fair chance at getting to present a paper.

One should be careful of self-citing, both how and how often one does it. Citing your own work too much can appear to be an attempt to bump up one's own citation rate. Cite your own works (and others) only when they are more than tangentially relevant to the current study. In addition, citing yourself too much can give away the authorship, compromising the blind review process. It is customary to put in-text citations of one's own work along the lines of "Author blinded." Full citations should be included once the paper is accepted.

## PILOT STUDIES

As has been explained previously in this book, there is some variation in the use of some terms in experimentation; among those are *pilot studies, pretests,* and *manipulation checks.* In the interest of semantic clarity, this book uses the term *pilot study* to mean the small-scale experiment that precedes a larger actual experiment. These are designed to work out the problems in a study design so that it can be refined before launching the larger study. Pilot studies may be used with methods other than experiments, but they are considered a best practice in experimentation.[60] Pilot studies have many uses, among them one that is relevant to the previous discussion—the ability to discover any unanticipated harm to subjects, things that offend them, or objections they may have. In addition to ethical issues, the pilot study is the place where researchers can discover other issues with their experiment that they had not anticipated—for example, if the instrument is working properly, if the measures have adequate range to avoid ceiling effects, the time it actually takes, the instruction wording, experimenter's demeanor, and how important subjects believe the study to be. Pilot studies also are good for testing the internal validity of new constructs. If deception is involved, a pilot study can be used to determine how believable the experiment is. Pilot studies are an opportunity for researchers to conduct a "test run" that will allow them to improve the actual experiment before conducting it, thus saving time and money.

Pilot studies should be conducted exactly as one intends to conduct the actual study but with more opportunity for subjects to give feedback on what is working and what is not. Open- and closed-ended questions can be added to the instrument to gather this feedback, as well as having experimenters interview subjects about the procedure itself. Experimenters' own impressions of how the study could be improved also should be sought, for example, if they observed subjects' attention wandering because the study was too long.

Subjects should be chosen from the population that will be studied in the actual experiment but should be excluded from later runs, as having been in the study previously may influence their behavior.

There is some disagreement over whether pilot studies should be used to determine whether a study is even worth conducting and for use in determining a sample size for the actual study.[61] Westlund and Stuart[62] maintain that pilot study results should be one data point among many in making these decisions. They offer reasons for not using pilot studies for these two purposes, including because pilot studies are typically underpowered with small sample sizes.[63]

There are few clear guidelines for conducting pilot studies, which some maintain is why more are not conducted.[64] Finally, one other misuse of the term pilot study is as a label researchers give to an experiment as post hoc justification for failing to achieve traditional significance levels or a small sample size. Pilot studies should be reported along with the actual larger experiment or in a white paper to a funding agency if required by a grant.

Once IRB approval has been secured, a pilot study can be launched. After carefully considering the lessons learned in the pilot study, adjustments should be made to the actual study, and then it is ready to run.

The aim of this book is to walk new experimentalists through the steps of designing an experiment. Not all the steps will proceed in the exact order of this book; for example, researchers may develop instruments and stimuli concurrently, and will certainly reconsider various aspects of the study, modifying previously completed phases as they go along. As promised, this book stops at the data analysis point, recognizing there are many good books and courses to help one learn to analyze the data collected in an experiment. Rather, the goal of this book is to "secure adequate and proper data,"[65] as the quote from W. A. McCall in the preface to this book says. Having secured that data, the final step is writing up the results; pointers and examples on this are provided in How To Do It box 11.3.

## Writing Up the Results Section

The results section is where the answers to the hypotheses and research questions are given. This is a "just the facts, ma'am" type of section, not the place to speculate about why the results came out the way they did or what it means; reserve that for the discussion and conclusions. Instead, data and statistical tests should be presented matter-of-factly and a statement given of whether the hypothesis was supported or not. For example:

"The first hypotheses predicted that regular advertisements are more likely to activate schemas associated with the concept of advertisement (H1a) and persuasion (H1b) than advertorials. Independent-sample $t$-tests comparing LDT mean scores for advertisement-related words between the regular advertisement condition ($M = 637.68$, $SD = 184.18$) and the unlabeled advertorial condition ($M = 619.70$, $SD = 193.47$) were not significantly different, $t$ (225) = 1.07, $p = ns$, suggesting that advertorials did not slow the activation of schema associated with the concept of advertisement. H1a was not supported (Figure 1)."[66]

As you can see from this example, reporting results can be a pretty short affair. The statistical test value is reported, in this case a $t$ test because there were two groups, a treatment and control, with degrees of freedom in parentheses followed by the $p$ value. Some journals prefer that $p$ values be given precisely—for example $p = .005$—while others prefer that only when the effect is not significant (e.g., $p = .69$), with significant $p$ values being rounded to the conventional levels (e.g., $p < .05$, $p < .01$, $p < .001$). Others use "$p = ns$" when the result is not significant. Means and standard deviations also are given in parentheses.

Here is another example:

"H1 predicted threats to positive face from rejection and criticism on social media would elicit greater self-reported negative affect, compared with nonaversive comments. Partial support was found for this hypothesis, $F$ (2, 75) = 7.37, $p = .001$, $\eta2 = .16.2$. Using Scheffe post hoc corrections, results show people in the rejection condition ($M = 2.11$, $SD = .70$, $p = .01$) and criticism condition ($M = 2.17$, $SD = .61$, $p = .01$) felt significantly more self-reported negative affect than those in the control condition ($M = 1.59$, $SD = .50$). No statistically significant difference was found between rejection and criticism, answering RQ1. No significant differences were found between conditions for self-reported positive affect, where lower values would indicate increased negative affect, $F$ (2, 75) = .21, $p = .81$, $\eta2 = .01$. These findings show partial support for H1 by offering evidence of an increase in self-reported negative affect in response to two types of threats to positive face, rejection and criticism, compared with the control."[67]

Note in this example that analysis of variance is used because there were more than two groups, so the $F$ test reports two degrees of freedom in parentheses, the first for the number of groups and the second for the total number of subjects. This example also reports effect sizes using eta-squared with the symbol $\eta2$. In addition, this reports partial support of the hypothesis; another possibility is to find significance but in the opposite direction that is predicted. Here is another example of reporting of effect sizes using Cohen's $d$:

"However, responses to persuasion-related words were faster after reading labeled advertorials ($M = 634.09$, $SD = 131.69$) than those exposed to the same advertorials without a label ($M = 672.59$, $SD = 144.09$), $t$ (211) = 2.06, $p < .05$, with a small magnitude in the effect size (Cohen's $d = .28$), supporting H2b (Figure 1)."[68]

Many articles begin their results section with descriptive statistics about the sample, DVs, and important covariates. Some journals include these in the methods section, so consult the journal's style guide. Here is an example of how this is reported:

"There were 337 MTurk workers in total ($N_{reg.ad}$ = 124; $N_{labeled advertorials}$ = 110; $N_{unlabeled advertorials}$ = 103), with 56% classified as male. The average age was 31.5 years old ($SD$ = 11.58), with a quartile range between 23 to 37 years old. The sample ($N$ = 337) consisted of White ($n$ = 263, 78%), Asian ($n$ = 47, 13.9%), African American ($n$ = 22, 6.5%), Hispanic/Latino ($n$ = 16, 4.7%), American Indian or Alaska Native ($n$ = 3, 0.9%), and Native Hawaiian or other Pacific Islander ($n$ = 1, 0.3%)."[69]

As shown, capital N refers to the entire sample, and lower-case n refers to groups.

Here is another example that reports summary statistics for the DVs:

"In the dictator treatment of game 2, students chose the selfish option 83% (90/108) of the time compared to 61% (68/111) of the time for adult industry professionals."[70]

And here is a final example with more demographics reported:

"Results

"Sample Characteristics

"Table 1 presents the baseline demographic and socioeconomic characteristics for all participants with disabilities ($N$ = 336), distinguishing results by treatment status. The mean age was about 38 years. About 80 percent of the participants were female, less than half were Caucasian, and slightly more than 20 percent were married. More than two-thirds of participants had some college or more, and, on average, participants' monthly household income was about $1,400. Three-fourths of participants reported having children in the household. The sample is balanced with respect to most of the variables except homeownership, public housing assistance, and ownership of a bank account. Compared with the control group members, treatment participants were 8 percentage points more likely to receive Section 8 public housing assistance (23 percent vs. 15 percent; $p < .05$), 9 percentage points more likely to own a bank account (88 percent vs. 79 percent; $p < .05$), and 9 percentage points less likely to own a home at baseline (18 percent vs. 27 percent; $p < .05$). Overall, the treatment group seems more socio-economically disadvantaged than the control group. As previous ADD studies noted (e.g., Mills et al. 2008), the Tulsa IDA program's sample was not representative of low-income households eligible for the program."[71]

Internal consistency tests are required for indexes (Cronbach's alpha, factor analyses), and some journals put them in the results section, while others include them in methods.

Tables and figures should be used when a graphic display is more easily understood than in-text descriptions—for example, when there are many results to report. When this is the case, the most important findings should be summarized in the results section, with the rest displayed in tables that are referenced in the text. For example:

"Returning to Table 2, we compare trust in the two populations adding controls for gender and beliefs. As column 3 of that table shows, trust is correlated with positive beliefs about trustworthiness. However, even with this control, the level of trust shown by domain traders is 24 percentage points higher than that by students. Once again, gender has no effect on trust."[72]

Structural equation models are also typically reported in graphics, with statistics in the graphics and the caption. For example:[73]

*(Continued)*

(Continued)

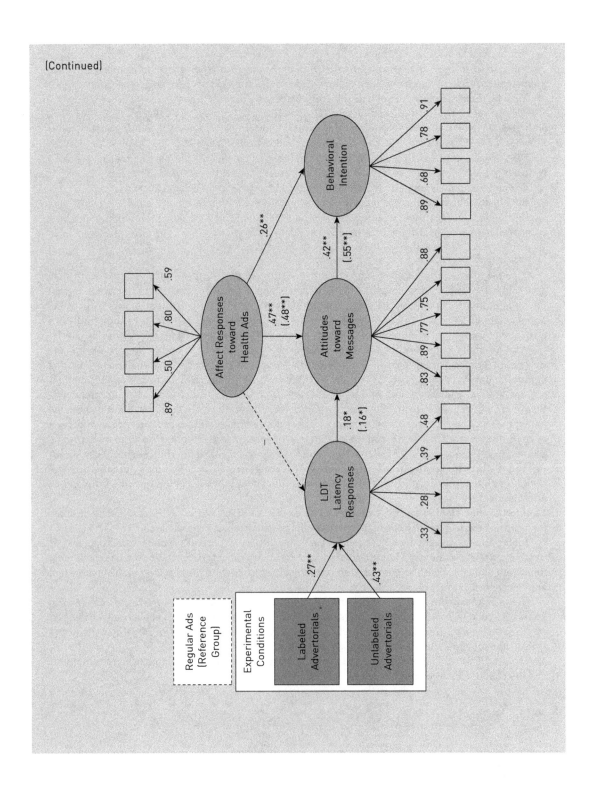

Results from PROCESS and regression models are best reported in tables, with basic information in text. For example:

| | Mediators | | | | | | Outcome variables | | | | | |
| | Negative affect | | | Positive affect | | | Retaliatory aggression | | | | | |
| | | | | | | | Virtual bombs | | | Virtual smiles | | |
| | Coeff. | SE | p | Coeff. | SE | p | Coeff. | SE | p | Coeff. | SE | p |
|---|---|---|---|---|---|---|---|---|---|---|---|---|
| Rejection and criticism | .56 | .15 | .00 | .02 | .18 | .91 | .69 | .32 | .03 | −.20 | .09 | .04 |
| Negative affect | | | | | | | .46 | .23 | .05 | −.10 | .07 | .16 |
| Positive affect | | | | | | | .05 | .19 | .78 | .05 | .05 | .40 |
| | $R^2 = .16$ F(1,76) = 14.78, $p = .00$ | | | $R^2 = .00$ F(1,76) = .01, $p = .91$ | | | $R^2 = .17$ F(3,74) = 5.03, $p = .00$ | | | $R^2 = .13$ F(3,74) = 3.60, $p = .02$ | | |

Note: Coeff. = Unstandardized regression coefficients derived from PROCESS model 4. SE = standard error.

*(Continued)*

(Continued)

"PROCESS (Hayes, 2013) model 4 was used to test the proposed model, a parallel mediation model with the experimental manipulation proposed to directly lead to affect and retaliatory aggression as well as to lead indirectly to retaliatory aggression through affect. To test this, negative and positive affect were treated as parallel mediators in the model, and the two measures of retaliatory aggression were examined separately. Bias-corrected bootstrap confidence intervals based on 5,000 bootstrap samples were used to test indirect effects."[74]

For multiple experiments within one paper, reporting can take the form of reporting results for each study separately—Study 1, Study 2, Study 3, for example. This is frequently used when different hypotheses are posited for each study. When multiple studies test the same hypotheses under different conditions, it may be clearer to present the results according to hypothesis with all the studies' results under each one (e.g., H1, Study 1 results, Study 2 results; H2, Study 1 results, Study 2 results). When this is the case, a global summary at the end helps readers follow along; for example, one study says this after presenting the results of three studies:

"To summarize, adult professionals lie slightly less when the tradeoff is between lying and shame, and significantly less when the tradeoff is between lying and money."[75]

When covariates are used, such as in analysis of covariance, their effects are also reported as either significant or not, and using language such as "after controlling for . . . ." For example:

"This hypothesis was supported. Public health framing ($M = 4.0$, $SD = 1.1$) was significantly more likely to cause people to say they intended to change their own behavior than traditionally ($M = 3.6$, $SD = 0.94$) framed stories ($F = 4.5$, $p < .05$) after controlling for demographic covariates. Significant covariates included gender ($F = 20.4$, $p < .001$) and race ($F = 8.58$, $p < .05$). Women ($M = 4.1$, $SD = 0.86$; men $M = 3.2$, $SD = 1.10$) and Hispanics ($M = 4.5$, $SD = 1.2$) were the most likely to change their behavioral intentions."[76]

MANCOVA, or multiple analysis of covariance, used with more than one dependent variable and covariates, is treated the same except that both MANCOVA and multiple analysis of variance (MANOVA, a significance test for multiple DVs but without the covariates) require the reporting of an omnibus or overall significance test with all the DVs considered together. Only if the overall analysis is significant does the researcher then report univariate significance tests for the individual DVs. For example:

"The public journalism-graphics DVs (issues and analysis, citizens views, mobilizing information, ways to contact the media, and common ground and solutions) were first entered together in a MANCOVA with the authorship covariate. Using Wilks' Lambda, the analysis showed a significant effect for the dependent variables considered together ($F = 4.87$, $df = 5$, 641, $p < .001$, $\eta2 = .037$). The authorship covariate was significant ($F = 50.3$, $df = 5$, 641, $p < .001$, $\eta2 = .068$). When the dependent measures' univariate analyses were examined, significant effects were obtained for two items, issues and analysis and common ground."[77]

Finally, while statistical software may generate output that indicates "$p = 0.000$," it is inappropriate to report this or even $p < .000$. Instead, it should be rounded to the highest conventional level, $p < .001$. The reason for this is elegantly explained in Lilienfeld et al.[78]—briefly, that it implies a zero probability of falsely rejecting a true null hypothesis, which is virtually impossible.

Of course, there are many more ways to report results of an experiment than are illustrated here; this represents the most basic. Read experiments in your discipline to see how others have written their results.

Finally, the best advice on conducting experiments comes from Campbell and Stanley's classic monograph from 1963: "Most experiments will be disappointing."[79] They also include "tedious" and "painful." So steel yourself against this reality and be relentless. Take comfort in small successes, for knowledge evolves. Design the very best experiment possible, which will still not be perfect. Go ahead with it and interpret it, fully aware of its imperfections.[80] In spite of these drawbacks, I have found experiments to be the most exciting way to learn about cause and effect, and to solve important problems in the social world. Enjoy the journey.

## Common Mistakes

- Using deception because it would be more time consuming or more difficult to avoid it

- Not submitting a research project to the IRB soon enough. Never start collecting data before receiving approval.

- Failing to close out a study with the IRB; reporting the wrong number of subjects studied; failing to file an amendment for changes in a study's protocol if required.

- Sloppy practices in taking notes and writing up papers that result in inadvertent plagiarism. Not rewriting one's own words from previous papers.

## Test Your Knowledge

1. The purpose of an IRB is to:
   a. Award federal funds for human subjects research
   b. Review research proposals to ensure that researchers treat subjects ethically and do not cause them harm
   c. Apply biomedical research standards to social science
   d. Slow down the research process so scientists can improve their studies

2. Which of the following is NOT one of the principles in the *Belmont Report*?
   a. Respect for persons
   b. Beneficence
   c. Justice
   d. Loyalty

3. The *least* preferred way to keep subjects from guessing the hypothesis of the experiment is to use:

   a. Unobtrusive instruments

   b. Deception

   c. Distractor questions

   d. Manipulation checks

4. When two researchers had a research assistant pretend to be a subject and tell prospective subjects that a study was interesting and important when it was not, they were using:

   a. An unobtrusive instrument

   b. A pilot study

   c. A confederate

   d. Distractor tasks

5. When answering questions on an experiment about one's political views is similar to talking to others about political opinions, this is an example of:

   a. Invasion of privacy

   b. Loss of confidentiality

   c. Lack of informed consent

   d. Risk of harm that is no greater than in everyday life

6. One way to minimize harm in social science experiments is:

   a. To allow subjects to skip questions

   b. To allow subjects to withdraw from a study

   c. By warning subjects about the risk of harm in the informed consent process

   d. All of these

7. When a researcher has control over a subject in some way—for example, his or her grades—that is an example of:

   a. Random assignment

   b. Abuse of power

   c. Loss of privacy

   d. Data manipulation

8. Allowing students to earn extra credit by doing an essay instead of being in an experiment is an example of:

   a. Grade inflation

   b. Coercion

   c.  A way to avoid abuse of power

   d.  Random assignment

9.  A study is considered anonymous when:

   a.  Information is de-identified

   b.  No identifying information is collected

   c.  Data are kept on a password-protected laptop

   d.  Results are reported in aggregate

10.  Confidentiality is maintained when:

   a.  Information is de-identified

   b.  Data are kept on a password-protected laptop

   c.  Results are reported in aggregate

   d.  All of these

## Answers

| | | | |
|---|---|---|---|
| 1. b | 4. c | 7. b | 9. b |
| 2. d | 5. d | 8. c | 10. d |
| 3. b | 6. d | | |

## Application Exercises

1.   If you have not done so already, take your institution's IRB training. You will need this to submit a research proposal and receive approval to conduct the pilot study. If you do not have an IRB, then read the *Belmont Report* and the regulations at the U.S. Department of Health and Human Services Office for Human Research Protections website, https://www.hhs.gov/ohrp/regulations-and-policy/regulations/45-cfr-46/index.html

    The *Belmont Report* and regulations are not long, but for a summary, see: Shelton, James D. (1999). How to Interpret the Federal Policy for the Protection of Human Subjects or Common Rule (Part A). *IRB: A review of human subjects research* 21: 6–9.

2.   File a research proposal with your institution's IRB. Consult with your instructor for directions and to secure a faculty sponsor if necessary. Respond to all the requests for changes. If you do not have an IRB, then follow the guidelines at the U.S. Department of Health and Human Services website.

Create an informed consent document for subjects to be given as either a paper copy or an online cover letter. If using student subjects, develop an alternate incentive. Follow all of the guidelines described in this chapter.

3. Once your study has been approved, plan and then conduct a pilot study. Remember, this is a small-scale version of your actual study with the intention of seeing what works and what does not so that you can make changes before collecting real data. Be sure to build in open-ended questions for subjects to answer about the procedures and to talk to them afterward about their impressions of the study.

## Suggested Readings

American Psychological Association. 2009. *Publication Manual of the American Psychological Association*, 6th edition. Washington, DC: Author.

For ethical guidelines, read Chapter 1, "Writing for the Behavioral and Social Sciences," starting with page 11 through page 20. For more on plagiarism, read Chapter 6, "Crediting Sources."

For another overview, see:

Hegtvedt, Karen A. 2014. "Ethics and Experiments." In *Laboratory Experiments in the Social Sciences*, edited by Murray Webster and Jane Sell, 22–51. London: Elsevier.

For codes of ethics specific to your discipline, check out your professional association's website.

For more on the call for different IRB rules for different disciplines, see:

La Noue, George R., and Alexander Bush. 2010. "Institutional Review Board Rules: Should One Size Fit All Disciplines?" *International Journal of Interdisciplinary Social Sciences* 5 (8): 239–258.

For more on P-hacking, see:

Aschwanden, Christie. 2015. "Science Isn't Broken: It's Just a Hell of a Lot Harder Than We Give It Credit For." http://fivethirtyeight.com/features/science-isnt-broken/

For a dissenting opinion on the ethics of random assignment, see:

Fives, Allyn, Daniel W. Russell, John Canavan, Rena Lyons, Patricia Eaton, Carmel Devaney, Norean Kearns, and Aoife O'Brien. 2015. "The Ethics of Randomized Controlled Trials in Social Settings: Can Social Trials Be Scientifically Promising and Must There Be Equipoise?" *International Journal of Research & Method in Education* 38 (1): 56–71.

For more on authorship, see:

Fine, Mark A., and Lawrence A. Kurdek. 1993. "Reflections on Determining Authorship Credit and Authorship Order on Faculty-Student Collaborations." *American Psychologist* 48 (11): 1141–1147.

For more on pilot studies, see:

**Westlund, Erik, and Elizabeth A. Stuart. 2017. "The Nonuse, Misuse, and Proper Use of Pilot Studies in Experimental Evaluation Research."** *American Journal of Evaluation* **38 (2): 246–261**

# Notes

1. A. Lijphart, "Comparative Politics and the Comparative Method," *American Political Science Review* 65, no. 3 (1971): 682–693.

2. Colin F. Camerer, G. Lowenstein, and D. Prelec, "Neuroeconomics: Why Economics Needs Brains," *Scandinavian Journal of Economics* 106, no. 3 (2004); James N. Druckman et al., "The Growth and Development of Experimental Research in Political Science," *American Political Science Review* 100, no. 4 (2006): 627–635; Cengiz Erisen, Elif Erisen, and Binnur Ozkececi-Taner, "Research Methods in Political Psychology," *Turkish Studies* 13, no. 1 (2013): 13–33; Susan D. Hyde, "Experiments in International Relations: Lab, Survey, and Field," *Annual Reviews of Political Science* 18 (2015): 403–424; Yair Levy, Timothy J. Ellis, and Eli Cohen, "A Guide for Novice Researchers on Experimental and Quasi-Experimental Studies in Information Systems Research," *Interdisciplinary Journal of Information, Knowledge and Management* 6 (2011): 151–161.

3. National Commission for the Protection of Human Subjects of Biomedical and Behavioral Research, *The Belmont Report*, ed. Department of Health, Education, and Welfare (Washington, DC: U.S. Government Printing Office, 1978).

4. Stanley Milgram, "Behavioral Study of Obedience," *Journal of Abnormal and Social Psychology* 67, no. 4 (1963): 371–378; Philip Zimbardo, *The Lucifer Effect: Understanding How Good People Turn Evil* (New York: Random House, 2007).

5. Mark H. Ashcraft and Jeremy A. Krause, "Social and Behavioral Researchers' Experiences With Their IRBs," *Ethics & Behavior* 17, no. 1 (2007): 1–17; Robert Klitzman, *The Ethics Police? The Struggle to Make Human Research Safe* (Oxford: Oxford University Press, 2015); J. Michael Oakes, "Risks and Wrongs in Social Science Research: An Evaluator's Guide to the IRB," *Evaluation Review* 26, no. 5 (2002): 443–479.

6. Ibid., 447.

7. Ibid., 449.

8. Ibid., 454.

9. Ibid., 467.

10. Federal changes to IRB regulations were pending as of this writing. For the most up-to-date information, consult the Federal Register at https://www.federal-register.gov/documents/2017/01/19/2017-01058/federal-policy-for-the-protection-of-human-subjects.

11. Rebecca B. Morton and Joshua A. Tucker, "Experiments, Journals, and Ethics," *Journal of Experimental Political Science* 1, no. 2 (2015): 99–103.

12. Benjamin G. Serfas, Oliver B. Büttner, and Arnd Florack, "Eyes Wide Shopped: Shopping Situations Trigger Arousal in Impulsive Buyers," *PLoS ONE* 9, no. 12 (2014): 1–9.

13. Morton and Tucker, "Experiments, Journals, and Ethics."

14. Serfas, Büttner, and Florack, "Eyes Wide Shopped," 3.

15. Lee Wilkins and Renita Coleman, *The Moral Media: How Journalists Reason About Ethics* (Mahwah: NJ: Erlbaum, 2005).

16. Immo Fritsche and Volker Linneweber, "Nonreactive (Unobtrusive) Methods," in *Handbook of Psychological Measurement—A Multimethod Perspective*, ed. M. Eid and E. Diener (Washington, DC: American Psychological Association, 2004).

17. Karen A. Hegtvedt, "Ethics and Experiments," in *Laboratory Experiments in the Social Sciences*, ed. Murray Webster and Jane Sell (London: Elsevier, 2014), 23–51.

18. Milgram, "Behavioral Study of Obedience."

19. L. Festinger and J. M. Carlsmith, "Cognitive Consequences of Forced Compliance," *Journal of*

*Abnormal and Social Psychology* 58, no. 2 (1959): 203–210.

20. T. Rogers et al., "Artful Paltering: The Risks and Rewards of Using Truthful Statements to Mislead Others," *Journal of Personality and Social Psychology* 112 (3), 456–473. http://dx.doi.org/10.1037/pspi0000081.

21. Oakes, "Risks and Wrongs in Social Science Research."

22. Hegtvedt, "Ethics and Experiments."

23. Morton and Tucker, "Experiments, Journals, and Ethics."

24. Ibid.

25. Hegtvedt, "Ethics and Experiments."

26. S. A. McLeod, "Psychology Research Ethics," *Simply Psychology* http://www.simplypsychology.org/Ethics.html Accessed Dec. 10, 2017 (2007).

27. Milgram, "Behavioral Study of Obedience."

28. Hegtvedt, "Ethics and Experiments."

29. Ibid.

30. Gary W. Ritter and Marc J. Holley, "Lessons for Conducting Random Assignment in Schools," *Journal of Children's Services* 3, no. 2 (2008): 28–39; Gary W. Ritter and Rebecca A. Maynard, "Using the Right Design to Get the 'Wrong' Answer? Results of a Random Assignment Evaluation of a Volunteer Tutoring Programme," *Journal of Children's Services* 3, no. 2 (2008): 4–16.

31. Richard A. Berk, Gordon K. Smyth, and Lawrence W. Sherman, "When Random Assignment Fails: Some Lessons From the Minneapolis Spouse Abuse Experiment," *Journal of Quantitative Criminology* 4, no. 3 (1988): 209–223; Sameer B. Srivastava, "Network Intervention: Assessing the Effects of Formal Mentoring on Workplace Networks," *Social Forces* 94, no. 1 (September 2015): 427–452.

32. Gerry Stoker, "Exploring the Promise of Experimentation in Political Science: Micro-Foundational Insights and Policy Relevance," *Political Studies* 58 (2010): 300–319.

33. Elizabeth J. Robinson et al., "Lay Conceptions of the Ethical and Scientific Justifications for Random Allocation in Clinical Trials," *Social Science & Medicine* 58, no. 4 (2004): 811.

34. R. J. Lilford and J. Jackson, "Equipoise and Randomisation," *Journal of the Royal Society of Medicine* 88 (1995): 552–559.

35. Robinson et al., "Lay Conceptions of the Ethical and Scientific Justifications."

36. J. A. Chard and R. J. Lilford, "The Use of Equipoise in Cultural Trials," *Social Science & Medicine* 47, no. 7 (1998): 891.

37. Allyn Fives et al., "The Ethics of Randomized Controlled Trials in Social Settings: Can Social Trials Be Scientifically Promising and Must There Be Equipoise?" *International Journal of Research & Method in Education* 38, no. 1 (2015): 56–71.

38. Hegtvedt, "Ethics and Experiments."

39. Oakes, "Risks and Wrongs in Social Science Research."

40. American Psychological Association, "Ethical Principles of Psychologists and Code of Conduct," *American Psychologist* 57, no. 12 (2002): 1060–1073.

41. Morton and Tucker, "Experiments, Journals, and Ethics."

42. J. Sieber, *Planning Ethically Responsible Research: A Guide for Students and Internal Review Boards* (Newbury Park, CA: Sage, 1992).

43. Hegtvedt, "Ethics and Experiments."

44. Ibid.

45. Oakes, "Risks and Wrongs in Social Science Research."

46. Explorable, "Confidentiality," *Privacy in research* (2017). https://explorable.com/privacy-in-research. Accessed Dec. 10, 2017.

47. M. J. Müller, B. Landsberg, and J. Ried, "Fraud in Science: A Plea for a New Culture in Research," *European Journal of Clinical Nutrition* 68, no. 4 (2014): 411–415.

48. Christie Aschwanden, "Science Isn't Broken: It's Just a Hell of a Lot Harder Than We Give It Credit For," *FiveThirtyEight* (2015); Tara Haelle, "P-Hacking, Self-Plagiarism Concerns Plague News-Friendly Nutrition Lab," *Association of Health Care Journalists* http://healthjournalism.org/blog/2017/03/p-hacking-self-plagiarism-concerns-plague-news-friendly-nutrition-lab/ (March 9, 2017). Accessed December 10, 2017.

49. Aschwanden, "Science Isn't Broken."

50. Haelle, "P-Hacking, Self-Plagiarism Concerns."

51. Müller, Landsberg, and Ried, "Fraud in Science."

52. Susan T. Fiske, "How to Publish Rigorous Experiments in the 21st Century," *Journal of Experimental Social Psychology* 66 (2016): 145–147.

53. Ibid.

54. Ibid., 147.

55. Ibid.

56. Morton and Tucker, "Experiments, Journals, and Ethics."

57. Louisa Ha, "Pressure to Publish, Transparency and Significant Knowledge Contribution," *Journalism and Mass Communication Quarterly* 94, no. 3 (2017): 637–640.

58. R. K. Goodyear, C. A. Crego, and M. W. Johnston, "Ethical Issues in the Supervision of Student Research: A Study of Critical Incidents," *Professional Psychology: Research and Practice* 23 (1992): 203–210.

59. Mark A. Fine and Lawrence A. Kurdek, "Reflections on Determining Authorship Credit and Authorship Order on Faculty-Student Collaborations," *American Psychologist* 48, no. 11 (1993): 1141–1147.

60. Erik Westlund and Elizabeth A. Stuart, "The Nonuse, Misuse, and Proper Use of Pilot Studies in Experimental Evaluation Research," *American Journal of Evaluation* 38, no. 2 (2017): 246–261.

61. Ibid.

62. Ibid.

63. Ibid.

64. Ibid.

65. W. A. McCall, *How to Experiment in Education* (New York: MacMillan, 1923). Preface.

66. Sunny Jung Kim and Jeffrey T. Hancock, "How Advertorials Deactivate Advertising Schema," *Communication Research* 44, no. 7 (2016): 1019–1045

67. Gina Masullo Chen, "Losing Face on Social Media," *Communication Research* 42, no. 6 (2013): 819–838.

68. Kim and Hancock, "How Advertorials Deactivate Advertising Schema."

69. Ibid., 8.

70. Mitchell Hoffman and John Morgan, "Who's Naughty? Who's Nice? Experiments on Whether Pro-Social Workers Are Selected Out of Cutthroat Business Environments," *Journal of Economic Behavior & Organization* 109 (2015): 173–187.

71. Jin Huang et al., "Individual Development Accounts and Homeownership among Low-Income Adults with Disabilities: Evidence from a Randomized Experiment," *Journal of Applied Social Science* 10, no. 1 (2016): 61.

72. Hoffman and Morgan, "Who's Naughty? Who's Nice?" 180.

73. Kim and Hancock, "How Advertorials Deactivate Advertising Schema," 10.

74. Chen, "Losing Face on Social Media."

75. Hoffman and Morgan, "Who's Naughty? Who's Nice?" 180.

76. Renita Coleman, Esther Thorson, and Lee Wilkins, "Testing the Impact of Public Health Framing and Rich Sourcing in Health News Stories," *Journal of Health Communication* 16, no. 9 (October 2011): 941–954.

77. Renita Coleman and Ben Wasike, "Visual Elements in Public Journalism Newspapers in an Election: A Content Analysis of the Photographs and Graphics in Campaign 2000," *Journal of Communication* 54, no. 3 (2004): 456–473.

78. Scott O. Lilienfeld et al., "Fifty Psychological and Psychiatric Terms to Avoid: A List of Inaccurate, Misleading, Misused, Ambiguous, and Logically Confused Words and Phrases," *Frontiers in Psychology* 6, no. 1100 (2015).

79. D. T. Campbell and J. C. Stanley, *Experimental and Quasi-Experimental Designs for Research.* (Chicago: Rand McNally, 1963), 3.

80. Ibid., 3.

# GLOSSARY

**A priori power analysis:** An analysis performed before data are collected to determine the appropriate sample size for an experiment.

**Ad blindness:** When subjects subconsciously tune out advertisements.

**Alternative hypothesis:** The hypothesis an experiment is testing that proposes a difference between or among treatment conditions; can also predict a direction.

**Analysis of variance:** A statistical technique used to test differences among groups. Abbreviated as ANOVA.

**Anonymous:** When researchers collect no demographic data that could identify subjects.

**Attention check:** Questions on a survey or questionnaire designed to detect when subjects are distracted and not answering the questions appropriately. Used to reduce response error.

**Attitude scales:** Ratings scales used to measure subjects' attitudes on various concepts.

**Attrition:** When subjects drop out of a study. A study's conclusions can be threatened if subjects drop out systematically, such as from one group more than the other, or for reasons such as treatment difficulty. Attrition threatens to create nonequivalent groups or an unbalanced design. In medical studies, this is often called "loss to follow-up."

**Belmont Report:** A set of basic ethical principles and guidelines for research with human subjects. Issued September 30, 1978, by the National Commission for the Protection of Human Subjects of Biomedical and Behavioral Research in response to experimental abuses such as the Tuskegee Syphilis Study.

**Between-subjects design:** An experimental factor where each subject is assigned to receive one and only one type of treatment.

**Blind:** A study that ensures subjects are unaware of whether they are receiving the treatment or not.

**Blocking, matched pairs:** Subjects are matched on important variables and then assigned to treatment and control groups as a pair or block. Matched pairs is a type of blocking design that involves grouping subjects into pairs. Blocking, also called *randomized block design*, consists of three or more subgroups.

**Carry-over effects:** When subjects are likely to react to receiving one type of treatment because of receiving another before it (e.g., taking a test more than once causes carry-over effects due to practice).

**Causation:** The reason why changing one thing causes something to happen to another thing.

**Ceiling effects:** When a variable has not been measured highly enough and so scores bunch up at the top because subjects cannot respond any higher—for example, with income that tops out at $100,000.

**Complete factorials:** See fully crossed factorial designs.

**Concept:** A general idea about something that has many specific characteristics.

**Conceptual definition:** An abstract, theoretical description of something using general qualitative terms.

**Conceptual replication:** Repeating a study and also extending it in some theoretically meaningful way, deliberately varying subjects, settings, variables, or interventions.

**Confederate:** An accomplice of the experimenter, someone who knows something about the study that the subject does not.

**Confidentiality:** When data are stored and reported to protect subjects' privacy (e.g., on a password-protected computer, locked in a researcher's office).

**Confound:** Something that could be causing an effect other than what you are studying, possibly providing a plausible alternative explanation.

**Constant:** Something that does not vary.

**Construct validity:** When an instrument measures what it claims to measure; that is, the variable represents the theoretical ideas or concepts behind it.

**Contingent conditions:** Situations under which a particular theory works or not.

**Continuous response instruments:** Instruments that allow subjects to report their feelings or valence of thoughts and attitudes moment by moment, typically with a dial on a handheld device.

**Control group:** A group of study subjects that gets no treatment, a treatment that is the status quo, or a treatment that is not related to what is being studied and serves as a comparison. A baseline measure of something that has not yet had a treatment or intervention.

**Convenience samples:** Subjects that are easily available rather than those randomly sampled from a population.

**Correlation:** When two or more things vary together, but one thing does not necessarily cause the other.

**Counterbalancing:** Randomly assigning or rotating the order of something, such as the stimuli, to avoid carry-over effects. This serves to offset or cancel out effects of an extraneous variable.

**Covary, covariate:** When two things vary together. A covariate is used to predict variance in the outcome or dependent variable that is not due to the treatment.

**Data mining:** Exploring data in an effort to find interesting or important results, often when one's hypotheses are not supported. Also called P-hacking and HARKing, or hypothesizing after the results are known.

**Data slicing:** Writing more than one paper from a single data set with only minor variations.

**Debriefing:** Telling subjects at the end of the experiment what it was really about, reassuring them, and getting data on other variables such as the psychological stress they endured.

**Demand characteristics:** When subjects change their behavior because they know they are being observed and want to please the researchers.

**Dependent variable:** The outcome that is expected to change with an experimental treatment.

**Design table:** A graphic representation of a factorial design, used to determine the characteristics of the stimuli and the number of subjects in each condition, represented by the "cells," or individual boxes.

**Direct or exact replication:** Studies that duplicate the methods and procedures of the original study; designed to test the operationalization of a study.

**Double-blinding:** When neither the subjects nor the observers know who is getting the treatment and control so as not to bias the study.

**Ecological validity:** How realistic an experiment is; how well it reflects real-life experiences.

**Effect size:** A statistic that describes the strength of the relationship between the independent variable (IV) and the dependent variable (DV), or the amount of variance in the DV that is explained or accounted for by the IV. The effect size statistic serves as a complement to the statistical significance represented by the $p$ value, referring to the practical significance of a relationship.

**Equipoise:** When researchers have no preference between two or more treatments.

**Equivalent:** Equal on average, or probabilistically equal, not identical.

**Experimental control:** When the stimuli themselves are designed to be free of confounds.

**Explicate, explication:** Explaining or interpreting.

**Exploratory:** Research conducted in the preliminary stages of studying a phenomenon, occurring before enough is known to posit hypotheses or relationships.

**External replication:** When independent, outside researchers repeat the results of a study of another researcher.

**External validity:** The extent to which the results of an experiment can be generalized to other people, settings, and treatments.

**F test:** The statistic used in analysis of variance.

**Face validity:** When something is what it appears to be.

**Factor:** An independent variable manipulated by a researcher in an experiment that has two or more values or levels. For example, if three sizes of weights are used in a study, the factor is weight, and it has three levels.

**Factorial design:** An experiment that manipulates more than one independent variable, each with two or more levels.

**Factorial notation:** The shorthand way to describe the number of factors and levels in a factorial design (e.g., 2 x 2, 2 x 3, 3 x 4, etc.).

**Field experiments:** Experiments that occur in a natural environment and also have random assignment of subjects to conditions.

**Fixed factors:** Factors whose levels are limited or the levels are chosen by researchers.

**Floor effects:** When the response choices do not go low enough, so scores bunch up at the bottom.

**fMRI (functional magnetic resonance imaging):** A noninvasive brain scanner that is used to identify areas of the brain associated with certain mental processes such as trusting or when experiencing emotions such as fear.

**Fractional factorials:** See *incomplete factorials*.

**Full factorials:** See *fully crossed factorial designs*.

**Fully crossed factorial designs:** All combinations of the levels and factors of an experiment have subjects assigned to them.

**Generalizability:** How the effects found apply beyond the specific study. For artificial experiments, this also means how well the effects translate to real life.

**HARKing:** Hypothesizing after results are known. See *data mining*.

**Homogeneous:** Subjects who are similar to each other—for example, college students are all the same age, about the same intelligence, and familiar with psychological experiments.

**Human Intelligence Tasks (HITs):** Tasks that computers cannot perform, such as writing book summaries, comments, or captions, identifying items in photographs, and transcribing audio and grocery receipts. Taking surveys and participating in research experiments has become one of the major tasks done by workers on Amazon's Mechanical Turk.

**Hypothesis:** A prediction that a certain treatment or manipulation will cause some specified effect.

**Impact factor:** A measurement of the average yearly citations of articles published in that journal. Impact factors are designed to help understand how important a journal is in its field.

**Implicit tests:** Instruments that make it so the subject is not necessarily consciously aware of his or her responses (e.g., psychological or physical responses such as heart rate, but also indirect questions or procedures such as thought listing).

**Incomplete factorial designs:** A design that leaves one or more of the cells in the design table empty and does not assign subjects to them.

**Independent variable:** The variable to be manipulated; the cause of some effect.

**Index:** Multiple questions that are combined to measure an abstract or multidimensional concept such as credibility, persuasion, or anxiety.

**Inductive:** A type of reasoning that infers general laws from specific cases; bottom-up logic. Different from deductive reasoning, or top-down logic, which uses general rules to reach a specific conclusion.

**Informed consent:** Telling research subjects about the risks of participating in the study and getting their approval to use their data.

**Institutional Review Boards:** A committee that reviews research with people—human subjects—and animals to ensure that researchers do not harm them, or expose them to minimal risk of harm.

**Instrument:** The device, tool, or procedure used to measure a response to a stimuli; the method of collecting data.

**Interaction:** The effects of two IVs or factors considered together; when one depends on the other. An effect that is between factors, not levels of one factor.

**Internal validity:** The extent to which the effects in an experiment are actually caused by the treatment.

**Interrater reliability:** A means of measuring how similar two judges are in scoring, observing, or rating the same thing.

**Intervening variables:** Causal mechanisms that come between the treatment and the outcome in an experiment and are indirectly responsible for effects.

**Items:** Individual questions in a questionnaire.

**Laboratory experiments:** Experiments not conducted in a natural setting that use random assignment of subjects to conditions.

**Latency:** A time interval or delay, such as the length of time it takes subjects to react before performing some behavior, such as pressing a switch to deliver shocks.

**Latency response:** An instrument that measures how quickly people respond to a question or stimulus to implicitly gauge memory, implicit attitudes, attitude accessibility, and cognitive processing. Also called reaction time.

**Latent:** Not obvious or on the surface. Latent variables are frequently not seen but have the potential to create effects. Opposite of "manifest."

**Latin Square:** A counterbalancing strategy for ordering treatments to compensate for systematic error or control nuisance variation instead of randomizing. It equalizes the number of positions under which each treatment occurs, with each occurring once per row and once per column. Used to control order effects.

**Levels:** The discrete values of an independent variable.

**Likert scale:** A fixed-choice response format that measures levels of agreement, frequency, importance, or likelihood. Usually 5 or 7 points.

**Logical inference:** The idea that reasonable conclusions can be drawn on the basis of common sense rather than mathematically calculated confidence levels.

**Longitudinal:** A study conducted across some period of time.

**Main effects:** The ability for the different levels in one factor alone to cause a change in the outcome variables; the difference between *levels* within one factor.

**Manipulation, manipulate:** Systematically changing something to see if it causes changes in the outcome variable. Also called an intervention or treatment.

**Manipulation check:** A way to determine if the treatment or manipulation is perceived by the subjects the way the researcher intends it to be.

**Matched pairs:** See *blocking*.

**Matching:** A strategy to reduce the effects of individual differences that involves pairing up subjects with similar characteristics and then assigning one to the treatment group and the other to the control group. Sometimes used when random assignment is not possible.

**Mechanical Turk, MTurk:** An online crowdsourcing platform where people are paid to perform various tasks that computers cannot.

**Mediator:** A variable that is influenced by the independent variable and then influences the dependent variable.

**Message variance:** When more than one message or stimulus is used to represent each treatment level.

**Mixed-factorial design:** A combination of between- and within-subjects designs in the same experiment. One independent variable is treated as a between-subjects factor so that subjects get only one level of that treatment, and the other is given as a within-subjects factor so that those subjects get all levels of that treatment.

**Moderator:** A third variable that, when combined with the independent variable, has an effect on the strength of the relationship to the dependent variable. Observable traits that exist before the intervention, not caused by it.

**Multiple-message design:** A design that employs message variance by using more than one message per treatment level. Also referred to as a *repetition factor*.

**Naïve subject:** A person participating in an experiment who does not know what the experiment is really about and is being deceived.

**Natural experiments:** Experiments that occur in a natural environment but do not have random assignment of subjects to conditions.

**Noise:** See *random variation*.

**Nonreactive or unobtrusive measures:** Tests that leave subjects unaware that they are being studied, unsuspecting of what is being measured, or unable to alter their responses.

**Nonresponse bias:** Meaningful differences between subjects who refuse to participate or don't answer questions and those who do.

**Null hypothesis:** The supposition that there will be no difference between those who get the treatment and those who do not.

**Observed power:** A power analysis conducted after data have been collected, typically in response to a nonsignificant finding in order to determine if low power played a part. These are widely misused, and experts recommend confidence intervals and other measures instead. Also called *post hoc power, a posteriori power,* and *retrospective power.*

**One-factor design:** See *single-factor design*.

**One-way design:** See *single-factor design*.

**Open-ended questions:** Questions that are answered in narrative form rather than yes or no, or by choosing from a predetermined set of responses.

**Open-ended responses:** Questions that have no set answers or scales for subjects to choose from but allow them to answer in their own words—for example, questions such as "Why did you choose this answer?" or "Tell me about . . . ."

**Operationalizations:** Redefines a concept into the specific, concrete way it is measured. Also called operational definitions.

**Opt-in participant panels:** Commercial survey and marketing research firms that provide respondents for research studies. Respondents are provided with incentives by the firms and choose which studies they want to participate in.

**Order effects:** When the order in which something is presented influences the outcome.

**P-hacking:** See *data mining*.

**Participant pools:** See *subject pools*.

**Pilot studies:** Small studies that precede a larger actual study. These are designed to work out the problems in a study design so that it can be refined before launching the larger study.

**Plagiarism:** Not giving proper credit to words and ideas that are not the researcher's own.

**Plausible alternative explanations:** Other believable explanations for why an effect occurred other than the one proposed.

**Post hoc power:** See *observed power*.

**Power:** The probability of supporting a hypothesis, or rejecting a false null hypothesis, when the alternative hypothesis is true. The probability of achieving statistical significance when an effect actually exists. The concept behind Type 2 errors.

**Power analysis:** A statistical technique to determine how many subjects a particular study needs.

**Pretest:** When an observation is made on subjects before the treatment is given. This same observation, or a similar one in an alternative form, is repeated after the treatment and is called the posttest.

**Primacy:** The tendency for things that are presented earlier to be better remembered or more influential on the outcome than things presented later.

**Privacy:** Protecting subjects by means of the data that are are collected. When no demographic data are collected, the study is anonymous; when demographic data are collected, it is confidential.

**Projective tests:** Ambiguous tests or questions that are designed to reveal something hidden within the person; for example, the ink blots in psychology are thought to reveal underlying thoughts and emotions.

**Qualitative measures:** Data that are not numerical measurement—for example, statements in interviews or focus groups.

**Quasi experiment:** Experiments that do not use random assignment of subjects to conditions.

**Questionnaire:** A set of questions, which may be printed, written, or spoken, that gives the set of answer choices.

**Random assignment:** A way of placing subjects into the different treatment groups so that individual differences are spread evenly across all the groups.

**Random factors:** Factors that represent a sample of a larger population rather than every conceivable level within that population.

**Random variation** or **noise:** Variation on things that are not of interest to the experiment as a result of random chance. Irregular and erratic fluctuations that cannot be anticipated.

**Randomization:** A process of assigning subjects to groups that ensures the groups are equivalent on various characteristics; it helps ensure that effects are not due to differences inherent in the inequality of groups rather than the treatment or manipulation.

**Recency:** The tendency for things that are presented at the end to be better remembered or more influential than things presented earlier.

**Regression to the mean:** When extreme scorers tend to move toward the average.

**Repetition factor:** See *multiple-message design*.

**Replicate, replication:** To repeat a study in order to see if the same results are found.

**Requesters:** Those who post tasks on MTurk and hire workers; researchers are among this group.

**Research question:** Used instead of a hypothesis when theory and prior evidence prevent a researcher from making a prediction.

**Response choices or scales:** The answers that a respondent can choose from on a survey or questionnaire. For example, *strongly agree, agree, neutral, disagree, strongly disagree*, is a common response choice set.

**Robust/Rigorous:** An accurate and unbiased or valid study design.

**Sample size:** The number of subjects in a study, indicated by *N* for the total number of subjects, and *n* for the number of subjects in each group.

**Scale:** The choice of responses an experimenter gives to subjects—for example, 7 points ranging from strongly agree to strongly disagree.

**Secondary data:** Existing data that were previously collected by someone other than the researcher.

**Secondary reaction task:** Similar to latency response in that time between a stimulus and response is measured; however, with secondary reaction tasks, there is the addition of a "distractor" task. Measures attention.

**Selection bias:** When subjects self-select the groups to be in, or researchers select subjects for some subjective reason such as because they are most in need or to improve the chances of supporting a hypothesis. Random assignment is not achieved.

**Self-plagiarism:** Using words or phrases verbatim from one's own previous writing.

**Self-replication:** When a researcher repeats his or her own study.

**Self-reports:** A form of instrument where the subjects answer questions about themselves.

**Seminal studies:** The classic studies, often the first in a program of research or ones that establish a new model or theory and influence future research.

**Single-factor design:** An experimental design that manipulates only one independent variable, with two or more levels.

**Single-item indicator:** When one question is used to measure a concrete construct such as age, education, or overall assessments.

**Single-message design:** An experiment that uses only one message per treatment level.

**Skin conductance:** Instruments that measure fluctuations in the skin including sweating, voltage, and resistance to provide measures of emotion, arousal, and attention. Also known as galvanic skin response and electrodermal response.

**Social desirability bias:** The tendency for subjects to give the "correct" answer according to social norms.

**Split plot designs:** A type of randomization that arose from studying crops, where an entire plot of land was split into sections so that different treatments could be applied to smaller sections.

**Standard error:** The estimate of the average difference between the sample and the population statistic. The standard deviation of the sampling statistic.

**Statistical control:** When it is not possible to control something in the stimuli of the study, researchers measure it and use it as a covariate in the statistical analysis.

**Statistical inference:** When a confidence level or interval can be mathematically calculated to determine the fit between the sample and larger population.

**Stimuli, Stimulus:** The materials used to convey the treatment, such as stories, messages, or teaching techniques, for example. Something that causes a response or reaction from a subject; the vehicle that an experimenter uses to deliver the manipulation hypothesized to cause some effect.

**Stratified random assignment:** A method of ensuring a sample contains key characteristics whereby multiple related variables are combined into a single variable, similar to the factors created by factor analysis. The one overarching factor can be measured for equivalence after units are randomly assigned instead of measuring numerous variables separately.

**Subject pools:** Lists of research volunteers, usually students, who are required to sign up to take part in a certain number of research studies per semester for course credit.

**Survey experiments:** Experiments conducted online using survey methodology.

**Treatment variance:** Variance in the stimuli based on the treatment or manipulation—that is, of the independent variables of theoretical interest to the study.

**Triangulation:** Studying the same phenomenon using different methods, typically both qualitative and quantitative.

**True experiments:** See *laboratory experiments*.

**Two-step randomization model:** Subjects are first randomly sampled from a population and then randomly assigned to a treatment group.

**Type 1 error:** When the null hypothesis is rejected but should not be. Also called a false positive.

**Type 2 error:** When the null hypothesis is not rejected but should be; that is, the alternative hypothesis should be supported but it is not. Also called a false negative.

**Unbalanced design:** When there are unequal numbers of observations, measurements, or subjects in each group.

**Univariate:** One variable.

**Unmasking:** Researchers who engage in policing other authors' perceived violations, often by reanalyzing their publicly available data and coming up with different results or uncovering inappropriate use of data.

**Validity:** That the conclusions of research are true, accurate, or authoritative.

**Vary, variation:** Things that change or are different.

**Within-subjects design:** An experimental design where each subject is included in all the groups and receives all treatments.

# INDEX